# We the Students

# WE THE

SUPREME COURT DECISIONS FOR
AND ABOUT STUDENTS

# STUDENTS

## Second Edition

JAMIN B. RASKIN

*American University*
*Washington College of Law*

COSPONSORED BY THE SUPREME COURT HISTORICAL SOCIETY

CQ PRESS

A DIVISION OF CONGRESSIONAL QUARTERLY INC.
WASHINGTON, D.C.

CQ Press
1255 22nd Street, N.W., Suite 400
Washington, D.C. 20037
202-729-1900; toll-free, 1-866-4CQ-PRESS (1-866-427-7737)
www.cqpress.com

⊛The paper used in this publication meets the minimum requirements of the American National Standard for Information Sciences—Permanence of Paper for Printed Library Materials, ANSI Z39.48-1992.

Cover photo by the Associated Press
Cover design by Debra Naylor
Interior design by Jill Shimabukuro

Printed and bound in the United States of America

07  06  05     5  4  3  2

Library of Congress Cataloging-in-Publication Data

Raskin, Jamin B.
    We the students : Supreme Court decisions for and about students / Jamin B. Raskin.—2nd ed.
        p.  cm.
Includes bibliographical references and index.
    ISBN 1-56802-797-4 (hardback: alk. paper)—ISBN 1-56802-798-2 (paperback: alk. paper)
    1. Students—Legal status, laws, etc.—United States—Cases. 2. Students—Civil rights—United States—Cases. 3. Educational law and legislation—United States—Cases. I. Title.
    KF4150.A7R37 2003
    344.73'079—dc21                                                    2003001206

# Contents

# Preface

"A people who mean to be their own governors, must arm themselves with the power knowledge gives."
JAMES MADISON (1822)

"In our system, state-operated schools may not be enclaves of totalitarianism. School officials do not possess absolute authority over their students. Students in school as well as out of school are 'persons' under our Constitution. They are possessed of fundamental rights which the State must respect, just as they themselves must respect their obligations to the State." JUSTICE ABE FORTAS, *TINKER V. DES MOINES INDEPENDENT COMMUNITY SCHOOL DISTRICT* (1969)

This casebook brings together two of America's great institutions: the high school and the high court. My subject is the Constitution of the United States and how the Supreme Court has interpreted it to govern the lives and experiences of America's public school students.

The cases presented here—some famous and some obscure—form a platform from which to launch young minds on a voyage of constitutional discovery. I invite America's students to learn to read and speak the language of constitutional law by studying cases that have affected them—and will continue to affect them—directly.

In the fall of 1999 twenty-five law students at American University's Washington College of Law, with the blessings of Mrs. Thurgood Marshall and Mrs. William J. Brennan Jr., went out to teach the Constitution in the public high schools of the District of Columbia. High school students rose to the occasion and developed their singular constitutional visions and voices. The Marshall-Brennan Fellowship Program was born—and so was this book.

Today the Marshall-Brennan program is thriving. Sixty fellows teach hundreds of high school students in Washington, D.C., and Maryland and coach them every spring in essay, creative arts, moot court, and poetry competitions about the meaning of the Constitution. With the support of the Open Society Institute we have launched the Marshall-Brennan Urban Debate League and brought debate skills to hundreds of high school students in the Washington area. Marshall-Brennan fellows at Rutgers Law School are passionately engaged in teaching in the Camden, New Jersey, public schools; there is an ambitious statewide "we the students" constitutional literacy effort led in Texas by

The 1999–2000 Marshall-Brennan fellows at American University, with Mrs. Thurgood Marshall, Mrs. William J. Brennan Jr. (both seated, center), and professor Jamin B. Raskin (far right).

United States District Court judge Royal Furgeson and the Texas State Bar called "What's Up With My Rights?"; and exciting sister projects are popping up all over America.

This casebook has been immeasurably improved not only by the ideas and contributions of the hundreds of Marshall-Brennan fellows who have served over the years, but also by the high school students I have met in the Marshall-Brennan program and while traveling across the United States talking about student rights. I first got interested in the rights of students when I represented a group of students at Blair High School in Montgomery County, Maryland, whose cable television show was censored when they sponsored a debate over gay marriage. (The details of this case are on pages 64–66.) It was that difficult and exhilarating experience, as well as my work with the wonderful Supreme Court Institute convened by the Street Law Program, which has been promoting law-related education for decades, that gave me the resolve to write a constitutional casebook for and about high school students.

*We the Students* is designed specifically for use by high school and college instructors in social studies, history, civics, and government classes. The explanatory historical material, glossary definitions, biographical sketches, class exercises, and discussion questions provide classroom teachers with all the material necessary to guide their students toward constitutional literacy. As late Supreme Court justice William J. Brennan Jr. noted thirty-five years ago in a remarkable address at the University of Pennsylvania calling for constitutional education in our high schools, "A teacher need not be a lawyer to teach

Stanford Law School's class of 1952. Future Supreme Court justice Sandra Day O'Connor is in the first row, second from left; future chief justice William Rehnquist is at far left in the back row.

effectively in this area. The teacher's job is not so much to supply the kind of answer a lawyer would give, but rather to raise the difficult questions to get his students worrying and thinking about the values and interests at stake."

## Constitutional Knowledge, Critical Thinking, Persuasive Argument, and Values Clarification

To approach the cases in this book with an inquiring and logical mind, you must first learn the basics of what the Constitution is and how the legal system works. Why does the Court decide a case one way rather than the other? Who has the better argument in a Supreme Court decision, the majority or the dissenters, and why? What makes an argument relevant or irrelevant? How does the Supreme Court go about the business of interpreting words? Is it always consistent? Should it be? Is constitutional law about facts, rules, values, or some complex interaction of all three? Why does law change over time, and what makes it change?

Pretty soon you will discover that there are few right answers when it comes to interpreting difficult constitutional issues. This ambiguity requires us to make persuasive

Future Supreme Court Justice Ruth Bader Ginsburg in her high school yearbook in 1950.

Future Supreme Court Justice Clarence Thomas compares notes with a fellow high school student at St. John's in Georgia.

arguments about the meaning of the Constitution based on the different methods of interpretation. As you practice writing and arguing about the Constitution, you will improve your oral communication skills and persuasiveness and your written communication skills, including clarity, cogency, and subtlety.

I hope that you will see that every great legal conflict has at its heart a clash over values and principles. Learning the Constitution in this way enables you to clarify what your own values are and to engage in real dialogue with other people about the rules of our common life.

I hope finally that you will gain from this text a love and appreciation for a document that has bound us together for more than two centuries. As Chief Justice John Marshall wrote in *McCulloch v.*

*Maryland* in 1819, "We must never forget, that it is a constitution we are expounding." It belongs to all of us.

## Becoming a Democratic Citizen: Rights and Responsibilities

I have written this casebook with one driving conviction: You cannot be an effective citizen without knowing your Constitution. Learning about the Constitution is not only a birthright but also a rite of passage that should be as important to your transition to adulthood as learning about the economy or how to drive a car.

It is a splendid and wonderful thing to learn your rights as a citizen, but rights exist only in the context of a working democratic community where we all assume corresponding responsibilities. Just as each of us has a legal right to speak and be heard, we have a complementary moral obligation to listen to one another in a respectful way. Just as we have a right to insist that government not violate our rights and securities as individuals, government has the right to insist that each of us respect the rights and securities of our fellow citizens (and students). It is this tension between rights and responsibilities that creates much of the excitement of this text.

Marshall-Brennan fellows Bruce Halloway Cork and Theresa Steed with their Banneker High School students at the Supreme Court.

I assume that the young readers of this book are mature and wise. You will find nothing in this casebook as a license for irresponsibility; rather, you will view the material presented here as a complex challenge to fulfill the highest calling of democracy: to be an active, engaged, educated, and responsible citizen. When you think and talk seriously about the problems and cases raised in this book, you will fine-tune your moral and political sensibilities as a citizen of the nation and your community. And who knows? Perhaps, even now, this book is in the hands of a future U.S. president or Supreme Court justice.

# Acknowledgments

This book is a labor of love that is part of a broader movement to raise the level of constitutional literacy in America. I wish to thank first the hundreds of dedicated Marshall-Brennan fellows who over the past five years have road tested, developed, refined, and improved these materials in the Maryland, New Jersey, and Washington, D.C., public schools. I would like to thank Mrs. Thurgood Marshall and the late Mrs. William J. Brennan Jr. for their generous support from the first day we walked this path; the magnificent agitator for peace and justice Mary Beth Tinker, a living American hero (whose name can be mentioned in the same breath as Rosa Parks's) who is a special friend of the Marshall-Brennan program and an unjaded champion of student rights; Michelle Carhart, the stalwart and inspired administrator of the program; Maryam Ahranjani, a former fellow who has transformed the program with her vision and equanimity as our academic coordinator; the public school systems of the District of Columbia, Montgomery County, and Prince George's County and their many devoted teachers and students; two deeply engaged and creative public servants—Kevin Chavous, chair of the D.C. Council's Education Committee, and Mike Subin, president of the Montgomery County Council—for their extraordinary support and commitment; Stephanie Joseph and Zack Rosenburg, two lawyers and former Marshall-Brennan fellows with deep commitment; D.C. schools superintendent Paul Vance, former chief of staff Steve Seleznow, and social studies content specialist Roceal Duke for their crucial help; the staff of the Supreme Court Historical Society, including consulting editor Jennifer Lowe, publications committee chair E. Barrett Prettyman, and sensational managing editor Clare Cushman, who gave invaluable editorial suggestions on the first edition; Lee Arbetman and Ed O'Brien of the National Institute for Citizen Education in the Law; my cherished colleague and codirector Steve Wermiel, who has been instrumental at every turn of this project; Mark Niles and Angela Davis, two beloved colleagues who give me great hope for the future; my beloved dean—Claudio Grossman—and my colleagues Muneer Ahmad, Cynthia Jones, Robert Vaughn, Tom Sargentich, Joshua Sarnoff, David Jaffe, Ann Shalleck, and the late and dearly missed Peter Cicchino; Terry Hickey at the Community Law in Action program at the University of Maryland School of Law; Chris Salamone, Christine Mason, and all the good people at LeadAmerica who are trying to bring the message of constitutional literacy and democratic leadership to every young person in the United States; the gifted Ron George, who has brought constitutional literacy to Haverhill, Massachusetts, and his students to Washington, D.C.; Rutgers clinical professor Traci Overton, whose vision and hard work brought Marshall-Brennan to New Jersey; the playwright and scholar Paula

Mary Beth Tinker (left) and Mrs. Thurgood Marshall watch students arguing in the 2002 "We the Students" William Karchmer Constitutional Law Moot Court Competition at American University.

Caplan, whose passionate support has been immeasurably important; Kim Rappaport, Sue Lyndrup, and the good people at Arnold and Porter who have brought their knowledge and commitment to our high school students; Eden Segal, a gifted teacher and organizer; Sam Chaltain, a scholar-activist whose First Amendment Schools project at the Freedom Forum is of surpassing importance; Elinor Hart and Elaine Melmed with the League of Women Voters; Carol Lange; Jocelyn Odle of We the People; Kenny Carroll and his troupe of soaring young slam poets at the D.C. Writers' Corps; Athelia Knight and Dorothy Gilliam of the *Washington Post,* who are bringing the skills of journalism to the young people of Washington; Marc Baiocco and Aaron Banks of Yonkers, New York; Liz Armstrong; and the great Bob Moses and Charles Cobb.

I would also like to thank the able and hardworking research assistants who pushed this project along, including the late Michelle Priestly, Danielle Fagre, Justin Antonipillai, Wilder Leavitt, Kara Mather, Ben Jackson, Eva Lopez-Paredes, Jennifer McKeever, Molly Crawford, Om Gillett, Addy Schmitt, Benjamin Sigel, Jennifer Beall, Ryan Borho, Ashley Kushner, Sheila Moreira, Christopher Caple, Tali Neuwirth, Micah Caldwell, and Oliver Tomas; and my very fine editors at CQ Press, Christopher Anzalone, Grace Hill, Molly Lohman, and Daphne Levitas.

On a personal note I would like to thank J. P. and Dina Sarbanes, Doug and Laura Gansler, Mark Plotkin, Christopher Hitchens, and Carol Blue for their friendship and generosity; Dar Williams for her musical inspiration and support; my friends Kate Bennis and Hal Movius for their loving solidarity; my dear mother, Barbara Raskin (1935–1999), who showed me how words could become windows to ideas and feelings; my beloved father, Marcus Raskin, who showed me how ideas can change things; my utterly indispensable brother, Noah Raskin; my brothers-in-law, Keith Littlewood and Kenneth Bloom; my great sisters, Eden Raskin and Erika Raskin Littlewood; and my sisters-in-law, Mina Raskin and Abby Bloom; my three naughty and wonderful children, Hannah Grace, Thomas Bloom, and Tabitha Claire, whose precocious (though admittedly compulsory) readings of this book have given me infinite satisfaction; my beloved nieces and nephews, Emily Blair, Zachary Gaylin, Maggie Ryan, Mariah Sophia, Phoebe Rose, and

Boman Grant; Lynn Raskin; and my ubiquitous mother-in-law, Arlene, and father-in-law, Herbert Bloom.

This book is dedicated to my wife, Sarah Bloom Raskin, the beautiful and mysterious woman who sat across from me in professor Laurence Tribe's constitutional law class at Harvard in Langdell North in the fall of 1986. It seems like yesterday.

## For Further Information

If you have a question that you cannot answer, consult your school librarian or a law librarian at a nearby law school or university. There are also extensive bibliographies and suggestions for other contacts at the end of each chapter and at the end of the book. You may also call the Student Press Law Center at (703) 807-1904 if your question relates to the free speech or free press rights of students. Or you may email me at *raskin@wcl. american.edu,* and I will get back to you with an answer as soon as I can. The website for the Marshall-Brennan program can be found at *www.wcl.american.edu/wethestudents.* We have a national high school students' moot court competition every spring and invite you to to come to Washington, D.C., to participate. To find out more, email Michelle Carhart at *mcarhart@wcl.american.edu.*

Remember: It's your Constitution, and it's up to you to learn it, to teach it, to quote it, to change it, to make it real.

Jamin B. Raskin
Professor of Law
Washington College of Law
American University
Washington, D.C.

# Foreword

This is a book for students everywhere, especially if you have ever looked at our world, as I have, and said, "There must be a better way!" *We the Students* is full of true stories of young people just like you who used the Bill of Rights and the Constitution to stand up for their rights and change history.

If you are like some people and think the Constitution and the Bill of Rights are dull and boring, you are in for a big surprise! Do you think you have a right to say something in class that your teacher disagrees with? Do you have the right to talk about sex in school? Do you have the right to wear a shirt that says "No war in Iraq" or one with a picture of Malcolm X? What about a shirt with a Confederate flag? Can you be searched in school? Can you have a religious club in school? A gay club? Can you be forced to give a urine sample to play sports? A blood sample? Do have the right to talk about controversial things in your school paper, or even to have a school paper at all?

You will learn about all of these things and more as you study the constitutional law cases in this book. They are about students like you who wanted the right to be treated fairly.

When I was thirteen years old, in 1968, I didn't know anything about my rights. But I knew something was wrong with the world. When I came home from school every night, there was news on TV about the civil rights movement and the war in Vietnam. When we saw pictures of African Americans being attacked with water hoses for trying to vote, my parents went to Mississippi to try to help. They didn't think it was right.

The 1960s followed a decade in which people were afraid to dissent. In the 1950s there was a senator who claimed to be patriotic. His name was Joseph McCarthy, and he accused everyone who didn't agree with him of being unpatriotic Communists. Workers in labor unions—or people working for racial equality and peace—were accused of being unpatriotic. No one was safe. McCarthy's friends in the FBI accused even Martin Luther King Jr. of being a Communist. All over the country people lost their jobs, and families and communities were destroyed.

Even as a child in Iowa, I was affected by this intolerance. My father tried to integrate the all-white swimming pool in our small town. That was considered too controversial; we had to move out of town. Later, the effects of McCarthyism continued.

In the 1960s, when I saw pictures on TV of Vietnamese kids getting bombed by the United States with a gooey gel called napalm, I didn't think that was right, and it mobilized me to action. The napalm would burn the kids like gasoline, but it was sticky and they couldn't get it off. It was chemical warfare. Kids in our neighborhood were also being sent to the war. Robert Kennedy, the brother of President John F. Kennedy, called for a Christmas truce. My brother and a group of our friends thought us kids should do something to support the truce. We decided to wear black armbands to school.

The school officials said we didn't have a right to do that. They suspended me. As you will see, they turned out to be wrong. In this book you will learn about the constitutional case that was fought and the First Amendment victory that was won for kids everywhere when the Supreme Court of the United States ruled in our favor. But it was not an easy victory. When we wore the armbands for peace to school, some people thought we weren't being patriotic and threw red paint at our house to suggest that we must be "reds." One woman even threatened to kill me. Many people supported us as well.

If you, like me, are shocked at the news on TV, or feel outraged or sad at the way the world is, you are not alone. When you read about the law cases in this book, you will see that there have always been ordinary people that felt the same way. When ordinary people take a stand to change things that make them outraged or sad, history is made. It may not be popular, and it is never easy. But if there was ever a time when ordinary people need to take a stand, it is now. And if there was ever a time when kids need to stand up for their rights, it is now.

It's hard to remember a time when young people have been blamed so much, so unfairly, for the problems of adult society. By teaching about real constitutional cases involving public school kids, *We the Students* is a powerful tool to help you stand up to injustice. It will also help inform adults who want you to be able to accomplish change. You will learn about the Constitution, not just to pass a test or write a paper, but so you can use it to change the world.

Thurgood Marshall was the first black justice on the Supreme Court, and one of the greatest. He used the Constitution to end segregation in the public schools. William Brennan Jr. was also a Supreme Court justice known for his rock-solid integrity and commitment to justice. To honor these men, their wives helped Jamin Raskin, the author of this book, start the Marshall-Brennan law project so that high school students could learn and use the Constitution in their own lives. As you read this book, you can feel fortunate to follow in the tradition of these two great Supreme Court justices who cared about young people and wanted you to have everything you need to become active, respected citizens.

When I was little, I read a story called "The Emperor's New Clothes." It was about a stupid, selfish emperor who spent all the kingdom's wealth on an invisible robe for himself. When he strolled down the road naked, no one dared to say anything, except a little boy who cried out: "The emperor is naked!" At last, all the people had the courage to say what they really thought. They all yelled out: "The emperor is naked, the emperor is naked!" and the world was changed forever.

I always liked that story because it's about the power of a child. That story and the book you are holding in your hands have a lot in common. They are both about young people like you, and the power you have, if you will only dare to use it. The cases reviewed have one thing in common: hope. Join us and lead us with your youthful energy and creativity in this lifelong struggle for justice and democracy. That is *our* hope. You will never regret it!

Mary Beth Tinker
October 29, 2002

# THE CONSTITUTION AND THE COURTS OF THE UNITED STATES

# 1

## The Constitution: What Is It?

The U.S. Constitution sets forth our nation's governing structure, establishing both the powers of government and the basic rights of the people. The modern world's first written constitution, it is the glue that has held the nation together through civil war; recession; depression; world war; the terrorist attacks of September 11, 2001; and profound social, economic, political, racial, sectional, and cultural conflict.

When the delegates to the Constitutional Convention in Philadelphia approved the Constitution on September 17, 1787, its provisions principally concerned structural issues—namely, the separation of powers, which refers to the distribution of powers among the legislative, executive, and judicial branches of the national government, and federalism, or the allocation of powers between the national government and the states.

Three years later, in 1791, the Constitution expanded to address individual liberty. In that year the states ratified the first ten amendments, called the Bill of Rights, laying down the constitutional rights of the people. The Bill of Rights had been championed by Anti-Federalists, who feared a tyrannical central government. Under these amendments, Congress could not establish a church or deny free exercise of religion, deny the right to assemble and petition for a redress of grievances, violate free speech or free press, conduct unreasonable or warrantless searches and seizures, or punish people twice for the same offense (double jeopardy).

Read through the Constitution and Bill of Rights in the Appendix and ask yourself: What values were important to our Founders? What would our Constitution be like without the Bill of Rights and later amendments? Do you think anything is missing in the Constitution today? If you were to add an amendment, what would it be? Do you have a class constitution? Can you write one?

## The Constitution: Whose Is It?

The Constitution begins "We the People," and these may be the three most important words in the document. Our Constitution incorporated the ideas of John Locke and Thomas Paine by assuming that all people begin with inalienable rights and that people create governments only to secure those rights and promote the common good. As Thomas Jefferson put it earlier in the Declaration of Independence, governments derive "their just Powers from the Consent of the Governed." The Constitution belongs to all of us, and we are all bound and protected by it.

President Abraham Lincoln returned to this democratic principle in the Gettysburg Address, perhaps the greatest speech in our history, when he poetically proclaimed his devotion to the idea that "government of the people, by the people, for the people, shall not perish from the earth." It was the Civil War and the resulting Thirteenth, Fourteenth, and Fifteenth Amendments that ended the horrors of slavery and launched the American people on a path toward equality for all citizens.

Congress and the people of the states have the power to amend the Constitution on "great and extraordinary occasions," as urged by James Madison in *Federalist* No. 49. And in fact, Americans have exercised this power seventeen times since the Bill of Rights was ratified, almost always to expand our rights. But, constitutional amending aside, it is the Supreme Court that is normally the final interpreter of the meaning of the Constitution. This court—along with the lower federal courts and state courts—acts as the guardian of our civil rights by striking down unconstitutional laws. This is the power of *judicial review,* by which the courts may declare unconstitutional any federal or state laws and policies that violate rights, rules, or principles set forth in the Constitution.

The principle and practice of judicial review were first established in the great case of *Marbury v. Madison* (1803), where the chief justice of the United States, John Marshall, declared: "[i]t is emphatically the province and duty of the judicial department to say what the law is." The Supreme Court thus has the power to strike down laws—even laws passed by an overwhelming majority in Congress or the state legislatures. In your opinion, does this make judicial review undemocratic? Or does it just enrich our understanding of democracy by incorporating irrevocable commitments that we have made as a people to certain fundamental rights?

The Constitution defined the structure and powers of the national government and, in short order, set forth a Bill of Rights for the people. Here the Founders take turns signing their names.

THE FOUNDATION OF AMERICAN GOVERNMENT

# The Constitution: What Does It Mean?

In some places, the Constitution seems very clear and specific, such as where it says that citizens must be thirty-five years old to become president. In other places, the Constitution speaks in broad, majestic generalities, such as where it says that states may not deprive persons of "equal protection of the laws" or abridge the "freedom of speech."

How exactly the Supreme Court and other courts should interpret broad constitutional terms is an issue of enduring and fascinating controversy. To interpret the Constitution, the Supreme Court draws on

- the text of the Constitution itself;
- *precedent,* or rulings from factually similar cases that illuminate the Constitution's meaning;
- the intentions of the Framers;
- the history of the nation and its institutions;
- the general structure of the constitutional design based on the division of national, state, and local powers through federalism and the separation of powers among the legislative, executive, and judicial branches at the national level;
- the spirit and values of the Constitution embodied in the Bill of Rights; and
- practical concerns and requirements.

The Constitution does not enforce itself, nor do judges go out searching for constitutional violations. If people think that their constitutional rights are being violated, they must summon the courage to bring a case to court. Under the Constitution's case-or-controversy requirement, which is set out in Article III's description of the judicial branch, the federal courts may take only those cases brought by people who have an active controversy involving an actual injury, that is, a violation of their legally protected rights. Our Court is not permitted to issue an advisory opinion, which is an opinion that states how the Court would rule on a legal matter that is not actually ripe. Ripeness is a doctrine requiring that a case or controversy be present—as opposed to hypothetical or potential—in order for it to be heard. At the same time, a case cannot be moot, or no longer fit for judicial resolution, because no actual controversy exists anymore. If there is no real injury alleged in a plaintiff's complaint, or the government is not responsible for it, or there is nothing the Court can do about it anyway, the Court will say that the plaintiff lacks standing. If the Court believes that it does not have proper jurisdiction over an issue because the Constitution leaves the resolution of that issue entirely up to the executive or legislative branches, the Court may decline to decide the case because it presents a political question.

## The Three Branches of the National Government

The Constitution distributes power at the national level of government among three branches. Article I defines the composition and powers of the legislative branch—Congress—which is divided between the House of Representatives and the Senate. Article II defines the powers of the executive branch, which consists of the president, the cabinet, and other officials appointed by the president. Article III sets up the judicial branch, which includes the Supreme Court and other federal courts that Congress may establish.

This structure places the lawmaking power in Congress, the bicameral (two-chamber) body that is today supposed to represent the will of the people as they elect their senators and House members. (Before ratification of the Seventeenth Amendment in 1913, state legislatures appointed U.S. senators.) The president is then charged with executing and enforcing the laws and policies that Congress adopts. The Supreme Court adjudicates cases and controversies involving the interpretation of the Constitution and federal laws.

The powers of the branches are not completely distinct and detached. For example, the Senate must confirm (or reject) the president's nominations to the Supreme Court and other judgeships. The House has power to impeach the president, which it did to President Bill Clinton in 1998, and the Senate has power to convict him and remove him from office, which it refused to do in Clinton's case. In impeachment trials in the Senate, the Chief Justice presides (as William Rehnquist did in Clinton's case). Each branch has a distinct function, but the Constitution overlaps and blends these functions.

### The National Government and the States

The Constitution makes federal law supreme to state law whenever they come into conflict, but the Constitution also implicitly leaves major areas of responsibility to the states. According to the Tenth Amendment, the powers not delegated to the United States by the Constitution "are reserved to the States respectively, or to the people." Many domains of social life have been left in large part to the states, including family law and land use, but none is more important than public education, where the role of localities and states has always been preeminent. The U.S. Department of Education contributes some funds to local school districts and pushes certain policies along with them, but the vast portion of resources in the public schools is raised in the states and their political subdivisions: the counties, cities and towns.

One of the recurring issues in the Supreme Court's education cases is whether the Court's searching review of local school district decisions is appropriate. Some people argue that the Court should not sit as a "super–school board" second-guessing local educators who know their schools and students best. Others believe that the Court should always aggressively defend basic federal constitutional values, like freedom of speech and due process, against tyranny at the local level. The images of federalism and the profound controversies over it linger close to the surface in these cases.

# The Incorporation of the Bill of Rights

Although the provisions of the Bill of Rights originally applied only against Congress ("*Congress* shall make no law . . ."), the Supreme Court has decided that the Bill of Rights binds all of the states and localities as well. Why? In 1868 the Fourteenth Amendment was added to the Constitution; its due process clause provides that "No state shall . . . deprive any person of life, liberty, or property, without due process of law; nor deny to any person within its jurisdiction the equal protection of the laws." The Court has found that the liberty guaranteed by due process of law includes almost all of the specific rights granted to the people against Congress by the Bill of Rights. Thus state governments cannot abridge the rights recognized in the Bill of Rights—such as the right to speak, publish a newspaper, practice religion, or be free from unreasonable searches and seizures—any

The Constitution's opening words, "We the People," may be not only the largest but also the most important in the document, infusing the meaning of the entire text.

more than Congress can. This assimilation of Bill of Rights protections to citizens facing state power is called "incorporation" through the due process clause.

## The State Action Requirement

It is important to remember that, although the Constitution applies against both Congress and the states (and localities), it applies only to government actions. Specifically, it applies to what we call a state action—an action undertaken by a government agency or actor, whether federal, state, or local. This is known as the state action requirement. A private entity is not ordinarily subject to constitutional restraints. (One exception is the Thirteenth Amendment's ban on slavery and involuntary servitude even where the offending actor is a private person or entity).

Thus, unlike public schools, which are an arm of government, private schools are not bound directly by the Constitution. Private schools may be found to be in violation of a *statute*, or law passed by a federal or state legislature, such as those forbidding job discrimination on the basis of race or gender or requiring "reasonable accommodation" for disabled persons. But private schools may not themselves be found to be in direct violation of the U.S. Constitution.

## Judicial Architecture: How Our Court System Works

To understand the cases that appear in the chapters that follow, some background information will be useful, beginning with an overview of the judicial process.

There are two major branches of the judicial system in the United States: the federal courts and the state courts. Depicted graphically, our judiciary looks something like this:

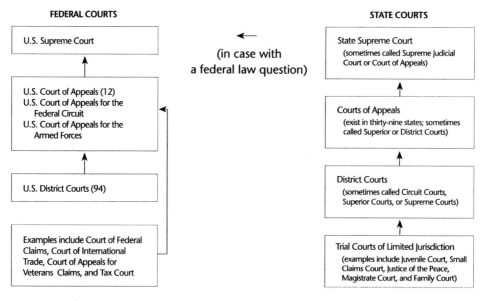

Source: Adapted from Lee Epstein and Thomas G. Walker, *Constitutional Law for a Changing America: Rights, Liberties, and Justice*, 2d ed. (Washington, D.C.: CQ Press, 1995), 865.

The U.S. Supreme Court is housed in a beautiful building across the street from the Capitol in Washington, D.C. When the Court is in session the plaza in front is filled, both before and after oral arguments, with interested parties, journalists, spectators, lawyers, and, sometimes, protesters.

Federal courts decide issues of federal law, which means controversies relating to the United States Constitution, federal laws (or statutes) passed by Congress, and regulations issued by federal agencies. The federal system has three levels of courts. The United States District Courts are trial courts that make findings of fact and law in civil cases and render verdicts in federal criminal cases. The United States Circuit Courts of Appeal are those courts where people appeal decisions and verdicts reached in district courts. In the courts of appeals, there are no juries; judges decide all the issues.

The United States Supreme Court is the highest court of appeals. The Supreme Court is the final step in the appeals process; its decisions become the supreme law of the land on constitutional issues. However, the Supreme Court may reject the vast majority of certiorari petitions it receives. . . . In fact, the Court agrees to hear fewer than 1 percent of the cases people try to bring before it.

The handsome Supreme Court building conveys the greatness and majesty of law, but the Court did not even have a home of its own for the first 146 years of its existence. After inhabiting relatively undignified quarters in New York and Philadelphia, the Court came to Washington when the city became the nation's capital at the start of the nineteenth century. Congress let it use space in the Capitol, where it decided such great cases as *Marbury v. Madison* (1803) and *McCulloch v. Maryland* (1819). In 1929 Chief Justice William Howard Taft, who had been president of the United States from 1909 to 1913, finally convinced Congress to build a permanent home for the Court. Today the Court attracts visitors and protestors alike. Ironically, there has been a good deal of First Amendment litigation about rules restricting First Amendment activity on the plaza in front of the Court, which remains generally unenthusiastic about political free speech on its doorstep.

Like the federal system, the state system usually has three levels of courts, comprised of trial, appellate, and supreme courts. The decisions of the state supreme courts may be appealed to the United States Supreme Court if there is a federal question involved. State courts may decide issues relating to both state law and federal law. In most cases, however, the issues that come before state courts deal with state law. Most crimes, such as assault, murder, rape, and burglary, are prosecuted in state court. Each state also has its own constitution, which provides citizens with additional protections beyond those afforded by the U.S. Constitution.

Courts hear two types of cases: criminal and civil. In a criminal prosecution charges are brought by a government prosecutor against a person who has allegedly violated a state or federal criminal statute. For example, if you attack your neighbor, the county or district attorney will prosecute you for violating the state's criminal code; if you are convicted, you might go to jail. Civil suits, in contrast, are brought by one person, company, or government entity against another for a civil wrong, property invasion, or breach of contract. For example, if you don't take care of your tree, and it falls on your neighbor's house, he can bring a negligence action against you for damages. This is called a *tort*. You cannot be sent to jail for committing a tort, although you can be forced to pay money damages to another party.

Courts will hear the facts and legal claims presented by two parties. The petitioner, or plaintiff, is the party that initiates the lawsuit; the respondent, or defendant, is the party that responds to the lawsuit. (In a case that has been appealed, the appealing party is known as the appellant and the responding party as the appellee.) The courts will then either dismiss the case or grant relief—that is, some monetary benefit or other restitution—based on the evidence and the arguments presented. Depending on the kind of case, courts tap different resources to reach their verdicts and make decisions. Courts analyze the Constitution and other relevant rules of law, such as a statutory law, which is passed by the state legislatures or Congress; an ordinance, which is enacted by a city, suburb, town, municipality or other local entity; or the common law, which is developed over time from the judgment of courts, as well as case precedent (decisions from earlier cases).

## Majority and Dissenting Opinions

You will notice that most of the case excerpts in this book present both majority and dissenting opinions. A majority opinion typically will first summarize the procedure of the case, which is the path the case took to get to the Supreme Court, and then the facts of the case—that is, what happened that led the parties to a court battle. The procedure and facts are normally followed by the justice's analysis of the issues posed in the case. The majority opinion represents the views of a majority of the justices on the nine-member Court. Occasionally another justice will write a concurring opinion, in which he or she agrees with the majority's result but offers a different analysis or gives the law or facts a different emphasis. A dissenting opinion expresses a different point of view on major or minor issues in the case and rejects the result reached by the majority of the Court.

It is important to read dissenting opinions along with majority opinions. Many decisions are decided on the slender margin of 5–4, and the simple change of one justice's mind—or the replacement of an outgoing or deceased justice with a newly appointed one—can create a new 5–4 majority in the opposite direction. Well-argued dissenting opinions are often the seeds of a later reversal. An example of a realignment of views took place

The justices of the Supreme Court, top row from left, Ruth Bader Ginsburg, David H. Souter, Clarence Thomas, and Stephen G. Breyer; bottom row from left, Antonin Scalia, John Paul Stevens, Chief Justice William H. Rehnquist, Sandra Day O'Connor, and Anthony M. Kennedy.

between 1940 and 1943. In *Minersville School Dist. v. Gobitis* (1940) the Supreme Court upheld compulsory flag salute rituals. But a strong dissenting opinion laid the groundwork for a reversal that followed three years later in *West Virginia v. Barnette* (1943) (see Chapter 2). In the latter case, the Court overruled *Gobitis,* finding that the First Amendment does not allow public schools to force students to pledge allegiance to the flag.

Dissenting opinions register the diversity of legal and political thought in our society and remind us that the law is not a "hard science." A court is not a computer that prints out right answers once you enter all of the facts. The law is a field of contests among competing theories, ideas, analogies, values, interpretations, and beliefs. As Justice Robert H. Jackson once said, "We are not final because we are infallible, but we are infallible only because we are final" (*Brown v. Allen,* 344 U.S. 443, 540 [1953]).

## How to Brief a Case

When law students read cases, they often take notes on them and outline them in a way that has come to be known as "briefing a case." You might find it useful to brief cases as you start your own habits of case reading and analysis. To effectively brief a case, you must do the following:

*State the procedure*—Where did this case come from? A state supreme court after a state appeals court after a state district court? A federal appeals court after a federal district court? What happened in those lower courts? Who won? Who lost? The procedural history of the case is a very quick statement about the path the case has followed in the courts.

***Name the parties***—Who is the plaintiff? Who is the defendant?

***State the facts***—Write down the facts of what happened to the parties. What is the story between them? Who did what to whom? What happened of legal significance? That is, what happened that is relevant to deciding the legal issues?

***State the issue (or issues)***—What are the legal issues that the court must decide to arrive at a decision?

***State the holding***—What does the court hold or decide? What is the "rule" that it comes up with in answer to the legal issues posed?

***State the court's reasoning or rationale***—Why does the court decide the way it does? What is the logic or rationale of its holding? What is its analysis?

There is no single right way to brief a case, but these basic features might be useful to you as you dip your toes in the water. If you become really interested in the process of case briefing and outlining—and do it as part of a study group—consider renting the classic 1973 movie about students at Harvard Law School called *The Paper Chase.* It might make you determined to go to law school—or to avoid the experience at all costs! If you don't want to wait for law school to engage your passion for the law, contact the Marshall-Brennan Fellows Program at American University's Washington College of Law for information about the annual high school student moot court and essay competitions. Check out the website at www.wcl.american.edu/wethestudents.

**Read On**

Cushman, Clare. *The Supreme Court Justices: Illustrated Biographies, 1789–1995.* 2d ed. Washington, D.C.: Congressional Quarterly, 1995.

Hall, Kermit. *The Oxford Companion to the Supreme Court of the United States.* New York: Oxford University Press, 1992.

Turow, Scott. *One L: The Turbulent True Story of a First Year at Harvard Law School.* New York: Farrar, Straus, and Giroux, reissued ed., 1988.

# THE HEART AND SOUL OF THE CONSTITUTION: FREEDOM OF EXPRESSION

2

"Congress shall make no law ... abridging the freedom of speech...." THE FIRST AMENDMENT

"If there is any principle of the Constitution that more imperatively calls for attachment than any other it is the principle of free thought—not free thought for those who agree with us but freedom for the thought that we hate." JUSTICE OLIVER WENDELL HOLMES, DISSENTING IN *UNITED STATES V. SCHWIMMER* (1929)

"Those who won our independence believed that the final end of the state was to make men free to develop their faculties, and that in its government the deliberative forces should prevail over the arbitrary. They valued liberty both as an end and as a means. They believed liberty to be the secret of happiness and courage to be the secret of liberty. They believed that freedom to think as you will and to speak as you think are means indispensable to the discovery and spread of political truth...." JUSTICE LOUIS BRANDEIS, CONCURRING IN *WHITNEY V. CALIFORNIA* (1927)

"In our system, students may not be regarded as closed-circuit recipients of only that which the State chooses to communicate. They may not be confined to the expression of those sentiments that are officially approved. In the absence of a specific showing of constitutionally valid reasons to regulate their speech, students are entitled to freedom of expression of their views...." JUSTICE ABE FORTAS, *TINKER V. DES MOINES INDEPENDENT COMMUNITY SCHOOL DISTRICT* (1969)

Many people today believe that the First Amendment captures what it means to be an American. This deep identification with the First Amendment is ironic because free speech received almost no protection from the Supreme Court until the middle of the twentieth century. Originally, the First Amendment applied only to congressional actions, and even then it was thought to be restricted to cases involving prior restraints by government against political speech. (Prior restraint refers to official restriction of speech or press publication before it occurs.)

Nonetheless, today the First Amendment both represents and guarantees a much more thoroughgoing commitment to freedom of speech, thought, and conscience. Since the 1940s the Supreme Court has upheld the right of citizens to engage in speech that is sexual, offensive, indecent, hostile, radical, reactionary, antiwar, unpopular, and even aggressively antigovernment in content. But the Court has also permitted government to censor and punish obscenity, fighting words (the kind of speech that people would experience as a verbal punch in the nose, like accusing a stranger in a bar of an incestuous relationship with his mother), and incitement of imminent lawless activity (like encouraging an angry mob in front of city hall to attack the mayor). Still, the United States of America protects more freedom of expression than almost any other nation on Earth.

The text of the First Amendment reads:

Congress shall make no law respecting an establishment of religion, or prohibiting the free exercise thereof; or abridging the freedom of speech, or of the press, or of the right of the people peaceably to assemble, and to petition the Government for a redress of grievances.

Although the First Amendment refers to Congress, the rights contained in the text apply also against states and localities. This is the effect of the "incorporation" doctrine discussed in Chapter 1.

There are six major rights protected by the First Amendment. These can be readily recalled by thinking of the word *GRAPES:*

*G*rievances, Right to petition for a redress of
*R*eligion, Right to no establishment of
*A*ssembly, Right to peaceful
*P*ress, Freedom of the
*E*xercise, Freedom of religious
*S*peech, Freedom of

What images does the First Amendment evoke in your mind? Can you make a collage, painting, or other artistic work that expresses your sense of the First Amendment?

**POINTS TO PONDER**

*How does the basic First Amendment liberty of free expression apply to students in public schools?*

- Should students be required to salute and pledge allegiance to the American flag?
- Should students be prevented from wearing clothing with political messages?
- Should students be allowed to wear their hair however they please?
- Should students be able to make speeches and presentations with vulgar or profane language?

## Expressive Conduct and the Right Not to Speak

The right to "speak" actually implies a broader right of free expression. The First Amendment protects not only written or spoken words, but what the Court calls *expressive conduct,* that is, actions that do not literally involve speaking or writing but that nonetheless send a message. Picketing a store, wearing a political button, or painting a picture are all examples of expressive conduct.

The decision in *West Virginia State Board of Education v. Barnette* (1943), one of many Supreme Court cases dealing with flags and political expression, articulated the idea that the First Amendment protects not just speech and written words but actions that communicate meaning. The case also established that free speech includes a right *not* to speak when a citizen so chooses.

In *Barnette* the Court found that public school students who choose not to join in the Pledge of Allegiance flag salute ritual for reasons of conscience cannot be forced to participate. The case reversed the Supreme Court's earlier decision in *Minersville School District v. Gobitis* (1940), which upheld the expulsion of the child of a Jehovah's Witness who refused to join in the pledge ritual.

The *Barnette* decision was of extraordinary importance because it set a precedent for defending liberty of conscience in the middle of World War II, when the United States and its Allies were struggling to defeat fascism and Nazism. In the three years between *Gobitis* and the Court's change of heart in *Barnette*, the children of Jehovah's Witnesses in public schools across the country faced widespread persecution and harassment for their continuing refusal to salute the flag during the nation's emergency mobilization against Adolph Hitler and the Axis powers. The Jehovah's Witnesses saw flag salutes as violating the prohibitions in the Ten Commandments against idol worship and graven images. They also wanted to show solidarity with Jehovah's Witnesses in Germany who had refused to participate in the "Heil Hitler" salute.

The Court's dramatic turnaround on the flag salute was a landmark statement that the values of the Constitution apply during wartime and peacetime alike. The case also illustrates that, when it comes to critical questions, the Court has often changed its mind about

The author of the landmark *Barnette* opinion, **JUSTICE ROBERT H. JACKSON** (1892–1954), was born and raised in the farm country outside Jamestown, New York. He graduated from two high schools, Frewsburg High and Jamestown High, where he spent an extra year. He never went to college, but he finished a two-year course at Albany Law School in only one year. He learned the practice of law through apprenticeship, and always considered himself a country lawyer. After a distinguished career during Franklin Delano Roosevelt's New Deal administration that included stints as *general counsel* of the Internal Revenue Bureau, *solicitor general of the United States*, and *attorney general*, Jackson was appointed to the Supreme Court by FDR in 1941. He served until 1954.

HIGHLIGHTS

➤   President Roosevelt tried to entice Jackson into electoral politics, encouraging him to run for governor of New York in 1938. His name was even floated as a potential vice presidential running mate for FDR, but Jackson's true passion was law, not electoral politics.

➤   Speaking of his high school English teacher Mary Willard, who inspired in him a love of language and oratory, Justice Jackson would later say: "Her influence would be hard to overestimate."

what the Constitution provides. Although we might be tempted to think of the Court as operating like a computer—plug in the facts and the legal answer prints out—in truth the concepts of the Constitution develop over time in reaction to events and in response to new legal arguments about how to define democracy and make the Constitution serve justice.

The Jehovah's Witnesses argued their case as if it were primarily about the rights of religious free exercise. Justice Jackson quickly shifted the terms of the discussion away from religion and toward free speech and free thought.

—  —

## WEST VIRGINIA STATE BOARD OF EDUCATION
### v.
## BARNETTE

*Supreme Court of the United States*
Argued March 11, 1943.
Decided June 14, 1943.

Justice JACKSON delivered the opinion of the Court.

... The Board of Education on January 9, 1942, ... order[ed] that the salute to the flag become "a regular part of the program of activities in the public schools," that all teachers and pupils "shall be required to participate in the salute honoring the Nation represented by the Flag; provided, however, that refusal to salute the Flag be regarded as an Act of insubordination, and shall be dealt with accordingly."

The resolution originally required the "commonly accepted salute to the Flag" which it defined. Objections to the salute as "being too much like Hitler's" were raised by the Parent and Teachers Association, the Boy and Girl Scouts, the Red Cross, and the Federation of Women's Clubs. Some modification appears to have been made in deference to these objections, but no concession was made to Jehovah's Witnesses. What is now required is the "stiff-arm" salute, the saluter to keep the right hand raised with palm turned up while the following is repeated: "I pledge allegiance to the Flag of the United States of America and to the Republic for which it stands; one Nation, indivisible, with liberty and justice for all."

Failure to conform is "insubordination" dealt with by expulsion. Readmission is denied by statute until compliance. Meanwhile the expelled child is "unlawfully absent" and may be proceeded against as a delinquent. His parents or guardians are liable to prosecution, and if convicted are subject to a fine not exceeding $50 and jail term not exceeding thirty days.

... [C]itizens of the United States and of West Virginia, brought suit in the United States District Court for themselves and others similarly situated asking its *injunction* to restrain enforcement of these laws and regulations against Jehovah's Witnesses. The Witnesses are an unincorporated body teaching that the obligation imposed by law of God is superior to that of laws enacted by temporal government. Their religious beliefs include a literal version of Exodus, Chapter 20, verses 4 and 5, which says: "Thou shalt not make unto thee any graven image, or any likeness of anything that is in heaven above, or that is in the earth beneath, or that is in the water under the earth; thou shalt not bow down thyself to them nor serve them." They consider that the flag is an "image" within this command. For this reason they refuse to salute it.

Children of this faith have been expelled from school and are threatened with exclusion for no other cause. Officials threaten to send them to reformatories maintained for criminally inclined juveniles. Parents of such children have been prosecuted and are threatened with prosecutions for causing delinquency.

... [T]he compulsory flag salute and pledge requires affirmation of a belief and an attitude of mind. It is not clear whether the regulation contemplates that pupils forego any contrary convictions of their own and become unwilling converts to the prescribed ceremony or whether it will be acceptable if they simulate assent by words without belief and by a gesture barren of meaning. It is now a commonplace that censorship or suppression of expression of opinion is tolerated by our Constitution only when the expression presents a clear and present danger of action of a kind the State is empowered to prevent and punish. It would seem that involuntary affirmation could be commanded only on even more immediate and urgent grounds than silence. But here the power of compulsion is invoked without any allegation that remaining passive during a flag salute ritual creates a clear and present danger that would justify an effort even to muffle expression. To sustain the compulsory flag salute we are required to say that a Bill of Rights which guards the individual's right to speak his own mind, left it open to public authorities to compel him to utter what is not in his mind.

... Nor does the issue as we see it turn on one's possession of particular religious views or the sincerity with which they are held. While religion supplies appellees' motive for enduring the discomforts of making the issue in this case, many citizens who do not share these religious views hold such a compulsory rite to infringe constitutional liberty of the individual. It is not necessary to inquire whether non-conformist beliefs will exempt from the duty to salute unless we first find power to make the salute a legal duty.

... The question which underlies the flag salute controversy is whether such a ceremony so touching matters of opinion and political attitude may be imposed upon the individual by official authority under powers committed to any political organization under our Constitution.

... The very purpose of a Bill of Rights was to withdraw certain subjects from the vicissitudes of political controversy, to place them beyond the reach of majorities and officials and to establish them as legal principles to be applied by the courts. One's right to life, liberty, and property, to free speech, a free press, freedom of worship and assembly, and other fundamental rights may not be submitted to vote; they depend on the outcome of no elections.

... National unity as an end which officials may foster by persuasion and example is not in question. The problem is whether under our Constitution compulsion as here employed is a permissible means for its achievement.

Struggles to coerce uniformity of sentiment in support of some end thought essential to their time and country have been waged by many good as well as by evil men. Nationalism is a relatively recent phenomenon but at other times and places the ends have been racial or territorial security, support of a dynasty or regime, and particular plans for saving souls. As first and moderate methods to attain unity have failed, those bent on its accomplishment must resort to an ever-increasing severity. As governmental pressure toward unity becomes greater, so strife becomes more bitter as to whose unity it shall be. Probably no deeper division of our people could proceed from any provocation than from finding it necessary to choose what doctrine and whose program public educational officials shall compel youth to unite in embracing. Ultimate futility of such attempts to compel coherence is the lesson of every such effort from the Roman drive to stamp out Christianity as

**JUSTICE FRANK MURPHY** (back row, second from left; 1890–1949) wrote a concurring opinion in *Barnette*. He was born and raised in Harbor Beach, Michigan, and graduated from the University of Michigan law school. He was mayor of Detroit and was elected governor of Michigan in 1936 at a time of tremendous labor unrest, which occupied much of his attention. President Franklin Delano Roosevelt appointed Murphy to the Supreme Court in 1940. He served until 1949 as a champion of freedom of expression, workers' rights, civil liberties, and the rights of Native Americans, Japanese Americans, and other miniorities.

HIGHLIGHTS

➤ As governor, Murphy was credited with the peaceful resolution of the nation's first sit-down strike at General Motors in 1937. "Nothing in the world is going to get the governor of Michigan off the position of working it out peacefully," he said.

➤ On the Court, Justice Murphy was known as a perfect gentleman, full of humanity, kindness, and humility. Clarence Darrow, who appeared before Murphy when he was a trial court judge in Michigan, said Murphy was "the kindliest and most understanding man I have ever happened to meet on the Bench."

a disturber of its pagan unity, the Inquisition, as a means to religious and dynastic unity, the Siberian exiles as a means to Russian unity, down to the fast failing efforts of our present totalitarian enemies. Those who begin coercive elimination of dissent soon find themselves exterminating dissenters. Compulsory unification of opinion achieves only the unanimity of the graveyard.

It seems trite but necessary to say that the First Amendment to our Constitution was designed to avoid these ends by avoiding these beginnings. There is no mysticism in the American concept of the State or of the nature or origin of its authority. We set up government by consent of the governed, and the Bill of Rights denies those in power any legal opportunity to coerce that consent. Authority here is to be controlled by public opinion, not public opinion by authority.

The case is made difficult not because the principles of its decision are obscure but because the flag involved is our own. Nevertheless, we apply the limitations of the Constitution with no fear that freedom to be intellectually and spiritually diverse or even contrary will disintegrate the social organization. To believe that patriotism will not flourish if patriotic ceremonies are voluntary and spontaneous instead of a compulsory routine is to make an unflattering estimate of the appeal of our institutions to free minds. We can have intellectual individualism and the rich cultural diversities that we owe to exceptional minds only at the price of occasional eccentricity and abnormal attitudes. When they are so harmless to others or to the State as those we deal with here, the price is not too great. But freedom to differ is not limited to things that do not matter much. That would be a mere shadow of freedom. The test of its substance is the right to differ as to things that touch the heart of the existing order.

If there is any fixed star in our constitutional constellation, it is that no official, high or petty, can prescribe what shall be orthodox in politics, nationalism, religion, or other matters of opinion or force citizens to confess by word or act their faith therein. If there are any circumstances which permit an exception, they do not now occur to us.

We think the action of the local authorities in compelling the flag salute and pledge transcends constitutional limitations on their power and invades the sphere of intellect and spirit which it is the purpose of the First Amendment to our Constitution to reserve from all official control.... 

*Affirmed.*

Justice MURPHY, concurring.

I agree with the opinion of the Court and join in it.

The complaint challenges an order of the State Board of Education which requires teachers and pupils to participate in the prescribed salute to the flag.... In effect compliance is compulsory and not optional. It is the claim of appellees that the regulation is invalid as a restriction on religious freedom and freedom of speech, secured to them against State infringement by the First and Fourteenth Amendments to the Constitution of the United States.

A reluctance to interfere with considered state action, the fact that the end sought is a desirable one, the emotion aroused by the flag as a symbol for which we have fought and are now fighting again, all of these are understandable. But there is before us the right of freedom to believe, freedom to worship one's Maker according to the dictates of one's conscience, a right which the Constitution specifically shelters. Reflection has convinced me that as a judge I have no loftier duty or responsibility than to uphold that spiritual freedom to its farthest reaches.

The right of freedom of thought and of religion as guaranteed by the Constitution against State action includes both the right to speak freely and the right to refrain from speaking at all, except insofar as essential operations of government may require it for the preservation of an orderly society, as in the case of compulsion to give evidence in court. Without wishing to disparage the purposes and intentions of those who hope to inculcate sentiments of loyalty and patriotism by requiring a declaration of allegiance as a feature of public education, or unduly belittle the benefits that may accrue therefrom, I am impelled to conclude that such a requirement is not essential to the maintenance of effective government and orderly society. ... Official compulsion to affirm what is contrary to one's religious beliefs is the antithesis of freedom of worship which, it is well to recall, was achieved in this country only after what Jefferson characterized as the "severest contests in which I have ever been engaged."

Justice FRANKFURTER, dissenting.

One who belongs to the most vilified and persecuted minority in history is not likely to be insensible to the freedoms guaranteed by our Constitution. Were my purely personal attitude relevant I should whole-heartedly associate myself with the general libertarian views in the Court's opinion, representing as they do the thought and action of a lifetime. But as judges we are neither Jew nor Gentile, neither Catholic nor agnostic. We owe equal attachment to the Constitution and are equally bound by our judicial obligations whether we derive our citizenship from the earliest or the latest immigrants to these shores. As a member of this Court I am not justified in writing my private notions of policy into the Constitution, no matter how deeply I may cherish them or how mischievous I may deem their disregard. The duty of a judge who must decide which of two claims before the Court shall prevail, that of a State to enact and enforce laws within its general competence or that of an individual to refuse obedience because of the demands of his conscience, is not that

The dissenter in *Barnette,* JUSTICE FELIX FRANKFURTER (1882–1965), was born in Vienna, Austria. With his family he left Vienna at age twelve for the United States. He attended the City College of New York and Harvard Law School, an institution where he taught for more than two decades and which he loved with the same passion he had for the Supreme Court. After Frankfurter's numerous jobs in Washington and his many years of teaching at Harvard, President Franklin Delano Roosevelt appointed him to the Court in 1939, where he served until 1962.

HIGHLIGHTS

➤   As a professor at Harvard Law School, Frankfurter was deeply involved in the celebrated Sacco-Vanzetti case, in which two Italian American anarchists, Nicola Sacco and Bartolomeo Vanzetti, were prosecuted on murder charges. Though they proclaimed their innocence, Sacco and Vanzetti were convicted in a politically charged trial and executed by the state of Massachusetts. Frankfurter helped fight, unsuccessfully, to have their convictions overturned, and he wrote a book critical of the unfairness of their criminal trial. The experience led Frankfurter to join others in establishing the American Civil Liberties Union, now America's leading civil liberties organization.

➤   During the post–World War I Paris Peace Conference, Frankfurter represented Dr. Chaim Weizmann and the Zionist leaders in negotiations with the Arab states. Frankfurter was himself Jewish, which he alludes to in the *Barnette* case, and a lifelong Zionist supporter of Israel.

➤   Although he was seen as a liberal when he was a law professor, Justice Frankfurter's career on the Court actually pleased conservatives because of his interest in federalism and judicial restraint, wherein judges defer to the political branches and decline to invalidate democratically chosen public policies and laws.

of the ordinary person. It can never be emphasized too much that one's own opinion about the wisdom or evil of a law should be excluded altogether when one is doing one's duty on the bench. The only opinion of our own even looking in that direction that is material is our opinion whether legislators could in reason have enacted such a law. In the light of all the circumstances, including the history of this question in this Court, it would require more daring than I possess to deny that reasonable legislators could have taken the action which is before us for review. Most unwillingly, therefore, I must differ from my brethren with regard to legislation like this. I cannot bring my mind to believe that the "liberty" secured by the Due Process Clause gives this Court authority to deny to the State of West Virginia the attainment of that which we all recognize as a legitimate legislative end, namely, the promotion of good citizenship, by employment of the means here chosen.

---

EXERCISE 2.1. In *Barnette,* the Court held that the First Amendment prevents school officials from compelling a student to stand and salute the flag during the Pledge of Allegiance. Although public schools may continue to have a Pledge of Allegiance ceremony every morning, students may not be forced to participate or be punished for not participating. Do you think this decision was right? Why or why not? Write a one-page statement on your assessment of the majority's opinion in *West Virginia State Board of Education v. Barnette* (1943). Read your reactions aloud and talk about them.

EXERCISE 2.2. What does the American flag represent to you? Does the flag have a single meaning or multiple meanings? If someone decides to sit out a flag salute, does it diminish the meaning of the flag in your eyes? Does it diminish the person in your eyes? What reasons might a student have for not joining in a flag salute? Do you think that

Gregory Johnson holds an American flag while another man sets it on fire. In *Texas v. Johnson* (1989) the Supreme Court on First Amendment grounds overturned Johnson's conviction for flag burning. In 1990 the Court reaffirmed its decision by ruling the Flag Protection Act unconstitutional.

businesses like Ralph Lauren, Speedo, and Tommy Hilfiger should be able to use the American flag as part of their clothing and advertising and to put it on products like underarm deodorant? Explore the use of the flag in advertising and popular culture.

EXERCISE 2.3. In *Texas v. Johnson* (1989) the Supreme Court upheld the right of the people under the First Amendment to use the American flag for expressive purposes, including even the burning of a flag at a political demonstration. In that case Gregory Johnson, a member of the Revolutionary Communist Youth Brigade, set fire to an American flag at the 1984 Republican National Convention in Dallas to demonstrate his opposition to the reelection of President Ronald Reagan. The youthful Johnson was convicted of violating a state law making it a crime to "deface, damage or otherwise physically mistreat" the American flag "in a way that the actor knows will seriously offend one or more persons likely to observe or discover his action." A 5–4 majority on the Supreme Court found that Johnson was engaged in an act of symbolic speech and that the Texas flag desecration statute he was charged under was impermissibly directed at censoring political expression. Writing for the majority, Justice William Brennan wrote: "If there is a bedrock principle underlying the First Amendment, it is that the Government may not prohibit the expression of an idea simply because society finds the idea itself offensive or disagreeable." The majority thus struck down Johnson's conviction under the statute as a violation of the First Amendment.

In his dissenting opinion, Justice John Paul Stevens argued: "Even if flag burning could be considered just another species of symbolic speech under the logical application of the rules that the Court has developed in its interpretation of the First Amendment in other contexts, this case has an intangible dimension that makes those rules inapplicable." Justice Stevens, who is ordinarily a strong champion of free speech, likened the asserted right to burn flags in protest to "a federal right to post bulletin boards and graffiti on the Washington Monument." Is this a perceptive analogy? Why or why not? Make a list of the ways in which this analogy is either accurate or misleading.

Since *Texas v. Johnson* was decided there have been several attempts to add to the Constitution language that would give Congress power to enact a law making it a crime to burn or desecrate the flag. Congress has voted several times on versions of the following proposed amendment:

> Congress shall have power to prohibit physical desecration of the flag of the United States.

Although the proposed "Flag Amendment" has repeatedly won two-thirds majorities in the House of Representatives, it has consistently fallen just short of the two-thirds mark in the Senate. (Article V of the Constitution provides that new amendments must be passed by a two-thirds vote in both the House of Representatives and the Senate and then ratified by three-fourths of the states.)

The issue of flag desecration is not going away. But what does "desecration" mean? Look it up. Is it clear that flag burning is a form of desecration? Federal law today actually recommends burning flags as the proper form of disposal. Indeed, any Boy Scout or Girl

Scout knows that this is proper flag protocol. There are undoubtedly students reading this book right now who have burned flags!

Pretend that you and your classmates are senators considering the proposed Flag Desecration Amendment. Research *Texas v. Johnson* and the pros and cons of the proposed constitutional amendment to ban flag desecration. (Check magazine and newspaper articles, as well as Internet commentary.) Prepare a one-minute speech on how you plan to vote and why. Be sure to consider whether use of the flag by companies like Ralph Lauren and Speedo for commercial advertising would be permitted under the amendment. The first generation of flag patriots, the Union's Civil War veterans in the Grand Army of the Republic, considered commercial use of the flag the worst kind of desecration. What about the use of flags in art, in theater, in personal clothing? Also consider more mainstream political uses of the flag, such as writing "Vote for Jones, not Smith" on a flag design poster or "Boycott oil from Saudi Arabia" on a flag. Earlier flag protectors thought it was desecration to use the flag in any partisan way since it was the symbol of the whole country. Will such political flag uses be allowed? What *is* a flag exactly?

EXERCISE 2.4. The combustible mix of public schools, the Pledge of Allegiance, and religion exploded once more in June 2002 when a three-judge panel on the Ninth Circuit ruled, in *Newdow v. U.S. Congress,* that public schools cannot conduct the Pledge of Allegiance with the words "under God" included in the script. We will return to this problem in Chapter 4, but think about this question: What function do the words "under God" now have in the pledge for students who choose to say it?

---

**FOR THE CLASS**

CHANNEL FUN. The Medium County Public School System has installed a television in every one of its schools' classrooms. The televisions were donated by the for-profit corporation Channel Fun in return for Medium County Schools' promise to broadcast daily in each homeroom at least seven minutes' worth of substantive Channel Fun programming—including news, features, and sports reports—and three minutes of commercials for fast food, soft drinks, and candy. Ninth-graders Sandy Sassy and Robert Rad walk out of the classroom whenever the commercials appear, saying that they "refuse to be part of this commercial sellout of our education." The school principal tells Sandy and Robert to stop their protest, but they continue to walk out whenever commercials come on. Sandy and Robert are suspended from school. They now appeal their suspensions to federal district court.

Form two teams of students and argue whether the suspensions of Sandy and Robert should be struck down on First Amendment grounds or whether the school acted reasonably within its powers. What language in *Barnette* do you cite for your position? Select a panel of three federal appeals court judges to determine whether *Barnette* protects the students' right to walk out.

---

# The Right to Speak Freely and Protest (But Not to Disrupt)

Just as students have a First Amendment right *not* to be forced to profess their belief in officially approved ideas, they also have a First Amendment right *to* express their own ideas, at least if they do so in a way that does not fundamentally interfere with their school's functions. This was the holding of the Court in *Tinker v. Des Moines School District* (1969), the dramatic high point of the Supreme Court's commitment to free speech in the schools.

The *Tinker* case arose in the heat of national controversy over the Vietnam War, the United States' military action in Indochina in the 1960s and 1970s that caused great political division across the country. Many people supported the war as an intervention on behalf of a besieged ally, South Vietnam, that was resisting Communist aggression. Others considered the long war both unjust and *illegal*—that is, a violation of the Constitution. They maintained that such an aggressive intervention in the affairs of another country, which Congress never declared as a war, took place at huge human and moral cost. Historians and politicians continue to debate the Vietnam War, perhaps our most divisive military experience outside of the Civil War.

Many young Americans joined the public debate over the morality and justice of the Vietnam War. This case had its origins in November 1965 when a group of people from Iowa traveled to Washington, D.C., to join a peace march that was organized by the National Committee for a Sane Nuclear Policy and that featured speeches by Coretta Scott King and Dr. Benjamin Spock. The Iowa marchers included teenagers Christopher Eckhardt and John Tinker, both fifteen years old and in the tenth grade at Des Moines public high schools. The boys' families were steeped in progressive causes such as civil rights and the peace movement.

Upon the boys' return to Iowa, Eckhardt and Tinker decided with Tinker's sister Mary Beth, a thirteen-year-old in eighth grade, to express their opposition to the war. Specifi-

Mary Beth Tinker, here with her mother, Lorena, and younger brother Paul, protested the Vietnam War in 1965 with her brother John by wearing black armbands to school. After they were suspended by school authorities, the Supreme Court held that public school students have First Amendment rights of political expression that were violated in their case.

cally, they wore black armbands to school as a way to mourn the loss of life in Vietnam and to support Sen. Robert F. Kennedy's proposal for an extended truce in the war. When dozens of other students joined in this silent protest, school authorities moved to stop the protests and isolate and punish the students who wore the armbands. Even in the face of this official hostility (and taunting by other students), the Tinkers and Christopher Eckhardt stood their ground and became the plaintiffs in this famous case.

————

# TINKER
## v.
## DES MOINES INDEPENDENT COMMUNITY SCHOOL DISTRICT

*Supreme Court of the United States*
Argued Nov. 12, 1968.
Decided Feb. 24, 1969.

Justice FORTAS delivered the opinion of the Court.

Petitioner John F. Tinker, 15 years old, and Christopher Eckhardt, 16 years old, attended high schools in Des Moines, Iowa. Petitioner Mary Beth Tinker, John's sister, was a 13-year-old student in junior high school.

In December 1965, a group of adults and students in Des Moines held a meeting at the Eckhardt home. The group determined to publicize their objections to the hostilities in Vietnam and their support for a truce by wearing black armbands during the holiday season and by fasting on December 16 and New Year's Eve. Petitioners and their parents had previously engaged in similar activities, and they decided to participate in the program.

The principals of the Des Moines schools became aware of the plan to wear armbands. On December 14, 1965, they met and adopted a policy that any student wearing an armband to school would be asked to remove it, and if he refused he would be suspended until he returned without the armband. Petitioners were aware of the regulation that the school authorities adopted.

On December 16, Mary Beth and Christopher wore black armbands to their schools. John Tinker wore his armband the next day. They were all sent home and suspended from school until they would come back without their armbands. They did not return to school until after the planned period for wearing armbands had expired—that is, until after New Year's Day. . . .

## I

The District Court recognized that the wearing of an armband for the purpose of expressing certain views is the type of symbolic act that is within the Free Speech Clause of the First Amendment. As we shall discuss, the wearing of armbands in the circumstances of this case was entirely divorced from actually or potentially disruptive conduct by those participating in it. It was closely akin to "pure speech" which, we have repeatedly held, is entitled to comprehensive protection under the First Amendment.

First Amendment rights, applied in light of the special characteristics of the school environment, are available to teachers and students. It can hardly be argued that either students or teachers shed their constitutional rights to freedom of speech or expression at the schoolhouse gate. This has been the unmistakable holding of this Court for almost 50 years. . . .

. . . Our problem lies in the area where students in the exercise of First Amendment rights collide with the rules of the school authorities.

II

The problem posed by the present case does not relate to regulation of the length of skirts or the type of clothing, to hair style, or deportment. It does not concern aggressive, disruptive action or even group demonstrations. Our problem involves direct, primary First Amendment rights akin to "pure speech."

The school officials banned and sought to punish petitioners for a silent, passive expression of opinion, unaccompanied by any disorder or disturbance on the part of petitioners. There is here no evidence whatever of petitioners' interference, actual or nascent, with the schools' work or of collision with the rights of other students to be secure and to be let alone. Accordingly, this case does not concern speech or action that intrudes upon the work of the schools or the rights of other students.

Only a few of the 18,000 students in the school system wore the black armbands. Only five students were suspended for wearing them. There is no indication that the work of the schools or any class was disrupted. Outside the classrooms, a few students made hostile remarks to the children wearing armbands, but there were no threats or acts of violence on school premises.

The District Court concluded that the action of the school authorities was reasonable because it was based upon their fear of a disturbance from the wearing of the armbands. But, in our system, undifferentiated fear or apprehension of disturbance is not enough to overcome the right to freedom of expression. Any departure from absolute regimentation may cause trouble. Any variation from the majority's opinion may inspire fear. Any word spoken, in class, in the lunchroom, or on the campus, that deviates from the views of another person may start an argument or cause a disturbance. But our Constitution says we must take this risk[,] and our history says it is this sort of hazardous freedom—this kind of openness—that is the basis of our national strength and of the independence and vigor of Americans who grow up and live in this relatively permissive . . . society.

In order for the State in the person of school officials to justify prohibition of a particular expression of opinion, it must be able to show that its action was caused by something more than a mere desire to avoid the discomfort and unpleasantness that always accompany an unpopular viewpoint. Certainly where there is no finding and no showing that engaging in the forbidden conduct would "materially and substantially interfere with the requirements of appropriate discipline in the operation of the school," the prohibition cannot be sustained.

In the present case, the District Court made no such finding, and our independent examination of the record fails to yield evidence that the school authorities had reason to anticipate that the wearing of the armbands would substantially interfere with the work of the school or impinge upon the rights of other students. Even an official memorandum prepared after the suspension that listed the reasons for the ban on wearing the armbands made no reference to the anticipation of such disruption.

On the contrary, the action of the school authorities appears to have been based upon an urgent wish to avoid the controversy which might result from the expression, even by the silent symbol of armbands, of opposition to this Nation's part in the conflagration in Vietnam. . . .

It is also relevant that the school authorities did not purport to prohibit the wearing of all symbols of political or controversial significance. The record shows that students in some of the schools wore buttons relating to national political campaigns, and some even wore the Iron Cross, traditionally a symbol of Nazism. The order prohibiting the wearing of armbands did not extend to these. Instead, a particular symbol—black armbands worn to exhibit opposition to this Nation's involvement in Vietnam—was singled out for prohibition. Clearly, the prohibition of expression of one particular opinion, at least without evidence that it is necessary to avoid material and substantial interference with schoolwork or discipline, is not constitutionally permissible.

In our system, state-operated schools may not be enclaves of totalitarianism. School officials do not possess absolute authority over their students. Students in school as well as out of school are "persons" under our Constitution. They are possessed of fundamental rights which the State must respect, just as they themselves must respect their obligations to the State. In our system, students may not be regarded as closed-circuit recipients of only that which the State chooses to communicate. They may not be confined to the expression of those sentiments that are officially approved. In the absence of a specific showing of constitutionally valid reasons to regulate their speech, students are entitled to freedom of expression of their views....

The principle of these cases is not confined to the supervised and ordained discussion which takes place in the classroom. The principal use to which the schools are dedicated is to accommodate students during prescribed hours for the purpose of certain types of activities. Among those activities is personal intercommunication among the students. This is not only an inevitable part of the process of attending school; it is also an important part of the educational process. A student's rights, therefore, do not embrace merely the classroom hours. When he is in the cafeteria, or on the playing field, or on the campus during the authorized hours, he may express his opinions, even on controversial subjects like the conflict in Vietnam, if he does so without "materially and substantially interfer(ing) with the requirements of appropriate discipline in the operation of the school" and without colliding with the rights of others. But conduct by the student, in class or out of it, which for any reason—whether it stems from time, place, or type of behavior—materially disrupts classwork or involves substantial disorder or invasion of the rights of others is, of course, not immunized by the constitutional guarantee of freedom of speech....

As we have discussed, the record does not demonstrate any facts which might reasonably have led school authorities to forecast substantial disruption of or material interference with school activities, and no disturbances or disorders on the school premises in fact occurred. These petitioners merely went about their ordained rounds in school. Their deviation consisted only in wearing on their sleeve a band of black cloth, not more than two inches wide. They wore it to exhibit their disapproval of the Vietnam hostilities and their advocacy of a truce, to make their views known, and, by their example, to influence others to adopt them. They neither interrupted school activities nor sought to intrude in the school affairs or the lives of others. They caused discussion outside of the classrooms, but no interference with work and no disorder. In the circumstances, our Constitution does not permit officials of the State to deny their form of expression....

*Reversed and remanded.*

Justice BLACK, dissenting.

... While the absence of obscene remarks or boisterous and loud disorder perhaps justifies the Court's statement that the few armband students did not actually "disrupt" the classwork, I think the record overwhelmingly shows that the armbands did exactly what the elected school officials and principals foresaw they would, that is, took the students' minds off their classwork and diverted

**JUSTICE ABE FORTAS** (1910–1982) wrote the opinion for the majority in *Tinker*. Born in Memphis, Tennessee, Justice Fortas was the youngest of five children. He went to Southwestern College in Memphis and Yale Law School, where he studied under another future justice, William O. Douglas. His good friend, President Lyndon Johnson, appointed Fortas to the Court in 1965. Fortas, an accomplished violinist, served on the Court for only four years. Fortas was a brilliant lawyer.

HIGHLIGHTS

➤ When Fortas was a partner at the prestigious Washington, D.C., firm of Arnold and Porter, Fortas became the court-appointed advocate for Clarence Earl Gideon, the appellant in *Gideon v. Wainwright* (1963). This case established that the government must appoint lawyers for indigent criminal defendants who cannot otherwise afford one.

➤ Justice Fortas wrote the Court's opinion in *In re Gault* (1967), holding that young people in juvenile proceedings enjoy many of the same constitutional protections as adults, including the right to counsel and the right against self-incrimination.

➤ Justice Fortas resigned from the Court on May 14, 1969, amid allegations of financial improprieties that led to calls for his impeachment.

them to thoughts about the highly emotional subject of the Vietnam war. And I repeat that if the time has come when pupils of state-supported schools, kindergartens, grammar schools, or high schools, can defy and flout orders of school officials to keep their minds on their own schoolwork, it is the beginning of a new revolutionary era of permissiveness in this country fostered by the judiciary. The next logical step, it appears to me, would be to hold unconstitutional laws that bar pupils under 21 or 18 from voting, or from being elected members of the boards of education. . . .

Change has been said to be truly the law of life but sometimes the old and the tried and true are worth holding. The schools of this Nation have undoubtedly contributed to giving us tranquility and to making us a more law-abiding people. Uncontrolled and uncontrollable liberty is an enemy to domestic peace. We cannot close our eyes to the fact that some of the country's greatest problems are crimes committed by the youth, too many of school age. School discipline, like parental discipline, is an integral and important part of training our children to be good citizens—to be better citizens. Here a very small number of students have crisply and summarily refused to obey a school order designed to give pupils who want to learn the opportunity to do so. One does not need to be a prophet or the son of a prophet to know that after the Court's holding today some students in Iowa schools and indeed in all schools will be ready, able, and willing to defy their teachers on practically all orders. This is the more unfortunate for the schools since groups of students all over the land are already running loose, conducting break-ins, sit-ins, lie-ins, and smash-ins. Many of these student groups, as is all too familiar to all who read the newspapers and watch the television news programs, have already engaged in rioting, property seizures, and destruction. They have picketed schools to force students not to cross their picket lines and have too often violently attacked earnest but frightened students who wanted an education that the pickets did not want them to get. Students engaged in such activities are apparently confident that they

Mary Beth Tinker (right) with high school students at the 2002 "We the Students" William Karchmer Constitutional Law Moot Court Competition at American University.

know far more about how to operate public school systems than do their parents, teachers, and elected school officials.... I dissent.

Building on *Barnette,* the Court in *Tinker* established several principles. First, it established that students do not surrender their constitutional rights simply by entering a public school; second, that symbolic dress worn for political reasons is expression protected by the First Amendment; and, third, that student expression can only be curtailed or censored where the school can show it threatens "material and substantial interference" with the school's effective operation or the rights of other students.

These principles were sharply limited in *Hazelwood School District v. Kuhlmeier* (1988), where the Court held that all student expression associated with official academic activities, such as the school newspaper, the school yearbook, assemblies, the student council, and athletic teams, may be regulated or censored in the interests of serving the school's reasonable academic missions and objectives. (We will explore this major caveat to the *Tinker* principle in Chapter 3.)

---

EXERCISE 2.5. Do you think that "political" discussion and nonviolent protests have a proper place in public schools? Should high school students be shielded from the discomforting turbulence of political controversy or should they be educated for active participation as democratic citizens in the rough-and-tumble of American society? What about junior high school students? Elementary school students? Is there any way to avoid political controversy in school? Write a one-page essay answering these questions.

---

SOFT DRINKS, HARD CHOICES. This exercise requires you to integrate your knowledge of the *Barnette* and *Tinker* cases and apply it to a contemporary problem. Hypothetical High School, which has been having financial problems, enters a national competition sponsored by Coca-Cola in which it tries to show its "Coca-Cola pride" to win educational tools worth tens of thousands of dollars, including televisions, VCRs, computers, and printers. On the appointed day, all Hypothetical High students wear a Coca-Cola T-shirt (donated by the company) to school—that is, all students except senior class clown Randy Rabblerouser, who wears a Pepsi T-shirt. When told by the principal to take it off and put on a Coca-Cola T-shirt, he says, "I'm no robot, man." The principal has invited executives from the Coca-Cola Corporation and local media to drop in at the school throughout the day and has also asked one of the art teachers to videotape students in their Coca-Cola garb. The principal is afraid that Randy's Pepsi T-shirt will be seen by the visiting corporate executives and news reporters or may be picked up on videotape. He gives Randy one more chance to take off his T-shirt and put on the Coca-Cola shirt, saying, "You are being disruptive of our mission, Randall. There's a lot at stake here." But Randy says, "You can't make me wear the flag of Coke." The principal has a hearing in his office where Randy talks about Mary Beth Tinker and Martin Luther King. The principal says, "If you want to be a civil disobedient, then you pay the price." He suspends Randy for three days for refusing to follow the rules and policies of the school. Randy goes to federal court to ask for an injunction against his suspension.

Divide the classroom into two teams of students and argue before a panel of three (student) federal district judges whether the suspension is constitutional or not. How do you rule and why?

An increasing number of public high schools are signing contracts with large corporations to sell and market their products on campus and at athletic events. For example, the Martin County, Florida, school district in the 1990s okayed a $155,000 contract between South Fork High School and Pepsi-Cola in which South Fork contracted to "make its best effort to maximize all sales opportunities for Pepsi-Cola products."

---

EXERCISE 2.6. In 1990 school teachers in McMinnville, Oregon, went on a lawful strike to protest for better pay and working conditions. The school fired them and replaced them. Many students were upset by this action, and two students, Chandler and Depweg (first names not available), were especially angry because their fathers were among the dismissed teachers. They wore buttons to school—and distributed them to other students—that said "No scabs," "I'm not listening scab," "Do scabs bleed?," "Scab we will never forget," "Students united for a fair settlement," and "We want our real teachers back." (*Scab* is derogatory slang for someone who takes the job of a striking worker.) The two students were suspended for refusing to take the buttons off. They brought a First Amendment action alleging that they had a right to wear the buttons and that they were disciplined for protesting the school's actions. The District Court upheld the discipline, saying that the buttons were "offensive" and "inherently disruptive." Chandler and Depweg appealed, arguing that their speech was political, passive, non-violent and nondisruptive. The case went to the Ninth Circuit Court of Appeals.

Set up teams to argue and decide the case. How do you decide? The actual decision is found at *Chandler v. McMinnville School District,* 978 F. 2d 524 (1992), and your teacher will know the outcome.

---

# The Confederate Flag and Other Racially Provocative Symbols

As we saw in *West Virginia v. Barnette* people can get touchy about flags. As we saw in *Tinker v. Des Moines Independent Community School District,* people become concerned about what students wear to school. Put flags and clothes together, and you get an explosive mix.

In *Melton v. Young* (1972), the Sixth Circuit Court of Appeals upheld the suspension of a Brainerd High School student in Chattanooga, Tennessee, for wearing to school a jacket with the Confederate battle flag emblem sewn on his sleeve. Prior to the incident, there had been racial antagonism and repeated fights and disturbances among students over the school's use of the Confederate flag as an official school symbol. In response, the school had decided to drop the Confederate flag and the song "Dixie" from its school functions (although it kept "the Rebels" for its team name). Student Rod Melton

Mississippi governor Ross Barnett smiles while Confederate flags wave in the background at a University of Mississippi football game. The Confederate battle flag made a strong reappearance in the South after the Supreme Court's desegregation holding in *Brown v. Board of Education* in 1954.

protested these changes by wearing his Confederate flag symbol to school. When he refused to take it off, he was suspended. The formerly all-white school was integrated in 1966 (twelve years after *Brown v. Board of Education of Topeka, Kansas,* which declared the segregation of public schools unconstitutional). In 1969 the student body consisted of 170 black and 1,224 white students. The Sixth Circuit majority found that, given the violent reactions to prior displays of the Confederate flag at school, school authorities did not violate the *Tinker* rule by suspending Melton since his expressive conduct threatened material and substantial disruption of the educational process.

A dissenting judge in the case, William E. Miller, took his colleagues to task for failing to distinguish between the school's official use of the Confederate emblem, which had indeed caused violent unrest in the past, and a student's personal use of the insignia, which he said was never linked to violent trouble at the school. Judge Miller emphasized that the Confederate flag patch "was small; it was worn as a part of an article of clothing; and it had no inherent qualities for causing disruption or disturbance." Moreover, he argued that, like Mary Beth Tinker's armband, the "emblem was worn by the student in a quiet, peaceful and dignified manner with no untoward gestures or remarks." But the majority thought the potential for violence was clear.

The Tenth Circuit Court of Appeals handed down a similar decision in *West v. Derby Unified School District No. 260* (2000). In that case a middle school student, who had been involved in racial incidents in the past, was suspended for violating a racial harassment and intimidation policy when he drew a Confederate flag design on a piece of paper during class. The court found the school system acted reasonably in predicting disruption from this incident based on past racial violence and hate group activities at the school.

---

FOR THE CLASS

HOW DISRUPTIVE IS THE CONFEDERATE FLAG? Imagine a school in Lancaster, Pennsylvania, where there has been no racial violence in anyone's memory and a very small minority student population until recently. After an influx of new students from El Salvador, a high school senior, John Rebell, wears a blue jean jacket with a Confederate Flag patch on the back to school. When several classmates complain, he is told by the principal to remove the patch but he refuses. He is suspended for violating a rule against "disruptive conduct or conduct that will violate the rights of other students." Do you think his suspension is acceptable within the *Tinker* rule? Is it like the *Melton* and *Derby* cases? Should a school have to wait for a disruption to occur before it limits students' rights? Why or why not? Should there be different presumptions about the potential for violence in southern and northern school districts?

*Melton* was a court of appeals case that the student tried to bring to the Supreme Court through a petition for a *writ of certiorari,* which the Court issues to direct a lower court to deliver a case for review. The Supreme Court has discretion to choose the cases it hears. When the Court declines to hear a case, as it did in *Melton,* it "denies certiorari." The Court denies certiorari in more than 99 percent of the cases in which it is sought.

Although it is hard to get a case heard before the Supreme Court, it is relatively easy to go hear someone else's Supreme Court case being argued. Arguments are open to the public, so you may want to organize a class trip to Washington to see one; it is an unforgettable experience.

The Supreme Court is in session between October and April and accommodates about fifty spectators on a first-come-first-served basis. The Supreme Court website, www.supremecourtus.gov, has information about visiting. Groups of thirty or more should write at least one month in advance to:

Office of the Marshall
Supreme Court of the United States of America
1 First Street N.E.
Washington, D.C. 20543

EXERCISE 2.7. Some people see the Confederate battle flag as a symbol of slavery, secession from the Union, and white supremacy. Others see it as a symbol of regional and historic pride. Who is right? Can the same symbol mean different things to different people? Semioticians—people who study the meaning of signs—often describe flags as "polysemous," meaning that they have multiple meanings. What if someone wore a Confederate flag emblem to your school? What kind of effect do you think it would have? What message might that person be sending?

EXERCISE 2.8. Do you think that racist and sexist symbols enjoy less First Amendment protection than other speech? Does the Fourteenth Amendment principle of equal protection give government more power to censor racist expression? Why or why not? Does the fact that the United States fought a war against the Confederacy in which hundreds of thousands of Americans died make any difference?

**FOR THE CLASS**

TINKER-ING WITH UNIFORM POLICIES. Imagine this scenario taking place in your school district: Parents and school authorities are concerned about an upsurge in student misbehavior throughout the schools as well as competition among students to see who can wear the "coolest" clothes, often meaning the most expensive designer clothing and athletic footwear. The school board votes to impose a mandatory school uniform policy in all elementary, junior high, and high schools that requires students to wear solid-color polo-type shirts with collars, oxford-type shirts, or blouses with collars in one of two colors (white or navy blue); khaki pants; and loafers. Boys must wear blue blazers and red ties. Blue jeans, denim, striped materials, checkered materials, and shirts with written messages on them are all prohibited by the new uniform policy. A group of students goes to federal court to try to stop the policy, arguing that it violates the First Amendment by denying students their expressive freedom as guaranteed in *Tinker*. They also argue that there are a lot of other ways to deal with student discipline problems. The school district argues that student dress is not an aspect of First Amendment freedom under *Tinker* and, even if it is, departures from a reasonable dress code threaten material and substantial disruption where there are ongoing problems with student discipline and fashion competition.

Divide the class into two teams of lawyers and a team of justices. Conduct a mock Supreme Court argument where lawyers for the students argue that the policy violates the First Amendment and lawyers for the school district defend it. The justices should ask intelligent questions of both sides.

(For your information, the Fifth Circuit Court of Appeals has upheld similar mandatory uniform policies in Bossier Parish, Louisiana, and Forney, Texas, against student lawsuits.)

A MYSTICAL BAN ON BLUE JEANS. In a Mystic, Connecticut, local newspaper, a report appears on Friday that annual "National Coming Out Day" is the following Thursday, May 5. The story states that gays and lesbians and their supporters will wear blue jeans to show their support for gay rights. The Mystic school board learns that many high school students intend to wear blue jeans (which are ordinarily allowed) and that another group of students plans to wear buttons that say "God Made Adam and Eve, Not Adam and Steve" provided by a local conservative group. The school board announces that "any student who wears blue jeans to school on May 5 or wears a button expressing an opinion about homosexuality will be sent home for the rest of the day." Can the school board do this under Supreme Court case law?

Divide the class into two groups, then take turns making arguments on both sides. Do you think the school board dealt well with the expected expression from students? How would you have handled it if you were on the school board?

---

# A Hirsute Lawsuit:
# Do Boys Have the Right to Wear Long Hair?

According to *Tinker*, students can choose their own dress as long as their choices do not threaten "material" and "substantial" disruption to school activities. In *Karr v. Schmidt* (1972), the Fifth Circuit considered a claim that a student's hairstyle represents a symbolic and expressive choice that deserves First Amendment protection. The plaintiff was Chesley Karr, a sixteen-year-old boy at Coronado High School in El Paso, Texas, who was not allowed to enroll in his junior year of high school because he had grown his hair long and refused to cut it despite his school's repeated demands that he do so.

Karr argued that his hairstyle was deeply personal and integrally related to his sense of style and personal values. He went to federal court and challenged the "boy hair" provisions in the following dress code:

> The matter of student grooming is of utmost concern to parents who realize the importance of seeing that children are properly attired when they leave for school each day. Also, student behavior is influenced by proper dress and grooming. Consequently, student grooming is the proper concern of school administrators and teachers. In order to help ensure proper acceptable behavior on the part of the students, it becomes necessary to establish certain guidelines to aid parents and students in selecting the proper attire for the school year. Schools also recog-

nize that parents are basically responsible for their children's dress and general appearance. The role of the school is one of guidance for pupils in an effort for total education and the development of proper attitudes. Student dress will be considered acceptable if it does not violate any of the three following principles: 1. Clothing worn is not to be suggestive or indecent. 2. Clothing and general appearance is not to be of the type that would cause a disturbance or interfere with the instructional program. 3. Clothing and general appearance is to be such as not to constitute a health or safety hazard. Guidelines for dress and grooming are:

FOR BOYS

Hair may be blocked, but is not to hang over the ears or the top of the collar of a standard dress shirt and must not obstruct vision. No artificial means to conceal the length of the hair is to be permitted; i.e., ponytails, buns, wigs, combs, or straps....

Cleanliness of body and clothing is expected of all students at all times. No child shall be admitted to school or shall be allowed to continue in school who fails to conform to the proper standards of dress.

Karr won a First Amendment and Equal Protection victory in federal district court in Texas. The court found that "the presence and enforcement of the hair-cut rule causes far more disruption of the classroom instructional process than the hair it seeks to prohibit."

The district court rejected the different reasons offered by the school to support the rule against long hair. For example, the school argued that the rule was necessary to guarantee cleanliness, but the district court found that the length of a student's hair is unrelated to "habits of personal hygiene." That is, a person can have long hair that is clean or short hair that is dirty.

The district court also rejected the claim that long hair creates a safety hazard in science laboratories; if true, the court said, this would mean that the rule should apply to girls as well as boys. The court also found that, even though fights occurred between long- and short-haired students, the proper course of action for the school board was to "[teach] tolerance" and stop the fighting rather than interfere with personal liberty.

However, when the school system appealed this judgment, the Fifth Circuit Court of Appeals reversed and found in the school's favor. According to this holding, personal decisions about hair length are not protected by the First Amendment. Schools can make boys cut their hair. What do you think of the reasoning in the following decision? Would the same decision be made today?

# KARR
## v.
## SCHMIDT

*United States Court of Appeals*
*Fifth Circuit*
April 28, 1972.

LEWIS R. MORGAN, Circuit Judge....

### III

... Is there a constitutionally protected right to wear one's hair in a public high school in the length and style that suits the wearer? We hold that no such right is to be found within the plain meaning of the Constitution....

A. The First Amendment.—The most frequently asserted basis for a constitutional right to wear long hair lies in the First Amendment. It is argued that the wearing of long hair is symbolic speech by which the wearer conveys his individuality, his rejection of conventional values, and the like. Accordingly, it is argued that the wearing of hair is subject to the protection of the First Amendment....

We find considerable difficulty, however, with the First Amendment approach to this question. First, we think it doubtful that the wearing of long hair has sufficient communicative content to entitle it to the protection of the First Amendment.... For some, no doubt, the wearing of long hair is intended to convey a discrete message to the world. But for many, the wearing of long hair is simply a matter of personal taste or the result of peer group influence. Appellee Karr, for example, has brought this suit not because his hair conveys a message but "because I like my hair long." Surely if we are to have workable rules of constitutional law, the validity of the regulation cannot turn on the plaintiff's subjective motivation in wearing his hair long.

For these reasons, we think it inappropriate that the protection of the First Amendment be extended to the wearing of long hair. Moreover, it is our belief that the Supreme Court's decision in *Tinker* supports this view....

> The problem posed by the present case does not relate to regulation of the length of skirts or the type of clothing, to hair style, or deportment.... Our problem involves direct, primary First Amendment rights akin to pure speech.

The conclusion is inescapable that this paragraph was intended to delimit the outer reach of the court's holding. We read this language as indicating that the right to style one's hair as one pleases in the public schools does not inherit the protection of the First Amendment....

In this case, it is evident from the record that the school authorities seek only to accomplish legitimate objectives in promulgating the hair regulation here in question. The record nowhere suggests that their goals are other than the elimination of classroom distraction, the avoidance of violence between long and short haired students, the elimination of potential health hazards, and the elimination of safety hazards resulting from long hair in the science labs....

*Reversed.*

... Circuit Judges, join, dissenting.

Hair styles change. A high school boy if he chooses should be able to wear his hair as Yul Brynner does or as Joe Namath does without fear of being deprived of an education by a majority of school board members who grew up at a time when the crew-cut was fashionable.

Individual rights never seem important to those who tolerate their infringement. Yet the Bill of Rights and the Fourteenth Amendment were designed to limit the reach of majority control over fundamental personal rights. Many young men and boys regard long hair as an expression of affinity with their peers and disapproval of the older generations' handling of the Vietnam War and current social problems. Some may wear their hair long because the girls like it long. Either way, the right to wear one's hair as one pleases is a fundamental right implicit "within the commodious concept of liberty, embracing freedoms great and small." ...

I

... To me the right to wear one's hair as one pleases, although unspecified in our Bill of Rights, is a "fundamental" right protected by the Due Process Clause. Hair is a purely personal matter—a matter of personal style which for centuries has been one aspect of the manner in which we hold ourselves out to the rest of the world. Like other elements of costume, hair is a symbol: of elegance, of efficiency, of affinity and association, of non-conformity and rejection of traditional values. A person shorn of the freedom to vary the length and style of his hair is forced against his will to hold himself out symbolically as a person holding ideas contrary, perhaps, to ideas he holds most dear. Forced dress, including forced hair style, humiliates the unwilling complier, forces him to submerge his individuality in the "undistracting" mass, and in general, smacks of the exaltation of organization over member, unit over component, and state over individual. I always thought this country does not condone such repression. ...

I ask: What is the important state interest that permits a public school board to deny an education to a boy whose hair is acceptably long to his parents but too long to suit a majority of the School Board of El Paso, Texas?

I submit that under the First and Fourteenth Amendments, if a student wishes to show his disestablishmentarianism by wearing long hair or has the whim to wear long hair, antidisestablishmentarians on public school boards have no constitutional authority to prevent it.

---

EXERCISE 2.9. What statement are you making (if any) with your hairstyle? Are you making it consciously or unconsciously? What do the style, color, and cut of your hair express about you? The French semiologist Roland Barthes argued that people inevitably make statements with their clothing and hairstyle, and there is no way around it. Do you agree?

EXERCISE 2.10. If a public high school can ban *long* hair for boys because it may cause fights between long- and short-haired students, can it ban *short* hair for girls by the same rationale? Can a school with a feminist agenda require boys to grow long hair and girls to have short hair to "change outmoded sexist stereotypes"?

EXERCISE 2.11. Write a one- or two-page essay explaining why hair length and style *should* or *should not* be protected by the First Amendment. Should the same rules hold for both boys and girls?

---

**JUSTICE WARREN E. BURGER** (1907–1995) was born on Constitution Day (September 17) in St. Paul, Minnesota, where he went to high school, college, and night law school at the St. Paul College of Law (now the William Mitchell College of Law). After a career at the Justice Department and service as a judge on the U.S. Court of Appeals for the District of Columbia Circuit, Burger was appointed to the Supreme Court by President Richard Nixon in 1969. Burger remained on the Court until 1986, when he left to devote himself fully to the Commission on the Bicentennial of the Constitution, a post from which he argued for pervasive constitutional education in American schools and colleges.

HIGHLIGHTS

➤    In high school Burger was president of the student council, a reporter on the student newspaper, and a well-rounded athlete. He was forced to turn down a partial scholarship to Princeton because his family could not afford to pay the difference. Burger married schoolteacher Elvera Stromberg, and future Supreme Court justice Harry Blackmun was best man at his wedding.

➤    The chief justice is the presiding officer of the Supreme Court who votes in every case along with the other justices. When he is part of the majority, he assigns the task of writing opinions to the other justices. He is also the chief administrative officer of the federal judicial branch.

➤    As chief justice, Burger shrunk the time allotted to Supreme Court litigants from two hours per case to one hour per case.

# Double Entendres and Double Standards:
# Lewd and Suggestive Language in a Student Government Campaign Speech

One of the things that makes people most nervous about free speech in school is the undeniable fact that teenagers frequently talk about sex and sexuality, sometimes in irreverent and crude ways. In *Bethel School District v. Fraser* (1986), the Supreme Court's anxiety about adolescent sexual innuendo led to a major retreat from its earlier free speech decision in *Tinker*.

The case began when Matthew Fraser, a popular student and class clown at Bethel High School in Pierce County, Washington, gave a nominating speech for a fellow student running for a student government position. The theme of the speech was a sophomoric sexual metaphor that included the following sentences:

> I know a man who is firm—he's firm in his pants, he's firm in his shirt, his character is firm—but most . . . of all, his belief in you, the students of Bethel, is firm. . . . Jeff Kuhlman is a man who takes his point and pounds it in. If necessary, he'll take an issue and nail it to the wall. He doesn't attack things in spurts—he drives hard, pushing and pushing until finally—he succeeds. . . . Jeff is a man who will go to the very end—even the climax, for each and every one of you. . . . So vote for Jeff for A.S.B. vice-president—he'll never come between you and the best our high school can be.

The Court found that the school did nothing wrong in disciplining Fraser for this speech. What is the Court's reasoning? How would you have decided this case?

— —

## BETHEL SCHOOL DISTRICT NO. 403
### v.
### FRASER

*Supreme Court of the United States*
Argued March 3, 1986.
Decided July 7, 1986.

Chief Justice BURGER delivered the opinion of the Court.

We granted certiorari to decide whether the First Amendment prevents a school district from disciplining a high school student for giving a lewd speech at a school assembly.

I

A

On April 26, 1983, respondent Matthew N. Fraser, a student at Bethel High School in Pierce County, Washington, delivered a speech nominating a fellow student for student elective office. Approximately 600 high school students, many of whom were 14-year-olds, attended the assembly. Students were required to attend the assembly or to report to the study hall. The assembly was part of a school-sponsored educational program in self-government. . . . During the entire speech, Fraser referred to his candidate in terms of an elaborate, graphic, and explicit sexual metaphor.

Two of Fraser's teachers, with whom he discussed the contents of his speech in advance, informed him that the speech was "inappropriate and that he probably should not deliver it," and that his delivery of the speech might have "severe consequences."

During Fraser's delivery of the speech, a school counselor observed the reaction of students to the speech. Some students hooted and yelled; some by gestures graphically simulated the sexual activities pointedly alluded to in respondent's speech. Other students appeared to be bewildered and

Matthew Fraser stands in front of Bethel High School, which suspended him for his sexually suggestive nomination speech for a fellow student in 1983. The Court found that the school acted within its powers to discipline Fraser, because he gave his saucy speech at a school-sponsored event.

embarrassed by the speech. One teacher reported that on the day following the speech, she found it necessary to forgo a portion of the scheduled class lesson in order to discuss the speech with the class.

A Bethel High School disciplinary rule prohibiting the use of obscene language in the school provides:

> "Conduct which materially and substantially interferes with the educational process is prohibited, including the use of obscene, profane language or gestures."

The morning after the assembly, the Assistant Principal called Fraser into her office and notified him that the school considered his speech to have been a violation of this rule. Fraser was presented with copies of five letters submitted by teachers, describing his conduct at the assembly; he was given a chance to explain his conduct, and he admitted to having given the speech described and that he deliberately used sexual innuendo in the speech. Fraser was then informed that he would be suspended for three days, and that his name would be removed from the list of candidates for graduation speaker at the school's commencement exercises.

Fraser sought review of this disciplinary action through the School District's grievance procedures. The hearing officer determined that the speech given by respondent was "indecent, lewd, and offensive to the modesty and decency of many of the students and faculty in attendance at the assembly." The examiner determined that the speech fell within the ordinary meaning of "obscene," as used in the disruptive-conduct rule, and affirmed the discipline in its entirety. Fraser served two days of his suspension, and was allowed to return to school on the third day.

B

... [Fraser] alleged a violation of his First Amendment right to freedom of speech and sought both injunctive relief and monetary damages. ... The District Court held that the school's sanctions violated respondent's right to freedom of speech under the First Amendment to the United States Constitution, that the school's disruptive-conduct rule is unconstitutionally vague and overbroad, and that the removal of respondent's name from the graduation speaker's list violated the Due Process Clause of the Fourteenth Amendment because the disciplinary rule makes no mention of such removal as a possible sanction. The District Court awarded [Fraser] $278 in damages, $12,750 in litigation costs and attorney's fees, and enjoined the School District from preventing [him] from speaking at the commencement ceremonies. [Fraser], who had been elected graduation speaker by a write-in vote of his classmates, delivered a speech at the commencement ceremonies on June 8, 1983.

The Court of Appeals for the Ninth Circuit affirmed the judgment of the District Court, holding that [Fraser's] speech was indistinguishable from the protest armband in *Tinker v. Des Moines Independent Community School Dist.* . . .

We granted certiorari. We reverse.

## II

. . . The Court of Appeals . . . appears to have proceeded on the theory that the use of lewd and obscene speech in order to make what the speaker considered to be a point in a nominating speech for a fellow student was essentially the same as the wearing of an armband in *Tinker* as a form of protest or the expression of a political position.

The marked distinction between the political "message" of the armbands in *Tinker* and the sexual content of respondent's speech in this case seems to have been given little weight by the Court of Appeals. In upholding the students' right to engage in a nondisruptive, passive expression of a political viewpoint in *Tinker,* this Court was careful to note that the case did "not concern speech or action that intrudes upon the work of the schools or the rights of other students."

. . . [W]e turn to consider the level of First Amendment protection accorded to Fraser's utterances and actions before an official high school assembly attended by 600 students.

## III

. . . The undoubted freedom to advocate unpopular and controversial views in schools and classrooms must be balanced against the society's countervailing interest in teaching students the boundaries of socially appropriate behavior. Even the most heated political discourse in a democratic society requires consideration for the personal sensibilities of the other participants and audiences.

In our Nation's legislative halls, where some of the most vigorous political debates in our society are carried on, there are rules prohibiting the use of expressions offensive to other participants in the debate. Senators have been censured for abusive language directed at other Senators. . . . Can it be that what is proscribed in the halls of Congress is beyond the reach of school officials to regulate?

The First Amendment guarantees wide freedom in matters of adult public discourse. A sharply divided Court upheld the right to express an antidraft viewpoint in a public place, albeit in terms highly offensive to most citizens. It does not follow, however, that simply because the use of an offensive form of expression may not be prohibited to adults making what the speaker considers a political point, the same latitude must be permitted to children in a public school. . . .

Surely it is a highly appropriate function of public school education to prohibit the use of vulgar and offensive terms in public discourse. . . . The determination of what manner of speech in the classroom or in school assembly is inappropriate properly rests with the school board. . . .

The pervasive sexual innuendo in Fraser's speech was plainly offensive to both teachers and students—indeed to any mature person. By glorifying male sexuality, and in its verbal content, the

**JUSTICE THURGOOD MARSHALL** (1908–1994), the first African American Supreme Court justice, was born in Baltimore, Maryland, which he later described as "the most segregated city in the United States." He graduated from a segregated high school and went north to all-black Lincoln University in Pennsylvania. He could not go to law school in Maryland because the state school was for whites only, so he rose before dawn every morning and commuted to Howard Law School in Washington, D.C., where he studied under Dean Charles Hamilton Houston, the architect of the legal strategy to end Jim Crow segregation. Marshall's distinguished career as a civil rights lawyer led to his appointment as solicitor general of the United States, a position from which he argued eighteen cases before the Supreme Court, and later as a federal appeals court judge. President Lyndon Johnson appointed Marshall to the Supreme Court in 1967, and he served until 1991.

HIGHLIGHTS

➤   As head of the NAACP Legal Defense Fund, Marshall argued along with other civil rights attorneys for the plaintiff black children in *Brown v. Board of Education*, the landmark case that discredited the doctrine of separate but equal and ended legalized apartheid in America.

speech was acutely insulting to teenage girl students. The speech could well be seriously damaging to its less mature audience, many of whom were only 14 years old and on the threshold of awareness of human sexuality. Some students were reported as bewildered by the speech and the reaction of mimicry it provoked. . . .

We hold that petitioner School District acted entirely within its permissible authority in imposing sanctions upon Fraser in response to his offensively lewd and indecent speech. Unlike the sanctions imposed on the students wearing armbands in *Tinker*, the penalties imposed in this case were unrelated to any political viewpoint. The First Amendment does not prevent the school officials from determining that to permit a vulgar and lewd speech such as respondent's would undermine the school's basic educational mission. A high school assembly or classroom is no place for a sexually explicit monologue directed towards an unsuspecting audience of teenage students. Accordingly, it was perfectly appropriate for the school to disassociate itself to make the point to the pupils that vulgar speech and lewd conduct is wholly inconsistent with the "fundamental values" of public school education. . . .

*Reversed.*

Justice MARSHALL, dissenting.

. . . I dissent from the Court's decision . . . because in my view the School District failed to demonstrate that respondent's remarks were indeed disruptive. The District Court and Court of Appeals conscientiously applied *Tinker v. Des Moines Independent Community School Dist.* and concluded that the School District had not demonstrated any disruption of the educational process. I recognize that the school administration must be given wide latitude to determine what forms of conduct are inconsistent with the school's educational mission; nevertheless, where speech is involved, we may not unquestioningly accept a teacher's or administrator's assertion that certain pure speech interfered with education. . . .

EXERCISE 2.12. The *Fraser* Court found that schools could censor and punish students for "lewd, indecent, or offensive" speech, at least in school-sponsored functions. While reaffirming that high school students have First Amendment rights, it held that such rights are not equal to the rights of adult citizens. After all, grown-ups do have the right to make lewd, indecent, and offensive remarks in public. (Think about *Saturday Night Live, Beavis and Butthead,* Howard Stern, and other raunchy comedies or comedians on TV and radio.)

What was wrong with Fraser's nominating speech? If you were the principal of Bethel High School, how would you have handled it? Do you think that suspension is an effective and appropriate response? What else could have been done?

EXERCISE 2.13. Chief Justice Burger drew out a gender dimension to the legal conflict and wrote, "By glorifying male sexuality, and in its verbal content, the speech was acutely insulting to teenage girl students." Do you agree with this point? Was it more insulting to girls than to boys? Should girls (must girls) in high school be protected from the hyperactive sexual imaginations of teenage boys?

**FOR THE CLASS**

SAFE CAMPAIGNING. Consider the real 1999 case of Adam Henery, a sophomore at St. Charles High School in Missouri. Henery was running for junior class president in an upcoming student council election. He signed a contract binding him to follow the school's election rules, including the requirement that all flyers and posters be approved before distribution. Henery got approval for his campaign slogan, "Adam Henery: The Safe Choice." But on election day, Henery passed out to fellow students condoms that had his campaign slogan written on the wrapping. After a student complained, the school principal ruled that Henery would be disqualified from holding office since he failed to clear the distribution of the condoms with the appropriate school official. Henery took the position that the preclearance rule applied only to flyers and posters and argued that his message was protected by the First Amendment under the *Tinker* rule. A subsequent count of the votes found that Henery had a majority of votes but the school refused to allow him to take office. Henery went to court alleging a First Amendment violation and asking to be placed into the office of class president his junior year. Who's right here? Is this a case of vulgarity and indecency? To find out what happened, look up *Henery v. City of St. Charles,* 200 F.3d 1128 (8th Circuit) (1999). Your teacher knows the outcome.

# Coed Naked Civil Liberties

Although *Fraser* gave schools authority to censor and punish "lewd, indecent and offensive" student speech, many states have given student speakers the same free speech rights

After Jeffrey Pyle (left) was sent home for wearing a suggestive T-shirt, he and his brother Jonathan (right) challenged their school's rapidly evolving dress code by designing and wearing a series of sexually provocative and politically pointed T-shirts to class. Today the Pyle brothers are both lawyers.

that adults enjoy. The Supreme Court sets a basic floor for constitutional rights—not a ceiling on them—and the state legislatures and state courts can always decide to offer citizens (adults and minors) *more* rights and liberties under state law than they enjoy directly under the U.S. Constitution.

Consider the Student Free Expression Act passed by the Massachusetts legislature in 1974:

> The rights of students to freedom of expression in the public schools of the Commonwealth shall not be abridged, provided that such right shall not cause any disruption or disorder within the school. Freedom of expression shall include without limitation the rights and responsibilities of students, collectively and individually, (a) to express their views through speech and symbols, (b) to write, publish, and disseminate their views. . . .

In a very interesting case, *Pyle v. South Hadley School Committee* (1996), the Supreme Judicial Court of Massachusetts interpreted this statute to allow students at South Hadley High School in Western Massachusetts to wear T-shirts with funny sexual subtexts that may be offensive to other students.

The *Pyle* case started when high school senior Jeffrey Pyle wore a shirt to gym class that his mother had given him bearing this message: "Coed Naked Band. Do It to the Rhythm." The shirt featured an illustration of closely intertwined musical instruments. He was told not to wear it again, but he did and was promptly sent home for violating the school's dress code, which made it a violation to wear a message that would "harass, threaten, intimidate, or demean an individual or group of individuals because of sex, color, race, religion, handicap, national origin or sexual orientation."

Pyle and his brother Jon were outraged and won the support of their mother and father (a professor of constitutional law at Mount Holyoke College) in an irreverent campaign to test the limits of the school's policy. The boys began to wear T-shirts of the same general type to school, including:

See Dick Drink/See Dick Drive/See Dick Die/Don't Be a Dick
Coed Naked Gerbils [Front] Some People Will Censor Anything [Back]
Coed Naked Civil Liberties [Front] Do It to the First Amendment [Back]
Legalize It [with a drawing of a marijuana plant]
A Century of Women On Top/Smith College Centennial/1875–1975
Boring Teacher-Approved Non-Suggestive T-Shirt
Coed Naked Censorship [Front] They Do It in South Hadley [Back]

The Pyle brothers were disciplined for violating a provision of a new, hastily adopted dress code prohibiting students from wearing clothing that "has comments, pictures, slogans, or designs that are obscene, profane, lewd, or vulgar."

On July 25, 1996, the Massachusetts Supreme Judicial Court upheld the Pyle brothers' claim that state law absolutely protected the expression of their message, even if considered "vulgar" by some, so long as that expression causes no material disruption of the educational program. "The statute is unambiguous," the court held, "and must be construed as written.... *Our Legislature is free to grant greater rights to the citizens of this Commonwealth than would otherwise be protected under the United States Constitution.*" The court thus stuck very closely to the *Tinker* standard and proclaimed broad free speech rights for students in Massachusetts.

---

EXERCISE 2.14. Many teachers and students saw Jeffrey Pyle's first T-shirt ("Coed Naked Band. Do It to the Rhythm") as sexist or sexually harassing. Do you agree? Why or why not? Should students be allowed to wear sexist T-shirts? T-shirts with pictures of nude women (or men)?

EXERCISE 2.15. Should people have a right to wear "offensive" clothing? How do we know what "offensive" is? Who defines it? What do you find offensive? What do you wear that other people find offensive? (The late comedian Lenny Bruce once said, "My parents came to America to be offensive.")

EXERCISE 2.16. No student complained to the school administration about any of the Pyle brothers' T-shirts. Is that relevant in trying to decide whether such T-shirts are really "disruptive"? How does *Tinker* approach this problem?

EXERCISE 2.17. Did the Pyle brothers make a mountain out of a mole hill? Or did they do the right thing by standing up for their rights? What would you have done?

---

**FOR THE CLASS**

DRAFT A DRESS CODE. Break the class into groups of three. Each group should write a dress code for your school that deals with both general standards of dress and specific standards for "message clothing." Come back together as a class. Read the codes and compare their virtues and flaws in a class discussion. See if you can come up with a dress code for the school that achieves unanimous support in your class.

---

Although *Tinker* suggested that students might be treated like adult citizens in terms of the right to speak, the *Fraser* decision signaled the Court's second thoughts about relatively unrestrained expression in public schools. In Chapter 3 we will examine cases dealing with the rights of student newspaper reporters and the like. There, we will see how the Supreme Court in the 1980s turned away from broad student rights, substantially limiting the reach of *Tinker,* and upheld broad powers of school authorities to censor and regulate student expression in school.

## Thought Control or Quality Control?
## The Problem of Library Book Removal

The First Amendment protects not only the right to speak but also the right to receive information. Citizens have a right to information even when the government thinks the information in question may be dangerous and prefers to suppress its availability. In the public school context, the principle of free access to information loses some of its clarity because the Supreme Court has recognized that a school system controls its curriculum, its libraries, and the selection of textbooks. Yet, the general control over information exercised by the school system is not unlimited. For example, school officials cannot ban specific library books for political reasons. Consider the events that culminated in *Board of Education, Island Trees Union Free School District #26 v. Pico,* a 1982 case that established this principle.

After several members of the Island Trees Board of Education went to a conference of the conservative Parents of New York United (PONYU), they returned home with a list of books that the board members considered "objectionable" and "improper fare." The list of dangerous books included a number that were already in the Island Trees school libraries, among them the following:

> *Slaughterhouse-five,* by Kurt Vonnegut Jr.
> *The Naked Ape,* by Desmond Morris
> *Down These Mean Streets,* by Piri Thomas
> *Best Short Stories of Negro Writers,* edited by Langston Hughes
> *Go Ask Alice,* by anonymous
> *Laughing Boy,* by Oliver LaFarge
> *Black Boy,* by Richard Wright
> *A Hero Ain't Nothin' but a Sandwich,* by Alice Childress
> *Soul on Ice,* by Eldridge Cleaver
> *A Reader for Writers,* edited by Jerome Archer
> *The Fixer,* by Bernard Malamud

Because these books had been described at the conference as "anti-American, anti-Christian, anti-Semitic, and just plain filthy," the Board of Education ordered public school librarians to deliver the books to the board so they could be examined. The board then formed a parent/teacher Book Review Committee to advise it on which books should be taken out of the libraries and which kept in the stacks. The Committee recommended the removal of only two books, but the board went ahead without any further explanation and removed nine of the books from the public school libraries, making one other book available only with parental consent.

When a group of students brought a suit alleging violation of their First Amendment rights, the District Court threw the suit out and held for the Board of Education, finding that it had only targeted books that were "vulgar." But a panel of the Second Circuit—and then a closely divided Supreme Court (5–4)—found that the students had a right to go to trial in the case to show that the books were removed as part of an official effort at thought control rather than an attempt to regulate student access to vulgar materials.

There was no majority opinion in *Board of Education v. Pico*, but Justice Brennan announced the judgment of the Supreme Court in an opinion that was joined in full by Justices Marshall and Stevens and in part by Justice Blackmun. Essentially, Justice Brennan found that this case was special because it did not involve textbooks but library books, and did not involve selection of books in the first instance but ad hoc removal of books that were already selected and purchased. Justice Brennan wrote:

> [We] think that the First Amendment rights of students may be directly and sharply implicated by the removal of the books from the shelves of a school library.... [W]e have held that in a variety of contexts "the Constitution protects the right to receive information and ideas." *Stanley v. Georgia.* [W]e do not deny that local school boards have a substantial legitimate role to play in the determination of school library content. [But] that discretion may not be exercised

Steven Pico (forefront) and members of the Island Trees Board of Education stand outside the Supreme Court in 1982. From left, Frank Martin, Richard Ahrens, Richard Michaels, Christina Fasulo, Patrick Hughes, Richard Melchers, and Louis Nessim.

in a narrowly partisan or political manner. If a Democratic school board, motivated by party affiliation, ordered the removal of all books written by or in favor of Republicans, few would doubt that the order violated the constitutional rights of students denied access to those books. The same conclusion would surely apply if an all-white school board, motivated by racial animus, decided to remove all books authored by blacks or advocating racial equality or integration. Our Constitution does not permit the official suppression of ideas.

Justice Rehnquist vigorously dissented from the Court's decision. He wrote:

> I can cheerfully concede [that a Democratic school board could not, for political reasons, remove all books by or in favor of Republicans, and that an all-white school board, motivated by racial animus, could not remove all books authored by blacks or advocating racial equality], but as in so many other cases the extreme examples are seldom the ones that arise in the real world of constitutional litigation. In this case the facts taken most favorably to respondents suggest that nothing of this sort happened. The nine books removed undoubtedly did contain "ideas," but in the light of the excerpts from them ... it is apparent that eight of them contained demonstrable amounts of vulgarity and profanity and the ninth contained nothing that could be considered partisan or political.

---

EXERCISE 2.18. Do you agree with the implication that the Island Trees Board of Education could have refused to purchase these books in the first place? If not, does that mean the board had a *constitutional obligation* to order these books? Does it have a constitutional obligation to order new copies when these become too beat up to use? Or does the decision simply stand for the proposition that books cannot be kept out of libraries for the wrong reasons? What are the right reasons to deny books a place in the library? Should children have access to any books that adults can obtain?

EXERCISE 2.19. There have been frequent efforts to get Mark Twain's classic *Huckleberry Finn* removed from high school curricula and libraries because of its alleged racism and frequent use of the word "nigger." Using your school library and the Internet, research the debate over *Huckleberry Finn* and write a two- to three-page paper about various perspectives expressed on this subject. Do you think that Twain's book should be removed from the schools? If not, how should it be taught with respect to its language, which is undoubtedly experienced as demeaning and painful by many students? Is school the right place to learn how to participate in a civil discourse when one is feeling injured and insulted? Consider Harvard Law Professor Randall Kennedy's book *Nigger* (2002), in which he explores the history, legal effect, and social meaning of this still ubiquitous and incendiary word. Do you agree that we should not try to suppress books, articles, songs, and cases where the word appears, or do you think we should do everything in our power to ban it?

---

LITERATURE AND VULGARITY IN THE HIGH SCHOOL LIBRARY. Do you agree with the premise, apparently shared by justices in both the majority and the dissent in *Pico*, that it is fine to remove books from the library when they are vulgar? Literature, films, and art described as "vulgar" are generally protected under the First Amendment. But should the general rules apply in the school setting? Are there dangers to having vulgar literature in a school library? Are there dangers to removing vulgar literature from a school library? Assume that there is a proposal in your school district to remove from the high school curriculum and the school libraries the eleven books at issue in *Pico* on the grounds that they are all vulgar. Transform yourselves into members of the school board and debate whether or not the books should indeed be removed. Can you speak about what the books say? Take a vote.

---

# Viewpoint Neutrality and Religious Speech: Good News for the Free Speech Rights of Religious Americans

When a public school opens its doors in the after-school hours to community groups for educational and civic meetings, it must allow all groups to use the facilities on an equal basis without regard to their politics or philosophical viewpoint. In First Amendment terms, we say that in a "public forum," the government must have a policy of "viewpoint neutrality" toward speech.

Yet, some public schools and universities have thought that they can exclude organizations and speakers with a religious perspective from public speech forums. Indeed, many schools have thought they *must* exclude religious speakers from their facilities on the supposition that it would violate the establishment clause to let them participate.

But in a string of cases the Supreme Court has made clear that religiously oriented speakers and groups have every equal right to use the facilities and resources of public universities and schools when they are opened up to the public. The Court first began to define this principle in *Widmar v. Vincent* (1981), which ruled that religiously oriented student groups must be given equal rights to meet in public school as other student groups. This constitutional principle is also embodied in Congressional statute: The Equal Access Act requires that public high schools receiving federal funds grant equal access to student groups who want to meet on campus without discriminating on the basis of the "religious, political, philosophical or other content of the speech."

In *Lamb's Chapel v. Center Moriches Union Free School District* (1993), the Court then considered whether a public school district violated the First Amendment when it opened its doors after school to outside groups but refused to allow a parents' group to show a film that dealt with family values from a religious perspective. The Court saw this exclusion as discriminating against speakers because of their religious viewpoint and found the group must be given access.

Then, in *Rosenberger v. Rector and Visitors of the University of Virginia* (1995), the Court struck down the University of Virginia's practice of funding all student-organized publications on campus except those written from a religious perspective. The plaintiff in that case was a student newspaper, *Wide Awake,* that considered issues like dating, academic competition, and athletics from a fundamentalist Christian perspective. Justice Kennedy, writing for the majority in *Rosenberger,* found that religion provides a distinct perspective and vantage point from which to analyze society, politics, and culture.

Thus, by the time the Court came to consider *Good News Club v. Milford Central School* in 2001, the die had been cast. The question was whether Milford Central School violated the free speech rights of the Good News Club, a Christian group for children ages six to twelve, by selectively rejecting its application to use the facilities because the group's members were engaged in religious-type activities. Justice Clarence Thomas first considered whether the policy violated the club's free speech rights and then, finding that it did, dealt with the argument that the establishment clause somehow required it.

---

## GOOD NEWS CLUB
### v.
## MILFORD CENTRAL SCHOOL

*Supreme Court of the United States*
Argued February 28, 2001.
Decided June 11, 2001.

Justice THOMAS delivered the opinion of the Court.

This case presents two questions. The first question is whether Milford Central School violated the free speech rights of the Good News Club when it excluded the Club from meeting after hours at the school. The second question is whether any such violation is justified by Milford's concern that permitting the Club's activities would violate the Establishment Clause. We conclude that Milford's restriction violates the Club's free speech rights and that no Establishment Clause concern justifies that violation.

I

The State of New York authorizes local school boards to adopt regulations governing the use of their school facilities. In particular, N.Y. Educ. Law § 414 . . . enumerates several purposes for which local boards may open their schools to public use. In 1992 . . . Milford Central School (Milford) enacted a community use policy adopting seven of § 414's purposes for which its building could be used after school. . . . Two of the stated purposes are relevant here. First, district residents may use the school for "instruction in any branch of education, learning or the arts." . . . Second, the school is available for "social, civic and recreational meetings and entertainment events, and other uses pertaining to the welfare of the community, provided that such uses shall be nonexclusive and shall be opened to the general public." . . .

Stephen and Darleen Fournier reside within Milford's district and therefore are eligible to use the school's facilities as long as their proposed use is approved by the school. Together they are sponsors of the local Good News Club, a private Christian organization for children ages 6 to 12. Pursuant to Milford's policy, in September 1996 the Fourniers submitted a request to Dr. Robert McGruder, interim superintendent of the district, in which they sought permission to hold the Club's weekly afterschool meetings in the school cafeteria.... The next month, McGruder formally denied the Fourniers' request on the ground that the proposed use—to have "a fun time of singing songs, hearing a Bible lesson and memorizing scripture"... was "the equivalent of religious worship."... According to McGruder, the community use policy, which prohibits use "by any individual or organization for religious purposes," foreclosed the Club's activities....

In response to a letter submitted by the Club's counsel, Milford's attorney requested information to clarify the nature of the Club's activities. The Club sent a set of materials used or distributed at the meetings and the following description of its meeting:

"The Club opens its session with Ms. Fournier taking attendance. As she calls a child's name, if the child recites a Bible verse the child receives a treat. After attendance, the Club sings songs. Next Club members engage in games that involve, *inter alia,* learning Bible verses. Ms. Fournier then relates a Bible story and explains how it applies to Club members' lives. The Club closes with prayer. Finally, Ms. Fournier distributes treats and the Bible verses for memorization."...

McGruder and Milford's attorney reviewed the materials and concluded that "the kinds of activities proposed to be engaged in by the Good News Club were not a discussion of secular subjects such as child rearing, development of character and development of morals from a religious perspective, but were in fact the equivalent of religious instruction itself."... In February 1997, the Milford Board of Education adopted a resolution rejecting the Club's request to use Milford's facilities "for the purpose of conducting religious instruction and Bible study."...

... The Club alleged that Milford's denial of its application violated its free speech rights under the First and Fourteenth Amendments....

II

Because the parties have agreed that Milford created a limited public forum when it opened its facilities in 1992 ... we simply will assume that Milford operates a limited public forum.

When the State establishes a limited public forum, the State is not required to and does not allow persons to engage in every type of speech. The State may be justified "in reserving [its forum] for certain groups or for the discussion of certain topics."... The State's power to restrict speech, however, is not without limits. The restriction must not discriminate against speech on the basis of viewpoint, and the restriction must be "reasonable in light of the purpose served by the forum." ...

III

Applying this test, we first address whether the exclusion constituted viewpoint discrimination. We are guided in our analysis by two of our prior opinions, *Lamb's Chapel [v. Center Moriches Union Free School District]* and *Rosenberger [v. Rector and Visitor of Univ. of Va. ]*. In *Lamb's Chapel*, we held that a school district violated the Free Speech Clause of the First Amendment when it excluded a private group from presenting films at the school based solely on the films' discussions of family values from a religious perspective. Likewise, in *Rosenberger,* we held that a university's refusal to fund a student publication because the publication addressed issues from a religious perspective violated the Free Speech Clause. Concluding that Milford's exclusion of the Good News Club based on its religious nature is indistinguishable from the exclusions in these cases, we hold that the exclusion con-

Members of the Good News Club stand outside Milford Central School. The club won the right to meet there after the Supreme Court ruled that public schools cannot deny religiously oriented groups an equal right to meet on campus.

stitutes viewpoint discrimination. Because the restriction is viewpoint discriminatory, we need not decide whether it is unreasonable in light of the purposes served by the forum....

Milford has opened its limited public forum to activities that serve a variety of purposes, including events "pertaining to the welfare of the community.".... Milford interprets its policy to permit discussions of subjects such as child rearing, and of "the development of character and morals from a religious perspective.".... For example, this policy would allow someone to use Aesop's Fables to teach children moral values.... Additionally, a group could sponsor a debate on whether there should be a constitutional amendment to permit prayer in public schools ... and the Boy Scouts could meet "to influence a boy's character, development and spiritual growth.".... In short, any group that "promote[s] the moral and character development of children" is eligible to use the school building....

Just as there is no question that teaching morals and character development to children is a permissible purpose under Milford's policy, it is clear that the Club teaches morals and character development to children. For example, no one disputes that the Club instructs children to overcome feelings of jealousy, to treat others well regardless of how they treat the children, and to be obedient, even if it does so in a nonsecular way. Nonetheless, because Milford found the Club's activities to be religious in nature—"the equivalent of religious instruction itself" ... it excluded the Club from use of its facilities.

Applying *Lamb's Chapel* ... we find it quite clear that Milford engaged in viewpoint discrimination when it excluded the Club from the afterschool forum....

Like the church in *Lamb's Chapel*, the Club seeks to address a subject otherwise permitted under the rule, the teaching of morals and character, from a religious standpoint.... The only apparent difference between the activity of Lamb's Chapel and the activities of the Good News Club is that the Club chooses to teach moral lessons from a Christian perspective through live storytelling and prayer, whereas Lamb's Chapel taught lessons through films. This distinction is inconsequential. Both modes of speech use a religious viewpoint. Thus, the exclusion of the Good News Club's activities, like the exclusion of Lamb's Chapel's films, constitutes unconstitutional viewpoint discrimination....

Milford argues that, even if its restriction constitutes viewpoint discrimination, its interest in not violating the Establishment Clause outweighs the Club's interest in gaining equal access to the school's facilities. In other words, according to Milford, its restriction was required to avoid violating the Establishment Clause. We disagree....

We rejected Establishment Clause defenses similar to Milford's in two previous free speech cases, *Lamb's Chapel* and *Widmar* [*v. Vincent*]. In particular, in *Lamb's Chapel,* we explained that "[t]he showing of th[e] film series would not have been during school hours, would not have been sponsored by the school, and would have been open to the public, not just to church members.".... Accordingly, we found that "there would have been no realistic danger that the community would think that the District was endorsing religion or any particular creed.".... Likewise, in *Widmar,* where the university's forum was already available to other groups, this Court concluded that there was no Establishment Clause problem....

The Establishment Clause defense fares no better in this case. As in *Lamb's Chapel,* the Club's meetings were held after school hours, not sponsored by the school, and open to any student who obtained parental consent, not just to Club members. As in *Widmar,* Milford made its forum available to other organizations. The Club's activities are materially indistinguishable from those in *Lamb's Chapel* and *Widmar.* Thus, Milford's reliance on the Establishment Clause is unavailing.

Milford attempts to distinguish *Lamb's Chapel* and *Widmar* by emphasizing that Milford's policy involves elementary school children. According to Milford, children will perceive that the school is endorsing the Club and will feel coercive pressure to participate, because the Club's activities take place on school grounds, even though they occur during nonschool hours.... This argument is unpersuasive....

First, we have held that "a significant factor in upholding governmental programs in the face of Establishment Clause attack is their neutrality towards religion.".... Milford's implication that granting access to the Club would do damage to the neutrality principle defies logic. For the "guarantee of neutrality is respected, not offended, when the government, following neutral criteria and evenhanded policies, extends benefits to recipients whose ideologies and viewpoints, including religious ones, are broad and diverse.".... The Good News Club seeks nothing more than to be treated neutrally and given access to speak about the same topics as are other groups....

Second, to the extent we consider whether the community would feel coercive pressure to engage in the Club's activities ... the relevant community would be the parents, not the elementary school children. It is the parents who choose whether their children will attend the Good News Club meetings. Because the children cannot attend without their parents' permission, they cannot be coerced into engaging in the Good News Club's religious activities. Milford does not suggest that the parents of elementary school children would be confused about whether the school was endorsing religion. Nor do we believe that such an argument could be reasonably advanced.

Third, whatever significance we may have assigned in the Establishment Clause context to the suggestion that elementary school children are more impressionable than adults ... we have never extended our Establishment Clause jurisprudence to foreclose private religious conduct during nonschool hours merely because it takes place on school premises where elementary school children may be present....

Fourth, even if we were to consider the possible misperceptions by schoolchildren in deciding whether Milford's permitting the Club's activities would violate the Establishment Clause, the facts of this case simply do not support Milford's conclusion. There is no evidence that young children are permitted to loiter outside classrooms after the schoolday has ended. Surely even young children are aware of events for which their parents must sign permission forms. The meetings were held in a combined high school resource room and middle school special education room, not in an elementary school classroom. The instructors are not schoolteachers. And the children in the group are not all the same age as in the normal classroom setting; their ages range from 6 to 12.... In sum, these circumstances simply do not support the theory that small children would perceive endorsement here....

Finally, even if we were to inquire into the minds of schoolchildren in this case, we cannot say the danger that children would misperceive the endorsement of religion is any greater than the danger that they would perceive a hostility toward the religious viewpoint if the Club were excluded from the public forum. This concern is particularly acute given the reality that Milford's building is not used only for elementary school children. Students, from kindergarten through the 12th grade, all attend school in the same building. There may be as many, if not more, upperclassmen than elementary school children who occupy the school after hours. For that matter, members of the public writ large are permitted in the school after hours pursuant to the community use policy. Any bystander could conceivably be aware of the school's use policy and its exclusion of the Good News Club, and could suffer as much from viewpoint discrimination as elementary school children could suffer from perceived endorsement....

We cannot operate, as Milford would have us do, under the assumption that any risk that small children would perceive endorsement should counsel in favor of excluding the Club's religious activity. We decline to employ Establishment Clause jurisprudence using a modified heckler's veto, in which a group's religious activity can be proscribed on the basis of what the youngest members of the audience might misperceive.... There are countervailing constitutional concerns related to rights of other individuals in the community. In this case, those countervailing concerns are the free speech rights of the Club and its members....

We are not convinced that there is any significance in this case to the possibility that elementary school children may witness the Good News Club's activities on school premises.... Accordingly, we conclude that permitting the Club to meet on the school's premises would not have violated the Establishment Clause....

V

When Milford denied the Good News Club access to the school's limited public forum on the ground that the Club was religious in nature, it discriminated against the Club because of its religious viewpoint in violation of the Free Speech Clause of the First Amendment. Because Milford has not raised a valid Establishment Clause claim, we do not address the question whether such a claim could excuse Milford's viewpoint discrimination....

Justice SOUTER, with whom Justice GINSBURG joins, dissenting.

I

This case, like Lamb's Chapel, properly raises no issue about the reasonableness of Milford's criteria for restricting the scope of its designated public forum. Milford has opened school property for, among other things, "instruction in any branch of education, learning or the arts" and for "social, civic and recreational meetings and entertainment events and other uses pertaining to the welfare of the community, provided that such uses shall be nonexclusive and shall be opened to the general public."... But Milford has done this subject to the restriction that "[s]chool premises shall not be used ... for religious purposes."... As the District Court stated, Good News did "not object to the reasonableness of [Milford]'s policy that prohibits the use of [its] facilities for religious purposes."...

The sole question before the District Court was, therefore, whether, in refusing to allow Good News's intended use, Milford was misapplying its unchallenged restriction in a way that amounted to imposing a viewpoint-based restriction on what could be said or done by a group entitled to use the forum for an educational, civic, or other permitted purpose. The question was whether Good News was being disqualified when it merely sought to use the school property the same way that the Milford Boy and Girl Scouts and the 4-H Club did....

... Good News's classes open and close with prayer. In a sample lesson considered by the District Court, children are instructed that "[t]he Bible tells us how we can have our sins forgiven by receiving the Lord Jesus Christ. It tells us how to live to please Him.... If you have received the Lord Jesus as your Saviour from sin, you belong to God's special group—His family."... The lesson plan instructs the teacher to "lead a child to Christ," and, when reading a Bible verse, to "[e]mphasize that this verse is from the Bible, God's Word" and is "important—and true—because God said it." The lesson further exhorts the teacher to "[b]e sure to give an opportunity for the 'unsaved' children in your class to respond to the Gospel" and cautions against "neglect[ing] this responsibility."...

While Good News's program utilizes songs and games, the heart of the meeting is the "challenge" and "invitation," which are repeated at various times throughout the lesson. During the challenge, "saved" children who "already believe in the Lord Jesus as their Savior" are challenged to "stop and ask God for the strength and the 'want' ... to obey Him."... They are instructed that "[i]f you know Jesus as your Savior, you need to place God first in your life. And if you don't know Jesus as Savior and if you would like to, then we will—we will pray with you separately, individually.... And the challenge would be, those of you who know Jesus as Savior, you can rely on God's strength to obey Him."...

During the invitation, the teacher "invites" the "unsaved" children "to trust the Lord Jesus to be your Savior from sin," and "receiv[e][him] as your Savior from sin."... The children are then instructed that "[i]f you believe what God's Word says about your sin and how Jesus died and rose again for you, you can have His forever life today. Please bow your heads and close your eyes. If you have never believed on the Lord Jesus as your Savior and would like to do that, please show me by raising your hand. If you raised your hand to show me you want to believe on the Lord Jesus, please meet me so I can show you from God's Word how you can receive His everlasting life."...

It is beyond question that Good News intends to use the public school premises not for the mere discussion of a subject from a particular, Christian point of view, but for an evangelical service of worship calling children to commit themselves in an act of Christian conversion.... The majority avoids this reality only by resorting to the bland and general characterization of Good News's activity as "teaching of morals and character, from a religious standpoint."... If the majority's statement ignores reality, as it surely does, then today's holding may be understood only in equally generic terms. Otherwise, indeed, this case would stand for the remarkable proposition that any public school opened for civic meetings must be opened for use as a church, synagogue, or mosque.

---

EXERCISE 2.20. The Good News Club engaged its student members in "education" and "learning" from a religious perspective. But what if it had applied for use of the school's facilities for "religious worship and services"? Many school districts have actually decided to allow their buildings to be used for religious worship on weekends and after hours. But do they have to? Would Milford Central School be violating the free speech (or religious free exercise) rights of the Good News Club by denying it space at school to engage in religious worship ceremonies? These are open questions. Debate them.

EXERCISE 2.21. Assume that a local atheists' group in your community issues a statement saying that, "*Good News Club* is a terrible decision. Our public schools should never allow religious clubs in for any purpose at all because it violates the separation between church and state. Let's make it our policy to keep all religious groups out." A local television news station comes to interview your class about the proposal and you have to explain the logic of the Good News Club case. What do you say?

---

### Read On

Abraham, Henry J., and Barbara Perry. *Freedom and the Court: Civil Rights and Liberties in the United States*. New York: Oxford University Press, 1998.

Bosmajian, Haig. *The Freedom Not to Speak*. New York: New York University Press, 1999.

Fish, Stanley. *There's No Such Thing as Free Speech and It's a Good Thing Too*. New York: Oxford University Press, 1994.

Johnson, John W. *The Struggle for Student Rights: Tinker v. Des Moines and the 1960's*. Lawrence: University Press of Kansas, 1997.

Kennedy, Randall. *Nigger: The Strange Career of a Troublesome Word*. New York: Pantheon, 2002.

### For Further Information

Student Press Law Center, www.splc.org

American Civil Liberties Union, www.aclu.org

First Amendment Center, www.freedomforum.org/first/welcome.asp

# ALL THE NEWS FIT TO PRINT AT SCHOOL: FREEDOM OF THE STUDENT PRESS

3

"Congress shall make no law . . . abridging the freedom of speech, or of the press. . . ."   THE FIRST AMENDMENT

"Were it left to me to decide whether we should have a government without newspapers, or newspapers without a government, I should not hesitate a moment to choose the latter."
THOMAS JEFFERSON (JANUARY 16, 1787)

From the country's beginnings, Americans have prided themselves on a tradition of spirited and irreverent journalism. In the twentieth century the press achieved landmark victories when the Supreme Court handed down decisions declaring that the media must be free from government censorship. The Court has come to a constitutional understanding that a free press in a democracy is vital to holding government accountable.

In the public school setting, however, the student press does not enjoy the same kind of autonomy. Although the *Tinker* case implied that student writers and editors might have a right to publish anything that would not substantially disrupt school functions, the Court in *Hazelwood School District v. Kuhlmeier* (1988) articulated a much narrower understanding of the rights of student journalists working on school-sponsored newspapers, magazines, and yearbooks. According to *Hazelwood,* the school may act as the editor of student speech in these contexts and may censor school-sponsored student expression for reasonable educational purposes.

As you read *Hazelwood* and the cases that follow, consider whether you think student journalists should have the same rights as adult journalists. Has the Supreme Court struck the right balance between the rights of students and the interest that school systems have in regulating the content of materials that go out under their name?

*How does the basic First Amendment liberty of freedom of the press apply to student publications?*

- Should school officials have the authority to review, regulate, and censor the content of school-sponsored student publications?
- Should school officials have the authority to censor student publications produced outside of school but distributed on school property?
- Should school officials have the authority to punish students for posting critical statements about other students or teachers on the Internet?

# Freedom of the Student Press in Official School-Sponsored Activities

When a school sponsors an activity in which students express themselves, how much control can it exert over the students' expression? In the following landmark case, a school principal censored two articles in the school's student newspaper because he felt that they dealt inappropriately with sensitive themes related to sex and family. The students tried to invoke their *Tinker* rights, asserting that their articles were educationally sound and would not cause "substantial" or "material" disruption of the school program.

But the Court found that *Tinker* was the wrong standard to use when the school is sponsoring and promoting the activity, which in this case was the school newspaper. The Court asked only whether the censorship is "reasonably related to legitimate pedagogical concerns." This is a much easier standard for schools to meet. Read the following case and think about how *Bethel v. Fraser* was a bridge to this decision. Do you think that the Court went too far in allowing principals and teachers to act as censors, or do you agree that when the school's name is implicated, the school should get to pick and choose what is published?

# HAZELWOOD SCHOOL DISTRICT
## v.
## KUHLMEIER

*Supreme Court of the United States*
Argued Oct. 13, 1987.
Decided Jan. 13, 1988.

Justice WHITE delivered the opinion of the Court.

This case concerns the extent to which educators may exercise editorial control over the contents of a high school newspaper produced as part of the school's journalism curriculum.

I

... [T]hree former Hazelwood East students who were staff members of Spectrum, the school newspaper ... contend that school officials violated their First Amendment rights by deleting two pages of articles from the May 13, 1983, issue of Spectrum. Spectrum was written and edited by the Journalism II class at Hazelwood East. The newspaper was published every three weeks or so during the 1982–1983 school year. More than 4,500 copies of the newspaper were distributed during that year to students, school personnel, and members of the community....

The practice at Hazelwood East during the spring 1983 semester was for the journalism teacher to submit page proofs of each Spectrum issue to Principal Reynolds for his review prior to publication. On May 10, Emerson delivered the proofs of the May 13 edition to Reynolds, who objected to

Robert Reynolds, principal of Hazelwood East High, stands in front of his school in January 1988 holding a copy of *Spectrum,* the student newspaper that was censored in *Hazelwood.* The Court's decision gave school authorities broad new powers to regulate the content of school-sponsored newspapers and yearbooks for "reasonable" pedagogical purposes.

two of the articles scheduled to appear in that edition. One of the stories described three Hazelwood East students' experiences with pregnancy; the other discussed the impact of divorce on students at the school.

Reynolds was concerned that, although the pregnancy story used false names "to keep the identity of these girls a secret," the pregnant students still might be identifiable from the text. He also believed that the article's references to sexual activity and birth control were inappropriate for some of the younger students at the school. In addition, Reynolds was concerned that a student identified by name in the divorce story had complained that her father "wasn't spending enough time with my mom, my sister and I" prior to the divorce, "was always out of town on business or out late playing cards with the guys," and "always argued about everything" with her mother. Reynolds believed that the student's parents should have been given an opportunity to respond to these remarks or to consent to their publication. He was unaware that Emerson had deleted the student's name from the final version of the article.

Reynolds believed that there was no time to make the necessary changes in the stories before the scheduled press run and that the newspaper would not appear before the end of the school year if printing were delayed to any significant extent. He concluded that his only options under the circumstances were to publish a four-page newspaper instead of the planned six-page newspaper, eliminating the two pages on which the offending stories appeared, or to publish no newspaper at all. Accordingly, he directed Emerson to withhold from publication the two pages containing the stories on pregnancy and divorce. He informed his superiors of the decision, and they concurred. . . .

II

Students in the public schools do not "shed their constitutional rights to freedom of speech or expression at the schoolhouse gate." *Tinker.* They cannot be punished merely for expressing their personal views on the school premises—whether "in the cafeteria, or on the playing field, or on the campus during the authorized hours"—unless school authorities have reason to believe that such expression will "substantially interfere with the work of the school or impinge upon the rights of other students."

We have nonetheless recognized that the First Amendment rights of students in the public schools "are not automatically coextensive with the rights of adults in other settings," and must be "applied in light of the special characteristics of the school environment." *Tinker.* A school need not tolerate student speech that is inconsistent with its "basic educational mission," even though the government could not censor similar speech outside the school. Accordingly, we held in *Fraser* that a student could be disciplined for having delivered a speech that was "sexually explicit" but not legally obscene at an official school assembly, because the school was entitled to "disassociate itself" from the speech in a manner that would demonstrate to others that such vulgarity is "wholly inconsistent with the 'fundamental values' of public school education." We thus recognized that "[t]he determination of what manner of speech in the classroom or in school assembly is inappropriate properly rests with the school board," rather than with the federal courts. . . .

The question whether the First Amendment requires a school to tolerate particular student speech—the question that we addressed in *Tinker*—is different from the question whether the First Amendment requires a school affirmatively to promote particular student speech. The former question addresses educators' ability to silence a student's personal expression that happens to occur on the school premises. The latter question concerns educators' authority over school-sponsored publications, theatrical productions, and other expressive activities that students, parents, and members of the public might reasonably perceive to bear the imprimatur of the school. These activities may fairly be characterized as part of the school curriculum, whether or not they occur in a traditional classroom setting, so long as they are supervised by faculty members and designed to impart particular knowledge or skills to student participants and audiences.

Educators are entitled to exercise greater control over this second form of student expression to assure that participants learn whatever lessons the activity is designed to teach, that readers or listeners are not exposed to material that may be inappropriate for their level of maturity, and that the views of the individual speaker are not erroneously attributed to the school. Hence, a school may in its capacity as publisher of a school newspaper or producer of a school play "disassociate itself," not only from speech that would "substantially interfere with [its] work . . . or impinge upon the rights of other students," *Tinker*, but also from speech that is, for example, ungrammatical, poorly written, inadequately researched, biased or prejudiced, vulgar or profane, or unsuitable for immature audiences. A school must be able to set high standards for the student speech that is disseminated under its auspices—standards that may be higher than those demanded by some newspaper publishers or theatrical producers in the "real" world—and may refuse to disseminate student speech that does not meet those standards. In addition, a school must be able to take into account the emotional maturity of the intended audience in determining whether to disseminate student speech on potentially sensitive topics, which might range from the existence of Santa Claus in an elementary school setting to the particulars of teenage sexual activity in a high school setting. A school must also retain the authority to refuse to sponsor student speech that might reasonably be perceived to advocate drug or alcohol use, irresponsible sex, or conduct otherwise inconsistent with "the shared values of a civilized social order," or to associate the school with any position other than neutrality on matters of political controversy. . . .

Accordingly, we conclude that the standard articulated in *Tinker* for determining when a school may punish student expression need not also be the standard for determining when a school may refuse to lend its name and resources to the dissemination of student expression. Instead, we hold that educators do not offend the First Amendment by exercising editorial control over the style and content of student speech in school-sponsored expressive activities so long as their actions are reasonably related to legitimate pedagogical concerns. . . .

We also conclude that Principal Reynolds acted reasonably in requiring the deletion from the May 13 issue of Spectrum of the pregnancy article, the divorce article, and the remaining articles that were to appear on the same pages of the newspaper. The initial paragraph of the pregnancy article declared that "[a]ll names have been changed to keep the identity of these girls a secret." The principal concluded that the students' anonymity was not adequately protected, however, given the other identifying information in the article and the small number of pregnant students at the school. . . . In addition, he could reasonably have been concerned that the article was not sufficiently sensitive to the privacy interests of the students' boyfriends and parents, who were discussed in the article but who were given no opportunity to consent to its publication or to offer a response. The article did not contain graphic accounts of sexual activity. The girls did comment in the article, however, concerning their sexual histories and their use or nonuse of birth control. It was not unreasonable for the principal to have concluded that such frank talk was inappropriate in a school-sponsored publication distributed to 14-year-old freshmen and presumably taken home to be read by students' even younger brothers and sisters.

The student who was quoted by name in the version of the divorce article seen by Principal Reynolds made comments sharply critical of her father. The principal could reasonably have concluded that an individual publicly identified as an inattentive parent—indeed, as one who chose "playing cards with the guys" over home and family—was entitled to an opportunity to defend himself as a matter of journalistic fairness. These concerns were shared by both of Spectrum's faculty advisers for the 1982–1983 school year, who testified that they would not have allowed the article to be printed without deletion of the student's name. . . .

In sum, we cannot reject as unreasonable Principal Reynolds' conclusion that neither the pregnancy article nor the divorce article was suitable for publication in Spectrum. Reynolds could reasonably have concluded that the students who had written and edited these articles had not sufficiently mastered those portions of the Journalism II curriculum that pertained to the treatment of controversial issues and personal attacks, the need to protect the privacy of individuals whose most intimate concerns are to be revealed in the newspaper, and "the legal, moral, and ethical restrictions imposed upon journalists within [a] school community" that includes adolescent subjects and readers. Finally, we conclude that the principal's decision to delete two pages of Spectrum, rather than to delete only the offending articles or to require that they be modified, was reasonable under the circumstances as he understood them. Accordingly, no violation of First Amendment rights occurred.

*Reversed.*

Justice BRENNAN, with whom Justice MARSHALL and Justice BLACKMUN join, dissenting.

When the young men and women of Hazelwood East High School registered for Journalism II, they expected a civics lesson. Spectrum, the newspaper they were to publish, "was not just a class exercise in which students learned to prepare papers and hone writing skills, it was a . . . forum established to give students an opportunity to express their views while gaining an appreciation of their rights and responsibilities under the First Amendment to the United States Constitution. . . ." [T]he student journalists published a Statement of Policy—tacitly approved each year by school authorities—announcing their expectation that "Spectrum, as a student-press publication, accepts all rights implied by the First Amendment. . . . Only speech that 'materially and substantially interferes with the requirements of appropriate discipline' can be found unacceptable and therefore prohibited." The school board itself affirmatively guaranteed the students of Journalism II an atmosphere conducive to fostering such an appreciation and exercising the full panoply of rights associated with a free student press. "School sponsored student publications," it vowed, "will not restrict free expression or diverse viewpoints within the rules of responsible journalism." . . .

In my view the principal broke more than just a promise. He violated the First Amendment's prohibitions against censorship of any student expression that neither disrupts classwork nor invades the rights of others, and against any censorship that is not narrowly tailored to serve its purpose.

I

. . . Free student expression undoubtedly sometimes interferes with the effectiveness of the school's pedagogical functions. Some brands of student expression do so by directly preventing the school from pursuing its pedagogical mission: The young polemic who stands on a soapbox during calculus class to deliver an eloquent political diatribe interferes with the teaching of calculus. And the student who delivers a lewd endorsement of a student government candidate might so extremely distract an impressionable high school audience as to interfere with the orderly operation of the school. Other student speech, however, frustrates the school's legitimate pedagogical purposes merely by expressing a message that conflicts with the school's, without directly interfering with the school's expression of its message: A student who responds to a political science teacher's question with the retort, "socialism is good," subverts the school's inculcation of the message that capitalism is better. Even the maverick who sits in class passively sporting a symbol of protest against a government policy, *Tinker*, or the gossip who sits in the student commons swapping stories of sexual escapade could readily muddle a clear official message condoning the government policy or condemning teenage sex. Likewise, the student newspaper that, like Spectrum, conveys a moral position at odds with the school's official stance might subvert the administration's legitimate inculcation of its own perception of community values.

If mere incompatibility with the school's pedagogical message were a constitutionally sufficient justification for the suppression of student speech, school officials could censor each of the students or student organizations in the foregoing hypotheticals, converting our public schools into "enclaves of totalitarianism," that "strangle the free mind at its source," *Barnette*. The First Amendment permits no such blanket censorship authority. While the "constitutional rights of students in public school are not automatically coextensive with the rights of adults in other settings," *Fraser*, students in the public schools do not "shed their constitutional rights to freedom of speech or expression at the schoolhouse gate," *Tinker*. Just as the public on the street corner must, in the interest of fostering "enlightened opinion," tolerate speech that "tempt[s] [the listener] to throw [the speaker] off the street," public educators must accommodate some student expression even if it offends them or offers views or values that contradict those the school wishes to inculcate.

In *Tinker*, this Court struck the balance. We held that official censorship of student expression—there the suspension of several students until they removed their armbands protesting the Vietnam war—is unconstitutional unless the speech "materially disrupts classwork or involves substantial disorder or invasion of the rights of others...."

## II

### A

The Court is certainly correct that the First Amendment permits educators "to assure that participants learn whatever lessons the activity is designed to teach...." That is, however, the essence of the *Tinker* test, not an excuse to abandon it. Under *Tinker*, school officials may censor only such student speech as would "materially disrup[t]" a legitimate curricular function. Manifestly, student speech is more likely to disrupt a curricular function when it arises in the context of a curricular activity—one that "is designed to teach" something—than when it arises in the context of a noncurricular activity. Thus, under *Tinker*, the school may constitutionally punish the budding political orator if he disrupts calculus class but not if he holds his tongue for the cafeteria. That is not because some more stringent standard applies in the curricular context. (After all, this Court applied the same standard whether the students in *Tinker* wore their armbands to the "classroom" or the "cafeteria.") It is because student speech in the noncurricular context is less likely to disrupt materially any legitimate pedagogical purpose.

I fully agree with the Court that the First Amendment should afford an educator the prerogative not to sponsor the publication of a newspaper article that is "ungrammatical, poorly written, inadequately researched, biased or prejudiced," or that falls short of the "high standards for ... student speech that is disseminated under [the school's] auspices...." But we need not abandon *Tinker* to reach that conclusion; we need only apply it. The enumerated criteria reflect the skills that the curricular newspaper "is designed to teach." The educator may, under *Tinker*, constitutionally "censor" poor grammar, writing, or research because to reward such expression would "materially disrup[t]" the newspaper's curricular purpose....

The author of the *Hazelwood* opinion, **JUSTICE BYRON R. WHITE**, was born in Fort Collins, Colorado, in 1917, and went to Wellington High School and the University of Colorado, where he earned varsity letters in football, basketball, and baseball and graduated as class valedictorian in 1938. After playing for the Pittsburgh Steelers for one year, "Whizzer" White went to Oxford on a Rhodes Scholarship, where he met George Bernard Shaw and John F. Kennedy. White left Oxford early for Yale Law School because of the onset of World War II. Before finishing law school, he played for the Detroit Lions and served in the Navy, where he would meet Kennedy again, before finally returning to Yale Law School after the war. In 1962, after White had served in the Kennedy Justice Department, President Kennedy appointed him to the Court. He served until 1993, making him one of the longest-serving justices in history.

HIGHLIGHTS

➤ In 1938, in his senior year of college, White was selected for Phi Beta Kappa and two days later scored all of Colorado's points in a 17–7 win over the Utah football team, a feat that included a 97-yard touchdown on a punt return. A standout athlete, he made the All-American team that year as a halfback.

The Court's second excuse for deviating from precedent is the school's interest in shielding an impressionable high school audience from material whose substance is "unsuitable for immature audiences." Specifically, the majority decrees that we must afford educators authority to shield high school students from exposure to "potentially sensitive topics" (like "the particulars of teenage sexual activity") or unacceptable social viewpoints (like the advocacy of "irresponsible se[x] or conduct otherwise inconsistent with 'the shared values of a civilized social order'") through school-sponsored student activities.

Tinker teaches us that the state educator's undeniable, and undeniably vital, mandate to inculcate moral and political values is not a general warrant to act as "thought police" stifling discussion of all but state-approved topics and advocacy of all but the official position. Otherwise educators could transform students into "closed-circuit recipients of only that which the State chooses to communicate," *Tinker,* and cast a perverse and impermissible "pall of orthodoxy over the classroom." . . . Thus, the State cannot constitutionally prohibit its high school students from recounting in the locker room "the particulars of [their] teen-age sexual activity," nor even from advocating "irresponsible se[x]" or other presumed abominations of "the shared values of a civilized social order." Even in its capacity as educator the State may not assume an Orwellian "guardianship of the public mind."

The mere fact of school sponsorship does not, as the Court suggests, license such thought control in the high school, whether through school suppression of disfavored viewpoints or through official assessment of topic sensitivity. The former would constitute unabashed and unconstitutional viewpoint discrimination. . . . Just as a school board may not purge its state-funded library of all books that "offen[d] [its] social, political and moral tastes," school officials may not, out of like motivation, discriminatorily excise objectionable ideas from a student publication. The State's prerogative to dissolve the student newspaper entirely (or to limit its subject matter) no more entitles it to dictate which viewpoints students may express on its pages, than the State's prerogative to close down the schoolhouse entitles it to prohibit the nondisruptive expression of antiwar sentiment within its gates. . . .

## C

. . . Dissociative means short of censorship are available to the school. It could, for example, require the student activity to publish a disclaimer, such as the "Statement of Policy" that Spectrum published each school year announcing that "[a]ll . . . editorials appearing in this newspaper reflect the opinions of the Spectrum staff, which are not necessarily shared by the administrators or faculty of Hazelwood East," or it could simply issue its own response clarifying the official position on the matter and explaining why the student position is wrong. Yet, without so much as acknowledging the less oppressive alternatives, the Court approves of brutal censorship. . . .

## IV

The Court opens its analysis in this case by purporting to reaffirm *Tinker's* time-tested proposition that public school students do not "shed their constitutional rights to freedom of speech or expression at the schoolhouse gate." That is an ironic introduction to an opinion that denudes high school students of much of the First Amendment protection that *Tinker* itself prescribed. Instead of "teach[ing] children to respect the diversity of ideas that is fundamental to the American system," and "that our Constitution is a living reality, not parchment preserved under glass," the Court today "teach[es] youth to discount important principles of our government as mere platitudes." *Barnette.* The young men and women of Hazelwood East expected a civics lesson, but not the one the Court teaches them today.

I dissent.

---

EXERCISE 3.1. Consider the outcomes in *Tinker, Fraser,* and *Hazelwood.* How have the Supreme Court's holdings changed? Is the Court expanding or narrowing the free speech rights of students?

EXERCISE 3.2. What was wrong with the student-written articles that Hazelwood East censored? Do you think that such articles are appropriate or important for students to write and read? If you were the principal, would you have censored the articles? Why or why not?

EXERCISE 3.3. Should school be a place where only teachers and administrators transmit knowledge and messages to students or a place where students also bring knowledge in and circulate their own messages to fellow students and teachers? How does *West Virginia v. Barnette* answer this question? How about *Hazelwood*? What image does Justice White have of high school students? What image does Justice Brennan have?

EXERCISE 3.4. Can school authorities at Hazelwood East censor articles that speak respectfully of the decision of high school students to go through with their pregnancies and have babies, but publish articles that condemn this decision and urge pregnant students to have abortions? Can school authorities censor one side in a political controversy? Generally, the First Amendment requires government to be *viewpoint neutral,* that is, scrupulously evenhanded among all sides in a political debate. Does *Hazelwood* respect that principle?

---

FOR THE CLASS

DRAFTING AN EDITORIAL POLICY FOR YOUR SCHOOL NEWSPAPER. The principal of your school has just appointed your class a school task force to come up with an editorial policy for your school newspaper that respects students' First Amendment rights but also prevents embarrassment of the school community and its members. Write a policy explaining what the newspaper will publish and what it will not. Do you leave it wide open? Are there categories of expression forbidden, such as obscene, libelous, dangerous, or disruptive speech? What will be the process for defining such categories? Do you attach a disclaimer? Do you forbid only articles that will materially and substantially disrupt school? Do you appoint faculty advisors who have free rein to censor articles for both grammatical and substantive reasons? Does the principal get final say? Bring your policies to class and discuss them as a task force, trying to find consensus for a final recommendation to the principal. Can you agree on the exact wording of a policy?

---

## Squelching Debate: A Different Sort of Blair Witch-Hunt

In October of 1996 an interesting sequence of events took place at Blair High School in Montgomery County, Maryland. Blair has an honors class that permits students to produce television news shows, commentaries, debates, and roundtable talk shows under the supervision of a teacher. They receive academic credit for their work. The TV news shows produced in the high school's studio are broadcast on the Montgomery County Public Schools' local cable channel.

The students have a monthly show called *Shades of Gray,* which has been airing for many years. In October 1996 the students planned and produced a debate format talk show on the subject of whether gays and lesbians should be allowed to marry. Two conservative adult guests appeared to oppose gay marriage and two liberal adult guests came to speak in favor of it. The show was taped; the teacher who oversees the class, Christopher Lloyd, praised the students' work, and the show was set to air.

At that point, however, officials in the school system who run the cable channel decided to preview the tape, which was not their ordinary practice. They notified Mr. Lloyd and the students that their show would not be broadcast because it was "inappropriate" for the station. A series of meetings and phone calls ensued in which the students tried to get the school authorities to explain what was wrong with their debate on gay marriage. On October 23, 1996, Barbara Wood, the program director for the cable channel, sent an email explaining the decision:

We felt that the gentleman who was a guest on the show [Dr. Frank Kameny] brought up the issue of religion and God in a very heated and controversial manner. . . . We both felt it would be inappropriate to air the program for that reason alone.

School authorities apparently reacted negatively when the student host asked a question about the basis of the guests' views about gay marriage. One of the conservative guests, Paula Govers, press secretary for Concerned Women for America, introduced religion into the discussion:

GOVERS: The Concerned Women for America believes that marriage is an institution sanctioned by God, licensed by the state, specifically between one man and one woman, and specifically for the purpose of procreation and should be a covenant between two people that should be a lifetime commitment.

This comment prompted the liberal guests, Dr. Frank Kameny of the Washington, D.C., Gay and Lesbian Activists Alliance and Judith Schaeffer of People for the American Way, to respond:

KAMENY: Paula, you said that the First Amendment guarantees us freedom of religion, and we all have our own views of God. My God gave us homosexuality as a blessing given to us by our creator God to be enjoyed to its fullest—exultantly, exuberantly, joyously. My God sanctifies same-sex marriage even if your God does not, and we are both American citizens and both Gods deserve equal recognition from our—not your—our government.
SCHAEFFER: That's exactly what the First Amendment requires. The government cannot legislate religious beliefs.
KAMENY: If you don't want to enter into a same-sex marriage, don't. But don't tell us just because your God doesn't sanctify it, my God is to be ignored.
GOVERS: Dr. Kameny, you said that your God does sanctify these unions. So your religious beliefs would say it's a good thing and our religious beliefs would say it's not. Why does your view get to trump ours?
KAMENY: It does not. If you believe that, you have an absolute right not to enter into a same-sex marriage.
KRIS ARDIZONNE [the other conservative guest and legal director of the Eagle Forum]: But my taxpayer dollars go to pay for the institution of marriage. And we don't believe in it.
KAMENY: And so do the tax dollars of gay people go to pay for marriage as well. . . .

Although the students' teacher and the principal of Blair High School saw this exchange of views as spirited and enlightening, the Montgomery County Public Schools officials thought it was inappropriate for the mostly adult audience of the cable channel.

The Blair students went to the Montgomery County Board of Education to appeal the school superintendent's decision to censor broadcast of the show. They made three arguments:

1. *The decision not to air the show violated the school system's own policy on student expression.* The student's guide to rights and responsibilities in Montgomery County Public School states: "School-sponsored publications such as newspapers, literary maga-

zines, and yearbooks will be encouraged. . . . Students have the right to decide on the contents of these publications, as long as the contents meet specific guidelines." The guidelines disallow only four categories of material: material that threatens the health and safety of students (such as use of illegal drugs), and material that is obscene, libelous, or disruptive.

2. *The decision to censor violated the First Amendment by discriminating against a speaker because of his religious views.* The students quoted the Supreme Court's 1995 decision in *Rosenberger v. University of Virginia,* which struck down the University of Virginia's practice of subsidizing student journals that had secular points of view but declining to subsidize those that had a religious point of view. The Court stated: "The government must abstain from regulating speech when the specific motivating ideology, or the opinion or perspective of the speaker, is the rationale for the restriction." The students argued that the school system was objecting to "the gentleman who was a guest on the show" who "brought up the issue of religion and God in a very heated and controversial manner."

3. *Because the educators in this case—the media teacher and the Blair principal—both favored broadcast of the show, the school system could not use to its advantage the* Hazelwood *finding that educators can censor when "their actions are reasonably related to legitimate pedagogical concerns."* The pedagogues in this case were *opposed* to censorship.

Meanwhile, the county superintendent argued that the school system's cable channel was government property within the absolute control of school system authorities. He maintained, in any event, that this was reasonable censorship within the meaning of *Hazelwood,* because the topic of gay marriage was sensitive and unsuitable for younger students.

The students never had to go to court because the school board voted 4–3 to reverse the superintendent and to air the show. The principal, Philip Gainous, subsequently won an award from the Freedom Forum in Virginia for standing up for the First Amendment rights of his students, and many of the students have since gone on to study media and broadcasting in college. Their case has given much force to arguments of students in other schools that they should have the same rights on video and television productions that they have in newspapers and yearbooks. Students in Montgomery County subsequently lobbied their school board to pass a set of guidelines on student speech that incorporates basic First Amendment ideas.

---

FOR THE CLASS

TOO HOT TO HANDLE? Do you think that high school students can handle discussion of controversial and sensitive topics like gay marriage, teen pregnancy, abortion rights, prayer in the public schools, parental divorce, and affirmative action? Should schools have the power to declare certain topics off limits to students journalists? Why or why not?

---

# Cyber Censors: Rising Conflicts over Internet Homepages

The *Hazelwood* decision has given school systems greater latitude to censor school newspapers, and many schools have used *Hazelwood* to censor student writings deemed offensive, subversive, mischievous, insubordinate, or inappropriate. Still, other schools have stood by policies that codify the old *Tinker* standard, which is much friendlier to student expression.

Censorship of school newspapers, combined with the rise of the Internet and desktop publishing, has led to the return of so-called "underground newspapers"—unofficial student-written, student-published, and privately circulated newspapers that were common in the 1960s. Many of today's underground newspapers are Web-based "'zines" where students express themselves in creative and uninhibited ways in cyberspace. Often students do not bother to design newspapers but simply publish diatribes, screeds, David Letterman–style "Top Ten" lists, or wicked satire on their Internet homepages.

In the 1970s court decisions about underground newspapers stayed true to the *Tinker* standard: They found that school authorities cannot censor privately distributed student newspapers and magazines unless the educational process is in danger of being disrupted. But today, because of the pervasiveness of the Internet and the immediacy of its power to communicate ideas, many schools are reacting against student speech on the Internet. In a typical case, a student posts stinging criticism of his principal or teachers on an Internet homepage and then school authorities retaliate by suspending him or punishing him academically.

Although no such case has made it to the Supreme Court, several lower courts have ruled on this kind of situation. In *Brandon Beussink v. Woodland R-IV School District* (1998), the United States District Court for the Eastern District of Missouri reversed Woodland High School's disciplinary action against Brandon Beussink, who was at the time a high school junior. Beussink had posted material "highly critical" of the school administration and "used vulgar language to convey his opinion regarding the teachers, the principal, and the school's own homepage."

Although Beussink designed his homepage at home and did not intend for it to be accessed at school, he did show it to a friend, Amanda Brown. Later, after the two friends had a falling out, Brown decided to get back at Beussink by showing his homepage to the school's computer teacher, who promptly reported it to the school principal, Yancy Poorman. Mr. Poorman said that he became "upset" by its contents and immediately suspended Beussink from school for five days. Then, as his anger apparently swelled, he "reconsidered" and suspended Beussink for ten days. Because of the school's absenteeism policy, this suspension would have resulted in Beussink's flunking all of his junior year classes.

Beussink went to court and won an injunction against his discipline on First Amendment grounds. The court found that Beussink's personal webpage caused no disruption in his classes—unlike the suspension itself—and that any fear of disruption was unreasonable. According to District Judge Sippel: "Disliking or being upset by the content of a student's speech is not an acceptable justification for limiting student speech under *Tinker.*"

In the following case from federal district court in western Pennsylvania, *Killion v. Franklin Regional School District*, another court considered the suspension of a student who had published on the Internet a "Top Ten" list of reasons that the school's athletic director was always in a grouchy mood.

10. The School Store doesn't sell twinkies.
9. He is constantly tripping over his own chins.
8. The girls at the 900 #'s keep hanging up on him.
7. For him, becoming Franklin's "Athletic Director" was considered "moving up in the world."
6. He has to use a pencil to type and make phone calls because his fingers are unable to hit only one key at a time.
5. As stated in previous list, he's just not getting any.
4. He is no longer allowed in any "All You Can Eat" restaurants.
3. He has constant flashbacks of when he was in high school and the athletes used to pick on him, instead of him picking on the athletes.
2. Because of his extensive gut factor, the "man" hasn't seen his own penis in over a decade.
1. Even it is wasn't for his gut, it would still take a magnifying glass and extensive searching to find it.

The school justified its discipline of this speech on the Web by arguing that it was disruptive, within the meaning of *Tinker,* and lewd and vulgar, within the meaning of *Fraser.* What does the court say? What do you think?

— —

## KILLION
### v.
### FRANKLIN REGIONAL SCHOOL DISTRICT

*United States District Court, Western District of Pennsylvania*
March 22, 2001.

ZIEGLER, District Judge.

... Plaintiff, Zachariah Paul ("Paul"), was a student at Franklin Regional High School during the 1998–1999 school year. During March of 1999, Paul, apparently angered by a denial of a student parking permit and the imposition of various rules and regulations for members of the track team (Paul was a member), compiled a "Top Ten" list about the athletic director, Robert Bozzuto. The Bozzuto list contained ... statements regarding Bozzuto's appearance, including the size of his genitals. After consulting with friends, Paul composed and assembled the list while at home after school hours. Thereafter, in late March or early April, Paul e-mailed the list to friends from his home computer.... Paul did not print or copy the list to bring it on school premises because, after copying and distributing similar lists in the past, he had been warned that he would be punished if he brought another list to school.

Several weeks later, several individuals found copies of the Bozzuto Top Ten list in the Franklin Regional High School teachers' lounge and the Franklin Regional Middle School. An undisclosed student had reformatted Paul's original e-mail and distributed the document on school grounds.

On or about May 3, 1999, Paul was called to a meeting with Richard Plutto (principal), Thomas Graham (assistant principal), and Robert Bozzuto (athletic director). Upon questioning, Paul admitted that he had created the contents of the Top Ten list, and that he had e-mailed it to the home computers of several friends from his home computer; however, Paul steadfastly denied bringing the list on school grounds. Plutto or Graham instructed Paul to bring a copy of the original e-mail message the next day....

The next day, shortly before Paul was scheduled to leave for a track meet, Plutto called Paul to his office. Paul, apparently anticipating that he might be disciplined, called his mother, who arrived shortly thereafter. Paul and Mrs. Killion went to the administrative offices where they met with Graham and Bozzuto. Graham and Bozzuto showed Mrs. Killion the Top Ten list, asked if she had seen it, and informed her that Paul was being suspended for ten days because the list contained offensive remarks about a school official, was found on school grounds, and that Paul admitted creating the list. Graham further informed Mrs. Killion that Paul could not participate in any school-related activities, including track and field events during the ten-day suspension.

... [P]laintiffs commenced an action in the Westmoreland County Court of Common Pleas, Pennsylvania, against the School District seeking immediate reinstatement. The parties subsequently entered a settlement agreement wherein plaintiffs agreed to withdraw the complaint in exchange for the School District's agreement to provide Paul with the due process outlined in the Pennsylvania School Code....

On May 12, plaintiffs Plutto and Graham met for the suspension hearing, which resulted in a ten day suspension. The same day, plaintiffs commenced a civil action in this court seeking a preliminary injunction for First ... Amendment violation, and requesting that Paul be allowed to return to school immediately....

Plaintiffs seek summary judgment contending that defendants violated Paul's First Amendment right of free expression by suspending Paul for speech that was made off school grounds and in the privacy of his home....

### B. First Amendment

#### 1. Freedom of Speech

... Although there is limited case law on the issue, courts considering speech that occurs off school grounds have concluded (relying on Supreme Court decisions) that school officials' authority over off-campus expression is much more limited than expression on school grounds....

... [W]e find that Paul's suspension violates the First Amendment because defendants failed to satisfy *Tinker's* substantial disruption test. First, defendants failed to adduce any evidence of actual disruption.... There is no evidence that teachers were incapable of teaching or controlling their classes because of the Bozzuto Top Ten list. Indeed, the list was on school grounds for several days before the administration became aware of its existence, and at least one week passed before defendants took any action....

Further, we note that the speech at issue was not threatening, and, although upsetting to Bozzuto, did not cause any faculty member to take a leave of absence.... Although the intended audience was undoubtedly connected to Franklin Regional High School, the absence of threats or actual disruption lead us to conclude that Paul's suspension was improper....

Admittedly, Bozzutto, Graham, Plutto and others found the list to be rude, abusive and demeaning.... However, "[d]isliking or being upset by the content of a student's speech is not an acceptable justification for limiting student speech. . . ." Indeed, "the mere desire to avoid 'discomfort' or 'unpleasantness' is not enough to justify restricting student speech. . . . However, if a school can point to a well-founded expectation of disruption—especially one based on past incidents arising out of similar speech—the restriction may pass constitutional muster." . . .

. . . [D]efendants apparently argue that the Bozzuto list could "impair the administration's ability to appropriately discipline the students." . . . We cannot accept, without more, that the childish and boorish antics of a minor could impair the administrators' abilities to discipline students and maintain control. . . .

. . . Defendants also argue that the suspension was appropriate because Paul's speech was lewd and obscene and therefore punishable. . . . Plaintiffs rejoin that, "[i]f the Bozzuto list could in fact be considered contraband . . . the defendants['] recourse would be to punish those students who actually brought the offending material to school. But to punish the author for work created outside of school is certainly beyond the First Amendment pale." . . .

Here, defendants argue that Paul's top ten list contained several lewd and vulgar statements. . . . Although we agree that several passages from the list are lewd, abusive, and derogatory, we cannot ignore the fact that the relevant speech . . . occurred within the confines of Paul's home, far removed from any school premises or facilities. Further, Paul was not engaged in any school activity or associated in any way with his role as a student when he compiled the Bozzuto Top Ten list.

. . . Given the out of school creation of the list, absent evidence that Paul was responsible for bringing the list on school grounds, and absent disruption . . . we hold . . . that defendants could not, without violating the First Amendment, suspend Paul for the mere creation of the Bozzuto Top Ten list. . . . Plaintiffs' motion for summary judgment must be granted.

---

EXERCISE 3.5. If schools cannot discipline students for posting disparaging comments about teachers on the Internet, can they discipline teachers for posting disparaging comments about students on the Internet? Make arguments in class both ways, assuming that Coach Bozzuto created a similar satirical "Top Ten" list about why Paul is always in a bad mood. How can schools create more positive dynamics among students and teachers? Can the Internet become a positive force for communication among students, teachers, and administrators in high schools? How?

---

### Read On

Hentoff, Nat. *Free Speech for Me—But Not for Thee.* New York: HarperCollins, 1992.
Bollinger, Lee C., and Geoffrey R. Stone, eds. *Eternally Vigilant: Free Speech in the Modern Era.* Chicago: University of Chicago Press, 2002.

### For Further Information

Electronic Frontier Foundation, www.eff.org
The Freedom Forum and First Amendment Schools Project, www.freedomforum.org
Society of Professional Journalists, http://spj.org
Student Press Law Center, www.splc.org

# PUBLIC SCHOOLS AND RELIGION UNDER THE CONSTITUTION

# 4

"Congress shall make no law respecting an establishment of religion, or prohibiting the free exercise thereof...."
THE FIRST AMENDMENT

"As long as there are math tests, there will be prayer in the public schools."   REV. JESSE JACKSON

The United States was founded by people fleeing religious persecution. They learned the hard way to distrust government-imposed religion. To ensure that our government never treats religious followers as other governments have, the religion clauses of the First Amendment give two commands: Congress may not "establish" a religion, nor may it prohibit the "free exercise" of religion. Government may neither sponsor nor endorse a religion of its own nor deliberately interfere with citizens' freedom to practice their own faiths.

The Framers thought that these two constitutional principles respecting church and state—the establishment clause and the free exercise clause—reinforced one another and stood best when they stood together. But sometimes the two principles come into conflict, or at least many people think they do. Many Americans feel that if we do everything we can to drive religion from the public square, we will be violating the free exercise of religiously oriented citizens and impoverishing our public life. Others believe that if we allow religion into public spaces and activities, we will invite sectarian conflict, hard feelings, and manipulation of religious sentiment by government leaders. What do you think?

There is no end to religious controversy in and around public schools. A recurring constitutional problem is organized school prayer, where teachers and administrators lead or encourage prayer among students. This practice clearly violates the establishment clause. On the other hand, public school students are always free to say quiet prayers on their own while at school so long as they are not disruptive. This is guaranteed by freedom of speech and religion. A more tricky problem is how to protect the free speech rights of students with religious viewpoints to meet and pray in public schools without violating the establishment clause. Yet another controversy focuses on the development by states and cities of school voucher plans that make public dollars available to families to send their children to private schools, including religious schools.

In this chapter we will learn where the Supreme Court has drawn different lines in this rocky field and ask how teachers and students can reconcile competing constitutional values in the classroom.

POINTS TO PONDER

**How do the First Amendment's religion clauses affect public school students?**

- Should school officials be able to establish a morning prayer for all students?
- Should nondenominational prayers be allowed during official school functions?
- Should public high school students be allowed to elect fellow students to make "solemnizing" invocations at football games?
- Should public school officials be allowed to post the Ten Commandments?
- Should government be allowed to ask students to pledge allegiance to the American flag "under God"?
- Should state and local governments be allowed to spend public dollars on school vouchers that families can use for tuition at private religious schools?
- Do student religious clubs and organizations have a right to meet in public schools?
- Do speakers with religious points of view have equal rights in public schools?
- Should religious beliefs ever excuse students from completing their state-required schooling?

# Freedom from Establishment of Religion at School

The Supreme Court has long tried to develop an easy test for deciding whether a government practice violates the establishment clause. The traditional test is found in *Lemon v. Kurtzman,* which provided that a challenged government practice must (1) have a primarily secular (not religious) purpose; (2) have a primarily secular effect; and (3) avoid "excessive entanglement" with religion. If a practice failed to meet any one of these requirements, it violated the establishment clause.

Most justices have expressed dissatisfaction with the *Lemon* test, but it is still in use; Justice Scalia even likened it to a Frankenstein monster that occasionally sits up in the coffin and scares the justices. But the Court has not been able to develop a consensus alternative. Justice O'Connor proposed her "endorsement" test, which suggests that any governmental endorsement of a specific religion or religion in general violates the establishment clause. Justice Kennedy's "coercion" test would invalidate on establishment clause grounds only those practices that actually coerce people into participating in religious exercises. Meantime, the most conservative justices have been promoting the acceptability of what they call "ceremonial deism," historically rooted public practices that invoke theistic belief, like "under God" in the Pledge of Allegiance or "In God We Trust" on the dollar bill, but do not directly try to establish a church. As you go through the cases in this chapter, think about which of these standards, or a new one you could develop, works best to effectuate establishment clause values.

Beginning in *Engel v. Vitale* in 1962, the Supreme Court has read the establishment clause to prevent governmental promotion of religion or departure from strict neutrality in matters of religion at school. In *Engel* the Court found it unconstitutional for school authorities to lead students in organized school prayer. Many politicians vehemently disagree with this holding and blame it for the nation's perceived moral demise. Some even link it to disasters like the 1999 Columbine High School killings in Littleton, Colorado. Others think the ban on organized school prayer is critical to maintaining Thomas Jefferson's "wall of separation" between church and state. Do you agree with the Court's decision that school-led prayers violate the establishment clause?

———

ENGEL

v.

VITALE

*Supreme Court of the United States*
Argued April 3, 1962.
Decided June 25, 1962.

Justice BLACK delivered the opinion of the Court.

The respondent Board of Education of Union Free School District No. 9, New Hyde Park, New York, acting in its official capacity under state law, directed the School District's principal to cause the following prayer to be said aloud by each class in the presence of a teacher at the beginning of each school day:

Almighty God, we acknowledge our dependence upon Thee, and we beg Thy blessings upon us, our parents, our teachers and our Country.

... [T]he parents of ten pupils brought this action in a New York State Court insisting that use of this official prayer in the public schools was

**JUSTICE HUGO L. BLACK** (1886–1971) wrote the majority opinion for this decision. He was the last of eight children born to a storekeeper and farmer in Clay County, Alabama. Skipping college, he went to the University of Alabama Law School, where he graduated with honors. After a distinguished career as a progressive reformer in public life, including stints as a judge, prosecutor, and U.S. senator, Black was appointed to the Supreme Court by President Franklin Delano Roosevelt in 1937. He served thirty-one years.

HIGHLIGHTS

➤ Justice Black attended medical school for one year at age seventeen.

➤ As a county prosecuting attorney in Alabama, he ran a successful grand jury investigation of the Bessamer, Alabama, police department, which was known for its barbaric torture chamber. Despite his brief membership in the Ku Klux Klan, Black's passionate concern for human rights later became a hallmark of his jurisprudence.

➤ Justice Black was an absolutist about the freedoms of speech and religion. He was fond of saying that "no law means *no law* abridging these rights." He was buried with a ten-cent pocket-size copy of the Constitution in his pocket.

contrary to the beliefs, religions, or religious practices of both themselves and their children. Among other things, these parents challenged the constitutionality of . . . the School District's regulation ordering the recitation of this particular prayer on the ground that these actions of official governmental agencies violate that part of the First Amendment of the Federal Constitution which commands that "Congress shall make no law respecting an establishment of religion." . . . The New York Court of Appeals . . . sustained an order of the lower state courts which had upheld the power of New York to use the Regents' prayer as a part of the daily procedures of its public schools so long as the schools did not compel any pupil to join in the prayer over his or his parents' objection. We think that by using its public school system to encourage recitation of the Regents' prayer, the State of New York has adopted a practice wholly inconsistent with the Establishment Clause. There can, of course, be no doubt that New York's program of daily classroom invocation of God's blessings as prescribed in the Regents' prayer is a religious activity. It is a solemn avowal of divine faith and supplication for the blessings of the Almighty. . . .

The petitioners contend among other things that the state laws requiring or permitting use of the Regents' prayer must be struck down as a violation of the Establishment Clause because that prayer was composed by governmental officials as a part of a governmental program to further religious beliefs. For this reason, petitioners argue, the State's use of the Regents' prayer in its public school system breaches the constitutional wall of separation between Church and State. We agree with that contention since we think that the constitutional prohibition against laws respecting an establishment of religion must at least mean that in this country it is no part of the business of government to compose official prayers for any group of the American people to recite as a part of a religious program carried on by government. . . .

. . . The First Amendment was added to the Constitution to stand as a guarantee that neither the power nor the prestige of the Federal Government would be used to control, support or influence the kinds of prayer the American people can say that the people's religions must not be subjected to the pressures of government for change each time a new political administration is elected to office.

Students in a San Antonio, Texas, classroom bow their heads in prayer in June 1962. Ever since *Engel v. Vitale* it has been unconstitutional for public school officials to conduct organized prayers in the classroom.

Under that Amendment's prohibition against governmental establishment of religion, as reinforced by the provisions of the Fourteenth Amendment, government in this country, be it state or federal, is without power to prescribe by law any particular form of prayer which is to be used as an official prayer in carrying on any program of governmentally sponsored religious activity.

There can be no doubt that New York's state prayer program officially establishes the religious beliefs embodied in the Regents' prayer. The respondents' argument to the contrary, which is largely based upon the contention that the Regents' prayer is "non-denominational" and the fact that the program, as modified and approved by state courts, does not require all pupils to recite the prayer but permits those who wish to do so to remain silent or be excused from the room, ignores the essential nature of the program's constitutional defects. Neither the fact that the prayer may be denominationally neutral nor the fact that its observance on the part of the students is voluntary can serve to free it from the limitations of the Establishment Clause, as it might from the Free Exercise Clause, of the First Amendment, both of which are operative against the States by virtue of the Fourteenth Amendment.

Although these two clauses may in certain instances overlap, they forbid two quite different kinds of governmental encroachment upon religious freedom. The Establishment Clause ... does not depend upon any showing of direct governmental compulsion and is violated by the enactment of laws which establish an official religion whether those laws operate directly to coerce nonobserving individuals or not.... When the power, prestige and financial support of government is placed behind a particular religious belief, the indirect coercive pressure upon religious minorities to conform to the prevailing officially approved religion is plain. But the purposes underlying the Establishment Clause go much further than that. Its first and most immediate purpose rested on the belief that a union of government and religion tends to destroy government and to degrade religion. ... The Establishment Clause thus stands as an expression of principle on the part of the Founders of our Constitution that religion is too personal, too sacred, too holy, to permit its "unhallowed perversion" by a civil magistrate. Another purpose of the Establishment Clause rested upon an awareness of the historical fact that governmentally established religions and religious persecutions go hand in hand. The Founders knew that only a few years after the Book of Common Prayer became the only accepted form of religious services in the established Church of England, an Act of Uniformity was passed to compel all Englishmen to attend those services and to make it a criminal offense to conduct or attend religious gatherings of any other kind....

It has been argued that to apply the Constitution in such a way as to prohibit state laws respecting an establishment of religious services in public schools is to indicate a hostility toward religion or toward prayer. Nothing, of course, could be more wrong.... It is neither sacrilegious nor antireligious to say that each separate government in this country should stay out of the business of writing or sanctioning official prayers and leave that purely religious function to the people themselves and to those the people choose to look to for religious guidance.

The judgment of the Court of Appeals of New York is reversed and the cause remanded for further proceedings not inconsistent with this opinion.

Justice STEWART, dissenting.

A local school board in New York has provided that those pupils who wish to do so may join in a brief prayer at the beginning of each school day, acknowledging their dependence upon God and asking His blessing upon them and upon their parents, their teachers, and their country. The Court today decides that in permitting this brief nondenominational prayer the school board has

**JUSTICE POTTER STEWART** (1915–1985) was born in Jackson, Michigan, on January 23, 1915. He went to prep school at Hotchkiss. Upon graduation from Yale University, Stewart went to Cambridge, England, on a Henry Fellowship and one year later entered Yale Law School. Stewart served active duty in the Navy, practiced privately, and was a judge on the United States Court of Appeals for the Sixth Circuit before President Dwight Eisenhower appointed him justice in 1958. He served until 1981.

HIGHLIGHTS

➤    During World War II, Stewart served as a deck officer on oil tankers.

➤    On the Court, Justice Stewart was well known for his pithy and witty statements in opinions. About obscenity, he said: "I shall not today further attempt to define the kinds of material I understand to be embraced within that shorthand description; and perhaps I could never succeed in intelligibly doing so. But I know it when I see it." In a capital punishment case, he wrote that arbitrary imposition of the death penalty is "cruel and unusual in the way that being struck by lightning is cruel and unusual."

violated the Constitution of the United States. I think this decision is wrong.

The Court does not hold, nor could it, that New York has interfered with the free exercise of anybody's religion. For the state courts have made clear that those who object to reciting the prayer must be entirely free of any compulsion to do so, including any "embarrassments and pressures." But the Court says that in permitting school children to say this simple prayer, the New York authorities have established "an official religion."

With all respect, I think the Court has misapplied a great constitutional principle. I cannot see how an "official religion" is established by letting those who want to say a prayer say it. On the contrary, I think that to deny the wish of these school children to join in reciting this prayer is to deny them the opportunity of sharing in the spiritual heritage of our Nation....

---

EXERCISE 4.1. Imagine that your class had to recite these words in unison every morning: "Almighty God, we acknowledge our dependence upon Thee, and we beg Thy blessings upon us, our parents, our teachers and our Country." How would that make you feel? Who might it make uncomfortable? Are there religious students who might be turned off to the prayer?

EXERCISE 4.2. The Supreme Court ruled in *Engel v. Vitale* that schools could not organize moments of prayer. In a later decision, *Wallace v. Jaffree* (1985), the Court allowed general "moments of silence" for meditation and reflection. Silence may be rare in a public school, but it is not unconstitutional! In Virginia, today, all students now begin the day with "the daily observance of one minute of silence in each classroom." State law provides that "each pupil may, in the exercise of his or her individual choice, meditate, pray or engage in any other silent activity which does not interfere with, distract or impede other pupils in the like exercise of individual choice."

Is it constitutional to mention religion in this way? Some students objected that Virginia's policy is a dressed-up form of school-endorsed prayer. Others clearly liked the chance to begin the day by focusing their minds and did not view the moment of silence as a religious imposition. What do you think of Virginia's policy? The Fourth Circuit Court of Appeals upheld the law against a challenge by some students and the American Civil Liberties Union in *Brown v. Gilmore* (2001).

## Saying a Benediction for Invocation

Even after *Engel v. Vitale,* many school systems tried to circumvent the Court's decision by having teachers and students read excerpts from the Bible rather than from a prayer composed by the school system. In Pennsylvania state law provided that "at least ten verses from the Holy Bible shall be read, without comment, at the opening of each public school on each school day." The Schempp family, who were Unitarians, challenged the practice of having students read passages from the New Testament and then recite in unison the Lord's Prayer.

In *Abington School District v. Schempp,* (1963), the Supreme Court found that this practice also violates the establishment clause by putting the government in the posture of leading a religious exercise. Indeed, because the schools were having students read from the

The Schempp family stands in front of the Supreme Court after hearing arguments in *School District of Abington v. Schempp* (1963). Justice Tom C. Clark's majority ruling overturned a state law that required a Bible reading at the start of each day in the public schools. From left, Edward Schempp, Donna Schempp, Roger Schempp, Sidney Schempp, Ellery Schempp, and Josephine Hallett, a family friend.

New Testament, the policy automatically excluded and offended Jewish students as well as atheists and students from other faiths. The Court emphasized that there is nothing wrong with a public school teaching about religion as a fact in the world, such as "the history of religion" or even the Bible as literature. But these inquiries into religion, "when presented objectively as part of a secular program of education," are a world apart from inviting (or requiring) students to participate in a sectarian religious ritual. Thus, whether the school system composes a prayer or selects Bible passages for reading, it is unconstitutional if the purpose is a kind of devotional worship rather than academic study and critique.

But even after *Schempp,* many local school system officials and teachers continued to lead students in group prayer at official ceremonial events, such as graduations and homecoming games. Then in 1992 the Supreme Court decided *Lee v. Weisman,* which held that public school officials could not invite clergy members to open graduation with an invocation prayer or close it with a benediction. Do you think that the Court was pushing things too far with this decision, as Justice Scalia suggests, or is this ruling necessary to allow all students, regardless of religious belief, to enjoy "one of life's most significant occasions," as Justice Kennedy argues?

—

# LEE
v.
# WEISMAN

*Supreme Court of the United States*
Argued Nov. 6, 1991.
Decided June 24, 1992.

Justice KENNEDY delivered the opinion of the Court.

School principals in the public school system of the city of Providence, Rhode Island, are permitted to invite members of the clergy to offer invocation and benediction prayers as part of the formal graduation ceremonies for middle schools and for high schools. The question before us is whether including clerical members who offer prayers as part of the official school graduation ceremony is consistent with the Religion Clauses of the First Amendment, provisions the Fourteenth Amendment makes applicable with full force to the States and their school districts.

I

Deborah Weisman graduated from Nathan Bishop Middle School, a public school in Providence, at a formal ceremony in June 1989.... For many years it has been the policy of the Providence School Committee and the Superintendent of Schools to permit principals to invite members of the clergy to give invocations and benedictions at middle school and high school graduations. Many, but not all, of the principals elected to include prayers as part of the graduation ceremonies. Acting for himself and his daughter, Deborah's father, Daniel Weisman, objected to any prayers at Deborah's middle school graduation, but to no avail. The school principal, petitioner Robert E. Lee, invited a rabbi

Daniel Weisman and his daughter, Deborah, challenged the practice of having a member of the clergy deliver invocation and benediction prayers at public school graduation exercises in Providence, Rhode Island. The Supreme Court ruled in their favor in *Lee v. Weisman* (1992).

to deliver prayers at the graduation exercises for Deborah's class. Rabbi Leslie Gutterman, of the Temple Beth El in Providence, accepted.

It has been the custom of Providence school officials to provide invited clergy with a pamphlet entitled "Guidelines for Civic Occasions," prepared by the National Conference of Christians and Jews. The Guidelines recommend that public prayers at nonsectarian civic ceremonies be composed with "inclusiveness and sensitivity," though they acknowledge that "[p]rayer of any kind may be inappropriate on some civic occasions." The principal gave Rabbi Gutterman the pamphlet before the graduation and advised him the invocation and benediction should be nonsectarian. Rabbi Gutterman's [invocation was] as follows:

> God of the Free, Hope of the Brave:
> For the legacy of America where diversity is celebrated and the rights of minorities are protected, we thank You. May these young men and women grow up to enrich it.
> For the liberty of America, we thank You. May these new graduates grow up to guard it.
> For the political process of America in which all its citizens may participate, for its court system where all may seek justice we thank You. May those we honor this morning always turn to it in trust.
> For the destiny of America we thank You. May the graduates of Nathan Bishop Middle School so live that they might help to share it.
> May our aspirations for our country and for these young people, who are our hope for the future, be richly fulfilled.
> AMEN ...

## B

... The District Court held that petitioners' practice of including invocations and benedictions in public school graduations violated the Establishment Clause of the First Amendment, and it enjoined petitioners from continuing the practice. The court applied the three-part Establishment

Clause test set forth in *Lemon v. Kurtzman*. Under that test as described in our past cases, to satisfy the Establishment Clause a governmental practice must (1) reflect a clearly secular purpose; (2) have a primary effect that neither advances nor inhibits religion; and (3) avoid excessive government entanglement with religion. The District Court held that petitioners' actions violated the second part of the test.... The court determined that the practice of including invocations and benedictions, even so-called nonsectarian ones, in public school graduations creates an identification of governmental power with religious practice, endorses religion, and violates the Establishment Clause....

On appeal, the United States Court of Appeals for the First Circuit affirmed.... We granted certiorari ... and now affirm.

II

These dominant facts mark and control the confines of our decision: State officials direct the performance of a formal religious exercise at promotional and graduation ceremonies for secondary schools. Even for those students who object to the religious exercise, their attendance and participation in the state-sponsored religious activity are in a fair and real sense obligatory, though the school district does not require attendance as a condition for receipt of the diploma.

... The government involvement with religious activity in this case is pervasive, to the point of creating a state-sponsored and state-directed religious exercise in a public school. Conducting this formal religious observance conflicts with settled rules pertaining to prayer exercises for students, and that suffices to determine the question before us.

The principle that government may accommodate the free exercise of religion does not supersede the fundamental limitations imposed by the Establishment Clause. It is beyond dispute that, at a minimum, the Constitution guarantees that government may not coerce anyone to support or participate in religion or its exercise.... The State's involvement in the school prayers challenged today violates these central principles....

The State's role did not end with the decision to include a prayer and with the choice of a clergyman. Principal Lee provided Rabbi Gutterman with a copy of the "Guidelines for Civic Occasions," and advised him that his prayers should be nonsectarian. Through these means the principal directed and controlled the content of the prayers....

Petitioners argue, and we find nothing in the case to refute it, that the directions for the content of the prayers were a good-faith attempt by the school to ensure that the sectarianism which is so often the flashpoint for religious animosity be removed from the graduation ceremony. The concern is understandable, as a prayer which uses ideas or images identified with a particular religion may foster a different sort of sectarian rivalry than an invocation or benediction in terms more neutral. The school's explanation, however, does not resolve the dilemma caused by its participation. The question is not the good faith of the school in attempting to make the prayer acceptable to most persons, but the legitimacy of its undertaking that enterprise at all when the object is to produce a prayer to be used in a formal religious exercise which students, for all practical purposes, are obliged to attend....

The degree of school involvement here made it clear that the graduation prayers bore the imprint of the State and thus put school-age children who objected in an untenable position. We turn our attention now to consider the position of the students, both those who desired the prayer and she who did not.

To endure the speech of false ideas or offensive content and then to counter it is part of learning how to live in a pluralistic society, a society which insists upon open discourse towards the end of a tolerant citizenry. And tolerance presupposes some mutuality of obligation. It is argued that our constitutional vision of a free society requires confidence in our own ability to accept or reject ideas of which we do not approve, and that prayer at a high school graduation does nothing more than offer a choice. By the time they are seniors, high school students no doubt have been required to attend classes and assemblies and to complete assignments exposing them to ideas they find distasteful or immoral or absurd or all of these. Against this background, students may consider it an odd measure of justice to be subjected during the course of their educations to ideas deemed offensive and irreligious, but to be denied a brief, formal prayer ceremony that the school offers in return. This argument cannot prevail, however. It overlooks a fundamental dynamic of the Constitution. The First Amendment protects speech and religion by quite different mechanisms. Speech is protected by ensuring its full expression even when the government participates, for the very object of some of our most important speech is to persuade the government to adopt an idea as its own. The method for protecting freedom of worship and freedom of conscience in religious matters is quite the reverse. In religious debate or expression the government is not a prime participant, for the Framers deemed religious establishment antithetical to the freedom of all. The Free Exercise Clause embraces a freedom of conscience and worship that has close parallels in the speech provisions of the First Amendment, but the Establishment Clause is a specific prohibition on forms of state intervention in religious affairs with no precise counterpart in the speech provisions. The explanation lies in the lesson of history that was and is the inspiration for the Establishment Clause, the lesson that in the hands of government what might begin as a tolerant expression of religious views may end in a policy to indoctrinate and coerce. A state-created orthodoxy puts at grave risk that freedom of belief and conscience which are the sole assurance that religious faith is real, not imposed.

The lessons of the First Amendment are as urgent in the modern world as in the 18th century when it was written. One timeless lesson is that if citizens are subjected to state-sponsored religious exercises, the State disavows its own duty to guard and respect that sphere of inviolable conscience and belief which is the mark of a free people. To compromise that principle today would be to deny our own tradition and forfeit our standing to urge others to secure the protections of that tradition for themselves.

As we have observed before, there are heightened concerns with protecting freedom of conscience from subtle coercive pressure in the elementary and secondary public schools. . . . What to most believers may seem nothing more than a reasonable request that the nonbeliever respect their religious practices, in a school context may appear to the nonbeliever or dissenter to be an attempt to employ the machinery of the State to enforce a religious orthodoxy.

We need not look beyond the circumstances of this case to see the phenomenon at work. The undeniable fact is that the school district's supervision and control of a high school graduation ceremony places public pressure, as well as peer pressure, on attending students to stand as a group or, at least, maintain respectful silence during the invocation and benediction. . . . There can be no doubt that for many, if not most, of the students at the graduation, the act of standing or remaining silent was an expression of participation in the rabbi's prayer. That was the very point of the religious exercise. It is of little comfort to a dissenter, then, to be told that for her the act of standing or remaining in silence signifies mere respect, rather than participation. What matters is that, given our social conventions, a reasonable dissenter in this milieu could believe that the group exercise signified her own participation or approval of it.

Finding no violation under these circumstances would place objectors in the dilemma of participating, with all that implies, or protesting. We do not address whether that choice is acceptable if the affected citizens are mature adults, but we think the State may not, consistent with the

Establishment Clause, place primary and secondary school children in this position. . . . To recognize that the choice imposed by the State constitutes an unacceptable constraint only acknowledges that the government may no more use social pressure to enforce orthodoxy than it may use more direct means. . . .

There was a stipulation in the District Court that attendance at graduation and promotional ceremonies is voluntary. . . . The argument lacks all persuasion. . . . Everyone knows that in our society and in our culture high school graduation is one of life's most significant occasions. . . .

The importance of the event is the point the school district and the United States rely upon to argue that a formal prayer ought to be permitted, but it becomes one of the principal reasons why their argument must fail. Their contention . . . is that the prayers are an essential part of these ceremonies because for many persons an occasion of this significance lacks meaning if there is no recognition, however brief, that human achievements cannot be understood apart from their spiritual essence. We think the Government's position that this interest suffices to force students to choose between compliance or forfeiture demonstrates fundamental inconsistency in its argumentation. It fails to acknowledge that what for many of Deborah's classmates and their parents was a spiritual imperative was for Daniel and Deborah Weisman religious conformance compelled by the State. . . . The Constitution forbids the State to exact religious conformity from a student as the price of attending her own high school graduation. This is the calculus the Constitution commands. . . .

We do not hold that every state action implicating religion is invalid if one or a few citizens find it offensive. People may take offense at all manner of religious as well as nonreligious messages, but offense alone does not in every case show a violation. We know too that sometimes to endure social isolation or even anger may be the price of conscience or nonconformity. But, by any reading of our cases, the conformity required of the student in this case was too high an exaction to withstand the test of the Establishment Clause. The prayer exercises in this case are especially improper because the State has in every practical sense compelled attendance and participation in an explicit religious exercise at an event of singular importance to every student, one the objecting student had no real alternative to avoid. . . .

. . . We recognize that, at graduation time and throughout the course of the educational process, there will be instances when religious values, religious practices, and religious persons will have some interaction with the public schools and their students. But these matters, often questions of accommodation of religion, are not before us. The sole question presented is whether a religious exercise may be conducted at a graduation ceremony in circumstances where, as we have found, young graduates who object are induced to conform. No holding by this Court suggests that a school can persuade or compel a student to participate in a religious exercise. That is being done here, and it is forbidden by the Establishment Clause of the First Amendment.

For the reasons we have stated, the judgment of the Court of Appeals is *Affirmed.*

Justice SCALIA, with whom The Chief Justice, Justice WHITE, and Justice THOMAS join, dissenting.

. . . In holding that the Establishment Clause prohibits invocations and benedictions at public school graduation ceremonies, the Court—with nary a mention that it is doing so—lays waste a tradition that is as old as public school graduation ceremonies themselves, and that is a component of an even more longstanding American tradition of nonsectarian prayer to God at public celebrations generally. . . .

Rabbi Leslie Gutterman, left, leads the prayer at the Nathan Bishop Middle School graduation in 1989. At right are principal Robert E. Lee and school board member Bruce Lundlun. The Court's decision in *Lee v. Weisman* has fueled the long-running controversy over prayer in schools.

I

... The history and tradition of our Nation are replete with public ceremonies featuring prayers of thanksgiving and petition....

From our Nation's origin, prayer has been a prominent part of governmental ceremonies and proclamations. The Declaration of Independence, the document marking our birth as a separate people, "appealed to the Supreme Judge of the world for the rectitude of our intentions" and avowed "a firm reliance on the protection of divine Providence." In his first inaugural address, after swearing his oath of office on a Bible, George Washington deliberately made a prayer a part of his first official act as President....

Such supplications have been a characteristic feature of inaugural addresses ever since....

II

... The Court's argument that state officials have "coerced" students to take part in the invocation and benediction at graduation ceremonies is, not to put too fine a point on it, incoherent.

The Court identifies two "dominant facts" that it says dictate its ruling that invocations and benedictions at public school graduation ceremonies violate the Establishment Clause. Neither of them is in any relevant sense true.

A

The Court declares that students' "attendance and participation in the [invocation and benediction] are in a fair and real sense obligatory." But what exactly is this "fair and real sense"? According to the Court, students at graduation who want "to avoid the fact or appearance of participation" in the invocation and benediction are *psychologically* obligated by "public pressure, as well as peer pressure ... to stand as a group or, at least, maintain respectful silence" during those prayers. This assertion— *the very linchpin of the Court's opinion*—is almost as intriguing for what it does not say as for what it says. It does not say, for example, that students are psychologically coerced to bow their heads, place their hands in a Dürer-like prayer position, pay attention to the prayers, utter "Amen," or in fact pray. (Perhaps further intensive psychological research remains to be done on these matters.) It claims only that students are psychologically coerced "to stand ... or, at least, maintain respectful silence." Both halves of this disjunctive (*both* of which must amount to the fact or appearance of participation in prayer if the Court's analysis is to survive on its own terms) merit particular attention.

To begin with the latter: The Court's notion that a student who simply sits in "respectful silence" during the invocation and benediction (when all others are standing) has somehow joined or would somehow be perceived as having joined in the prayers is nothing short of ludicrous. We indeed live in a vulgar age. But surely "our social conventions" have not coarsened to the point that anyone who does not stand on his chair and shout obscenities can reasonably be deemed to have assented to everything said in his presence. Since the Court does not dispute that students exposed to prayer at graduation ceremonies retain (despite "subtle coercive pressures") the free will to sit, there is absolutely no basis for the Court's decision. It is fanciful enough to say that "a reasonable dissenter," standing head erect in a class of bowed heads, "could believe that the group exercise signified her own participation or approval of it." It is beyond the absurd to say that she could entertain such a belief while pointedly declining to rise.

But let us assume the very worst, that the nonparticipating graduate is "subtly coerced" ... to stand! Even that half of the disjunctive does not remotely establish a "participation" (or an "appearance of participation") in a religious exercise. The Court acknowledges that "in our culture standing ... can signify adherence to a view or simple respect for the views of others." (Much more often the latter than the former, I think, except perhaps in the proverbial town meeting, where one votes by standing.) But if it is a permissible inference that one who is standing is doing so simply out of respect for the prayers of others that are in progress, then how can it possibly be said that a "reasonable dissenter ... could believe that the group exercise signified her own participation or approval"? Quite obviously, it cannot. I may add, moreover, that maintaining respect for the religious observances of others is a fundamental civic virtue that government (including the public schools) can and should cultivate so that even if it were the case that the displaying of such respect might be mistaken for taking part in the prayer, I would deny that the dissenter's interest in avoiding *even the false appearance of participation* constitutionally trumps the government's interest in fostering respect for religion generally.

The opinion manifests that the Court itself has not given careful consideration to its test of psychological coercion. For if it had, how could it observe, with no hint of concern or disapproval, that students stood for the Pledge of Allegiance, which immediately preceded Rabbi Gutterman's invocation? ...

I also find it odd that the Court concludes that high school graduates may not be subjected to this supposed psychological coercion, yet refrains from addressing whether "mature adults" may. I had thought that the reason graduation from high school is regarded as so significant an event is that it is generally associated with transition from adolescence to young adulthood. Many graduating seniors, of course, are old enough to vote. Why, then, does the Court treat them as though they were first-graders? Will we soon have a jurisprudence that distinguishes between mature and immature adults?

The other "dominant fac[t]" identified by the Court is that "[s]tate officials direct the performance of a formal religious exercise" at school graduation ceremonies. "Direct[ing] the performance of a formal religious exercise" has a sound of liturgy to it, summoning up images of the principal directing acolytes where to carry the cross, or showing the rabbi where to unroll the Torah. . . . All the record shows is that principals of the Providence public schools, acting within their delegated authority, have invited clergy to deliver invocations and benedictions at graduations; and that Principal Lee invited Rabbi Gutterman, provided him a two-page pamphlet, prepared by the National Conference of Christians and Jews, giving general advice on inclusive prayer for civic occasions, and advised him that his prayers at graduation should be nonsectarian. How these facts can fairly be transformed into the charges that Principal Lee "directed and controlled the content of [Rabbi Gutterman's] prayer," . . . is difficult to fathom. The Court identifies nothing in the record remotely suggesting that school officials have ever drafted, edited, screened, or censored graduation prayers, or that Rabbi Gutterman was a mouthpiece of the school officials.

These distortions of the record are, of course, not harmless error: without them the Court's solemn assertion that the school officials could reasonably be perceived to be "enforcing a religious orthodoxy," would ring as hollow as it ought.

## III

The deeper flaw in the Court's opinion does not lie in its wrong answer to the question whether there was state-induced "peer-pressure" coercion; it lies, rather, in the Court's making violation of the Establishment Clause hinge on such a precious question. The coercion that was a hallmark of historical establishments of religion was coercion of religious orthodoxy and of financial support *by force of law and threat of penalty.* . . .

Thus, while I have no quarrel with the Court's general proposition that the Establishment Clause "guarantees that government may not coerce anyone to support or participate in religion or its exercise," I see no warrant for expanding the concept of coercion beyond acts backed by threat of penalty. . . .

. . . [T]here is nothing in the record to indicate that failure of attending students to take part in the invocation or benediction was subject to any penalty or discipline. . . .

The Court relies on our "school prayer" cases . . . [b]ut whatever the merit of those cases, they do not support, much less compel, the Court's psycho-journey. . . . [W]e have made clear our understanding that school prayer occurs within a framework in which legal coercion to attend school (i.e., coercion under threat of penalty) provides the ultimate backdrop. . . . Voluntary prayer at graduation—a one-time ceremony at which parents, friends, and relatives are present—can hardly be thought to raise the same concerns.

## IV

. . . The narrow context of the present case involves a community's celebration of one of the milestones in its young citizens' lives, and it is a bold step for this Court to seek to banish from that occasion, and from thousands of similar celebrations throughout this land, the expression of gratitude to God that a majority of the community wishes to make. The issue before us today is not the abstract philosophical question whether the alternative of frustrating this desire of a religious majority is to be preferred over the alternative of imposing "psychological coercion," or a feeling of exclusion, upon nonbelievers. Rather, the question is *whether a mandatory choice in favor of the former has been imposed by the United States Constitution.* As the age-old practices of our people show, the answer to that question is not at all in doubt.

I must add one final observation: The Founders of our Republic knew the fearsome potential of sectarian religious belief to generate civil dissension and civil strife. And they also knew that nothing, absolutely nothing, is so inclined to foster among religious believers of various faiths a toleration—no, an affection—for one another than voluntarily joining in prayer together, to the God whom they all worship and seek. Needless to say, no one should be compelled to do that, but it is a shame to deprive our public culture of the opportunity, and indeed the encouragement, for people to do it voluntarily. The Baptist or Catholic who heard and joined in the simple and inspiring prayers of Rabbi Gutterman on this official and patriotic occasion was inoculated from religious bigotry and prejudice in a manner that cannot be replicated. To deprive our society of that important unifying mechanism, in order to spare the nonbeliever what seems to me the minimal inconvenience of standing or even sitting in respectful nonparticipation, is as senseless in policy as it is unsupported in law.

For the foregoing reasons, I dissent.

---

Even after *Lee v. Weisman,* many schools remained defiant about maintaining religious practices. School-organized prayers continued to be a common feature of athletic games throughout the 1990s. Nowhere was this practice more ingrained than in varsity high school football games in the South.

In 2000 the Supreme Court took a case involving a challenge to organized football game prayers in the Santa Fe Independent School District in Texas. For many years, this overwhelmingly Southern Baptist community had students elect a "student council chaplain" who prayed over the loud speaker before football games. After litigation forced the school to drop the student chaplain position, the school adopted a two-part policy. It first allowed students to have a pregame speaker to "solemnize" football games if they wanted. Second, if they decided to have such a solemnizing speaker, the policy allowed them to elect the student who would give the statement or prayer.

A Mormon family and a Catholic family brought suit against this policy, alleging that it was yet another assault on the establishment clause in a district where the rights of religious minorities were routinely violated. They claimed that the football field was part of the school and the school system should not be involved with religious prayer at all. Electing the student to give a prayerful invocation made matters worse by turning the different religious groups in the school into political parties. The school district answered that students did not have to choose to have a solemnizing statement, and the statement did not have to be a religious one. It said the case was premature and the plaintiffs were making a mountain out of a molehill. The Supreme Court majority disagreed. Do you?

# SANTA FE INDEPENDENT SCHOOL DISTRICT

### v.

## DOE

*Supreme Court of the United States*
Argued March 29, 2000.
Decided June 19, 2000.

Justice STEVENS delivered the opinion of the Court.

Prior to 1995, the Santa Fe High School student who occupied the school's elective office of student council chaplain delivered a prayer over the public address system before each varsity football game for the entire season. This practice, along with others, was challenged in District Court as a violation of the Establishment Clause of the First Amendment.... [T]he school district [then] adopted a different policy that permits, but does not require, prayer initiated and led by a student at all home games....

I

Respondents are two sets of current or former students and their respective mothers. One family is Mormon and the other is Catholic. The District Court permitted respondents (Does) to litigate anonymously to protect them from intimidation or harassment....

Respondents ... alleged that the District had engaged in several proselytizing practices, such as promoting attendance at a Baptist revival meeting, encouraging membership in religious clubs, chastising children who held minority religious beliefs, and distributing Gideon Bibles on school premises. They also alleged that the District allowed students to read Christian invocations and benedictions from the stage at graduation ceremonies, and to deliver overtly Christian prayers over the public address system at home football games.

On May 10, 1995, the District Court entered an interim order.... [T]he order provided that "nondenominational prayer" consisting of "an invocation and/or benediction" could be presented by a senior student or students selected by members of the graduating class. The text of the prayer was to be determined by the students, without scrutiny or preapproval by school officials. References to particular religious figures "such as Mohammed, Jesus, Buddha, or the like" would be permitted "as long as the general thrust of the prayer is non-proselytizing."...

In response ... the District adopted a series of policies over several months dealing with prayer at school functions....

The August policy, which was titled "Prayer at Football Games,"... authorized two student elections, the first to determine whether "invocations" should be delivered, and the second to select the spokesperson to deliver them.... it contained two parts, an initial statement that omitted any requirement that the content of the invocation be "nonsectarian and nonproselytising," and a fallback provision that automatically added that limitation if the preferred policy should be enjoined. On August 31, 1995 ... [t]he district's high school students voted to determine whether a student would deliver prayer at varsity football games.... The students chose to allow a student to say a prayer at football games.". . . A week later, in a separate election, they selected a student "to deliver the prayer at varsity football games.". . .

The . . . [October policy] is essentially the same as the August policy, though it omits the word "prayer" from its title, and refers to "messages" and "statements" as well as "invocations.". . .

. . . We conclude, as did the Court of Appeals, that . . . the District's policy permitting student-led, student-initiated prayer at football games violates the Establishment Clause.

## II

. . . The fact that the District's policy provides for the election of the speaker only after the majority has voted on her message identifies an obvious distinction between this case and the typical election of a "student body president, or even a newly elected prom king or queen.". . .

. . . While Santa Fe's majoritarian election might ensure that *most* of the students are represented, it does nothing to protect the minority; indeed, it likely serves to intensify their offense.

Moreover, the District has failed to divorce itself from the religious content in the invocations. It has not succeeded in doing so, either by claiming that its policy is "one of neutrality rather than endorsement". . . or by characterizing the individual student as the "circuit-breaker". . . in the process. Contrary to the District's repeated assertions that it has adopted a "hands-off" approach to the pregame invocation . . . its policy involves both perceived and actual endorsement of religion. . . . [T]he "degree of school involvement" makes it clear that the pregame prayers bear "the imprint of the State and thus put school-age children who objected in an untenable position.". . .

The District has attempted to disentangle itself from the religious messages by developing the two-step student election process. The text of the October policy, however, exposes the extent of the school's entanglement. The elections take place at all only because the school "board *has chosen to permit* students to deliver a brief invocation and/or message.". . . The elections thus "shall" be conducted "by the high school student council" and "[u]pon advice and direction of the high school principal.". . . The decision whether to deliver a message is first made by majority vote of the entire student body, followed by a choice of the speaker in a separate, similar majority election. Even

In *Santa Fe v. Doe*, the Court struck down school-organized and student-led prayer exercises at public high school football games. Private schools are not affected by the decision. Here, private school football players pray before a game in Rolling Fork, Mississippi, in August 2000.

though the particular words used by the speaker are not determined by those votes, the policy mandates that the "statement or invocation" be "consistent with the goals and purposes of this policy," which are "to solemnize the event, to promote good sportsmanship and student safety, and to establish the appropriate environment for the competition.". . .

In addition to involving the school in the selection of the speaker, the policy, by its terms, invites and encourages religious messages. The policy itself states that the purpose of the message is "to solemnize the event." A religious message is the most obvious method of solemnizing an event. Moreover, the requirements that the message "promote good sportsmanship" and "establish the appropriate environment for competition" further narrow the types of message deemed appropriate, suggesting that a solemn, yet nonreligious, message, such as commentary on United States foreign policy, would be prohibited. . . . Indeed, the only type of message that is expressly endorsed in the text is an "invocation"—a term that primarily describes an appeal for divine assistance. . . . In fact, as used in the past at Santa Fe High School, an "invocation" has always entailed a focused religious message. Thus, the expressed purposes of the policy encourage the selection of a religious message, and that is precisely how the students understand the policy. The results of the elections . . . make it clear that the students understood that the central question before them was whether prayer should be a part of the pregame ceremony. . . .

The actual or perceived endorsement of the message, moreover, is established by factors beyond just the text of the policy. Once the student speaker is selected and the message composed, the invocation is then delivered to a large audience assembled as part of a regularly scheduled, school-sponsored function conducted on school property. The message is broadcast over the school's public address system, which remains subject to the control of school officials. It is fair to assume that the pregame ceremony is clothed in the traditional indicia of school sporting events, which generally include not just the team, but also cheerleaders and band members dressed in uniforms sporting the school name and mascot. The school's name is likely written in large print across the field and on banners and flags. The crowd will certainly include many who display the school colors and insignia on their school T-shirts, jackets, or hats and who may also be waving signs displaying the school name. It is in a setting such as this that "[t]he board has chosen to permit" the elected student to rise and give the "statement or invocation."

In this context the members of the listening audience must perceive the pregame message as a public expression of the views of the majority of the student body delivered with the approval of the school administration. In cases involving state participation in a religious activity, one of the relevant questions is "whether an objective observer, acquainted with the text, legislative history, and implementation of the statute, would perceive it as a state endorsement of prayer in public schools.". . . Regardless of the listener's support for, or objection to, the message, an objective Santa Fe High School student will unquestionably perceive the inevitable pregame prayer as stamped with her school's seal of approval. . . .

According to the District, the secular purposes of the policy are to "foste[r] free expression of private persons . . . as well [as to] solemniz[e] sporting events, promot[e] good sportsmanship and student safety, and establis[h] an appropriate environment for competition.". . . [H]owever . . . the District's approval of only one specific kind of message, an "invocation," is not necessary to further any of these purposes. Additionally, the fact that only one student is permitted to give a content-limited message suggests that this policy does little to "foste[r] free expression." Furthermore, regardless of whether one considers a sporting event an appropriate occasion for solemnity, the use of an invocation to foster such solemnity is impermissible when, in actuality, it constitutes prayer sponsored by the school. . . .

School sponsorship of a religious message is impermissible because it sends the ancillary message to members of the audience who are nonadherents "that they are outsiders, not full members of the political community, and an accompanying message to adherents that they are insiders, favored members of the political community.".... The delivery of such a message—over the school's public address system, by a speaker representing the student body, under the supervision of school faculty, and pursuant to a school policy that explicitly and implicitly encourages public prayer—is not properly characterized as "private" speech.

III

The District next argues that its football policy ... does not coerce students to participate in religious observances. Its argument has two parts: first, that there is no impermissible government coercion because the pregame messages are the product of student choices; and second, that there is really no coercion at all because attendance at an extracurricular event, unlike a graduation ceremony, is voluntary.

... [T]he issue resolved in the first election was "whether a student would deliver prayer at varsity football games"... and the controversy in this case demonstrates that the views of the students are not unanimous on that issue.

One of the purposes served by the Establishment Clause is to remove debate over this kind of issue from governmental supervision or control.... [T]he "preservation and transmission of religious beliefs and worship is a responsibility and a choice committed to the private sphere.".... The two student elections authorized by the policy, coupled with the debates that presumably must precede each, impermissibly invade that private sphere. The election mechanism ... reflects a device the District put in place that determines whether religious messages will be delivered at home football games. The mechanism encourages divisiveness along religious lines in a public school setting, a result at odds with the Establishment Clause. Although it is true that the ultimate choice of student speaker is "attributable to the students"... the District's decision to hold the constitutionally problematic election is clearly "a choice attributable to the State"...

... Attendance at a high school football game, unlike showing up for class, is certainly not required in order to receive a diploma. Moreover, we may assume that the District is correct in arguing that the informal pressure to attend an athletic event is not as strong as a senior's desire to attend her own graduation ceremony.

There are some students, however, such as cheerleaders, members of the band, and, of course, the team members themselves, for whom seasonal commitments mandate their attendance, sometimes for class credit. The District also minimizes the importance to many students of attending and participating in extracurricular activities as part of a complete educational experience.... To assert that high school students do not feel immense social pressure, or have a truly genuine desire, to be involved in the extracurricular event that is American high school football is "formalistic in the extreme."...

... the delivery of a pregame prayer has the improper effect of coercing those present to participate in an act of religious worship.... "[W]hat to most believers may seem nothing more than a reasonable request that the nonbeliever respect their religious practices, in a school context may appear to the nonbeliever or dissenter to be an attempt to employ the machinery of the State to enforce a religious orthodoxy."... The constitutional command will not permit the District "to exact religious conformity from a student as the price" of joining her classmates at a varsity football game....

The judgment of the Court of Appeals is, accordingly, affirmed.

Chief Justice REHNQUIST, with whom Justice SCALIA and Justice THOMAS join, dissenting.

The Court distorts existing precedent to conclude that the school district's student-message program is invalid on its face under the Establishment Clause. But even more disturbing than its holding is the tone of the Court's opinion; it bristles with hostility to all things religious in public life. Neither the holding nor the tone of the opinion is faithful to the meaning of the Establishment Clause....

... [T]he Court ... holds that the "policy is invalid on its face because it establishes an improper majoritarian election on religion, and unquestionably has the purpose and creates the perception of encouraging the delivery of prayer at a series of important school events."... The Court's reliance on each of these conclusions misses the mark.

First, the Court misconstrues the nature of the "majoritarian election" permitted by the policy as being an election on "prayer" and "religion."... To the contrary, the election permitted by the policy is a two-fold process whereby students vote first on whether to have a student speaker before football games at all, and second, if the students vote to have such a speaker, on who that speaker will be.... It is conceivable that the election could become one in which student candidates campaign on platforms that focus on whether or not they will pray if elected. It is also conceivable that the election could lead to a Christian prayer before 90 percent of the football games. If, upon implementation, the policy operated in this fashion, we would have a record before us to review whether the policy, as applied, violated the Establishment Clause or unduly suppressed minority viewpoints. But it is possible that the students might vote not to have a pregame speaker, in which case there would be no threat of a constitutional violation. It is also possible that the election would not focus on prayer, but on public speaking ability or social popularity. And if student campaigning did begin to focus on prayer, the school might decide to implement reasonable campaign restrictions....

But the Court ignores these possibilities by holding that merely granting the student body the power to elect a speaker that may choose to pray, "regardless of the students' ultimate use of it, is not acceptable."... The Court so holds despite that any speech that may occur as a result of the election process here would be *private*, not *government*, speech. The elected student, not the government, would choose what to say. Support for the Court's holding cannot be found in any of our cases. And it essentially invalidates all student elections. A newly elected student body president, or even a newly elected prom king or queen, could use opportunities for public speaking to say prayers. Under the Court's view, the mere grant of power to the students to vote for such offices, in light of the fear that those elected might publicly pray, violates the Establishment Clause.

Second, with respect to the policy's purpose, the Court holds that "the simple enactment of this policy, with the purpose and perception of school endorsement of student prayer, was a constitutional violation."... But the policy itself has plausible secular purposes: "[T]o solemnize the event, to promote good sportsmanship and student safety, and to establish the appropriate environment for the competition."... Where a governmental body "expresses a plausible secular purpose" for an enactment, "courts should generally defer to that stated intent."... The Court grants no deference to—and appears openly hostile toward—the policy's stated purposes, and wastes no time in concluding that they are a sham....

... [T]he school district was acting diligently to come within the governing constitutional law. The District Court ordered the school district to formulate a policy ... which permitted a school district to have a prayer-only policy.... But the school district went further than required by the District Court order and eventually settled on a policy that gave the student speaker a choice to deliver either an invocation or a message. In so doing, the school district exhibited a willingness to comply with, and exceed, Establishment Clause restrictions. Thus, the policy cannot be viewed as having a sectarian purpose....

... Here ... the potential speech at issue, if the policy had been allowed to proceed, would be a message or invocation selected or created by a student. That is, if there were speech at issue here, it would be *private* speech. The "crucial difference between *government* speech endorsing religion, which the Establishment Clause forbids, and *private* speech endorsing religion, which the Free Speech and Free Exercise Clauses protect," applies with particular force to the question of endorsement....

Finally, the Court seems to demand that a government policy be completely neutral as to content or be considered one that endorses religion.... This is undoubtedly a new requirement, as our Establishment Clause jurisprudence simply does not mandate "content neutrality." That concept is found in our First Amendment *speech* cases....

---

EXERCISE 4.3. Suzie Smith was named valedictorian of your high school graduating class by virtue of her grade point average. She is a devout Muslim who has written her valedictorian address about the importance in her life of Mohammed and why she thinks students who abuse drugs and alcohol or belong to gangs need to discover Mohammed in their personal lives. She wants to finish by inviting her fellow graduates to come with her to her mosque before they leave for college or work. The principal is nervous about letting her give such a speech, but students in the past have always been allowed to speak about the topic of their choice, and their remarks are traditionally edited for length, clarity, and style only. The principal does not want to be sued by non-Muslim parents, but she also does not want to be sued by Suzie and her family.

Knowing that you are taking this class, the principal asks your advice on how to handle the situation without violating the establishment clause or Suzie's free speech and free exercise of religion rights. How will you advise the principal to act in this majority Christian community? (What if Suzie were a Methodist? A Jehovah's Witness? A Hare Krishna? A follower of Rev. Sun Myung Moon? Would that change your views?) Discuss the problem with your classmates and come up with what you think is sound legal and policy advice for the principal.

---

**FOR THE CLASS**

INTERVIEWING THE JUSTICES. Select two students to play the anchors of an evening television news talk show like *Nightline.* The anchors have an unusual assignment: they will be interviewing the nine Supreme Court justices about their opinions in *Santa Fe v. Doe.* Select one set of students to play Justice Stevens (who wrote the Court's majority opinion) and the five justices who agreed with him. Select a second set of students to play Chief Justice Rehnquist (who wrote the dissenting opinion) and the two justices who dissented alongside him. Try to get to the bottom of the views of each justice. Why did those who sided with the majority think that the football invocation violated the establishment clause? How did they think that such statements affected students, team players, cheerleaders, and fans? And why did the dissenters object to the majority's decision? The news anchors should invite additional student guests to play teachers and students to discuss their own thoughts about the case. (This exercise is for fun and learning; in reality, Supreme Court justices almost never discuss their opinions in public, and certainly never in a format like this.)

---

# Government Aid to Private Religious Schools: When Does It Cross the Establishment Line?

Government cannot give tax dollars directly to religious schools for the purpose of teaching religion. The First Amendment prevents the government from establishing religions or taxing the public to support them. Yet many public services and dollars are rendered to private religious institutions in a way that poses no constitutional problem. For example, if a church is on fire, the fire department can put the fire out without violating the First Amendment. Police officers can help churches, mosques, and synagogues if they have been vandalized or burglarized. Cities can provide sewerage and garbage collection. None of these forms of public aid is invalid; they are part of neutral and universal government services that do not bolster a specifically religious mission of the churches.

In the following case the Supreme Court considered the constitutionality of a New Jersey township's policy of reimbursing parents for the cost of sending their children to private school, including private religious school, on public buses. The plaintiffs attacking the policy argued that it was designed to make parochial school cheaper and to indirectly subsidize religious schools. The township argued that it was part of a universal policy to pay for all kids, whether in public or private school, to get to school safely and on time. What do you think? What does the Court decide?

---

## EVERSON
### v.
## BOARD OF EDUCATION OF THE TOWNSHIP OF EWING

*Supreme Court of the United States*
Argued Nov. 20, 1946.
Decided Feb. 10, 1947.

Justice BLACK delivered the opinion of the Court.

A New Jersey statute authorizes its local school districts to make rules and contracts for the transportation of children to and from schools. The appellee, a township board of education, acting pursuant to this statute, authorized reimbursement to parents of money expended by them for the bus transportation of their children on regular buses operated by the public transportation system. Part of this money was for the payment of transportation of some children in the community to

Catholic parochial schools. These church schools give their students, in addition to secular education, regular religious instruction conforming to the religious tenets and modes of worship of the Catholic Faith....

... The New Jersey statute is challenged as a "law respecting an establishment of religion." The First Amendment, as made applicable to the states by the Fourteenth, commands that a state "shall make no law respecting an establishment of religion, or prohibiting the free exercise thereof...." These words of the First Amendment reflected in the minds of early Americans a vivid mental picture of conditions and practices which they fervently wished to stamp out in order to preserve liberty for themselves and for their posterity. Doubtless their goal has not been entirely reached; but so far has the Nation moved toward it that the expression "law respecting an establishment of religion," probably does not so vividly remind present-day Americans of the evils, fears, and political problems that caused that expression to be written into our Bill of Rights....

The "establishment of religion" clause of the First Amendment means at least this: Neither a state nor the Federal Government can set up a church. Neither can pass laws which aid one religion, aid all religions, or prefer one religion over another. Neither can force nor influence a person to go to or to remain away from church against his will or force him to profess a belief or disbelief in any religion. No person can be punished for entertaining or professing religious beliefs or disbeliefs, for church attendance or non-attendance. No tax in any amount, large or small, can be levied to support any religious activities or institutions, whatever they may be called, or whatever form they may adopt to teach or practice religion....

We must consider the New Jersey statute in accordance with the foregoing limitations imposed by the First Amendment.... New Jersey cannot consistently with the "establishment of religion" clause of the First Amendment contribute tax-raised funds to the support of an institution which teaches the tenets and faith of any church. On the other hand, other language of the amendment commands that New Jersey cannot hamper its citizens in the free exercise of their own religion.... While we do not mean to intimate that a state could not provide transportation only to children attending public schools, we must be careful, in protecting the citizens of New Jersey against state-established churches, to be sure that we do not inadvertently prohibit New Jersey from extending its general state law benefits to all its citizens without regard to their religious belief. Measured by these standards, we cannot say that the First Amendment prohibits New Jersey from spending tax-raised funds to pay the bus fares of parochial school pupils as a part of a general program under which it pays the fares of pupils attending public and other schools.... That Amendment requires the state to be a neutral in its relations with groups of religious believers and non-believers; it does not require the state to be their adversary. State power is no more to be used so as to handicap religions than it is to favor them....

The First Amendment has erected a wall between church and state. That wall must be kept high and impregnable. We could not approve the slightest breach. New Jersey has not breached it here.

*Affirmed.*

Justice RUTLEDGE, with whom Justice FRANKFURTER, Justice JACKSON and Justice BURTON agree, dissenting....

I

Not simply an established church, but any law respecting an establishment of religion is forbidden. The Amendment was broadly but not loosely phrased. It is the compact and exact summation of its author's views formed during his long struggle for religious freedom....

... The funds used here were raised by taxation. The Court does not dispute, nor could it, that their use does in fact give aid and encouragement to religious instruction. It only concludes that this aid is not "support" in law.... Here parents pay money to send their children to parochial schools and funds raised by taxation are used to reimburse them. This not only helps the children to get to school and the parents to send them. It aids them in a substantial way to get the very thing which they are sent to the particular school to secure, namely, religious training and teaching....

New Jersey's action therefore exactly fits the type of exaction and the kind of evil at which Madison and Jefferson struck. Under the test they framed it cannot be said that the cost of transportation is no part of the cost of education or of the religious instruction given....

... Payment of transportation is no more, nor is it any the less essential to education, whether religious or secular, than payment for tuitions, for teachers' salaries, for buildings, equipment and necessary materials. Nor is it any the less directly related, in a school giving religious instruction, to the primary religious objective all those essential items of cost are intended to achieve. No rational line can be drawn between payment for such larger, but not more necessary, items and payment for transportation....

---

EXERCISE 4.4. *Everson* may have been an easy case because the city buses simply got the children to the schoolhouse door; government action did not follow students inside the religious schools. What would you think about a local policy of reimbursing all parents of children in public or private school for the cost of any schoolbooks they buy, including both secular and religious books? What would you think about a city policy, designed to make teaching a more attractive option for talented college graduates, that gave teachers a 10 percent bonus for working in the city at public or private schools, including religious schools?

---

# School Vouchers: Revolution in the Making?

In the 1990s several school districts developed school voucher policies that gave parents tuition vouchers redeemable at public, private, or religious schools. Critics attacked these programs as a violation of the establishment clause. Defenders said they passed constitutional muster on the grounds that the parents, not the government, decided whether to allocate the voucher money to religious schools in these programs.

The table was set for victory for voucher proponents in a series of cases upholding the constitutionality of universal and formally neutral programs whose benefits went heavily to religious institutions. In *Mueller v. Allen* (1983), the Supreme Court rejected an establishment clause attack on a Minnesota program authorizing tax deductions for various educational expenses, including private school tuition costs, even though 96 percent of the program's beneficiaries were parents of children in religious schools. The Court found it compelling that the class of beneficiaries was "all parents," including parents with "children [who] attend nonsectarian private schools or sectarian private schools."

The program thus respected the principle of private choice, since public funds were made available to religious schools "only as a result of numerous, private choices of individual parents of school-age children."

The Court employed the same logic in *Witters v. Washington Department of Services for the Blind* (1986) to reject an establishment clause challenge to a vocational scholarship program that provided tuition aid to a student studying at a religious institution to become a pastor. The Court observed that the state's scholarship program was open to all private and public schools and that "[a]ny aid . . . that ultimately flows to religious institutions does so only as a result of the genuinely independent and private choices of aid recipients."

Finally, in *Zobrest v. Catalina Foothills School District,* the Court refused an establishment clause challenge to a federal program that permitted sign-language interpreters to assist deaf children enrolled in religious schools. The Court stated that "government programs that neutrally provide benefits to a broad class of citizens defined without reference to religion are not readily subject to an establishment clause challenge." The program, the Court found, distributes sign-language or other interpretive benefits "neutrally to any child qualifying as 'disabled.'" . . . Its primary beneficiaries were "disabled children, not sectarian schools."

Thus, by the time the Court took up the school voucher question in 2002, it was easy for a majority on the Court to settle the constitutional controversy (though certainly not the political one). In *Zelman v. Simmons-Harris* (2002), the Court upheld the state of Ohio's educational voucher program for poor students in the Cleveland City School District, which had been failing and was finally placed under direct state control. When the state made the tuition vouchers available to less affluent families, fully 96 percent of those who transferred out of public schools enrolled their children in parochial religious schools. Yet the Court found that there was no constitutional problem with this transfer of public resources to private religious schools because the Ohio plan relied on the "private choice" of eligible families who could choose among public schools (with bolstered tutoring services), secular private schools, and religious private schools. The fact that most school vouchers were redeemed at religious schools was deemed incidental and not fatal to the program.

What do you think? Do you agree with the majority rationale, or do you agree with the dissenters who thought school vouchers are a clever way to channel public money directly into the coffers of religious institutions?

# ZELMAN
## v.
## SIMMONS-HARRIS

*Supreme Court of the United States*
Argued Feb 20, 2002.
Decided June 27, 2002.

Chief Justice REHNQUIST delivered the opinion of the Court.

The State of Ohio has established a pilot program designed to provide educational choices to families with children who reside in the Cleveland City School District. The question presented is whether this program offends the Establishment Clause of the United States Constitution. We hold that it does not.

There are more than 75,000 children enrolled in the Cleveland City School District. The majority of these children are from low-income and minority families. Few of these families enjoy the means to send their children to any school other than an inner-city public school. For more than a generation, however, Cleveland's public schools have been among the worst performing public schools in the Nation. . . .

. . . Ohio enacted . . . its Pilot Project Scholarship Program. . . .

The program provides two basic kinds of assistance to parents of children in a covered district. First, the program provides tuition aid for students in kindergarten through third grade, expanding each year through eighth grade, to attend a participating public or private school of their parent's choosing. . . Second, the program provides tutorial aid for students who choose to remain enrolled in public school. . . .

. . . Any private school, whether religious or nonreligious, may participate in the program and accept program students so long as the school is located within the boundaries of a covered district and meets statewide educational standards. . . . Participating private schools must agree not to discriminate on the basis of race, religion, or ethnic background, or to "advocate or foster unlawful behavior or teach hatred of any person or group on the basis of race, ethnicity, national origin, or religion.". . . Any public school located in a school district adjacent to the covered district may also participate in the program. . . .

The tutorial aid portion of the program provides tutorial assistance through grants to any student in a covered district who chooses to remain in public school. Parents arrange for registered tutors to provide assistance to their children and then submit bills for those services to the State for payment. . . . Students from low-income families receive 90% of the amount charged for such assistance up to $360. All other students receive 75% of that amount. . . .

The program has been in operation within the Cleveland City School District since the 1996–1997 school year. In the 1999–2000 school year, 56 private schools participated in the program, 46 (or 82%) of which had a religious affiliation. None of the public schools in districts adjacent to Cleveland have elected to participate. More than 3,700 students participated in the scholarship program, most of whom (96%) enrolled in religiously affiliated schools. Sixty percent of these students were from families at or below the poverty line. In the 1998–1999 school year, approximately 1,400 Cleveland public school students received tutorial aid. This number was expected to double during the 1999–2000 school year. . . .

In July 1999, respondents filed this action in United States District Court, seeking to enjoin the ... program on the ground that it violated the Establishment Clause.... In August 1999 the District Court issued a preliminary injunction barring further implementation of the program.... In December 1999, the District Court granted summary judgment for respondents.... In December 2000, a divided panel of the Court of Appeals affirmed the judgment of the District Court, finding that the program had the "primary effect" of advancing religion in violation of the Establishment Clause.... We granted certiorari ... and now reverse the Court of Appeals....

... While our jurisprudence with respect to the constitutionality of direct aid programs has "changed significantly" over the past two decades ... our jurisprudence with respect to true private choice programs has remained consistent and unbroken. Three times we have confronted Establishment Clause challenges to neutral government programs that provide aid directly to a broad class of individuals, who, in turn, direct the aid to religious schools or institutions of their own choosing. Three times we have rejected such challenges....

We believe that the program challenged here is a program of true private choice, consistent with *Mueller, Witters,* and *Zobrest,* and thus constitutional. As was true in those cases, the Ohio program is neutral in all respects toward religion. It is part of a general and multifaceted undertaking by the State of Ohio to provide educational opportunities to the children of a failed school district. It confers educational assistance directly to a broad class of individuals defined without reference to religion, *i.e.,* any parent of a school-age child who resides in the Cleveland City School District. The program permits the participation of *all* schools within the district, religious or nonreligious. Adjacent public schools also may participate and have a financial incentive to do so. Program benefits are available to participating families on neutral terms, with no reference to religion. The only preference stated anywhere in the program is a preference for low-income families, who receive greater assistance and are given priority for admission at participating schools.

There are no "financial incentive[s]" that "ske[w]" the program toward religious schools.... The program here in fact creates financial *dis*incentives for religious schools, with private schools receiving only half the government assistance given to community schools and one-third the assistance given to magnet schools. Adjacent public schools, should any choose to accept program students, are also eligible to receive two to three times the state funding of a private religious school.

As the Supreme Court heard oral arguments on February 20, 2002, about the constitutionality of school voucher plans, both supporters and opponents rallied outside.

Families too have a financial disincentive to choose a private religious school over other schools. Parents that choose to participate in the scholarship program and then to enroll their children in a private school (religious or nonreligious) must copay a portion of the school's tuition. Families that choose a community school, magnet school, or traditional public school pay nothing. Although such features of the program are not necessary to its constitutionality, they clearly dispel the claim that the program "creates ... financial incentive[s] for parents to choose a sectarian school.". . .

Respondents suggest that even without a financial incentive for parents to choose a religious school, the program creates a "public perception that the State is endorsing religious practices and beliefs.". . . But we have repeatedly recognized that no reasonable observer would think a neutral program of private choice, where state aid reaches religious schools solely as a result of the numerous independent decisions of private individuals, carries with it the *imprimatur* of government endorsement. . . .

. . . It is true that 82% of Cleveland's participating private schools are religious schools, but it is also true that 81% of private schools in Ohio are religious schools. . . To attribute constitutional significance to this figure . . . would lead to the absurd result that a neutral school-choice program might be permissible in some parts of Ohio, such as Columbus, where a lower percentage of private schools are religious schools . . . but not in inner-city Cleveland, where Ohio has deemed such programs most sorely needed, but where the preponderance of religious schools happens to be greater. . . .

. . . The constitutionality of a neutral educational aid program simply does not turn on whether and why, in a particular area, at a particular time, most private schools are run by religious organizations, or most recipients choose to use the aid at a religious school. As we said in *Mueller*, "[s]uch an approach would scarcely provide the certainty that this field stands in need of, nor can we perceive principled standards by which such statistical evidence might be evaluated.". . .

. . . In sum, the Ohio program is entirely neutral with respect to religion. It provides benefits directly to a wide spectrum of individuals, defined only by financial need and residence in a particular school district. It permits such individuals to exercise genuine choice among options public and private, secular and religious. The program is therefore a program of true private choice. In keeping with an unbroken line of decisions rejecting challenges to similar programs, we hold that the program does not offend the Establishment Clause.

The judgment of the Court of Appeals is reversed.

Justice SOUTER, with whom Justice STEVENS, Justice GINSBURG, and Justice BREYER join, dissenting.

The Court's majority holds that the Establishment Clause is no bar to Ohio's payment of tuition at private religious elementary and middle schools under a scheme that systematically provides tax money to support the schools' religious missions. The occasion for the legislation thus upheld is the condition of public education in the city of Cleveland. The record indicates that the schools are failing to serve their objective, and the vouchers in issue here are said to be needed to provide adequate alternatives to them. If there were an excuse for giving short shrift to the Establishment Clause, it would probably apply here. But there is no excuse. Constitutional limitations are placed on government to preserve constitutional values in hard cases, like these. . . .

Today, however, the majority holds that the Establishment Clause is not offended by Ohio's Pilot Project Scholarship Program, under which students may be eligible to receive as much as $2,250 in the form of tuition vouchers transferable to religious schools. In the city of Cleveland the overwhelming proportion of large appropriations for voucher money must be spent on religious schools if it is to be spent at all, and will be spent in amounts that cover almost all of tuition. The money will thus pay for eligible students' instruction not only in secular subjects but in religion as well, in schools that can fairly be characterized as founded to teach religious doctrine and to imbue teaching in all subjects with a religious dimension....

## II

### A

Consider first the criterion of neutrality. As recently as two Terms ago, a majority of the Court recognized that neutrality conceived of as evenhandedness toward aid recipients had never been treated as alone sufficient to satisfy the Establishment Clause.... But at least in its limited significance, formal neutrality seemed to serve some purpose. Today, however, the majority employs the neutrality criterion in a way that renders it impossible to understand.

Neutrality in this sense refers, of course, to evenhandedness in setting eligibility as between potential religious and secular recipients of public money... Thus, for example, the aid scheme in *Witters* provided an eligible recipient with a scholarship to be used at any institution within a practically unlimited universe of schools ... it did not tend to provide more or less aid depending on which one the scholarship recipient chose, and there was no indication that the maximum scholarship amount would be insufficient at secular schools. Neither did any condition of Zobrest's interpreter's subsidy favor religious education....

In order to apply the neutrality test, then, it makes sense to focus on a category of aid that may be directed to religious as well as secular schools, and ask whether the scheme favors a religious direction. Here, one would ask whether the voucher provisions, allowing for as much as $2,250 toward private school tuition (or a grant to a public school in an adjacent district), were written in a way that skewed the scheme toward benefiting religious schools.

This, however, is not what the majority asks. The majority looks not to the provisions for tuition vouchers ... but to every provision for educational opportunity: "The program permits the participation of *all* schools within the district, [as well as public schools in adjacent districts], religious or nonreligious."... The majority then finds confirmation that "participation of *all* schools" satisfies neutrality by noting that the better part of total state educational expenditure goes to public schools ... thus showing there is no favor of religion.

The illogic is patent. If regular, public schools (which can get no voucher payments) "participate" in a voucher scheme with schools that can, and public expenditure is still predominantly on public schools, then the majority's reasoning would find neutrality in a scheme of vouchers available for private tuition in districts with no secular private schools at all. "Neutrality" as the majority employs the term is, literally, verbal and nothing more. This, indeed, is the only way the majority can gloss over the very nonneutral feature of the total scheme covering "*all* schools": public tutors may receive from the State no more than $324 per child to support extra tutoring (that is, the State's 90% of a total amount of $360) ... whereas the tuition voucher schools (which turn out to be mostly religious) can receive up to $2,250....

### B

The majority addresses the issue of choice the same way it addresses neutrality, by asking whether recipients or potential recipients of voucher aid have a choice of public schools among secular alternatives to religious schools. Again, however, the majority asks the wrong question and misapplies the criterion. The majority has confused choice in spending scholarships with choice from the entire menu of possible educational placements, most of them open to anyone willing to attend a public school. . . The question is whether the private hand is genuinely free to send the money in either a secular direction or a religious one. . . .

. . . If "choice" is present whenever there is any educational alternative to the religious school to which vouchers can be endorsed, then there will always be a choice and the voucher can always be constitutional, even in a system in which there is not a single private secular school as an alternative to the religious school. And because it is unlikely that any participating private religious school will enroll more pupils than the generally available public system, it will be easy to generate numbers suggesting that aid to religion is not the significant intent or effect of the voucher scheme. . . .

There is, in any case, no way to interpret the 96.6% of current voucher money going to religious schools as reflecting a free and genuine choice by the families that apply for vouchers. The 96.6% reflects, instead, the fact that too few nonreligious school desks are available and few but religious schools can afford to accept more than a handful of voucher students. And contrary to the majority's assertion . . . public schools in adjacent districts hardly have a financial incentive to participate in the Ohio voucher program, and none has. . . . For the overwhelming number of children in the voucher scheme, the only alternative to the public schools is religious. And it is entirely irrelevant that the State did not deliberately design the network of private schools for the sake of channeling money into religious institutions. . . .

Justice BREYER, with whom Justice STEVENS and Justice SOUTER join, dissenting. . . .

V

The Court . . . turns the clock back. It adopts, under the name of "neutrality," an interpretation of the Establishment Clause that this Court rejected more than half a century ago. In its view, the parental choice that offers each religious group a kind of equal opportunity to secure government funding overcomes the Establishment Clause concern for social concord. An earlier Court found that "equal opportunity" principle insufficient; it read the Clause as insisting upon greater separation of church and state, at least in respect to primary education. . . . In a society composed of many different religious creeds, I fear that this present departure from the Court's earlier understanding risks creating a form of religiously based conflict potentially harmful to the Nation's social fabric. Because I believe the Establishment Clause was written in part to avoid this kind of conflict, and for reasons set forth by Justice SOUTER and Justice STEVENS, I respectfully dissent.

---

EXERCISE 4.5. The majority in *Zelman* found that Ohio's plan did not violate the establishment clause because the choice of where to send the children to school was made by parents, not the state. Thus, when 96 percent of the 3,700 participating students chose religious schools, this was a contingent, not necessary, feature of the program. Indeed, only forty-six of fifty-six participating private schools were religiously affiliated. But would the Court reach the same result if 100 percent of participating students went to religious schools and all fifty-six private schools had been religious? Would such a program still be constitutional? Conversely, would the dissenters still think the Ohio plan was unlawful if only five percent of participating students were in religious schools?

# The First Amendment and the Ten Commandments

We know that schools shape the educational experience of students not only by the words spoken in the classroom but also by the signs and messages displayed in the students' physical environment. Can a state require public school teachers to put up a display of the Ten Commandments in their classrooms? Consider the following landmark case, in which the Court said no.

A *per curiam* opinion is one handed down by the entire Court (or a majority of it) in which no single justice is given attribution for authorship. Do you prefer to know who writes the decision? Is that information important or distracting?

## STONE
v.
## GRAHAM

*Supreme Court of the United States*
Decided Nov. 17, 1980.

PER CURIAM.

A Kentucky statute requires the posting of a copy of the Ten Commandments, purchased with private contributions, on the wall of each public classroom in the State.

... We conclude that Kentucky's statute requiring the posting of the Ten Commandments in public schoolrooms had no secular legislative purpose, and is therefore unconstitutional.

The Commonwealth [of Kentucky] insists that the statute in question serves a secular legislative purpose, observing that the legislature required the following notation in small print at the bottom of each display of the Ten Commandments: "The secular application of the Ten Commandments is clearly seen in its adoption as the fundamental legal code of Western Civilization and the Common Law of the United States."

The trial court found the "avowed" purpose of the statute to be secular, even as it labeled the statutory declaration "self-serving." Under this Court's rulings, however, such an "avowed" secular purpose is not sufficient to avoid conflict with the First Amendment. In *Abington School District v. Schempp* this Court held unconstitutional the daily reading of Bible verses and the Lord's Prayer in the public schools, despite the school district's assertion of such secular purposes as "the promotion of moral values, the contradiction to the materialistic trends of our times, the perpetuation of our institutions and the teaching of literature."

The pre-eminent purpose for posting the Ten Commandments on schoolroom walls is plainly religious in nature. The Ten Commandments are undeniably a sacred text in the Jewish and Christian faiths, and no legislative recitation of a supposed secular purpose can blind us to that fact. The

Commandments do not confine themselves to arguably secular matters, such as honoring one's parents, killing or murder, adultery, stealing, false witness, and covetousness. Rather, the first part of the Commandments concerns the religious duties of believers: worshipping the Lord God alone, avoiding idolatry, not using the Lord's name in vain, and observing the Sabbath Day.

This is not a case in which the Ten Commandments are integrated into the school curriculum, where the Bible may constitutionally be used in an appropriate study of history, civilization, ethics, comparative religion, or the like. Posting of religious texts on the wall serves no such educational function. If the posted copies of the Ten Commandments are to have any effect at all, it will be to induce the schoolchildren to read, meditate upon, perhaps to venerate and obey, the Commandments. However desirable this might be as a matter of private devotion, it is not a permissible state objective under the Establishment Clause.

It does not matter that the posted copies of the Ten Commandments are financed by voluntary private contributions, for the mere posting of the copies under the auspices of the legislature provides the "official support of the State ... Government" that the Establishment Clause prohibits. Nor is it significant that the Bible verses involved in this case are merely posted on the wall, rather than read aloud ... for "it is no defense to urge that the religious practices here may be relatively minor encroachments on the First Amendment." [T]he judgment below is reversed.

Justice REHNQUIST, dissenting.

... The Court's summary rejection of a secular purpose articulated by the legislature and confirmed by the state court is without precedent in Establishment Clause jurisprudence. This Court regularly looks to legislative articulations of a statute's purpose in Establishment Clause cases and accords such pronouncements the deference they are due.... The fact that the asserted secular purpose may overlap with what some may see as a religious objective does not render it unconstitutional. As this Court stated in *McGowan v. Maryland,* in upholding the validity of Sunday closing laws, "the present purpose and effect of most of [these laws] is to provide a uniform day of rest for all citizens; the fact that this day is Sunday, a day of particular significance for the dominant Christian sects, does not bar the state from achieving its secular goals." ...

The Establishment Clause does not require that the public sector be insulated from all things which may have a religious significance or origin. This Court has recognized that "religion has been closely identified with our history and government," and that "[t]he history of man is inseparable from the history of religion...." Kentucky has decided to make students aware of this fact by demonstrating the secular impact of the Ten Commandments.

---

EXERCISE 4.6. If a teacher cannot post the Ten Commandments in the classroom, can she integrate a recitation of the Ten Commandments into a teaching unit on the tale of Exodus during a Western literature class? Can a public high school offer a course on the Bible and teach about various books and chapters so long as the material is presented from a literary perspective? Why or why not? What is the difference between posting the Ten Commandments in the front of the room and teaching about the Bible in literature class? Is there a danger of offending religious students by teaching the Bible as literature rather than the revealed word of God?

EXERCISE 4.7. Even for those who think that posting the Ten Commandments is a good idea and should be allowed under the First Amendment, there is a major problem: Which version should be displayed? There are multiple versions of the Ten Commandments, with different wordings and orderings used by different churches and religions. For example, here are the Ten Commandments according to the Russian Orthodox Church of Washington, D.C.[1]

1. Thou shalt have no other gods before Me.
2. Thou shalt not make unto thee any graven image, or any likeness of any thing that is in heaven above, or that is in the earth beneath, or that is in the water under the earth: thou shalt not bow down thyself to them, nor serve them.
3. Thou shalt not take the name of the Lord thy God in vain.
4. Remember the Sabbath day, to keep it holy. Six days shalt thou labor and do all thy work: but the seventh day is the Sabbath of the Lord thy God.
5. Honor thy father and thy mother: that thy days may be long upon the land which the Lord thy God giveth thee.
6. Thou shalt not kill.
7. Thou shalt not commit adultery.
8. Thou shalt not steal.
9. Thou shalt not bear false witness against thy neighbor.
10. Thou shalt not covet thy neighbor's house, thou shalt not covet thy neighbor's wife, nor his manservant, nor his maidservant, nor his ox, nor his ass, nor any thing that is thy neighbor's.

Contrast this version with the translation of the Ten Commandments that hung on the wall of Alabama state court judge Roy Moore's courtroom in the 1990s.[2] (A federal district court forced Judge Moore to take down the display, but the controversy propelled him to the position of chief justice of the Alabama state supreme court in March 2001. As chief justice he proceeded to erect another Ten Commandments display in the state supreme court building, only to have another federal court order him to take it down on November 18, 2002.)

1. You shall have no other gods before me
2. You shall not take the name of the Lord your God in vain
3. You shall not make unto yourself any graven image
4. Remember the sabbath day, to keep it holy
5. Honor your father and your mother: that your days may be long
6. You shall not kill
7. You shall not commit adultery
8. You shall not steal
9. You shall not bear false witness against your neighbour
10. You shall not covet.

Does the sheer variety in Ten Commandments presentations reinforce the sense that government should not be meddling in religion?

---

TALK SHOW DEBATE. On June 17, 1999, in the wake of continuing public concern about the April 20 massacre at Columbine High School in Littleton, Colorado—in which two students roamed the school with guns and shot fellow students and teachers—the U.S. House of Representatives passed a law purporting to give states the power to post the Ten Commandments in public buildings, including public schools. One representative, criticizing the Court's decision in *Stone v. Graham*, said that, had the Ten Commandments been posted on the wall at Columbine High, the massacre never would have happened. Do you agree? Set up a TV-style talk show in which a moderator has several guests on either side of the issue. Discuss whether having the Ten Commandments in the classroom will stop school violence.

# The Court's Agonizing Ambivalence over Christmas Nativity Displays

In 1984 the Supreme Court rendered a decision in *Lynch v. Donnelly,* a case testing the constitutionality of a Christmas display erected by the city of Pawtucket, Rhode Island, in a park in the heart of the city's shopping district. The Pawtucket display included many of the traditional figures and decorations associated with Christmas, including Santa Claus, reindeer, candy-striped poles, a Christmas tree, carolers, cutout figures of a clown, a dancing elephant, a robot, a teddy bear, hundreds of colored lights, a "seasons greetings" banner, and at its very center a Christmas crèche (nativity scene). This crèche, which had been part of the annual display for four decades, featured the infant Jesus, Mary and Joseph, angels, shepherds, kings, and barn animals. The Rhode Island American Civil Liberties Union (ACLU) challenged the city's practice of spending public money to prepare and stage the display.

Chief Justice Burger, for the majority, rejected the ACLU's establishment clause attack. He observed that our official history is "replete with official references to the value and invocation of Divine guidance," noting the observance of Thanksgiving and Christmas as religious holidays and the employment of congressional chaplains to conduct daily prayers in the House and Senate. Elaborating the theme of "ceremonial deism," he invoked the statutorily defined national motto "In God We Trust" on our dollars and the language "One nation under God" as part of the Pledge of Allegiance to the American flag. Declining to "take a rigid, absolutist view of the Establishment Clause," Chief Justice Burger found that the crèche scene in Pawtucket was no more religious than these ceremonial invocations upheld in the past and that the crèche had a legitimate secular purpose in celebrating the Christmas holiday and depicting its origins.

In Justice O'Connor's concurrence, she voted to uphold the display but reached the conclusion based on reasoning different from "ceremonial deism." For her, the critical question under the establishment clause was whether the practice constituted a governmental "endorsement" of religion. Government endorsement of religion violates the establishment clause because it sends "a message to nonadherents that they are outsiders, not full members of the political community, and an accompanying message to adherents that they are insiders, favored members of the political community." Justice O'Connor found that the "evident purpose of including the crèche in the larger display was not promotion of the religious content of the crèche but celebration of the public holiday through its traditional symbols." This "is a legitimate secular purpose." Moreover, the effect of having the crèche as part of the holiday display is not religious since "the overall holiday setting changes what viewers may fairly understand to be the purpose of the display." In other words, the reindeer, the robot, the elves, and the elephant dilute and counteract the religiosity of the manger scene.

The four dissenters in *Lynch*—Justices Brennan, Marshall, Blackmun and Stevens—considered the majority's opinion an outrageous betrayal of establishment clause principles. They saw the religious endorsement as clear. Justice Brennan could find no secular purpose in having the crèche at all and quoted testimony by town officials that its actual purpose was to "keep Christ in Christmas." The effect of the nativity scene, he argued, was "to place the government's imprimatur of approval on the particular religious beliefs exemplified by the crèche." He rejected the claim that the overall holiday context somehow removed the religious character of the central manger scene, for "the crèche retains a specifically Christian religious meaning," which is "the characteristically Christian belief that a divine savior was brought into the world and that the purpose of this miraculous birth was to illuminate a path toward salvation and redemption."

Justice O'Connor is often the swing vote on divisive issues and the power of her vote and her "endorsement" analysis became clear in *Allegheny County v. American Civil Liberties Union Greater Pittsburgh Chapter* (1989), when the Court considered two more holiday displays. The first one was a crèche nativity scene, complete with an angel and a banner proclaiming "Gloria in Excelsis Deo," placed on the grand staircase of the Allegheny County Courthouse. The second was a Hanukkah menorah placed next to a Christmas tree and a sign saluting liberty outside the City-County Building.

A five-person majority on the Court, including Justice O'Connor, voted to strike down the crèche because it was placed centrally inside the county courthouse and in such a way that its religious message was totally undiluted by secular holiday imagery like reindeer or dancing elephants. However, the majority upheld the outdoor display of the menorah and Christmas tree as a secular recognition "that both Christmas and Hanukkah are part of the same winter-holiday season." Justice Kennedy, writing for himself and Chief Justice Rehnquist and Justices White and Scalia, would have allowed both displays as less religious in nature than other cases of "ceremonial deism" accepted by the Court. Justices Brennan, Marshall, and Stevens would have struck down both displays as impermissible placement of "indisputably" religious symbols on public property for purely religious reasons.

Where would you come down on this tough problem?

Pretend your class is your city or county council and a group has proposed that you set up a holiday display in a major public park near a shopping center. Some people don't want it. Most people do. Some want a nativity scene and others do not. What creative responses can you come up with? What will you do? How will you make sure the display is constitutional?

DRAFT A SCHOOL BOARD POLICY ON HOLIDAY PROGRAMS. During the Christmas/Hanukkah/Kwanzaa period, public and secular private schools confront the complexities of how to properly observe a religiously saturated holiday season. No school wants to be the grinch that steals the joy of the holiday season, but how do you put on holiday programs that do not cross the line? After all, many religions—Judaism, Islam, Hinduism—do not celebrate Christmas at all, and even some that do, like the Greek Orthodox or Serbian Orthodox, celebrate Christmas at a different time altogether.

Many public schools have students sing songs and perform skits in holiday shows that celebrate Christmas because Christianity is (in many places) the majority religion. Should schools be required to offer a sampling of religious traditions so that every child's tradition is represented? What about atheist families that object to any religious overtones in official school programs? Should there be no mention of Christmas, Hanukkah, or Kwanzaa? Turn your class into a school board to discuss this problem. Vote on a systemwide policy for appropriate holiday programs and decorations.

# One Nation, under Canada, with Constitutional Controversy for All: The New Establishment Clause Conflict over the Pledge of Allegiance

The Supreme Court's landmark decision in *West Virginia v. Barnette* (1943) did not put an end to public controversy over the Pledge of Allegiance in public schools. Today we face deep controversy over whether the words "under God" violate the establishment clause.

The Pledge of Allegiance was written in 1892 (on the 400th anniversary of Christopher Columbus's arrival in America) and has been modified over the years. The original pledge was written by Francis Bellamy, a Baptist minister, socialist, and antiracist agitator who sought to unify the country around the American flag. He wanted to replace the continuing salutes and nostalgic rituals developing around the Confederate battle flag in the South with a culture of national allegiance to the flag of freedom. Bellamy was emphatic that his pledge not include mention of God, because he thought it would be socially divisive. The pledge proved hugely popular and spread across the country.

But in 1954, at the height of the cold war, and just several weeks after the Supreme Court's decision in *Brown v. Board of Education,* Congress added the words "under God" to the codified pledge of allegiance in federal law. President Dwight D. Eisenhower said, "In this way we are reaffirming the transcendence of religious faith in America's heritage and future; in this way we shall constantly strengthen those spiritual weapons which forever will be our country's most powerful resource in peace and war."

In the following remarkable case brought in the Ninth Circuit Court of Appeals, Dr. Michael Newdow argued that the addition of the words "under God" to the Pledge of Allegiance violated the establishment clause. After hearing the case a three-judge panel struck down government Pledge of Allegiance rituals with the words "under God" in them. The panel then stayed the decision, which would have applied in the western states, after the U.S. Senate voted 99–0 in June 2002 to denounce the decision and a firestorm of criticism swept the country. The full Ninth Circuit will decide all together ("*en banc*"), presumably in 2003, whether to change the 2–1 opinion of the panel. It is quite possible that the case could advance to the Supreme Court.

------

**NEWDOW**

**v.**

**U.S. CONGRESS**

*United States Court of Appeals, Ninth Circuit*
Argued March 14, 2002.
Decided June 26, 2002.

GOODWIN, Circuit Judge:

Michael Newdow appeals a judgment dismissing his challenge to the constitutionality of the words "under God" in the Pledge of Allegiance to the Flag. Newdow argues that the addition of these words by a 1954 federal statute to the previous version of the Pledge of Allegiance (which made no reference to God) and the daily recitation in the classroom of the Pledge of Allegiance, with the added words included, by his daughter's public school teacher are violations of the Establishment Clause of the First Amendment to the United States Constitution.

FACTUAL AND PROCEDURAL BACKGROUND

Newdow is an atheist whose daughter attends public elementary school in the Elk Grove Unified School District ("EGUSD") in California. In accordance with state law and a school district rule, EGUSD teachers begin each school day by leading their students in a recitation of the Pledge of Allegiance ("the Pledge"). The California Education Code requires that public schools begin each school day with "appropriate patriotic exercises" and that "[t]he giving of the Pledge of Allegiance to the Flag of the United States of America shall satisfy" this requirement.…

DISCUSSION

… D. Establishment Clause
… Over the last three decades, the Supreme Court has used three interrelated tests to analyze alleged violations of the Establishment Clause in the realm of public education: the three-prong test set forth in *Lemon v. Kurtzman;* the "endorsement" test, first articulated by Justice O'Connor in her concurring opinion in *Lynch v. Donnelly,* and later adopted by a majority of the Court in *County of Allegheny v. ACLU;* and the "coercion" test first used by the Court in *Lee v. Weisman.*

We are free to apply any or all of the three tests, and to invalidate any measure that fails any one of them. Although this court has typically applied the *Lemon* test to alleged Establishment Clause violations, we are not required to apply it if a practice fails one of the other tests. Nevertheless, for purposes of completeness, we will analyze the school district policy and the 1954 Act under all three tests.

Michael Newdow, a doctor and lawyer who argued his own case that resulted in the Pledge of Allegiance being called unconstitutional, talks to the press about the pledge at his home on June 27, 2002, in Sacramento, California. After the ruling against the "under God" language he received death threats on his answering machine.

We first consider whether the 1954 Act and the EGUSD's policy of teacher-led Pledge recitation survive the endorsement test.

In the context of the Pledge, the statement that the United States is a nation "under God" is an endorsement of religion. It is a profession of a religious belief, namely, a belief in monotheism. The recitation that ours is a nation "under God" is not a mere acknowledgment that many Americans believe in a deity. Nor is it merely descriptive of the undeniable historical significance of religion in the founding of the Republic. Rather, the phrase "one nation under God" in the context of the Pledge is normative. To recite the Pledge is not to describe the United States; instead, it is to swear allegiance to the values for which the flag stands: unity, indivisibility, liberty, justice, and—since 1954—monotheism. The text of the official Pledge, codified in federal law, impermissibly takes a position with respect to the purely religious question of the existence and identity of God. A profession that we are a nation "under God" is identical, for Establishment Clause purposes, to a profession that we are a nation "under Jesus," a nation "under Vishnu," a nation "under Zeus," or a nation "under no god," because none of these professions can be neutral with respect to religion. "[T]he government must pursue a course of complete neutrality toward religion." Furthermore, the school district's practice of teacher-led recitation of the Pledge aims to inculcate in students a respect for the ideals set forth in the Pledge, and thus amounts to state endorsement of these ideals. Although students cannot be forced to participate in recitation of the Pledge, the school district is nonetheless conveying a message of state endorsement of a religious belief when it requires public school teachers to recite, and lead the recitation of, the current form of the Pledge.

The Pledge, as currently codified, is an impermissible government endorsement of religion because it sends a message to unbelievers "that they are outsiders, not full members of the political community, and an accompanying message to adherents that they are insiders, favored members of the political community." . . . To be sure, no one is obligated to recite this phrase . . . but it borders on sophistry to suggest that the reasonable atheist would not feel less than a full member of the political community every time his fellow Americans recited, as part of their expression of patriotism and love for country, a phrase he believed to be false.

Similarly, the policy and the Act fail the coercion test. The policy and the Act place students in the untenable position of choosing between participating in an exercise with religious content or protesting. "What to most believers may seem nothing more than a reasonable request that the nonbeliever respect their religious practices, in a school context may appear to the nonbeliever or dissenter to be an attempt to employ the machinery of the State to enforce a religious orthodoxy." Although the defendants argue that the religious content of "one nation under God" is minimal, to an atheist or a believer in certain non-Judeo-Christian religions or philosophies, it may reasonably appear to be an attempt to enforce a "religious orthodoxy" of monotheism, and is therefore impermissible. The coercive effect of this policy is particularly pronounced in the school setting given the age and impressionability of schoolchildren, and their understanding that they are required to adhere to the norms set by their school, their teacher and their fellow students. The mere fact that a pupil is required to listen every day to the statement "one nation under God" has a coercive effect. The coercive effect of the Act is apparent from its context and legislative history, which indicate that the Act was designed to result in the daily recitation of the words "under God" in school classrooms. ... Therefore, the policy and the Act fail the coercion test.

Finally we turn to the *Lemon* test, the first prong of which asks if the challenged policy has a secular purpose. Historically, the primary purpose of the 1954 Act was to advance religion, in conflict with the first prong of the *Lemon* test. The federal defendants "do not dispute that the words 'under God' were intended to recognize a Supreme Being," at a time when the government was publicly inveighing against atheistic communism. Nonetheless, the federal defendants argue that the Pledge must be considered as a whole when assessing whether it has a secular purpose. They claim that the Pledge has the secular purpose of "solemnizing public occasions, expressing confidence in the future, and encouraging the recognition of what is worthy of appreciation in society."

The flaw in defendants' argument is that it looks at the text of the Pledge "as a whole," and glosses over the 1954 Act.

We apply the purpose prong of the *Lemon* test to the amendment that added the words "under God" to the Pledge, not to the Pledge in its final version. The legislative history of the 1954 Act reveals that the Act's *sole* purpose was to advance religion, in order to differentiate the United States from nations under communist rule. "[T]he First Amendment requires that a statute must be invalidated if it is entirely motivated by a purpose to advance religion." The purpose of the 1954 Act was to take a position on the question of theism, namely, to support the existence and moral authority of God, while "deny[ing] ... atheistic and materialistic concepts." Such a purpose runs counter to the Establishment Clause, which prohibits the government's endorsement or advancement not only of one particular religion at the expense of other religions, but also of religion at the expense of atheism.

[T]he Court has unambiguously concluded that the individual freedom of conscience protected by the First Amendment embraces the right to select any religious faith or none at all. This conclusion derives support not only from the interest in respecting the individual's freedom of conscience, but also from the conviction that religious beliefs worthy of respect are the product of a free and voluntary choice by the faithful, and from recognition of the fact that the political interest in forestalling intolerance extends beyond intolerance among Christian sects—or even intolerance among "religions"—to encompass intolerance of the disbeliever and the uncertain.

Similarly, the school district policy also fails the *Lemon* test. Although it survives the first prong of *Lemon* because, as even Newdow concedes, the school district had the secular purpose of fostering patriotism in enacting the policy, the policy fails the second prong. The second *Lemon* prong asks "whether the challenged government action is sufficiently likely to be perceived by adherents of the controlling denominations as an endorsement, and by the nonadherents as a disapproval, of their individual religious choices." Given the age and impressionability of schoolchildren, as discussed above, particularly within the confined environment of the classroom, the policy is highly likely to convey an impermissible message of endorsement to some and disapproval to others of their beliefs regarding the existence of a monotheistic God. Therefore the policy fails the effects prong of *Lemon,* and fails the *Lemon* test. In sum, both the policy and the Act fail the *Lemon* test as well as the endorsement and coercion tests. ...

# The Free Exercise Rights of Religious Americans

As we have seen, one significant issue that courts face is the extent to which schools can make religion a part of the educational experience of students. But another is the extent to which parents can use religion to keep their kids *out* of school or particular school activities. In this famous decision about the free exercise of religion, the Supreme Court upheld the right of Amish families to stop sending their children to school after the eighth grade. As you read this decision, ask yourself whether the holding applies broadly to people and children of *all* faiths, or whether there were unique, compelling facts about the Amish community that justified this constitutional exemption.

---

## WISCONSIN
## v.
## YODER

*Supreme Court of the United States*
Argued Dec. 8, 1971.
Decided May 15, 1972.

Chief Justice BURGER delivered the opinion of the Court....

Respondents Jonas Yoder and Wallace Miller are members of the Old Order Amish religion, and respondent Adin Yutzy is a member of the Conservative Amish Mennonite Church. They and their families are residents of Green County, Wisconsin. Wisconsin's compulsory school-attendance law required them to cause their children to attend public or private school until reaching age 16 but the respondents declined to send their children, ages 14 and 15, to public school after they complete the eighth grade. The children were not enrolled in any private school, or within any recognized exception to the compulsory attendance law, and they are conceded to be subject to the Wisconsin statute.

... [R]espondents were charged, tried, and convicted of violating the compulsory attendance law in Green County Court and were fined the sum of $5 each. Respondents defended on the ground that the application of the compulsory-attendance law violated their rights under the First and Fourteenth Amendments. The trial testimony showed that respondents believed, in accordance with the tenets of Old Order Amish communities generally, that their children's attendance at high school, public or private, was contrary to the Amish religion and way of life. They believed that by sending their children to high school, they would not only expose themselves to the danger of the censure of the church community, but ... also endanger their own salvation and that of their children. The State stipulated that respondents' religious beliefs were sincere....

A related feature of Old Order Amish communities is their devotion to a life in harmony with nature and the soil, as exemplified by the simple life of the early Christian era that continued in America during much of our early national life. Amish beliefs require members of the community to make their living by farming or closely related activities....

Amish objection to formal education beyond the eighth grade is firmly grounded in these central religious concepts. They object to the high school, and higher education generally, because the values they teach are in marked variance with Amish values and the Amish way of life; . . . The high school tends to emphasize intellectual and scientific accomplishments, self-distinction, competitiveness, worldly success, and social life with other students. Amish society emphasizes informal learning through doing; a life of "goodness," rather than a life of intellect; wisdom, rather than technical knowledge, community welfare, rather than competition; and separation from, rather than integration with, contemporary worldly society.

Formal high school education beyond the eighth grade is contrary to Amish beliefs, not only because it places Amish children in an environment hostile to Amish beliefs . . . but also because it takes them away from their community, physically and emotionally, during the crucial and formative adolescent period of life. During this period, the children must acquire Amish attitudes favoring manual work and self-reliance and the specific skills needed to perform the adult role of an Amish farmer or housewife. They must learn to enjoy physical labor. Once a child has learned basic reading, writing, and elementary mathematics, these traits, skills, and attitudes admittedly fall within the category of those best learned through example and "doing" rather than in a classroom. And, at this time in life, the Amish child must also grow in his faith and his relationship to the Amish community if he is to be prepared to accept the heavy obligations imposed by adult baptism. In short, high school attendance with teachers who are not of the Amish faith and may even be hostile to it interposes a serious barrier to the integration of the Amish child into the Amish religious community. . . .

. . . The testimony of Dr. Donald A. Erickson, an expert witness on education, showed that the Amish succeed in preparing their high school age children to be productive members of the Amish community. He described their system of learning through doing the skills directly relevant to their adult roles in the Amish community as "ideal" and perhaps superior to ordinary high school education. The evidence also showed that the Amish have an excellent record as law-abiding and generally self-sufficient members of society. . . .

I

There is no doubt as to the power of a State, having a high responsibility for education of its citizens, to impose reasonable regulations for the control and duration of basic education. . . . [A] State's interest in universal education, however highly we rank it, is not totally free from a balancing process when it impinges on fundamental rights and interests, such as those specifically protected by the Free Exercise Clause of the First Amendment, and the traditional interest of parents with respect to the religious upbringing of their children. . . .

It follows that in order for Wisconsin to compel school attendance beyond the eighth grade against a claim that such attendance interferes with the practice of a legitimate religious belief, it must appear either that the State does not deny the free exercise of religious belief by its requirement, or that there is a state interest of sufficient magnitude to override the interest claiming protection under the Free Exercise Clause. . . .

The essence of all that has been said and written on the subject is that only those interests of the highest order and those not otherwise served can overbalance legitimate claims to the free exercise of religion. . . .

II

We come then to the quality of the claims of the respondents concerning the alleged encroachment of Wisconsin's compulsory school-attendance statute on their rights and the rights of their children

In *Wisconsin v. Yoder* the Court upheld the right of Amish families to take their children out of school after the eighth grade.

to the free exercise of the religious beliefs they and their forbears have adhered to for almost three centuries. In evaluating those claims we must be careful to determine whether the Amish religious faith and their mode of life are, as they claim, inseparable and interdependent. A way of life, however virtuous and admirable, may not be interposed as a barrier to reasonable state regulation of education if it is based on purely secular considerations; to have the protection of the Religion Clauses, the claims must be rooted in religious belief.... Thus, if the Amish asserted their claims because of their subjective evaluation and rejection of the contemporary secular values accepted by the majority, much as Thoreau rejected the social values of his time and isolated himself at Walden Pond, their claims would not rest on a religious basis....

... [T]he record in this case abundantly supports the claim that the traditional way of life of the Amish is not merely a matter of personal preference, but one of deep religious conviction, shared by an organized group, and intimately related to daily living. That the Old Order Amish daily life and religious practice stem from their faith is shown by the fact that it is in response to their literal interpretation of the Biblical injunction from the Epistle of Paul to the Romans, "be not conformed to this world...." This command is fundamental to the Amish faith. Moreover, for the Old Order Amish, religion is not simply a matter of theocratic belief. As the expert witnesses explained, the Old Order Amish religion pervades and determines virtually their entire way of life, regulating it with the detail of the Talmudic diet through the strictly enforced rules of the church community....

The impact of the compulsory-attendance law on respondents' practice of the Amish religion is not only severe, but inescapable, for the Wisconsin law affirmatively compels them, under threat of criminal sanction, to perform acts undeniably at odds with fundamental tenets of their religious beliefs. Nor is the impact of the compulsory-attendance law confined to grave interference with important Amish religious tenets from a subjective point of view. It carries with it precisely the kind of objective danger to the free exercise of religion that the First Amendment was designed to prevent. As the record shows, compulsory school attendance to age 16 for Amish children carries with it a very real threat of undermining the Amish community and religious practice as they exist today;

they must either abandon belief and be assimilated into society at large, or be forced to migrate to some other and more tolerant region.

In sum, the unchallenged testimony of acknowledged experts in education and religious history, almost 300 years of consistent practice, and strong evidence of a sustained faith pervading and regulating respondents' entire mode of life support the claim that enforcement of the State's requirement of compulsory formal education after the eighth grade would gravely endanger if not destroy the free exercise of respondents' religious beliefs.

III

... We turn, then, to the State's broader contention that its interest in its system of compulsory education is so compelling that even the established religious practices of the Amish must give way. Where fundamental claims of religious freedom are at stake, however, we cannot accept such a sweeping claim; despite its admitted validity in the generality of cases, we must searchingly examine the interests that the State seeks to promote by its requirement for compulsory education to age 16, and the impediment to those objectives that would flow from recognizing the claimed Amish exemption.

The State advances two primary arguments in support of its system of compulsory education. It notes ... that some degree of education is necessary to prepare citizens to participate effectively and intelligently in our open political system if we are to preserve freedom and independence. Further, education prepares individuals to be self-reliant and self-sufficient participants in society. We accept these propositions.

However, the evidence adduced by the Amish in this case is persuasively to the effect that an additional one or two years of formal high school for Amish children in place of their long-established program of informal vocational education would do little to serve those interests. ... It is one thing to say that compulsory education for a year or two beyond the eighth grade may be necessary when its goal is the preparation of the child for life in modern society as the majority live, but it is quite another if the goal of education be viewed as the preparation of the child for life in the separated agrarian community that is the keystone of the Amish faith.

... No one can question the State's duty to protect children from ignorance but this argument does not square with the facts disclosed in the record. Whatever their idiosyncrasies as seen by the majority, this record strongly shows that the Amish community has been a highly successful social unit within our society, even if apart from the conventional "mainstream." Its members are productive and very law-abiding members of society; they reject public welfare in any of its usual modern forms. ...

The State, however, supports its interest in providing an additional one or two years of compulsory high school education to Amish children because of the possibility that some such children will choose to leave the Amish community, and that if this occurs they will be ill-equipped for life. ... However, on this record, that argument is highly speculative. There is no specific evidence of the loss of Amish adherents by attrition, nor is there any showing that upon leaving the Amish community Amish children, with their practical agricultural training and habits of industry and self-reliance, would become burdens on society because of educational shortcomings. Indeed, this argument of the State appears to rest primarily on the State's mistaken assumption, already noted, that the Amish do not provide any education for their children beyond the eighth grade, but allow them to grow in "ignorance." To the contrary, not only do the Amish accept the necessity for formal schooling through the eighth grade level, but continue to provide what has been characterized by the undisputed testimony of expert educators as an "ideal" vocational education for their children in the adolescent years. . . .

Insofar as the State's claim rests on the view that a brief additional period of formal education is imperative to enable the Amish to participate effectively and intelligently in our democratic process, it must fall. The Amish alternative to formal secondary school education has enabled them to function effectively in their day-to-day life under self-imposed limitations on relations with the world, and to survive and prosper in contemporary society as a separate, sharply identifiable and highly self-sufficient community for more than 200 years in this country. In itself this is strong evidence that they are capable of fulfilling the social and political responsibilities of citizenship without compelled attendance beyond the eighth grade at the price of jeopardizing their free exercise of religious belief. . . .

## V

. . . [W]e hold . . . that the First and Fourteenth amendments prevent the State from compelling respondents to cause their children to attend formal high school to age 16. . . .

*Affirmed.*

Justice DOUGLAS, dissenting in part.

## I

I agree with the Court that the religious scruples of the Amish are opposed to the education of their children beyond the grade schools, yet I disagree with the Court's conclusion that the matter is within the dispensation of parents alone. The Court's analysis assumes that the only interests at stake in the case are those of the Amish parents on the one hand, and those of the State on the other. The difficulty with this approach is that, despite the Court's claim, the parents are seeking to vindicate not only their own free exercise claims, but also those of their high-school-age children. . . .

Religion is an individual experience. It is not necessary, nor even appropriate, for every Amish child to express his views on the subject in a prosecution of a single adult. Crucial, however, are the views of the child whose parent is the subject of the suit. Frieda Yoder has in fact testified that her own religious views are opposed to high-school education. I therefore join the judgment of the Court as to respondent Jonas Yoder. But Frieda Yoder's views may not be those of Vernon Yutzy or Barbara Miller. I must dissent, therefore, as to respondents Adin Yutzy and Wallace Miller as their motion to dismiss also raised the question of their children's religious liberty.

## II

. . . These children are "persons" within the meaning of the Bill of Rights. We have so held over and over again.

In *Tinker v. Des Moines School District* we dealt with 13-year-old, 15-year-old, and 16-year-old students who wore armbands to public schools and were disciplined for doing so. We gave them relief, saying that their First Amendment rights had been abridged.

In *West Virginia State Board of Education v. Barnette* we held that school-children, whose religious beliefs collided with a school rule requiring them to salute the flag, could not be required to do so. While the sanction included expulsion of the students and prosecution of the parents, the vice of the regime was its interference with the child's free exercise of religion. We said: "Here . . . we are

**JUSTICE WILLIAM O. DOUGLAS** (1898–1980) was born poor and sickly in the town of Maine, Minnesota. Because he had polio, he was small and faced ridicule from other children. He turned to sports and outdoor activities to build up his body and self-esteem and thus began a lifelong passion for nature and the environment. He went to Whitman College in Walla Walla, Washington, and in the fall of 1922 hitchhiked his way across the country, sleeping and eating with hobos, to enter Columbia Law School, where he graduated second in his class. Douglas spent many years at the Securities and Exchange Commission and was a key component of the New Deal brain trust in Washington, D.C. President Franklin Delano Roosevelt appointed him to the Supreme Court in 1939. He served as a justice for thirty-six years, longer than any other justice.

HIGHLIGHTS

➤ Douglas was married four times. When he was sixty-eight years old he married a twenty-three-year-old college student.

➤ Douglas was the foremost naturalist, explorer, and hiker ever to serve on the Court, and frequently hiked the C&O Canal in Washington, D.C.

➤ A prolific writer, Justice Douglas was especially fond of writing about his adventuresome travels abroad.

dealing with a compulsion of students to declare a belief." ...

On this important and vital matter of education, I think the children should be entitled to be heard. While the parents, absent dissent, normally speak for the entire family, the education of the child is a matter on which the child will often have decided views. He may want to be a pianist or an astronaut or an oceanographer. To do so he will have to break from the Amish tradition.

It is the future of the student, not the future of the parents, that is imperiled by today's decision. If a parent keeps his child out of school beyond the grade school, then the child will be forever barred from entry into the new and amazing world of diversity that we have today. The child may decide that is the preferred course, or he may rebel. It is the student's judgment, not his parents', that is essential if we are to give full meaning to what we have said about the Bill of Rights and of the right of students to be masters of their own destiny.... The child, therefore, should be given an opportunity to be heard before the State gives the exemption which we honor today....

III

I think the emphasis of the Court on the "law and order" record of this Amish group of people is quite irrelevant. A religion is a religion irrespective of what the misdemeanor or felony records of its members might be. I am not at all sure how the Catholics, Episcopalians, the Baptists, Jehovah's Witnesses, the Unitarians, and my own Presbyterians would make out if subjected to such a test....

FOR THE CLASS

RELIGIOUS FREEDOM OR CHILD NEGLECT? As Justice Douglas suggests, this decision values highly the religious wishes of Amish parents but undervalues the rights of Amish children to a full-blown education that would prepare them to make their own fully aware decisions about their future. Who was right in this case, the Yoders or the state of Wisconsin?

It is not clear how *Yoder* would be decided today. In *Employment Division v. Smith* (1990), the Supreme Court rejected a free exercise challenge by members of the Native American Indian religion to state policies banning the ingestion of peyote, which the Indians saw as an important part of their sacrament. The Court found that *incidental* burdens on religious exercise do not trigger scrutiny. Neutral and universally applicable laws not undertaken for purposes of religious harassment are presumed to be legitimate. Thus, a truancy law like Wisconsin's would carry a heavy presumption of legitimacy.

---

# The Theory of Evolution and the Story of Creation: An Ongoing Duel in the Classroom

What happens in high school classrooms when science makes discoveries about the natural world that contradict the religious beliefs of a large number of citizens? Should such scientific theories be taught? Should they be censored? Should they be balanced with "equal time" for religiously based theories? Or is there no place at all for religious indoctrination in the classroom?

Nowhere has this problem been posed more dramatically than in the science classroom when it comes to teaching about human evolution and the doctrine that is sometimes called Darwinism. The classroom war between evolutionary science and religious creationism has gone on for more than seventy-five years.

One of the most famous trials in our nation's history was the so-called "Scopes Monkey Trial," which took place in the sweltering summer of 1925 in Tennessee. The case, which arose in the midst of rising religious fundamentalism, involved the criminal prosecution of John T. Scopes, a twenty-four-year-old science teacher and football coach, for teaching evolution in violation of a recently passed state law banning the theory of evolution from the classroom. Scopes had the support of the American Civil Liberties Union and was represented by the legendary Clarence Darrow, who wanted to show that the antievolution statute was an attempt to establish a religious law and substitute nonsense for knowledge. The lawyer for the state of Tennessee was the eloquent populist political leader William Jennings Bryan. A former secretary of state in the Woodrow Wilson administration, Bryan saw the trial as a showdown between evolution and Christianity.

The key moment in the trial arrived when Darrow called Bryan himself to the stand and examined him on whether or not he believed that everything recorded in the Bible was literally true. After interrogating him about biblical stories like the Tower of Babel and Jonah being swallowed by the whale, Darrow zeroed in on the origins of Earth:

Q: "Do you think the earth was made in six days?"
A: "Not six days of 24 hours.... My impression is they were periods...."
Q: "Now, if you call those periods, they may have been a very long time?"
A: "They might have been."

Q: "The creation might have been going on for a very long time?"
A: "It might have continued for millions of years...."

Thus Darrow exploded Bryan's determination not to depart from the biblical text and radically shifted public sentiment in favor of Scopes and evolution. Still, the jury returned with a guilty verdict and the judge ordered Scopes to pay a fine of $100, the lowest allowed under the law. In his parting words to the court, Scopes said: "Your Honor, I feel that I have been convicted of violating an unjust statute. I will continue in the future ... to oppose this law in any way I can. Any other action would be in violation of my idea of academic freedom." Scopes' conviction was later reversed in the Tennessee Supreme Court on technical grounds.

The Scopes trial did not put the controversy over teaching evolution to rest. In 1968 the issue finally reached the Supreme Court in the landmark case *Epperson v. Arkansas.* There the Court struck down a similar "antievolution" law in Arkansas that made it illegal for public school teachers "to teach the theory or doctrine that mankind ascended or descended from a lower order of animals." The Court found that this law violated the establishment clause of the First Amendment because it "selects from the body of knowledge a particular segment which it proscribes for the sole reason that it is deemed to conflict with a particular religious doctrine." The Court said that it was "clear that fundamentalist sectarian conviction was ... the law's reason for existence."

*Epperson* was a relatively easy case. But what about *Edward v. Aguillard,* a case that reached the Court almost twenty years later in 1987? In that decision, the Supreme Court struck down a Louisiana statute that prevented public school teachers from "teaching the

Don Aguillard, a teacher at Acadiana High School in Scott, Louisiana, filed suit against the state's equal time for creation science law in 1981. Six years later, in *Edwards v. Aguillard,* the Supreme Court found that law to be in violation of the establishment clause.

theory of evolution in public schools unless accompanied by instruction in 'creation science,'" the controversial scientific claims developed to support the belief in the biblical version of creation. Despite the fact that the stated purpose of this law was to enhance academic freedom, the Court considered this a "sham" since the law did "not grant teachers a flexibility that they did not already possess to supplement the present science curriculum with the presentation of theories, besides evolution, about the origin of life." Rather, the "primary purpose of the Creationism Act" was "to endorse a particular religious doctrine" and thus violated the establishment clause.

---

EXERCISE 4.8. Does the holding in *Epperson* make sense, because the clear purpose of the law struck down was to undermine the teaching of evolution with a wholly religious doctrine? Or has the Court unfairly taken sides in a legitimate scientific controversy by declaring one viewpoint religious and in effect banning it? Does the decision actually ban the teaching of creation science even when teachers undertake it voluntarily, or does it just forbid a mandatory "equal time" arrangement? Research "creation science" and "intelligent design theory," both of which are efforts to mobilize scientific evidence and principles in defense of biblical accounts of creation. Are they science?

---

**FOR THE CLASS**

EVOLUTION CONTROVERSY. Imagine a fundamentalist Christian student, Heather Bouler, whose parents do not want her to participate in biology class when evolution is being taught. The teacher is assigning a three-page research paper on the life of Charles Darwin and a final exam on modern evolutionary scientists like Stephen Jay Gould. Heather's parents refuse to send her to the class and the school is threatening to fail her for the whole semester if she does not do her evolution-related work. The family sues in federal court for an injunction against any moves to punish Heather and for her right to study creationism when the rest of the class is studying evolution. Does Heather have a free exercise right to opt out of the evolution section of the biology course? Form two teams and argue Heather's side and the school district's side. Heather's team will cite the *Yoder* decision, the school the *Smith* decision.

SCHOOL BOARD EXERCISE. Pretend that your class is a school board trying to define a policy governing the teaching of evolution and creation in high school classes. Consider the following options:

1. Teach only the theory of evolution.
2. Teach only the theory of evolution, but include scientific criticisms of it. Explain that many Christians believe in creation for religious reasons.
3. Teach both the theory of evolution and creation science as two equally plausible alternatives.

4. Allow each individual teacher to teach whatever he or she wants according to individual conscience and belief.
5. Allow each individual school to select its preferred curriculum.
6. Teach only creation science, explaining that while this practice is unconstitutional, the school will engage in it as a form of civil disobedience.
7. Teach only the theory of evolution, but allow individual teachers to state their personal beliefs about the origins of humanity.

After discussing the options (including any others you think of), try to form a majority consensus around a solution and take a vote. Do you think your plan is constitutional?

---

### Notes

1. Found at The Russian Orthodox Cathedral of St. John the Baptist in Washington, D.C., www. stjohndc.org/command/Command.htm, February 1, 2000.

2. Found at the Byzantine Catholic Churches of the Pacific Northwest, www.saintirene.org/davidf/essays/tencomm.htm, February 10, 2000.

### Read On

"A Teacher's Guide to Religion in the Public Schools," pamphlet published by the First Amendment Center. Call 1-800-830-3733 for copies.

"Religion in the Public Schools: A Joint Statement of Current Law," a pamphlet published by Religion in the Public Schools. Write 15 East 84th Street., Suite 501, New York, NY 10028 for copies.

"Religious Expression in Public Schools," pamphlet published by the U.S. Department of Education. Call 1-800-USA-LEARN for copies.

# THE FOURTH AMENDMENT: SEARCHES OF STUDENTS AND THEIR BELONGINGS 5

"The right of the people to be secure in their persons, houses, papers, and effects, against unreasonable searches and seizures, shall not be violated...." THE FOURTH AMENDMENT

It is natural to want to be free from inspection and surveillance by the police and other state agents. But we also want to live in safe environments, free from violence, and this means we will grant large powers to the police to protect our safety and property. Americans' desire for security intensified in the wake of the horrific terrorism of September 11, 2001; the diabolical anthrax attacks that followed; and random appalling acts of violence like the sniper killings in the fall of 2002 that terrified millions in Maryland, Virginia, and Washington, D.C.

At the same time, many Americans fear that the militarized and anxiety-ridden environment of the new century will embolden government to trample individual freedoms. This type of fear also animated the signers of our Constitution, who wrote the Bill of Rights to save us from tyrannical government. They wanted government to protect us against chaos and violence, but they also wanted the Constitution to protect us against the government. If you read through the Bill of Rights, you can pick out numerous ways that the Framers tried to protect us against unbridled and arbitrary police power.

The tension between our competing desires for security and freedom infuses the environment of public schools. While schools work to stop violence, students struggle to maintain not only their safety but also their liberty and privacy. This chapter examines when government authorities may invade students' expectations of privacy and liberty, and when they may not.

The Fourth Amendment does not protect against all government searches and seizures, only *unreasonable* ones. In the world outside of school, this means that the police and government agents cannot conduct a search of your home or person without a search warrant issued by a magistrate and based upon probable cause that a crime has been (or is being) committed. In practice, the Supreme Court has relaxed this warrant requirement. In *Terry v. Ohio* (1968), the Supreme Court authorized police officers to "stop and frisk" people on the street through a "patdown" of the outer garments of their clothing if the police have "reasonable suspicion" to believe that the individuals may be armed and dangerous. This holding has empowered the police in encounters with people on the street and has led to vigorous debate in recent years about whether law enforcement officers unfairly target citizens based on race, ethnicity, and age. What has been your experience?

In the context of public education, the Supreme Court has granted school authorities broad discretion to search students and their belongings. Many students feel that, under the Fourth Amendment, public officials should not be able to search their clothing, lockers, or persons without a search warrant and probable cause. Conversely, many school officials believe that there should be no limits on their authority to search students. But the Supreme Court comes down between these two polar positions. In *New Jersey v. T. L. O.* (1984), the Court did away with the need for schools to show probable cause and to get a search warrant when they want to search, but it did require them to have "reasonable suspicion" of an individual and to keep their searches related to their objects of suspicion. Many students believe that the decision went too far in sacrificing their rights.

Yet the Court went even further in the drug testing cases *Vernonia School District v. Acton* (1995) and *Pottawatomie County v. Earls* (2002) by abolishing the need for schools to have even reasonable suspicion of a particular individual before conducting drug tests of students participating in athletics and other extracurricular activities. What is your reaction?

We will examine one case, *Chicago v. Morales* (1999), in which the Supreme Court struck down a city ordinance that prohibited "loitering" (hanging around with no apparent purpose) by "street gang members" because the language of the ordinance was impermissibly vague and thus violated due process. Did the Court properly stand up for civil liberty in *Morales* or did it cave in to criminal lawlessness by taking from the Chicago police an important tool of juvenile crime fighting?

---

**POINTS TO PONDER**

***How does the right to be free from unreasonable searches and seizures apply to public school students?***

- Should school officials have the authority to search students' belongings without a search warrant or probable cause that a crime has been committed?
- Can school authorities require student athletes to participate in random drug testing?
- Can school authorities require anyone who participates in extracurricular activities to undergo random drug testing?
- Can school authorities subject students to strip searches?
- Should government have power to arrest and prosecute street gang members and their associates for loitering in public places?

---

## The Reduced Right of Students to Expect Privacy of Their Belongings

"Smokin' in the Boys' Room," a rock song from the 1970s, reminded America's youth that "smoking ain't allowed in school." In the following Supreme Court case, a high school freshman in New Jersey was caught smoking in the girls' room. This infraction triggered a series of escalating searches of the girl's belongings, and the high school's vice principal found marijuana in her purse. This discovery led to a lower court's finding that the girl—identified only as T. L. O.—was criminally delinquent. The Supreme Court took the case to determine whether the searches of T. L. O.'s purse were lawful. If not, the evidence would be excluded—this is the effect of the "exclusionary rule"—and the conviction reversed. Despite the fact that the school had no search warrant and no probable cause to search, the Court upheld the delinquency finding. Why? What is the standard governing searches of individual students by school authorities?

———

## NEW JERSEY
### v.
## T. L. O.

*Supreme Court of the United States*
Argued March 28, 1984.
Reargued October 2, 1984.
Decided January 15, 1985.

Justice WHITE delivered the opinion of the Court. . . .

I

On March 7, 1980, a teacher at Piscataway High School in Middlesex County, N.J., discovered two girls smoking in a lavatory. One of the two girls was . . . T. L. O., who at that time was a 14-year-old high school freshman. Because smoking in the lavatory was a violation of a school rule, the teacher took the two girls to the Principal's office, where they met with Assistant Vice Principal Theodore Choplick. In response to questioning by Mr. Choplick, T. L. O.'s companion admitted that she had violated the rule. T. L. O., however, denied that she had been smoking in the lavatory and claimed that she did not smoke at all.

Mr. Choplick asked T. L. O. to come into his private office and demanded to see her purse. Opening the purse, he found a pack of cigarettes, which he removed from the purse and held before T. L. O. as he accused her of having lied to him. As he reached into the purse for the cigarettes, Mr. Choplick also noticed a package of cigarette rolling papers. In his experience, possession of rolling papers by high school students was closely associated with the use of marihuana. Suspecting that a closer examination of the purse might yield further evidence of drug use, Mr. Choplick proceeded to search the purse thoroughly. The search revealed a small amount of marihuana, a pipe, a number of empty plastic bags, a substantial quantity of money in one-dollar bills, an index card that appeared to be a list of students who owed T. L. O. money, and two letters that implicated T. L. O. in marihuana dealing.

Mr. Choplick notified T. L. O.'s mother and the police, and turned the evidence of drug dealing over to the police. At the request of the police, T. L. O.'s mother took her daughter to police headquarters, where T. L. O. confessed that she had been selling marihuana at the high school. On the basis of the confession and the evidence seized by Mr. Choplick, the State brought delinquency charges against T. L. O. in the Juvenile and Domestic Relations Court of Middlesex County. Contending that Mr. Choplick's search of her purse violated the Fourth Amendment, T. L. O. moved to suppress the evidence found in her purse as well as her confession, which, she argued, was tainted by the allegedly unlawful search. The Juvenile Court denied the motion to suppress. Although the court concluded that the Fourth Amendment did apply to searches carried out by school officials, it held that

> a school official may properly conduct a search of a student's person if the official has a reasonable suspicion that a crime has been or is in the process of being committed, or reasonable cause to believe that the search is necessary to maintain school discipline or enforce school policies.

Applying this standard, the court concluded that the search conducted by Mr. Choplick was a reasonable one. The initial decision to open the purse was justified by Mr. Choplick's well-founded suspicion that T. L. O. had violated the rule forbidding smoking in the lavatory. Once the purse was open, evidence of marihuana violations was in plain view, and Mr. Choplick was entitled to conduct a thorough search to determine the nature and extent of T. L. O.'s drug-related activities. Having denied the motion to suppress, the court on March 23, 1981, found T. L. O. to be a delinquent and on January 8, 1982, sentenced her to a year's probation....

... [W]e are satisfied that the search did not violate the Fourth Amendment.

## II

In determining whether the search at issue in this case violated the Fourth Amendment, we are faced initially with the question whether that Amendment's prohibition on unreasonable searches and seizures applies to searches conducted by public school officials. We hold that it does....

... In carrying out searches and other disciplinary functions pursuant to such policies, school officials act as representatives of the State, not merely as surrogates for the parents, and they cannot claim the parents' immunity from the strictures of the Fourth Amendment.

## III

To hold that the Fourth Amendment applies to searches conducted by school authorities is only to begin the inquiry into the standards governing such searches. Although the underlying command of the Fourth Amendment is always that searches and seizures be reasonable, what is reasonable depends on the context within which a search takes place. The determination of the standard of reasonableness governing any specific class of searches requires "balancing the need to search against the invasion which the search entails." On one side of the balance are arrayed the individual's legitimate expectations of privacy and personal security; on the other, the government's need for effective methods to deal with breaches of public order.

We have recognized that even a limited search of the person is a substantial invasion of privacy. We have also recognized that searches of closed items of personal luggage are intrusions on protected privacy interests, for "the Fourth Amendment provides protection to the owner of every container that conceals its contents from plain view." A search of a child's person or of a closed purse or other bag carried on her person, no less than a similar search carried out on an adult, is undoubtedly a severe violation of subjective expectations of privacy.

... To receive the protection of the Fourth Amendment, an expectation of privacy must be one that society is "prepared to recognize as legitimate." The State of New Jersey has argued that because

Most students consider the contents of their lockers private, but the Court in *T.L.O.* held that even students' private property can be searched at school based on "reasonable suspicions" that school rules or laws are being violated. Lower courts have upheld school policies that treat lockers as school property searchable at any time.

of the pervasive supervision to which children in the schools are necessarily subject, a child has virtually no legitimate expectation of privacy in articles of personal property "unnecessarily" carried into a school. This argument has two factual premises: (1) the fundamental incompatibility of expectations of privacy with the maintenance of a sound educational environment; and (2) the minimal interest of the child in bringing any items of personal property into the school. Both premises are severely flawed.

Although this Court may take notice of the difficulty of maintaining discipline in the public schools today, the situation is not so dire that students in the schools may claim no legitimate expectations of privacy. We have recently recognized that the need to maintain order in a prison is such that prisoners retain no legitimate expectations of privacy in their cells, but it goes almost without saying that "[t]he prisoner and the schoolchild stand in wholly different circumstances, separated by the harsh facts of criminal conviction and incarceration." We are not yet ready to hold that the schools and the prisons need be equated for purposes of the Fourth Amendment.

Nor does the State's suggestion that children have no legitimate need to bring personal property into the schools seem well anchored in reality. Students at a minimum must bring to school not only the supplies needed for their studies, but also keys, money, and the necessaries of personal hygiene and grooming. In addition, students may carry on their persons or in purses or wallets such nondisruptive yet highly personal items as photographs, letters, and diaries. Finally, students may have perfectly legitimate reasons to carry with them articles of property needed in connection with extracurricular or recreational activities. In short, schoolchildren may find it necessary to carry with them a variety of legitimate, noncontraband items, and there is no reason to conclude that they have necessarily waived all rights to privacy in such items merely by bringing them onto school grounds.

Against the child's interest in privacy must be set the substantial interest of teachers and administrators in maintaining discipline in the classroom and on school grounds. Maintaining order in the classroom has never been easy, but in recent years, school disorder has often taken particularly ugly forms: drug use and violent crime in the schools have become major social problems. Even in schools that have been spared the most severe disciplinary problems, the preservation of order and a proper educational environment requires close supervision of schoolchildren, as well as the enforcement of rules against conduct that would be perfectly permissible if undertaken by an adult. . . .

How, then, should we strike the balance between the schoolchild's legitimate expectations of privacy and the school's equally legitimate need to maintain an environment in which learning can take place? It is evident that the school setting requires some easing of the restrictions to which searches by public authorities are ordinarily subject. The warrant requirement, in particular, is unsuited to the school environment: requiring a teacher to obtain a warrant before searching a child suspected of an infraction of school rules (or of the criminal law) would unduly interfere with the maintenance of the swift and informal disciplinary procedures needed in the schools. Just as we have in other cases dispensed with the warrant requirement when "the burden of obtaining a warrant is likely to frustrate the governmental purpose behind the search," we hold today that school officials need not obtain a warrant before searching a student who is under their authority.

The school setting also requires some modification of the level of suspicion of illicit activity needed to justify a search. Ordinarily, a search—even one that may permissibly be carried out without a warrant—must be based upon "probable cause" to believe that a violation of the law has occurred. However, "probable cause" is not an irreducible requirement of a valid search. . . .

We join the majority of courts that have examined this issue in concluding that the accommodation of the privacy interests of schoolchildren with the substantial need of teachers and administrators for freedom to maintain order in the schools does not require strict adherence to the requirement that searches be based on probable cause to believe that the subject of the search has violated or is violating the law. Rather, the legality of a search of a student should depend simply on the reasonableness, under all the circumstances, of the search. Determining the reasonableness of any search involves a twofold inquiry: first, one must consider "whether the . . . action was justified at its inception," second, one must determine whether the search as actually conducted "was reasonably related in scope to the circumstances which justified the interference in the first place." Under ordinary circumstances, a search of a student by a teacher or other school official will be "justified at its inception" when there are reasonable grounds for suspecting that the search will turn up evidence that the student has violated or is violating either the law or the rules of the school. Such a search will be permissible in its scope when the measures adopted are reasonably related to the objectives of the search and not excessively intrusive in light of the age and sex of the student and the nature of the infraction. . . .

IV

. . . The incident that gave rise to this case actually involved two separate searches, with the first—the search for cigarettes—providing the suspicion that gave rise to the second—the search for marihuana. Although it is the fruits of the second search that are at issue here, the validity of the search for marihuana must depend on the reasonableness of the initial search for cigarettes, as there would have been no reason to suspect that T. L. O. possessed marihuana had the first search not taken place. Accordingly, it is to the search for cigarettes that we first turn our attention.

The New Jersey Supreme Court pointed to two grounds for its holding that the search for cigarettes was unreasonable. First, the court observed that possession of cigarettes was not in itself illegal or a violation of school rules. Because the contents of T. L. O.'s purse would therefore have "no direct bearing on the infraction" of which she was accused (smoking in a lavatory where smoking was prohibited), there was no reason to search her purse. Second, even assuming that a search of T. L. O.'s purse might under some circumstances be reasonable in light of the accusation made against T. L. O., the New Jersey court concluded that Mr. Choplick in this particular case had no reasonable grounds to suspect that T. L. O. had cigarettes in her purse. At best, according to the court, Mr. Choplick had "a good hunch."

Both these conclusions are implausible. T. L. O. had been accused of smoking, and had denied the accusation in the strongest possible terms when she stated that she did not smoke at all. Surely it cannot be said that under these circumstances, T. L. O.'s possession of cigarettes would be irrelevant to the charges against her or to her response to those charges. T. L. O.'s possession of cigarettes, once it was discovered, would both corroborate the report that she had been smoking and undermine the credibility of her defense to the charge of smoking. To be sure, the discovery of the cigarettes would not prove that T. L. O. had been smoking in the lavatory; nor would it, strictly speaking, necessarily be inconsistent with her claim that she did not smoke at all. But it is universally recognized that evidence, to be relevant to an inquiry, need not conclusively prove the ultimate fact in issue, but only have "any tendency to make the existence of any fact that is of consequence to the determination of the action more probable or less probable than it would be without the evidence." The relevance of T. L. O.'s possession of cigarettes to the question whether she had been smoking and to the credibility of her denial that she smoked supplied the necessary "nexus" between the item searched for and the infraction under investigation. Thus, if Mr. Choplick in fact had a reasonable suspicion that T. L. O. had cigarettes in her purse, the search was justified despite the fact that the cigarettes, if found, would constitute "mere evidence" of a violation.

Of course, the New Jersey Supreme Court also held that Mr. Choplick had no reasonable suspicion that the purse would contain cigarettes. This conclusion is puzzling. A teacher had reported that T. L. O. was smoking in the lavatory. Certainly this report gave Mr. Choplick reason to suspect that T. L. O. was carrying cigarettes with her; and if she did have cigarettes, her purse was the obvious place in which to find them. Mr. Choplick's suspicion that there were cigarettes in the purse ... was the sort of "common-sense conclusio[n] about human behavior" upon which "practical people"—including government officials—are entitled to rely.... It cannot be said that Mr. Choplick acted unreasonably when he examined T. L. O.'s purse to see if it contained cigarettes.

Our conclusion that Mr. Choplick's decision to open T. L. O.'s purse was reasonable brings us to the question of the further search for marihuana once the pack of cigarettes was located. The suspicion upon which the search for marihuana was founded was provided when Mr. Choplick observed a package of rolling papers in the purse as he removed the pack of cigarettes. Although T. L. O. does not dispute the reasonableness of Mr. Choplick's belief that the rolling papers indicated the presence of marihuana, she does contend that the scope of the search Mr. Choplick conducted exceeded permissible bounds when he seized and read certain letters that implicated T. L. O. in drug dealing. This argument, too, is unpersuasive. The discovery of the rolling papers concededly gave rise to a reasonable suspicion that T. L. O. was carrying marihuana as well as cigarettes in her purse. This suspicion justified further exploration of T. L. O.'s purse, which turned up more evidence of drug-related activities: a pipe, a number of plastic bags of the type commonly used to store marihuana, a small quantity of marihuana, and a fairly substantial amount of money. Under these circumstances, it was not unreasonable to extend the search to a separate zippered compartment of the purse; and when a search of that compartment revealed an index card containing a list of "people who owe me money" as well as two letters, the inference that T. L. O. was involved in marihuana trafficking was substantial enough to justify Mr. Choplick in examining the letters to determine whether they contained any further evidence. In short, we cannot conclude that the search for marihuana was unreasonable in any respect....

*Reversed.*

Justice BRENNAN, with whom Justice MARSHALL joins, concurring in part and dissenting in part....

... Today's decision sanctions school officials to conduct full-scale searches on a "reasonableness" standard whose only definite content is that it *is not* the same test as the "probable cause" standard found in the text of the Fourth Amendment. In adopting this unclear, unprecedented, and unnecessary departure from generally applicable Fourth Amendment standards, the Court carves out a broad exception to standards that this Court has developed over years of considering Fourth Amendment problems....

Justice STEVENS, with whom Justice MARSHALL joins, and with whom Justice BRENNAN joins as to Part I, concurring in part and dissenting in part....

### III

... In this case, Mr. Choplick overreacted to what appeared to be nothing more than a minor infraction—a rule prohibiting smoking in the bathroom of the freshmen's and sophomores' building. It is, of course, true that he actually found evidence of serious wrongdoing by T. L. O., but no one claims that the prior search may be justified by his unexpected discovery. As far as the smoking infraction is concerned, the search for cigarettes merely tended to corroborate a teacher's eyewitness account of T. L. O.'s violation of a minor regulation designed to channel student smoking behavior into designated locations. Because this conduct was neither unlawful nor significantly disruptive of school order or the educational process, the invasion of privacy associated with the forcible opening of T. L. O.'s purse was entirely unjustified at its inception.

... Although I agree that school administrators must have broad latitude to maintain order and discipline in our classrooms, that authority is not unlimited.

### IV

The schoolroom is the first opportunity most citizens have to experience the power of government. Through it passes every citizen and public official, from schoolteachers to policemen and prison guards. The values they learn there, they take with them in life. One of our most cherished ideals is the one contained in the Fourth Amendment: that the government may not intrude on the personal privacy of its citizens without a warrant or compelling circumstance. The Court's decision today is a curious moral for the Nation's youth....

I respectfully dissent.

---

EXERCISE 5.1. The *T. L. O.* decision allows searches of students' property whenever school officials have "reasonable suspicion" that a particular individual is engaging in something criminal or impermissible under school rules. This degree of suspicion—which is lower than the "probable cause" required of police officers searching adults—is acceptable to the Court because of the school setting. Should school officials and teachers be authorized to search students when they are on school property but not in the school building? The Supreme Court has not treated this issue, but most lower courts permit it so long as reasonable suspicion exists that laws or school rules are being violated. What about searches of students' cars parked on school property? The general rule for cars on the street, as the Supreme Court elucidated in *California v. Acevedo* (1991), is that if police have probable cause to think there is criminal contraband inside a car, they can search the car without a search warrant. This is because the mobility of cars creates a kind of traveling exigency. Does this apply to a student's car in the school parking lot? Should the school have to show "probable cause" before searching it, or is "reasonable suspicion" enough? The Court has not decided this issue. What do you think?

EXERCISE 5.2. In determining whether or not a search is "reasonable" under *New Jersey v. T. L. O.*, the Court conducts a two-part analysis. First, the Court determines whether the search was "justified at its inception"—that is, whether there were reasonable grounds for suspecting the search would turn up evidence that the student was violating either the law or school rules. Second, the Court asks whether the search was reasonably related in scope to the purpose of the search and not overly intrusive in light of the student's age and sex and the nature of the infraction. To analyze this second issue, the Court must balance the importance of the government's interest against the level of violation of legitimate privacy rights.

Draw a line down the middle of a piece of paper and make two columns. At the top of the left-hand column, write "Level of Privacy Intrusion"; at the top of the right-hand column, write "Nature of Government Interest." To do a balancing test, you must compare the severity of the privacy intrusion against the weight of the government interest. (For example, in *Vernonia School District v. Acton,* which deals with drug testing of student athletes, there is a dignitary invasion against the normal solitude and privacy people enjoy in going to the bathroom, as well as an invasion of the privacy usually enjoyed in medical information contained in one's own body fluids. These privacy intrusions must be balanced against the government's interest in protecting students from harm in playing sports under the influence of drugs and its interest in establishing student athletes as school role models.)

Read through the following list of procedures established at various public high schools facing the problems of drug and alcohol use among students. In the "Intrusion" column of your chart, list what you think the intrusion is for each procedure and rank how intrusive you think the procedure is on a scale of one to ten (ten being the highest) and why. In the "Government Interest" column, write down what you think the government interest is in the drug testing policy and how high that interest ranks on a scale of one to ten. If you think one example is not a "search" at all, write it on your chart and explain why.

(a) Students entering the building at Madison High must walk through a metal detector.
(b) Students at Hamilton High must walk through a metal detector and put their book bags through an x-ray machine before entering the building.
(c) Jefferson High reserves the right to "tap" all the pay phones in the hallways of the school and listen in on conversations. Students are informed of this practice at the beginning of each school year.
(d) Martin Luther King High has a counselor available to talk to students about their problems. Any teacher can "sign out" from the counselor's office student files that contain notes kept on each student's sessions.

(e) Big City High has video cameras in the hallways filming the rows of student lockers. If students act suspiciously around their lockers, the principal searches their lockers for drugs or weapons. Videotapes are routinely turned over to the police.

(f) Small City High conducts random locker searches of all boys' lockers and has removed all doors from the toilet stalls in the girls' bathroom.

(g) At Kaynine High, trained police dogs sniff outside student lockers, and school officials open and search lockers when the dogs bark and alert teachers to the presence of narcotics.

(h) Southeast High has trained police dogs at school doorways sniffing each student's backpack or bookbag as students enter the building.

(i) Detection High places young-looking undercover police officers into the senior class to befriend students and uncover information about drug dealing and about students obtaining abortions without the parental consent required under state law. They turn in several of their "friends."

(j) As a requirement for advancing to the next grade at J. Edgar Hoover High, all students must take a polygraph ("lie-detector") test and answer one question: "Did you cheat on any of your final exams this year?"

(k) At Thurgood Marshall High's homecoming dance, all of the chaperones carry an alcohol tester. Throughout the dance, the chaperones may approach any student and have him or her blow into the machine. If alcohol is detected, a red light goes on and the student's parents are called to take the student home.

(l) At John Marshall High's homecoming dance, students who test positive using the same device are expelled.

---

## Drug Tests and Strip Searches

Although *New Jersey v. T. L. O.* gave schools much latitude to search the *belongings* of students, it did not directly deal with the question of when school officials can search the *bodies* of students. A case came before the Court that dealt with just this issue: *Vernonia School District v. Acton* (1995). James Acton, a seventh grader, went out for the football team at a public school in Oregon. He made the team but was denied the right to join it when he refused to sign forms giving his consent to urinalysis drug testing before the season began and periodically on a random basis throughout the season. The school cited two interests in the drug testing: protecting students from harm caused by mental impairment during athletic activity and maintaining athletes as proper "role models" for other students. In *Acton* (1995), the Court found that these interests important enough, and the privacy invasion slight enough, to permit the school district to maintain its drug testing policy.

The *Acton* decision was written narrowly, seemingly as if to allow drug testing only against interscholastic student athletes. But high school administrators across the country took the football and ran with it, so to speak; many imposed drug testing on students in *all* extracurricular activities, students on overnight field trips and camping trips, and students who run for student council. Compulsory drug testing was destined to return to

Tenth grader James Acton, center, along with friends and family members, leaves the Supreme Court on March 28, 1995, after the Court considered his challenge to Vernonia school district's compulsory urinalysis drug testing of student athletes, a policy to which he was subjected in junior high school. Although plaintiffs in a case like this may attend the Court's oral argument to see their lawyers argue on their behalf, the Court's rules forbid lawyers to introduce their clients to the Court.

the Court. In the following case, the Court considered the constitutionality of a high school testing all students who participate in competitive extracurricular activities, including the Academic Team, Future Farmers of America, band, choir, and cheerleading. The Court upheld the drug testing program. In hindsight, the Acton case looks less like a narrow exception for random compulsory drug testing of athletes and more like a foot in the door to randomly testing everyone. Is that going to be the next step after this case?

———

## BOARD OF EDUCATION OF INDEPENDENT SCHOOL DISTRICT NO. 92 OF POTTAWATOMIE COUNTY
### v.
### EARLS

*Supreme Court of the United States*
Argued March 19, 2002.
Decided June 27, 2002.

Justice THOMAS delivered the opinion of the Court.

The Student Activities Drug Testing Policy implemented by the Board of Education of Independent School District No. 92 of Pottawatomie County (School District) requires all students who participate in competitive extracurricular activities to submit to drug testing. Because this Policy reasonably serves the School District's important interest in detecting and preventing drug use among its students, we hold that it is constitutional.

The city of Tecumseh, Oklahoma, is a rural community located approximately 40 miles southeast of Oklahoma City. The School District administers all Tecumseh public schools. In the fall of 1998, the School District adopted the Student Activities Drug Testing Policy (Policy), which requires all middle and high school students to consent to drug testing in order to participate in any extracurricular activity. In practice, the Policy has been applied only to competitive extracurricular activities sanctioned by the Oklahoma Secondary Schools Activities Association, such as the Academic Team, Future Farmers of America, Future Homemakers of America, band, choir, pom-pom, cheerleading, and athletics. Under the Policy, students are required to take a drug test before participating in an extracurricular activity, must submit to random drug testing while participating in that activity, and must agree to be tested at any time upon reasonable suspicion. The urinalysis tests are designed to detect only the use of illegal drugs, including amphetamines, marijuana, cocaine, opiates, and barbiturates, not medical conditions or the presence of authorized prescription medications.

At the time of their suit, both respondents attended Tecumseh High School. Respondent Lindsay Earls was a member of the show choir, the marching band, the Academic Team, and the National Honor Society. Respondent Daniel James sought to participate in the Academic Team. Together with their parents, Earls and James ... challeng[ed] the Policy both on its face and as applied to their participation in extracurricular activities. They alleged that the Policy violates the Fourth Amendment as incorporated by the Fourteenth Amendment and requested injunctive and declarative relief. They also argued that the School District failed to identify a special need for testing students who participate in extracurricular activities, and that the "Drug Testing Policy neither addresses a proven problem nor promises to bring any benefit to students or the school." ...

II

... In *Vernonia* [*School Dist. 47J v. Acton*], this Court held that the suspicionless drug testing of athletes was constitutional. The Court, however, did not simply authorize all school drug testing, but rather conducted a fact-specific balancing of the intrusion on the children's Fourth Amendment rights against the promotion of legitimate governmental interests. Applying the principles of *Vernonia* to the somewhat different facts of this case, we conclude that Tecumseh's Policy is also constitutional.

A

We first consider the nature of the privacy interest allegedly compromised by the drug testing. As in *Vernonia*, the context of the public school environment serves as the backdrop for the analysis of the privacy interest at stake and the reasonableness of the drug testing policy in general....

A student's privacy interest is limited in a public school environment where the State is responsible for maintaining discipline, health, and safety. Schoolchildren are routinely required to submit to physical examinations and vaccinations against disease. Securing order in the school environment sometimes requires that students be subjected to greater controls than those appropriate for adults.

Respondents argue that because children participating in nonathletic extracurricular activities are not subject to regular physicals and communal undress, they have a stronger expectation of privacy than the athletes tested in *Vernonia*. This distinction, however, was not essential to our decision in *Vernonia*, which depended primarily upon the school's custodial responsibility and authority.

Lindsay Earls, second right; Graham Boyd, center, an attorney for the American Civil Liberties Union representing Tecumseh School District students challenging the district's random drug testing policy; and others listen to a reporter's question in front of the Supreme Court on March 19, 2002. Sharon Smith, holding sign, who supports the random testing, lost her daughter Angela, shown on sign, to drugs.

In any event, students who participate in competitive extracurricular activities voluntarily subject themselves to many of the same intrusions on their privacy as do athletes. Some of these clubs and activities require occasional off-campus travel and communal undress. All of them have their own rules and requirements for participating students that do not apply to the student body as a whole. For example, each of the competitive extracurricular activities governed by the Policy must abide by the rules of the Oklahoma Secondary Schools Activities Association, and a faculty sponsor monitors the students for compliance with the various rules dictated by the clubs and activities. This regulation of extracurricular activities further diminishes the expectation of privacy among school-children. We therefore conclude that the students affected by this Policy have a limited expectation of privacy.

B

Next, we consider the character of the intrusion imposed by the Policy. Urination is "an excretory function traditionally shielded by great privacy." But the "degree of intrusion" on one's privacy caused by collecting a urine sample "depends upon the manner in which production of the urine sample is monitored."

Under the Policy, a faculty monitor waits outside the closed restroom stall for the student to produce a sample and must "listen for the normal sounds of urination in order to guard against tampered specimens and to insure an accurate chain of custody." The monitor then pours the sample into two bottles that are sealed and placed into a mailing pouch along with a consent form signed by the student. This procedure is virtually identical to that reviewed in *Vernonia*, except that it additionally protects privacy by allowing male students to produce their samples behind a closed stall. Given that we considered the method of collection in *Vernonia* a "negligible" intrusion, the method here is even less problematic.

In addition, the Policy clearly requires that the test results be kept in confidential files separate from a student's other educational records and released to school personnel only on a "need to know" basis. Respondents nonetheless contend that the intrusion on students' privacy is significant because the Policy fails to protect effectively against the disclosure of confidential information and, specifically, that the school "has been careless in protecting that information: for example, the Choir teacher looked at students' prescription drug lists and left them where other students could see them." But the choir teacher is someone with a "need to know," because during off-campus trips she needs to know what medications are taken by her students. Even before the Policy was enacted the choir teacher had access to this information. In any event, there is no allegation that any other student did see such information. This one example of alleged carelessness hardly increases the character of the intrusion.

Moreover, the test results are not turned over to any law enforcement authority. Nor do the test results here lead to the imposition of discipline or have any academic consequences. Rather, the only consequence of a failed drug test is to limit the student's privilege of participating in extracurricular activities. Indeed, a student may test positive for drugs twice and still be allowed to participate in extracurricular activities. After the first positive test, the school contacts the student's parent or guardian for a meeting. The student may continue to participate in the activity if within five days of the meeting the student shows proof of receiving drug counseling and submits to a second drug test in two weeks. For the second positive test, the student is suspended from participation in all extracurricular activities for 14 days, must complete four hours of substance abuse counseling, and must submit to monthly drug tests. Only after a third positive test will the student be suspended from participating in any extracurricular activity for the remainder of the school year, or 88 school days, whichever is longer.

Given the minimally intrusive nature of the sample collection and the limited uses to which the test results are put, we conclude that the invasion of students' privacy is not significant.

C

Finally, this Court must consider the nature and immediacy of the government's concerns and the efficacy of the Policy in meeting them. This Court has already articulated in detail the importance of the governmental concern in preventing drug use by schoolchildren. The drug abuse problem among our Nation's youth has hardly abated since *Vernonia* was decided in 1995. In fact, evidence suggests that it has only grown worse. As in *Vernonia*, "the necessity for the State to act is magnified by the fact that this evil is being visited not just upon individuals at large, but upon children for whom it has undertaken a special responsibility of care and direction." The health and safety risks identified in *Vernonia* apply with equal force to Tecumseh's children. Indeed, the nationwide drug epidemic makes the war against drugs a pressing concern in every school.

Additionally, the School District in this case has presented specific evidence of drug use at Tecumseh schools. Teachers testified that they had seen students who appeared to be under the influence of drugs and that they had heard students speaking openly about using drugs. A drug dog found marijuana cigarettes near the school parking lot. Police officers once found drugs or drug paraphernalia in a car driven by a Future Farmers of America member. And the school board president reported that people in the community were calling the board to discuss the "drug situation." We decline to second-guess the finding of the District Court that "[v]iewing the evidence as a whole, it cannot be reasonably disputed that the [School District] was faced with a 'drug problem' when it adopted the Policy."

Respondents consider the proffered evidence insufficient and argue that there is no "real and immediate interest" to justify a policy of drug testing nonathletes. We have recognized, however, that "[a] demonstrated problem of drug abuse ... [is] not in all cases necessary to the validity of a testing regime," but that some showing does "shore up an assertion of special need for a suspicionless general search program." The School District has provided sufficient evidence to shore up the need for its drug testing program.

Furthermore, this Court has not required a particularized or pervasive drug problem before allowing the government to conduct suspicionless drug testing.... [T]he need to prevent and deter the substantial harm of childhood drug use provides the necessary immediacy for a school testing policy. Indeed, it would make little sense to require a school district to wait for a substantial portion of its students to begin using drugs before it was allowed to institute a drug testing program designed to deter drug use.

Given the nationwide epidemic of drug use, and the evidence of increased drug use in Tecumseh schools, it was entirely reasonable for the School District to enact this particular drug testing policy....

Respondents also argue that the testing of nonathletes does not implicate any safety concerns, and that safety is a "crucial factor" in applying the special needs framework... They contend that there must be "surpassing safety interests" or "extraordinary safety and national security hazards," in order to override the usual protections of the Fourth Amendment. Respondents are correct that safety factors into the special needs analysis, but the safety interest furthered by drug testing is undoubtedly substantial for all children, athletes and nonathletes alike. We know all too well that drug use carries a variety of health risks for children, including death from overdose.

We also reject respondents' argument that drug testing must presumptively be based upon an individualized reasonable suspicion of wrongdoing because such a testing regime would be less intrusive. In this context, the Fourth Amendment does not require a finding of individualized suspicion, and we decline to impose such a requirement on schools attempting to prevent and detect drug use by students. Moreover, we question whether testing based on individualized suspicion in fact would be less intrusive. Such a regime would place an additional burden on public school teachers who are already tasked with the difficult job of maintaining order and discipline. A program of individualized suspicion might unfairly target members of unpopular groups. The fear of lawsuits resulting from such targeted searches may chill enforcement of the program, rendering it ineffective in combating drug use. In any case, this Court has repeatedly stated that reasonableness under the Fourth Amendment does not require employing the least intrusive means, because "[t]he logic of such elaborate less-restrictive-alternative arguments could raise insuperable barriers to the exercise of virtually all search-and-seizure powers."

Finally, we find that testing students who participate in extracurricular activities is a reasonably effective means of addressing the School District's legitimate concerns in preventing, deterring, and detecting drug use. While in *Vernonia* there might have been a closer fit between the testing of athletes and the trial court's finding that the drug problem was "fueled by the 'role model' effect of athletes' drug use," such a finding was not essential to the holding. *Vernonia* did not require the school to test the group of students most likely to use drugs, but rather considered the constitutionality of the program in the context of the public school's custodial responsibilities. Evaluating the Policy in this context, we conclude that the drug testing of Tecumseh students who participate in extracurricular activities effectively serves the School District's interest in protecting the safety and health of its students.

Within the limits of the Fourth Amendment, local school boards must assess the desirability of drug testing schoolchildren. In upholding the constitutionality of the Policy, we express no opinion as to its wisdom. Rather, we hold only that Tecumseh's Policy is a reasonable means of furthering the School District's important interest in preventing and deterring drug use among its schoolchildren. Accordingly, we reverse the judgment of the Court of Appeals....

Justice GINSBURG, with whom Justice STEVENS, JUSTICE O'CONNOR, and Justice SOUTER join, dissenting.

Seven years ago, in *Vernonia School Dist. 47J v. Acton* this Court determined that a school district's policy of randomly testing the urine of its student athletes for illicit drugs did not violate the Fourth Amendment. In so ruling, the Court emphasized that drug use "increase[d] the risk of sports-related injury" and that Vernonia's athletes were the "leaders" of an aggressive local "drug culture" that had reached "epidemic proportions." Today, the Court relies upon *Vernonia* to permit a school district with a drug problem its superintendent repeatedly described as "not ... major" to test the urine of an academic team member solely by reason of her participation in a nonathletic, competitive extracurricular activity—participation associated with neither special dangers from, nor particular predilections for, drug use.

"[T]he legality of a search of a student," this Court has instructed, "should depend simply on the reasonableness, under all the circumstances, of the search." Although "'special needs' inhere in the public school context," those needs are not so expansive or malleable as to render reasonable any program of student drug testing a school district elects to install. The particular testing program upheld today is not reasonable, it is capricious, even perverse: Petitioners' policy targets for testing a student population least likely to be at risk from illicit drugs and their damaging effects. I therefore dissent.

I

A

... The *Vernonia* Court concluded that a public school district facing a disruptive and explosive drug abuse problem sparked by members of its athletic teams had "special needs" that justified suspicionless testing of district athletes as a condition of their athletic participation.

This case presents circumstances dispositively different from those of *Vernonia*. True, as the Court stresses, Tecumseh students participating in competitive extracurricular activities other than athletics share two relevant characteristics with the athletes of *Vernonia*. First, both groups attend public schools. "[O]ur decision in *Vernonia*," the Court states, "depended primarily upon the school's custodial responsibility and authority." Concern for student health and safety is basic to the school's caretaking, and it is undeniable that "drug use carries a variety of health risks for children, including death from overdose."

Those risks, however, are present for *all* schoolchildren. *Vernonia* cannot be read to endorse invasive and suspicionless drug testing of all students upon any evidence of drug use, solely because drugs jeopardize the life and health of those who use them. Many children, like many adults, engage in dangerous activities on their own time; that the children are enrolled in school scarcely allows government to monitor all such activities. If a student has a reasonable subjective expectation of privacy in the personal items she brings to school, surely she has a similar expectation regarding

A full-time police officer patrols the halls in Webster Groves High School in St. Louis, Missouri—evidence of a new security consciousness in high schools.

the chemical composition of her urine. Had the *Vernonia* Court agreed that public school attendance, in and of itself, permitted the State to test each student's blood or urine for drugs, the opinion in *Vernonia* could have saved many words.

The second commonality to which the Court points is the voluntary character of both interscholastic athletics and other competitive extracurricular activities. "By choosing to 'go out for the team,' [school athletes] voluntarily subject themselves to a degree of regulation even higher than that imposed on students generally." Comparably, the Court today observes, "students who participate in competitive extracurricular activities voluntarily subject themselves to" additional rules not applicable to other students.

The comparison is enlightening. While extracurricular activities are "voluntary" in the sense that they are not required for graduation, they are part of the school's educational program; for that reason, the petitioner (hereinafter School District) is justified in expending public resources to make them available. Participation in such activities is a key component of school life, essential in reality for students applying to college, and, for all participants, a significant contributor to the breadth and quality of the educational experience. Students "volunteer" for extracurricular pursuits in the same way they might volunteer for honors classes: They subject themselves to additional requirements, but they do so in order to take full advantage of the education offered them.

Voluntary participation in athletics has a distinctly different dimension: Schools regulate student athletes discretely because competitive school sports by their nature require communal undress and, more important, expose students to physical risks that schools have a duty to mitigate. For the very reason that schools cannot offer a program of competitive athletics without intimately affecting the privacy of students, *Vernonia* reasonably analogized school athletes to "adults who choose to participate in a closely regulated industry." Industries fall within the closely regulated category when the nature of their activities requires substantial government oversight. Interscholastic athletics similarly require close safety and health regulation; a school's choir, band, and academic team do not.

In short, *Vernonia* applied, it did not repudiate, the principle that "the legality of a search of a student should depend simply on the reasonableness, *under all the circumstances,* of the search." Enrollment in a public school, and election to participate in school activities beyond the bare minimum that the curriculum requires, are indeed factors relevant to reasonableness, but they do not on their own justify intrusive, suspicionless searches. *Vernonia,* accordingly, did not rest upon these factors; instead, the Court performed what today's majority aptly describes as a "fact-specific balancing." Balancing of that order, applied to the facts now before the Court, should yield a result other than the one the Court announces today.

B

*Vernonia* initially considered "the nature of the privacy interest upon which the search [there] at issue intrude[d]." The Court emphasized that student athletes' expectations of privacy are necessarily attenuated:

> Legitimate privacy expectations are even less with regard to student athletes. School sports are not for the bashful. They require "suiting up" before each practice or event, and showering and changing afterwards. Public school locker rooms, the usual sites for these activities, are not notable for the privacy they afford. The locker rooms in Vernonia are typical: No individual dressing rooms are provided; shower heads are lined up along a wall, unseparated by any sort of partition or curtain; not even all the toilet stalls have doors.... [T]here is an element of communal undress inherent in athletic participation.

Competitive extracurricular activities other than athletics, however, serve students of all manners: the modest and shy along with the bold and uninhibited. Activities of the kind plaintiff-respondent Lindsay Earls pursued—choir, show choir, marching band, and academic team—afford opportunities to gain self-assurance, to "come to know faculty members in a less formal setting than the typical classroom," and to acquire "positive social supports and networks [that] play a critical role in periods of heightened stress."

On "occasional out-of-town trips," students like Lindsay Earls "must sleep together in communal settings and use communal bathrooms." But those situations are hardly equivalent to the routine communal undress associated with athletics; the School District itself admits that when such trips occur, "public-like restroom facilities," which presumably include enclosed stalls, are ordinarily available for changing, and that "more modest students" find other ways to maintain their privacy.

After describing school athletes' reduced expectation of privacy, the *Vernonia* Court turned to "the character of the intrusion ... complained of." Observing that students produce urine samples in a bathroom stall with a coach or teacher outside, *Vernonia* typed the privacy interests compromised by the process of obtaining samples "negligible." As to the required pretest disclosure of prescription medications taken, the Court assumed that "the School District would have permitted [a student] to provide the requested information in a confidential manner—for example, in a sealed envelope delivered to the testing lab." On that assumption, the Court concluded that Vernonia's athletes faced no significant invasion of privacy.

In this case, however, Lindsay Earls and her parents allege that the School District handled personal information collected under the policy carelessly, with little regard for its confidentiality. Information about students' prescription drug use, they assert, was routinely viewed by Lindsay's choir teacher, who left files containing the information unlocked and unsealed, where others, including students, could see them; and test results were given out to all activity sponsors whether or not they had a clear "need to know." ...

Finally, the "nature and immediacy of the governmental concern" faced by the Vernonia School District dwarfed that confronting Tecumseh administrators. Vernonia initiated its drug testing policy in response to an alarming situation: "[A] large segment of the student body, particularly those involved in interscholastic athletics, was in a state of rebellion ... fueled by alcohol and drug abuse as well as the student[s'] misperceptions about the drug culture." Tecumseh, by contrast, repeatedly reported to the Federal Government during the period leading up to the adoption of the policy that "types of drugs [other than alcohol and tobacco] including controlled dangerous substances, are present [in the schools] but have not identified themselves as major problems at this time." ...

Not only did the Vernonia and Tecumseh districts confront drug problems of distinctly different magnitudes, they also chose different solutions: Vernonia limited its policy to athletes; Tecumseh indiscriminately subjected to testing all participants in competitive extracurricular activities. Urging that "the safety interest furthered by drug testing is undoubtedly substantial for all children, athletes and nonathletes alike," the Court cuts out an element essential to the *Vernonia* judgment. Citing medical literature on the effects of combining illicit drug use with physical exertion, the *Vernonia* Court emphasized that "the particular drugs screened by [Vernonia's] Policy have been demonstrated to pose substantial physical risks to athletes." We have since confirmed that these special risks were necessary to our decision in *Vernonia*.

At the margins, of course, no policy of *random* drug testing is perfectly tailored to the harms it seeks to address. The School District cites the dangers faced by members of the band, who must "perform extremely precise routines with heavy equipment and instruments in close proximity to other students," and by Future Farmers of America, who "are required to individually control and restrain animals as large as 1500 pounds." For its part, the United States acknowledges that "the linebacker faces a greater risk of serious injury if he takes the field under the influence of drugs than the drummer in the halftime band," but parries that "the risk of injury to a student who is under the influence of drugs while playing golf, cross country, or volleyball (sports covered by the policy in *Vernonia*) is scarcely any greater than the risk of injury to a student ... handling a 1500-pound steer (as [Future Farmers of America] members do) or working with cutlery or other sharp instruments (as [Future Homemakers of America] members do)." One can demur to the Government's view of the risks drug use poses to golfers ... for golfers were surely as marginal among the linebackers, sprinters, and basketball players targeted for testing in Vernonia as steer-handlers are among the choristers, musicians, and academic-team members subject to urinalysis in Tecumseh. Notwithstanding nightmarish images of out-of-control flatware, livestock run amok, and colliding tubas disturbing the peace and quiet of Tecumseh, the great majority of students the School District seeks to test in truth are engaged in activities that are not safety sensitive to an unusual degree. There is a difference between imperfect tailoring and no tailoring at all....

Nationwide, students who participate in extracurricular activities are significantly less likely to develop substance abuse problems than are their less-involved peers. Even if students might be deterred from drug use in order to preserve their extracurricular eligibility, it is at least as likely that other students might forgo their extracurricular involvement in order to avoid detection of their drug use. Tecumseh's policy thus falls short doubly if deterrence is its aim: It invades the privacy of students who need deterrence least, and risks steering students at greatest risk for substance abuse away from extracurricular involvement that potentially may palliate drug problems.

To summarize, this case resembles *Vernonia* only in that the School Districts in both cases conditioned engagement in activities outside the obligatory curriculum on random subjection to urinalysis. The defining characteristics of the two programs, however, are entirely dissimilar. The Vernonia district sought to test a subpopulation of students distinguished by their reduced expectation of privacy, their special susceptibility to drug-related injury, and their heavy involvement with drug use. The Tecumseh district seeks to test a much larger population associated with none of these factors. It does so, moreover, without carefully safeguarding student confidentiality and without regard to the program's untoward effects. A program so sweeping is not sheltered by *Vernonia;* its unreasonable reach renders it impermissible under the Fourth Amendment....

For the reasons stated, I would affirm the judgment of the Tenth Circuit declaring the testing policy at issue unconstitutional.

---

EXERCISE 5.3. The four dissenters in *Earls* describe the majority decision as "perverse," because studies show that students in competitive extracurricular activities are *less* prone to use drugs than students who are not involved at school in this way. Does this point resonate with you? Would it make more sense to drug test students *not* involved in extracurriculars? Would this be constitutional? Is it less defensible because everyone must go to school (according to the truancy laws) but no one must participate in an extracurricular program?

EXERCISE 5.4. How effective is random drug testing in preventing, deterring, and detecting drug use among students? Divide the class into three groups—parents, students, and teachers—and act out a community discussion about how best to counteract drug use. Consider drug testing along with other options, such as education by physicians and health trainers, free drug treatment, peer counseling, and so on. What is your plan? Is it constitutional?

---

# The Crime of Hanging Out with Gang Members: "Loitering with No Apparent Purpose" in Chicago

In many American cities, teenaged gangs are a way of life, and this tradition goes back decades if not centuries. Gangs become especially important to youngsters when family structures break down. Many gangs get involved in criminal activity, such as trafficking in guns and drugs, and not a few gang members die in the shocking rounds of violence America witnesses when turf fights take place. To outsiders who live and work near gangs, their habits and practices can be utterly terrifying. Often times gangs congregate around public high schools, causing problems in the school environment.

Fear of violent gangs led the Chicago City Council to pass an ordinance in 1992 against "loitering" by "criminal street gang members." The Council defined loitering as "remaining in any one place with no apparent purpose." This strange and inscrutable wording provoked a lawsuit after more than 42,000 people were arrested in Chicago for violating the terms of the ordinance. In *City of Chicago v. Morales,* Morales claimed that the language of the antiloitering ordinance was legally "vague" in that it did not define specifically what conduct was forbidden and in that it invited arbitrary and discriminatory enforcement by the police. Criminal laws that suffer from such vagueness violate due process under the Fourteenth Amendment. The Supreme Court agreed and struck it down. Was this a boon for liberty and the Bill of Rights or for criminal gangs and disorder on the street?

----

## CITY OF CHICAGO
## v.
## MORALES

*Supreme Court of the United States*
Argued December 9, 1998.
Decided June 10, 1999.

Justice STEVENS announced the judgment of the Court and delivered the opinion of the Court with respect to Parts I, II, and V, and an opinion with respect to Parts III, IV, and VI, in which Justice SOUTER and Justice GINSBURG join.

In 1992, the Chicago City Council enacted the Gang Congregation Ordinance, which prohibits "criminal street gang members" from "loitering" with one another or with other persons in any public place. The question presented is whether the Supreme Court of Illinois correctly held that the ordinance violates the Due Process Clause of the Fourteenth Amendment to the Federal Constitution.

I

Before the ordinance was adopted, the city council's Committee on Police and Fire conducted hearings to explore the problems created by the city's street gangs, and more particularly, the consequences of public loitering by gang members. . . .

The council found that a continuing increase in criminal street gang activity was largely responsible for the city's rising murder rate, as well as an escalation of violent and drug related crimes. It noted that in many neighborhoods throughout the city, "the burgeoning presence of street gang members in public places has intimidated many law abiding citizens." Furthermore, the council stated that gang members "establish control over identifiable areas . . . by loitering in those areas and intimidating others from entering those areas; and . . . [m]embers of criminal street gangs avoid arrest by committing no offense punishable under existing laws when they know the police are present. . . ." It further found that "loitering in public places by criminal street gang members creates a justifiable fear for the safety of persons and property in the area" and that "[a]ggressive action is necessary to preserve the city's streets and other public places so that the public may use such places without fear." Moreover, the council concluded that the city "has an interest in discouraging all persons from loitering in public places with criminal gang members."

The ordinance creates a criminal offense punishable by a fine of up to $500, imprisonment for not more than six months, and a requirement to perform up to 120 hours of community service. Commission of the offense involves four predicates. First, the police officer must reasonably believe that at least one of the two or more persons present in a "public place" is a "criminal street gang membe[r]." Second, the persons must be "loitering," which the ordinance defines as "remain[ing] in any one place with no apparent purpose." Third, the officer must then order "all" of the persons to disperse and remove themselves "from the area." Fourth, a person must disobey the officer's order. If any person, whether a gang member or not, disobeys the officer's order, that person is guilty of violating the ordinance.

Two months after the ordinance was adopted, the Chicago Police Department promulgated General Order 92-4 to provide guidelines to govern its enforcement. That order purported to establish limitations on the enforcement discretion of police officers "to ensure that the anti-gang loitering ordinance is not enforced in an arbitrary or discriminatory way." The limitations confine the authority to arrest gang members who violate the ordinance to sworn "members of the Gang Crime Section" and certain other designated officers, and establish detailed criteria for defining street gangs and membership in such gangs. In addition, the order directs district commanders to "designate areas in which the presence of gang members has a demonstrable effect on the activities of law abiding persons in the surrounding community," and provides that the ordinance "will be enforced only within the designated areas."

## II

During the three years of its enforcement, the police issued over 89,000 dispersal orders and arrested over 42,000 people for violating the ordinance....

This ordinance, for reasons that are not explained in the findings of the city council, requires no harmful purpose and applies to nongang members as well as suspected gang members. It applies to everyone in the city who may remain in one place with one suspected gang member as long as their purpose is not apparent to an officer observing them. Friends, relatives, teachers, counselors, or even total strangers might unwittingly engage in forbidden loitering if they happen to engage in idle conversation with a gang member.

Ironically, the definition of loitering in the Chicago ordinance not only extends its scope to encompass harmless conduct, but also has the perverse consequence of excluding from its coverage much of the intimidating conduct that motivated its enactment. As the city council's findings demonstrate, the most harmful gang loitering is motivated either by an apparent purpose to publicize the gang's dominance of certain territory, thereby intimidating nonmembers, or by an equally apparent purpose to conceal ongoing commerce in illegal drugs.... [W]e assume that the ordinance means what it says and that it has no application to loiterers whose purpose is apparent. The relative importance of its application to harmless loitering is magnified by its inapplicability to loitering that has an obviously threatening or illicit purpose....

## VI

... [T]he ordinance does not provide sufficiently specific limits on the enforcement discretion of the police "to meet constitutional standards for definiteness and clarity." We recognize the serious and difficult problems testified to by the citizens of Chicago that led to the enactment of this ordinance. "We are mindful that the preservation of liberty depends in part on the maintenance of social order." However, in this instance the city has enacted an ordinance that affords too much discretion to the police and too little notice to citizens who wish to use the public streets.

Accordingly, the judgment of the Supreme Court of Illinois is

*Affirmed. . . .*

Justice THOMAS, with whom THE CHIEF JUSTICE and Justice SCALIA join, dissenting.

The duly elected members of the Chicago City Council enacted the ordinance at issue as part of a larger effort to prevent gangs from establishing dominion over the public streets. By invalidating Chicago's ordinance, I fear that the Court has unnecessarily sentenced law-abiding citizens to lives of terror and misery. The ordinance is not vague. . . . Nor does it violate the Due Process Clause. The asserted "freedom to loiter for innocent purposes," is in no way "deeply rooted in this Nation's history and tradition." I dissent. . . .

At the outset, it is important to note that the ordinance does not criminalize loitering *per se.* Rather, it penalizes loiterers' failure to obey a police officer's order to move along. A majority of the Court believes that this scheme vests too much discretion in police officers. Nothing could be further from the truth. Far from according officers too much discretion, the ordinance merely enables police officers to fulfill one of their traditional functions. Police officers are not, and have never been, simply enforcers of the criminal law. They wear other hats—importantly, they have long been vested with the responsibility for preserving the public peace. Nor is the idea that the police are also *peace officers* simply a quaint anachronism. In most American jurisdictions, police officers continue to be obligated, by law, to maintain the public peace. . . .

In order to perform their peacekeeping responsibilities satisfactorily, the police inevitably must exercise discretion. Indeed, by empowering them to act as peace officers, the law assumes that the police will exercise that discretion responsibly and with sound judgment. That is not to say that the law should not provide objective guidelines for the police, but simply that it cannot rigidly constrain their every action. By directing a police officer not to issue a dispersal order unless he "observes a person whom he reasonably believes to be a criminal street gang member loitering in any public place," Chicago's ordinance strikes an appropriate balance between those two extremes. Just as we trust officers to rely on their experience and expertise in order to make spur-of-the-moment determinations about amorphous legal standards such as "probable cause" and "reasonable suspicion," so we must trust them to determine whether a group of loiterers contains individuals (in this case members of criminal street gangs) whom the city has determined threaten the public peace. . . .

In concluding that the ordinance adequately channels police discretion, I do not suggest that a police officer enforcing the Gang Congregation Ordinance will never make a mistake. Nor do I overlook the *possibility* that a police officer, acting in bad faith, might enforce the ordinance in an arbitrary or discriminatory way. But our decisions should not turn on the proposition that such an event will be anything but rare. Instances of arbitrary or discriminatory enforcement of the ordinance, like any other law, are best addressed when (and if) they arise, rather than prophylactically through the disfavored mechanism of a facial challenge on vagueness grounds. . . .

The plurality's conclusion that the ordinance "fails to give the ordinary citizen adequate notice of what is forbidden and what is permitted," is similarly untenable. There is nothing "vague" about an order to disperse. While "we can never expect mathematical certainty from our language," it is safe to assume that the vast majority of people who are ordered by the police to "disperse and remove themselves from the area" will have little difficulty understanding how to comply. . . .

Today, the Court focuses extensively on the "rights" of gang members and their companions. It can safely do so—the people who will have to live with the consequences of today's opinion do not live in our neighborhoods. Rather, the people who will suffer from our lofty pronouncements are people like Ms. Susan Mary Jackson; people who have seen their neighborhoods literally destroyed by gangs and violence and drugs. They are good, decent people who must struggle to overcome their desperate situation, against all odds, in order to raise their families, earn a living, and remain good citizens. As one resident described: "There is only about maybe one or two percent of the people in the city causing these problems maybe, but it's keeping 98 percent of us in our houses and off the streets and afraid to shop." By focusing exclusively on the imagined "rights" of the two percent, the Court today has denied our most vulnerable citizens the very thing that Justice STEVENS, elevates above all else—the "freedom of movement." And that is a shame. I respectfully dissent.

---

EXERCISE 5.5. The majority in *Morales* is eager to constrain the discretion of the police to order people to move from place to place in public. The dissenters are just as eager to empower the police to keep "public order" by clearing the streets. Do you think the police should have the power to tell people where to stand or congregate in public if no crime is being committed? Do you think most young people have positive or negative attitudes about the police? Why?

EXERCISE 5.6. Do citizens have a constitutional right to "hang out" in public places? Must there be an "apparent purpose"? (What if the "apparent purpose" is a criminal one, as the majority suggests?)

EXERCISE 5.7. Laws that are found to be "void for vagueness" are written in too obscure and confusing a way to give people actual notice of what is criminal activity and what is innocent activity. We say that vague laws violate due process because they [1] fail to give people proper notice of what they cannot do; and [2] invite arbitrary and discriminatory enforcement by the police. Which of the following prohibitions seem to be overly vague—and therefore unconstitutional—to you? Why?

1. "Students shall not loiter near school premises after hours in such a way as to disturb the neighbors."
2. "Only a reasonable number of students shall enter a convenience store at any one time."
3. "No more than one other person under the age of 18 may ride in a car driven by a person under the age of 18."
4. "No loud talking on the bus."
5. "It is a violation of the school's conduct code to do another student's homework for him or her, although it is not an offense to help another student understand the concepts."

---

**Read On**

Arbetman, Lee, and Edward O'Brien. *Street Law.* St. Paul, Minn.: West Educational Publishing, 1999.

Cole, David. *No Equal Justice: Race and Class in the American Criminal Justice System.* New York: New Press, 1999.

LaFave, Wayne R. *Search and Seizure.* 2d ed. St. Paul, Minn.: West Publishing, 1987.

# 6 DISCIPLINE AND PUNISHMENT: DUE PROCESS AND THE EIGHTH AMENDMENT

"[N]or shall any State deprive any person of life, liberty, or property, without due process of law...."
THE FOURTEENTH AMENDMENT

"Excessive bail shall not be required, nor excessive fines imposed, nor cruel and unusual punishment inflicted."
THE EIGHTH AMENDMENT

When students are disciplined for misbehaving at school, school authorities need not bring them to court to suspend or even expel them. Disciplinary sanctions like these are deemed civil, not criminal, in nature. Therefore, the school system can set up its own process to investigate, examine, and dispose of cases of student misconduct. But what kind of process *is* due to a student in trouble at school? Can a school suspend or expel students without telling them why or giving them a chance to explain their side of the story? Are there any kinds of discipline so severe that they violate the Eighth Amendment's ban on cruel and unusual punishment? We take up these questions here.

## POINTS TO PONDER

***Should procedural due process rights and Eighth Amendment protections against cruel and unusual punishment be extended to public school students?***

- What procedural rights to be heard do students have when facing suspension and other forms of discipline by school authorities?
- Should schoolteachers be allowed to use physical force to discipline students?

# Due Process

When school officials want to suspend students from school for several days or weeks, should the students first get a fair hearing in which they have an opportunity to tell their side of the story?

The opportunity to be heard is the foundation of procedural due process. Generally, constitutional due process requires some sort of official proceeding and hearing before any part of the government may take action against any person. The hearings and trial required before a person can be convicted of a crime are examples of procedural due process.

The events in the following case, *Goss v. Lopez,* occurred in Columbus, Ohio, in 1971 during a period of unrest in American high schools over school policies that many African Americans and other racial minorities saw as discriminatory. The widespread in-school civil disobedience that gave rise to the *Goss* decision occurred after a series of dramatic and polarizing events. Columbus was beset by racial conflict. A few weeks before civil rights protests by African American students began, authorities at Central High School cancelled a student-organized Black History Week assembly because they objected to its themes and to certain speakers invited by the students. The anger of African American students grew after two were shot by whites on the evening of February 25, 1971. The next day protests at high schools and junior high schools led to summary discipline—that is, suspensions without any measure of due process. Principals believed that they had this authority and, indeed, had exercised it for decades.

Yet in the famous *In re Gault* (1967) case, the Supreme Court had found that minors charged with criminal conduct could not be declared juvenile delinquents by states unless they had been given basic due process protections in court. Although the Court found that minors do not enjoy all of the same protections that apply to adult criminal defendants, minors had a right to be represented by counsel, to be notified of the charges against them, to have an adversarial hearing, and, perhaps most controversially, to remain silent and not testify against themselves in accordance with the Fifth Amendment's ban on compulsory self-incrimination. Change was in the air, and many civil rights and civil liberties groups believed that, if some form of due process should apply to young people being criminally prosecuted, it should also apply to young people facing academic discipline.

In most of the incidents discussed in *Goss v. Lopez,* school officials suspended students without filing formal charges, without giving them an opportunity to be heard or to challenge the administrators' conclusions, and without submitting the cases to any consideration by neutral third parties.

The Court struck down the discipline in these cases, which mostly involved ten-day suspensions, finding that there must be a fair hearing before a student is suspended or otherwise disciplined. Note that a hearing before a principal is nothing like a trial: there is no right to be represented by a lawyer, to cross-examine witnesses, or to produce evidence. But the idea of some due process—any due process—for high school students was revolutionary at the time, as evidenced by the vigorous dissent in this 5–4 case. Dissenting Justice Powell, a former president of the Richmond School Board, complained about the Court's intervention into the realm of local education and the majority's dangerous permissiveness toward juvenile insubordination.

G O S S

v.

L O P E Z

*Supreme Court of the United States*
Argued Oct. 16, 1974.
Decided Jan. 22, 1975.

Justice WHITE delivered the opinion of the Court. . . .

The nine named [students], each of whom alleged that he or she had been suspended from public high school in Columbus for up to 10 days without a hearing . . . filed an action . . . against the Columbus Board of Education and various administrators of the CPSS [Columbus, Ohio, Public School System]. The complaint sought a declaration that § 3313.66 [of an Ohio Law] was unconstitutional in that it permitted public school administrators to deprive plaintiffs of their rights to an education without a hearing of any kind, in violation of the procedural due process component of the Fourteenth Amendment. It also sought to enjoin the public school officials from issuing future suspensions . . . and to require them to remove references to the past suspensions from the records of the students in question.

. . . [T]he suspensions arose out of a period of widespread student unrest in the CPSS during February and March 1971. Six of the named plaintiffs, Rudolph Sutton, Tyrone Washington, Susan Cooper, Deborah Fox, Clarence Byars, and Bruce Harris, were students at the Marion-Franklin High School and were each suspended for 10 days on account of disruptive or disobedient conduct committed in the presence of the school administrator who ordered the suspension. One of these, Tyrone Washington, was among a group of students demonstrating in the school auditorium while a class was being conducted there. He was ordered by the school principal to leave, refused to do so, and was suspended. Rudolph Sutton, in the presence of the principal, physically attacked a police officer who was attempting to remove Tyrone Washington from the auditorium. He was immediately suspended. The other four Marion-Franklin students were suspended for similar conduct. None was given a hearing to determine the operative facts underlying the suspension, but each, together with his or her parents, was offered the opportunity to attend a conference, subsequent to the effective date of the suspension, to discuss the student's future.

Two named plaintiffs, Dwight Lopez and Betty Crome, were students at the Central High School and McGuffey Junior High School, respectively. The former was suspended in connection with a disturbance in the lunchroom which involved some physical damage to school property. Lopez testified that at least 75 other students were suspended from his school on the same day. He also testified below that he was not a party to the destructive conduct but was instead an innocent bystander. Because no one from the school testified with regard to this incident, there is no evidence in the record indicating the official basis for concluding otherwise. Lopez never had a hearing.

Betty Crome was present at a demonstration at a high school other than the one she was attending. There she was arrested together with others, taken to the police station, and released without being formally charged. Before she went to school on the following day, she was notified that she had been suspended for a 10-day period. Because no one from the school testified with respect to this incident, the record does not disclose how the McGuffey Junior High School principal went about making the decision to suspend Crome, nor does it disclose on what information the decision was based. It is clear from the record that no hearing was ever held. . . .

## II

At the outset, [the school administrators] contend that because there is no constitutional right to an education at public expense, the Due Process Clause does not protect against expulsions from the public school system. This position misconceives the nature of the issue and is refuted by prior decisions. The Fourteenth Amendment forbids the State to deprive any person of life, liberty, or property without due process of law. . . .

Here, on the basis of state law, [the students] plainly had legitimate claims of entitlement to a public education. . . . It is true that § 3313.66 of the Code permits school principals to suspend students for up to 10 days; but suspensions may not be imposed without any grounds whatsoever. All of the schools had their own rules specifying the grounds for expulsion or suspension. Having chosen to extend the right to an education to people of appellees' class generally, Ohio may not withdraw that right on grounds of misconduct, absent fundamentally fair procedures to determine whether the misconduct has occurred.

. . . "The Fourteenth Amendment, as now applied to the States, protects the citizen against the State itself and all of its creatures—Boards of Education not excepted." . . . [T]he State is constrained to recognize a student's legitimate entitlement to a public education as a property interest which is protected by the Due Process Clause and which may not be taken away for misconduct without adherence to the minimum procedures required by that Clause.

The Due Process Clause also forbids arbitrary deprivations of liberty. "Where a person's good name, reputation, honor, or integrity is at stake because of what the government is doing to him," the minimal requirements of the Clause must be satisfied. School authorities here suspended appellees from school for periods of up to 10 days based on charges of misconduct. If sustained and recorded, those charges could seriously damage the students' standing with their fellow pupils and their teachers as well as interfere with later opportunities for higher education and employment. It is apparent that the claimed right of the State to determine unilaterally and without process whether that misconduct has occurred immediately collides with the requirements of the Constitution. . . .

A short suspension is, of course, a far milder deprivation than expulsion. But, "education is perhaps the most important function of state and local governments," and the total exclusion from the educational process for more than a trivial period, and certainly if the suspension is for 10 days, is a serious event in the life of the suspended child. Neither the property interest in educational benefits temporarily denied nor the liberty interest in reputation, which is also implicated, is so insubstantial that suspensions may constitutionally be imposed by any procedure the school chooses, no matter how arbitrary.

III

"Once it is determined that due process applies, the question remains what process is due.". . .

. . . "The fundamental requisite of due process is the opportunity to be heard," a right that "has little reality or worth unless one is informed that the matter is ending and can choose for himself whether to . . . contest." At the very minimum, therefore, students facing suspension and the consequent interference with a protected property interest must be given some kind of notice and afforded *some* kind of hearing. "Parties whose rights are to be affected are entitled to be heard; and in order that they may enjoy that right they must first be notified."

. . . The student's interest is to avoid unfair or mistaken exclusion from the educational process, with all of its unfortunate consequences. The Due Process Clause will not shield him from suspensions properly imposed, but it disserves both his interest and the interest of the State if his suspension is in fact unwarranted. The concern would be mostly academic if the disciplinary process were a totally accurate, unerring process, never mistaken and never unfair. Unfortunately, that is not the case, and no one suggests that it is. Disciplinarians, although proceeding in utmost good faith, frequently act on the reports and advice of others; and the controlling facts and the nature of the conduct under challenge are often disputed. . . .

The difficulty is that our schools are vast and complex. Some modicum of discipline and order is essential if the educational function is to be performed. Events calling for discipline are frequent occurrences and sometimes require immediate, effective action. Suspension is considered not only to be a necessary tool to maintain order but a valuable educational device. The prospect of imposing elaborate hearing requirements in every suspension case is viewed with great concern, and many school authorities may well prefer the untrammeled power to act unilaterally, unhampered by rules about notice and hearing. But it would be a strange disciplinary system in an educational institution if no communication was sought by the disciplinarian with the student in an effort to inform him of his dereliction and to let him tell his side of the story in order to make sure that an injustice is not done. "[F]airness can rarely be obtained by secret, one-sided determination of facts decisive of rights. . . ."

"Secrecy is not congenial to truth-seeking and self-righteousness gives too slender an assurance of rightness. No better instrument has been devised for arriving at truth than to give a person in jeopardy of serious loss notice of the case against him and opportunity to meet it."

. . . Students facing temporary suspension have interests qualifying for protection of the Due Process Clause, and due process requires, in connection with a suspension of 10 days or less, that the student be given oral or written notice of the charges against him and, if he denies them, an explanation of the evidence the authorities have and an opportunity to present his side of the story. . . .

. . . We hold only that, in being given an opportunity to explain his version of the facts at this discussion, the student first be told what he is accused of doing and what the basis of the accusation is. . . .

Justice POWELL, with whom The Chief Justice, Justice BLACKMUN, and Justice REHNQUIST join, dissenting. . . .

II

C

One of the more disturbing aspects of today's decision is its indiscriminate reliance upon the judiciary, and the adversary process, as the means of resolving many of the most routine problems arising in the classroom. In mandating due process procedures the Court misapprehends the reality of the normal teacher-pupil relationship. There is an ongoing relationship, one in which the teacher must occupy many roles—educator, adviser, friend, and, at times, parent-substitute. It is rarely adversary in nature except with respect to the chronically disruptive or insubordinate pupil whom the teacher must be free to discipline without frustrating formalities.

... We have relied for generations upon the experience, good faith and dedication of those who staff our public schools, and the nonadversary means of airing grievances that always have been available to pupils and their parents. One would have thought before today's opinion that this informal method of resolving differences was more compatible with the interests of all concerned than resort to any constitutionalized procedure, however blandly it may be defined by the Court.

### D

... Nor does the Court's due process "hearing" appear to provide significantly more protection than that already available. The Court holds only that the principal must listen to the student's "version of the events," either before suspension or thereafter—depending upon the circumstances. Such a truncated "hearing" is likely to be considerably less meaningful than the opportunities for correcting mistakes already available to students and parents.

In its rush to mandate a constitutional rule, the Court appears to give no weight to the practical manner in which suspension problems normally would be worked out under Ohio law. One must doubt, then, whether the constitutionalization of the student-teacher relationship, with all of its attendant doctrinal and practical difficulties, will assure in any meaningful sense greater protection than that already afforded under Ohio law.

### III

No one can foresee the ultimate frontiers of the new "thicket" the Court now enters. Today's ruling appears to sweep within the protected interest in education a multitude of discretionary decisions in the educational process. Teachers and other school authorities are required to make many decisions that may have serious consequences for the pupil. They must decide, for example, how to grade the student's work, whether a student passes or fails a course, whether he is to be promoted, whether he is required to take certain subjects, whether he may be excluded from interscholastic athletics or other extracurricular activities, whether he may be removed from one school and sent to another, whether he may be bused long distances when available schools are nearby, and whether he should be placed in a "general," "vocational," or "college-preparatory" track.

In these and many similar situations claims of impairment of one's educational entitlement identical in principle to those before the Court today can be asserted with equal or greater justification. Likewise, in many of these situations, the pupil can advance the same types of speculative and subjective injury given critical weight in this case. The District Court, relying upon generalized opinion evidence, concluded that a suspended student may suffer psychological injury in one or more of the ways set forth in the margin below. The Court appears to adopt this rationale.

It hardly need be said that if a student, as a result of a day's suspension, suffers "a blow" to his "self esteem," "feels powerless," views "teachers with resentment," or feels "stigmatized by his teachers," identical psychological harms will flow from many other routine and necessary school decisions. The student who is given a failing grade, who is not promoted, who is excluded from certain extracurricular activities, who is assigned to a school reserved for children of less than average ability, or who is placed in the "vocational" rather than the "college preparatory" track, is unlikely to suffer any less psychological injury than if he were suspended for a day for a relatively minor infraction.

If, as seems apparent, the Court will now require due process procedures whenever such routine school decisions are challenged, the impact upon public education will be serious indeed. The discretion and judgment of federal courts across the land often will be substituted for that of the 50 state legislatures, the 14,000 school boards, and the 2,000,000 teachers who heretofore have been responsible for the administration of the American public school system. If the Court perceives a rational and analytically sound distinction between the discretionary decision by school authorities to suspend a pupil for a brief period, and the types of discretionary school decisions described above, it would be prudent to articulate it in today's opinion. Otherwise, the federal courts should prepare themselves for a vast new role in society.

## IV

Not so long ago, state deprivations of the most significant forms of state largesse were not thought to require due process protection on the ground that the deprivation resulted only in the loss of a state-provided "benefit." In recent years the Court, wisely in my view, has rejected the "wooden distinction between 'rights' and 'privileges,'" and looked instead to the significance of the state-created or state-enforced right and to the substantiality of the alleged deprivation. Today's opinion appears to abandon this reasonable approach by holding in effect that government infringement of any interest to which a person is entitled, no matter what the interest or how inconsequential the infringement, requires constitutional protection. As it is difficult to think of any less consequential infringement than suspension of a junior high school student for a single day, it is equally difficult to perceive any principled limit to the new reach of procedural due process.

---

EXERCISE 6.1. In Justice Powell's dissenting opinion, he suggests that a disciplinary suspension from school is no big deal. It "leaves no scars" and "affects no reputations." He even suggests that "it often may be viewed by the young as a badge of some distinction and a welcome holiday." Do you agree? Is suspension so commonplace and desirable that a school's decision to suspend should trigger no constitutional protections for students? Debate Justice Powell's position.

EXERCISE 6.2. What are the stages of the disciplinary process at your school? Are there published rules available from the school or the school board? Do you think that these rules comply with the (rather minimal) requirements of *Goss v. Lopez*? (Note that schools can give more protection than what is suggested by *Goss*, but not less.) Draft your own set of ideal rules for disciplinary proceedings in school. Would you give students more rights or fewer rights than they have now? Would you allow the testimony of witnesses? Opening and closing statements? The opportunity to open the hearing to the public and the media? Should students be involved in the process as judges, prosecutors, or defenders? Should the principal decide on the final action or should a panel of teachers and/or administrators and students make that decision? Compare your rules with those of your classmates.

EXERCISE 6.3. If you were suspended for ten days, how would you react? How would your parents and friends react? What would you do with your days during that time? Make a one-page schedule of how you would spend your time. Could you make productive use of your time away from school?

# Corporal Punishment

The Eighth Amendment protects citizens against cruel and unusual punishment. This right primarily comes into play when someone convicted of a crime claims that his or her punishment is exceptionally painful, disproportionate, or outrageous.

In the following case, students who were paddled on the buttocks multiple times by their teachers asserted that they had been subjected to cruel and unusual punishment. The Supreme Court disagreed. It found that the Eighth Amendment ban on cruel and unusual punishment does not apply to the application of corporal punishment in schools. Why not?

## INGRAHAM

v.

## WRIGHT

*Supreme Court of the United States*
Argued Nov. 2–3, 1976.
Decided April 19, 1977.

Justice POWELL delivered the opinion of the Court.

This case presents [a question] concerning the use of corporal punishment in public schools: ... whether the paddling of students as a means of maintaining school discipline constitutes cruel and unusual punishment in violation of the Eighth Amendment.

I

... In the 1970–1971 school year many of the 237 schools in Dade County used corporal punishment as a means of maintaining discipline pursuant to Florida legislation [Fla. Stat. Ann. §232.27 (1961)] and a local School Board regulation [Dade County School Board policy 5144].

The statute then in effect authorized limited corporal punishment by negative inference, proscribing punishment which was "degrading or unduly severe" or which was inflicted without prior consultation with the principal or the teacher in charge of the school. The regulation ... contained explicit directions and limitations. The authorized punishment consisted of paddling the recalcitrant student on the buttocks with a flat wooden paddle measuring less than two feet long, three

Willie Wright, shown here in April 1977, administered paddling to the rear ends of students in a Florida public school. The Court ruled that such corporal punishment was not "cruel and unusual" within the meaning of the Eighth Amendment.

Summery

Partly cloudy with highs in the 80s and lows in the 70s. Winds 15 to 29 m.p.h. (Details, Page 2A.)

TUESDAY'S TEMPERATURES

# The Miami Herald

Wednesday, April 20, 1977    *Florida's Complete Newspaper*
A Latin America Edition Is Published Daily

86 Pages

Final Edition

15 Cents

Newsstand price higher in air delivery cities

87th Year — No. 141

## *Corporal Punishment Not 'Cruel and Unusual'*

# High Court OKs Paddling

to four inches wide, and about one-half inch thick. The normal punishment was limited to one to five "licks" or blows with the paddle and resulted in no apparent physical injury to the student. School authorities viewed corporal punishment as a less drastic means of discipline than suspension or expulsion. Contrary to the procedural requirements of the statute and regulation, teachers often paddled students on their own authority without first consulting the principal.

... The evidence, consisting mainly of the testimony of 16 students, suggests that the regime at Drew [High School] was exceptionally harsh. The testimony of Ingraham and Andrews, in support of their individual claims for damages, is illustrative. Because he was slow to respond to his teacher's instructions, Ingraham was subjected to more than 20 licks with a paddle while being held over a table in the principal's office. The paddling was so severe that he suffered a hematoma requiring medical attention and keeping him out of school for several days. Andrews was paddled several times for minor infractions. On two occasions he was struck on his arms, once depriving him of the full use of his arm for a week....

II

... We ... begin by examining the way in which our traditions and our laws have responded to the use of corporal punishment in public schools.

The use of corporal punishment in this country as a means of disciplining schoolchildren dates back to the colonial period.... Despite the general abandonment of corporal punishment as a means of punishing criminal offenders, the practice continues to play a role in the public education of school children in most parts of the country.

At common law a single principle has governed the use of corporal punishment since before the American Revolution: Teachers may impose reasonable but not excessive force to discipline a child.... The basic doctrine has not changed. The prevalent rule in this country today privileges such force as a teacher or administrator "reasonably believes to be necessary for [the child's] proper control, training, or education." To the extent that the force is excessive or unreasonable, the educator in virtually all States is subject to possible civil and criminal liability.

... All of the circumstances are to be taken into account in determining whether the punishment is reasonable in a particular case. Among the most important considerations are the seriousness of the offense, the attitude and past behavior of the child, the nature and severity of the punishment, the age and strength of the child, and the availability of less severe but equally effective means of discipline.

Of the 23 States that have addressed the problem through legislation, 21 have authorized the moderate use of corporal punishment in public schools.... Only two States, Massachusetts and New Jersey, have prohibited all corporal punishment in their public schools.

Against this background of historical and contemporary approval of reasonable corporal punishment, we turn to the constitutional questions before us.

### III

The Eighth Amendment provides: "Excessive bail shall not be required, nor excessive fines imposed, nor cruel and unusual punishments inflicted." ... An examination of the history of the Amendment and the decisions of this Court construing the proscription against cruel and unusual punishment confirms that it was designed to protect those convicted of crimes. We adhere to this longstanding limitation and hold that the Eighth Amendment does not apply to the paddling of children as a means of maintaining discipline in public schools....

### B

... It is not surprising to find that every decision of this Court considering whether a punishment is "cruel and unusual" within the meaning of the Eighth and Fourteenth Amendments has dealt with a criminal punishment....

### C

Petitioners ... urge nonetheless that the prohibition should be extended to ban the paddling of schoolchildren. Observing that the Framers of the Eighth Amendment could not have envisioned our present system of public and compulsory education, with its opportunities for noncriminal punishments, petitioners contend that extension of the prohibition against cruel punishments is necessary lest we afford greater protection to criminals than to schoolchildren. It would be anomalous, they say, if schoolchildren could be beaten without constitutional redress, while hardened criminals suffering the same beatings at the hands of their jailers might have a valid claim under the Eighth Amendment. Whatever force this logic may have in other settings, we find it an inadequate basis for wrenching the Eighth Amendment from its historical context and extending it to traditional disciplinary practices in the public schools.

The prisoner and the schoolchild stand in wholly different circumstances, separated by the harsh facts of criminal conviction and incarceration. The prisoner's conviction entitles the State to

**JUSTICE LEWIS F. POWELL JR.** (1907–1998) was born in a suburb of Norfolk, Virginia. He went to Washington and Lee College for both undergraduate and law school study and also took a year at Harvard Law School. After service in World War II as an air force intelligence officer, he launched a career in corporate law in Virginia and became increasingly active in local affairs in Richmond. As chairman of the Richmond School Board between 1952 and 1961, he defended racial segregation in the schools during a time when much of the South had declared a policy of "massive resistance" to *Brown v. Board of Education.* President Richard Nixon appointed Powell to the Supreme Court in 1971. He retired in 1987.

HIGHLIGHTS

➤  Powell served in North Africa during World War II and was decorated with the Legion of Merit, the Bronze Star, and the French Croix de Guerre. He was instrumental in cracking the Nazis' secret ULTRA code.

➤  As a lawyer, Powell was a member of the board of directors of eleven large corporations, including Philip Morris.

classify him as a "criminal," and his incarceration deprives him of the freedom "to be with family and friends and to form the other enduring attachments of normal life." Prison brutality, as the Court of Appeals observed in this case, is "part of the total punishment to which the individual is being subjected for his crime and, as such, is a proper subject for Eighth Amendment scrutiny." Even so, the protection afforded by the Eighth Amendment is limited. After incarceration, only the "unnecessary and wanton infliction of pain," constitutes cruel and unusual punishment forbidden by the Eighth Amendment.

The schoolchild has little need for the protection of the Eighth Amendment. Though attendance may not always be voluntary, the public school remains an open institution. Except perhaps when very young, the child is not physically restrained from leaving school during school hours; and at the end of the school day, the child is invariably free to return home. Even while at school, the child brings with him the support of family and friends and is rarely apart from teachers and other pupils who may witness and protest any instances of mistreatment.

The openness of the public school and its supervision by the community afford significant safeguards against the kinds of abuses from which the Eighth Amendment protects the prisoner. In virtually every community where corporal punishment is permitted in the schools, these safeguards are reinforced by the legal constraints of the common law. Public school teachers and administrators are privileged at common law to inflict only such corporal punishment as is reasonably necessary for the proper education and discipline of the child; any punishment going beyond the privilege may result in both civil and criminal liability.

We conclude that when public school teachers or administrators impose disciplinary corporal punishment, the Eighth Amendment is inapplicable.

*Affirmed.*

Justice WHITE, with whom Justice BRENNAN, Justice MARSHALL, and Justice STEVENS join, dissenting.

Today the Court holds that corporal punishment in public schools, no matter how severe, can never be the subject of the protections afforded by the Eighth Amendment.

## I

## A

The Eighth Amendment places a flat prohibition against the infliction of "cruel and unusual punishments." This reflects a societal judgment that there are some punishments that are so barbaric and inhumane that we will not permit them to be imposed on anyone, no matter how opprobrious the offense. If there are some punishments that are so barbaric that they may not be imposed for the commission of crimes, designated by our social system as the most thoroughly reprehensible acts an individual can commit, then . . . similar punishments may not be imposed on persons for less culpable acts, such as breaches of school discipline. Thus, if it is constitutionally impermissible to cut off someone's ear for the commission of murder, it must be unconstitutional to cut off a child's ear for being late to class. Although there were no ears cut off in this case, the record reveals beatings so severe that if they were inflicted on a hardened criminal for the commission of a serious crime, they might not pass constitutional muster.

Nevertheless, the majority holds that the Eighth Amendment "was designed to protect [only] those convicted of crimes," relying on a vague and inconclusive recitation of the history of the Amendment. . . . Certainly the fact that the Framers did not choose to insert the word "criminal" into the language of the Eighth Amendment is strong evidence that the Amendment was designed to prohibit all inhumane or barbaric punishments, no matter what the nature of the offense for which the punishment is imposed.

No one can deny that spanking of schoolchildren is "punishment" under any reasonable reading of the word, for the similarities between spanking in public schools and other forms of punishment are too obvious to ignore. Like other forms of punishment, spanking of schoolchildren involves an institutionalized response to the violation of some official rule or regulation proscribing certain conduct and is imposed for the purpose of rehabilitating the offender, deterring the offender and others like him from committing the violation in the future, and inflicting some measure of social retribution for the harm that has been done. . . .

## C

. . . The essence of the majority's argument is that schoolchildren do not need Eighth Amendment protection because corporal punishment is less subject to abuse in the public schools than it is in the prison system. However, it cannot be reasonably suggested that just because cruel and unusual punishments may occur less frequently under public scrutiny, they will not occur at all. The mere fact that a public flogging or a public execution would be available for all to see would not render the punishment constitutional if it were otherwise impermissible. Similarly, the majority would not suggest that a prisoner who is placed in a minimum-security prison and permitted to go home to his family on the weekends should be any less entitled to Eighth Amendment protections than his counterpart in a maximum-security prison. In short, if a punishment is so barbaric and inhumane that it goes beyond the tolerance of a civilized society, its openness to public scrutiny should have nothing to do with its constitutional validity.

Nor is it an adequate answer that schoolchildren may have other state and constitutional remedies available to them. Even assuming that the remedies available to public school students are adequate under Florida law, the availability of state remedies has never been determinative of the coverage or of the protections afforded by the Eighth Amendment. The reason is obvious. The fact that a person may have a state-law cause of action against a public official who tortures him with a thumbscrew for the commission of an antisocial act has nothing to do with the fact that such official conduct is cruel and unusual punishment prohibited by the Eighth Amendment.

D

By holding that the Eighth Amendment protects only criminals, the majority adopts the view that one is entitled to the protections afforded by the Eighth Amendment only if he is punished for acts that are sufficiently opprobrious for society to make them "criminal."

The issue presented in this phase of the case is limited to whether corporal punishment in public schools can *ever* be prohibited by the Eighth Amendment. I am therefore not suggesting that spanking in the public schools is in every instance prohibited by the Eighth Amendment. My own view is that it is not. I only take issue with the extreme view of the majority that corporal punishment in public schools, no matter how barbaric, inhumane, or severe, is never limited by the Eighth Amendment. Where corporal punishment becomes so severe as to be unacceptable in a civilized society, I can see no reason that it should become any more acceptable just because it is inflicted on children in the public schools.

---

EXERCISE 6.4. Justice Powell, who had strong views about education, thought that students could not be compared with prisoners and schools could not be likened to prisons. Thus he found that the Eighth Amendment, which forbids "cruel and unusual punishment," should not apply to what happens to students in the school environment. But if we cannot define "corporal punishment" as a form of "punishment" for Eighth Amendment purposes, then what is it exactly? Is it a form of education? Justice Powell clearly thought that some kinds of corporal punishment could be fairly deemed "reasonably necessary for the proper education and discipline of the child." Does Justice White agree that punitive hitting can constitute part of a student's education? Do you?

EXERCISE 6.5. The Supreme Court has often said that the Eighth Amendment prohibits two kinds of government practices: those that were cruel and unusual when the Constitution was written, and those that offend the "evolving standards" of decency of the society. Do you think that the standards of American society have changed sufficiently in the last two decades such that corporal punishment today might violate the Eighth Amendment? Why or why not?

EXERCISE 6.6. Even though a specific action may not be unconstitutional, we can still say that it makes for *bad policy*. Does corporal punishment make for bad policy or good policy? Assume that the school board for your community asks you to draft a policy for teachers on the use of physical punishment in the classroom. Draft a policy on when, if ever, physical force or corporal punishment may be used against students in the classroom. (Remember that teachers and administrators sometimes act in self-defense and intervene to stop fights.) Present your policy to your classmates as if they were members of the school board, and give them the opportunity to ask questions.

---

# Corporal Punishment in the Aftermath of *Ingraham v. Wright*

*Ingraham v. Wright* was a huge disappointment to the opponents of corporal punishment in school, but they redoubled their efforts to ban the practice over the next two decades. At the time of the decision in 1977, only two states banned corporal punishment, but by 1998 twenty-five states banned corporal punishment outright, and even in those states that had not gotten rid of it, many counties and cities had adopted policies against the practice.

Furthermore, although *Ingraham* established that corporal punishment in schools does not violate the Eighth Amendment, a number of federal circuit courts have found that *excessive* physical force against students does violate their due process rights. In the 1980 case of *Hall v. Tawney,* the Fourth Circuit Court of Appeals allowed money damages to a seventh-grade student who had been beaten so severely with a thick rubber paddle that she had to receive emergency medical treatment and was hospitalized for ten days.

Similarly, the Tenth Circuit allowed for money damages in a civil rights lawsuit based on extreme corporal punishment in the 1987 case of *Garcia v. Miera.* The plaintiff in *Garcia,* a nine-year-old student, was held upside down by her ankles while the school principal beat her on the front of her legs with a paddle that was "split right down the middle, so it was two pieces, and when it hit it clapped and grabbed." After the paddling, the student's classroom teacher noticed blood coming through her clothes. The student's injuries left a permanent scar. Responding to complaints from the student's parents, the principal agreed not to spank the child again without first contacting her parents. But the student was again seriously injured a month later.

The Third Circuit, in the 1988 case of *Metzger v. Osbeck,* also allowed students to sue schools for injuries suffered in severe attacks by teachers. In *Metzger,* a teacher punished a student for using abusive language by choking the student while lifting him from the ground. The student lost consciousness and fell face down on a concrete floor suffering lip lacerations, a broken nose, broken teeth, and other injuries.

The courts have generally allowed students to recover money damages against schools where there is a severe injury and the force applied was wholly disproportionate to the underlying problem or misbehavior.

---

EXERCISE 6.7. Research how much violence there is in the schools in your community—among students and teachers or other employees—and then what sorts of things are being done to stop it. Based on your research and interviews, what strategies and policies can you suggest to reduce violence and "increase the peace" in your community?

EXERCISE 6.8. In states that still allow corporal punishment, the practice is often justified by virtue of the fact that the school is acting *in loco parentis*, in the place of the parents. Do you think that schools should therefore have to receive the written or oral authorization of the parents before hitting their children? Divide the class in half and debate such a proposal.

---

### Read On

Devine, John. *Maximum Security: The Culture of Violence in Inner-City Schools*. Chicago: University of Chicago Press, 1996.

Hyman, Irwin A. *Corporal Punishment in American Education: Readings in History, Practice, and Alternatives*. Philadelphia: Temple University Press, 1979.

Lantieri, Linda, and Janet Patti. *Waging Peace in Our Schools*. Boston: Beacon Press, 1998.

### For Further Information

Parents and Teachers Against Violence in Education (PTAVE), www.nospank.org

Keep Schools Safe Project, www.keepschoolssafe.org

# EQUAL PROTECTION: DRAWING LINES BY RACE, WEALTH, GENDER, CITIZENSHIP, AND SEXUAL ORIENTATION

7

"[N]or shall any State deprive any person of life, liberty, or property, without due process of law; nor deny to any person within its jurisdiction the equal protection of the laws." THE FOURTEENTH AMENDMENT

All laws draw lines. For example, we allow people age sixteen and older to drive cars, but we make it illegal for those fifteen and younger. The courts accept this classification even though some fifteen-and-a-half-year-olds might make excellent drivers and some seventeen-year-olds are poor drivers. The line drawn at age sixteen is thought to be reasonable, and the courts do not see classifications based on age as inherently suspicious or discriminatory.

Similarly, the vast majority of counties and municipalities allow people to register to vote in local elections or enroll their children in public school only if they live within the borders of the jurisdiction. The Supreme Court views residency as a reasonable qualification for voting and does not approach residency requirements as demanding any special government justification beyond a "rational basis."

But the Supreme Court's deference to government classifications falls away when those classifications are based on race or gender. The Fourteenth Amendment was added to the Constitution in 1868 as part of the post–Civil War effort to purge the Constitution of white supremacy and racism, and so the Court has made it clear that equal protection forbids the use of racial categorization to separate, demean, stigmatize, or disadvantage people. Although the framers of the Fourteenth Amendment did not intend it to protect women from discrimination, starting in the last quarter of the twentieth century the Court has taken the broad principle of equal protection and used it to strike down laws that treat women differently from men, barring some very good reason.

One kind of government line drawing that seems obviously legitimate, at least at first blush, is between U.S. citizens and noncitizens, whether they are permanent resident aliens, illegal aliens, or simply foreigners. However, in *Plyler v. Doe* (1982), the Supreme Court struck down a Texas law that denied a place in school to the children of illegal aliens. How does the Court arrive at this fascinating and controversial decision?

On the other hand, in the interesting 1979 case of *Ambach v. Norwick,* the Court upheld a New York state law forbidding schools to employ as teachers any permanent resident aliens who have the right to apply for full citizenship but decline to do so. Why does the Court reach a different conclusion in this case?

Finally, we will look at a case involving the Boy Scouts' decision to revoke the membership of a former Eagle Scout who publicly revealed his homosexuality. The New Jersey Supreme Court found that the Boy Scouts' exclusion of the young man violated the state's public accommodations law, which disallows discrimination on the basis of sexual orientation. But the Boy Scouts appealed to the Supreme Court, arguing that its members were a private expressive association and therefore had a right to decide with whom they would associate and on what grounds. The Supreme Court majority in this 5–4 decision found that the state of New Jersey had indeed violated the Boy Scouts' First Amendment rights by forcing them to associate with homosexuals.

**POINTS TO PONDER**

***How do the equal protection guarantees of the Fourteenth Amendment apply to students in public schools?***

- Are our schools today racially integrated? Do students have a right to attend integrated schools or just schools that are not formally segregated?
- Should public education be a fundamental right protected by the Constitution?
- Should states have to spend proportionately equal resources in local school districts?
- Should states be able to fund single-sex schools?
- Can states deny the children of undocumented workers—"illegal aliens"—the right to go to public school?
- Can states refuse to hire as public school teachers lawful resident aliens who are eligible to apply for United States citizenship but decline to do so?
- Can a state force private associations to accept gay members even if they want to express their opposition to homosexuality by excluding them?

# The Persistent Legacy of Slavery and Racism

Slavery was America's original sin. It was given the full force of law for centuries until the Civil War and the Thirteenth Amendment abolished it. Today, even though most Americans take pride in the diversity of our nation's population, we still grapple with the complicated legacies of racism and discrimination.

Children in African American and other minority communities have often been the victims of racial exclusion and violence. Yet the country has placed a large burden of hope on them to liberate America from the injustices of the past. *Brown v. Board of Education,* one of the most famous of the Supreme Court's twentieth-century rulings, deals with the rights of black schoolchildren not to be forced into segregated schools. The decision led to a period of intense struggle—and violence—in which children, especially African American children, were put on the front lines of the effort to create an integrated America.

Brown has become the central symbol of the nation's commitment to an interracial, integrated, and "color-blind" society. It marked a turning point for the Supreme Court, which historically has been a force for racial conservatism. For example, in 1857 the Court upheld the expansion of slavery in the infamous *Dred Scott* case and found that African Americans were not "persons" eligible to sue in federal court within the meaning of the Constitution. In 1896 the Court ruled in support of the Jim Crow doctrine of "separate but equal" in *Plessy v. Ferguson* by upholding racial segregation in public places and services. More than fifty years later the Court, in *Brown,* found that "in the field of public education the doctrine of 'separate but equal' has no place." The Court in 1954 ruled that "[s]eparate educational facilities are inherently unequal." Between 1896, when the Court found that the equal protection clause *allows* racially segregated public facilities, and 1954, when it found that the equal protection clause *disallows* racially segregated public facilities, the language of the Constitution did not change. So what changed the mind of the Court? Cultural attitudes? The war against fascism and Nazism? The emergence of the cold war? The stirrings of a civil rights movement? Why did the Supreme Court (with an entirely new membership) make a reversal in its reading of the Constitution? What does the reversal teach us about the nature of Supreme Court interpretation? Does it consist of science, logic, morality, rhetoric, emotion, politics, or some combination thereof?

---

### BROWN
### v.
### BOARD OF EDUCATION OF TOPEKA

*Supreme Court of the United States*
Argued Dec. 9, 1952.
Reargued Dec. 7–9, 1953.
Decided May 17, 1954.

Chief Justice WARREN delivered the opinion of the Court.

These cases come to us from the States of Kansas, South Carolina, Virginia, and Delaware.

In each of the cases, minors of the Negro race, through their legal representatives, seek the aid of the courts in obtaining admission to the public schools of their community on a nonsegregated basis. In each instance, they have been denied admission to schools attended by white children under laws requiring or permitting segregation according to race. This segregation was alleged to deprive the plaintiffs of the equal protection of the laws under the Fourteenth Amendment. [Segregation has been legally justified by] the so-called "separate but equal" doctrine announced by this Court in *Plessy v. Ferguson.* Under that doctrine, equality of treatment is accorded when the races are provided substantially equal facilities, even though these facilities be separate.

**JUSTICE HENRY BILLINGS BROWN** (1836–1913) authored the *Plessy v. Ferguson* opinion, which upheld the doctrine of "separate but equal." Brown was born into an affluent New England family and received his education at prep school, Yale University, and Harvard Law School. After a career as a marshal, United States Attorney, lawyer, and judge, Brown was appointed by President Benjamin Harrison to the Supreme Court in 1890. He served until 1906.

HIGHLIGHTS

➤ Justice Brown employed a substitute to avoid the draft during the Civil War.

➤ Late in his life, Justice Brown acknowledged that he had been naive to think that the Louisiana statute in *Plessy v. Ferguson* was not meant principally to keep African Americans out of white train cars.

The plaintiffs contend that segregated public schools are not "equal" and cannot be made "equal," and that hence they are deprived of the equal protection of the laws....

In the instant cases ... there are findings ... that the Negro and white schools involved have been equalized, or are being equalized, with respect to buildings, curricula, qualifications and salaries of teachers, and other "tangible" factors. Our decision, therefore, cannot turn on merely a comparison of these tangible factors in the Negro and white schools involved in each of the cases. We must look instead to the effect of segregation itself on public education.

In approaching this problem, we cannot turn the clock back to 1868 when the Amendment was adopted, or even to 1896 when *Plessy v. Ferguson* was written. We must consider public education in the light of its full development and its present place in American life throughout the Nation. Only in this way can it be determined if segregation in public schools deprives these plaintiffs of the equal protection of the laws.

Today, education is perhaps the most important function of state and local governments. Compulsory school attendance laws and the great expenditures for education both demonstrate our recognition of the importance of education to our democratic society. It is required in the performance of our most basic public responsibilities, even service in the armed forces. It is the very foundation of good citizenship. Today it is a principal instrument in awakening the child to cultural values, in preparing him for later professional training, and in helping him to adjust normally to his environment. In these days, it is doubtful that any child may reasonably be expected to succeed in life if he is denied the opportunity of an education. Such an opportunity, where the state has undertaken to provide it, is a right which must be made available to all on equal terms.

We come then to the question presented: Does segregation of children in public schools solely on the basis of race, even though the physical facilities and other "tangible" factors may be equal, deprive the children of the minority group of equal educational opportunities? We believe that it does.

Under the Jim Crow system of "separate but equal" racial segregation, African American children were segregated from whites and forced to go to underfunded schools with underpaid teachers and poor resources.

In *Sweatt v. Painter,* in finding that a segregated law school for Negroes could not provide them equal educational opportunities, this Court relied in large part on "those qualities which are incapable of objective measurement but which make for greatness in a law school." In *McLaurin v. Oklahoma State Regents,* the Court, in requiring that a Negro admitted to a white graduate school be treated like all other students, again resorted to intangible considerations: ". . . his ability to study, to engage in discussions and exchange views with other students, and, in general, to learn his profession." Such considerations apply with added force to children in grade and high schools. To separate them from others of similar age and qualifications solely because of their race generates a feeling of inferiority as to their status in the community that may affect their hearts and minds in a way unlikely ever to be undone. The effect of this separation on their educational opportunities was well stated by a finding in the Kansas case by a court which nevertheless felt compelled to rule against the Negro plaintiffs:

> Segregation of white and colored children in public schools has a detrimental effect upon the colored children. The impact is greater when it has the sanction of the law; for the policy of separating the races is usually interpreted as denoting the inferiority of the Negro group. A sense of inferiority affects the motivation of a child to learn. Segregation with the sanction of law, therefore, has a tendency to [retard] the educational and mental development of Negro children and to deprive them of some of the benefits they would receive in a racial[ly] integrated school system.

Whatever may have been the extent of psychological knowledge at the time of *Plessy v. Ferguson,* this finding is amply supported by modern authority. Any language in *Plessy v. Ferguson* contrary to this finding is rejected.

We conclude that in the field of public education the doctrine of "separate but equal" has no place. Separate educational facilities are inherently unequal. Therefore, we hold that the plaintiffs

**JUSTICE JOHN MARSHALL HARLAN** (1833–1911) disagreed with the Court majority in *Plessy v. Ferguson;* he wrote that the statute at issue "interfered with the personal freedom of citizens."

Justice Harlan was born in Boyle County, Kentucky. He studied nearby at Centre College and acquired his legal education from professors at Transylvania University. President Rutherford B. Hayes appointed him to the Supreme Court in 1877, where he remained until his death.

HIGHLIGHTS

➤ Harlan was named for then–chief justice John Marshall.

➤ Harlan opposed the secessionists during the Civil War, although he firmly believed in a slave owner's right to slaves as property.

➤ He also opposed the Emancipation Proclamation and Thirteenth Amendment, abolishing slavery.

➤ Harlan formed and fought with the 10th Kentucky Volunteers on the side of the Union during the Civil War.

➤ He was raised to defend slavery but came to abhor racists. He developed the metaphor of "color-blindness" to analyze the equal protection guarantee.

and others similarly situated for whom the actions have been brought are, by reason of the segregation complained of, deprived of the equal protection of the laws guaranteed by the Fourteenth Amendment.

... We have now announced that ... segregation is a denial of the equal protection of the laws.

EXERCISE 7.1. The *Brown* Court found segregation unconstitutional because it had such a negative effect on black children: "To separate them from others of similar age and qualifications solely because of their race generates a feeling of inferiority as to their status in the community that may affect their hearts and minds in a way unlikely ever to be undone." What do you think of this as the rationale for the Court's holding? Contrast it with the following hypothetical rationales that the Court might have used:

A. "To segregate white and black children solely because of their race generates a feeling of false inferiority in the black children and a feeling of false superiority in the white children that may affect their hearts and minds in a way unlikely ever to be undone."

B. "Segregation is a creation of white supremacy, which was invalidated by the Thirteenth Amendment's ban on slavery and the Fourteenth Amendment's guarantee of Equal Protection."

C. "The Constitution is color-blind, and so government may never take race into account for any purpose whatsoever."

D. "The premise of American democracy is freedom for all persons, but there is no freedom where the state segregates people on the basis of race."

EXERCISE 7.2. The Court in *Brown* seems to assume that all students are either black or white. Where do you suppose children who are neither "black" nor "white" fit into the pic-

Spottswood Bolling, shown here rejoicing with his mother, Sarah, was one of five Washington, D.C., youngsters to serve as plaintiffs in *Bolling v. Sharpe*, which struck down the congressionally authorized segregation of public schools in the District of Columbia.

ture? Do you think that the presence of millions of Hispanic, Asian American, and Native American children in the United States improves the prospects for good race relations? What about students who cannot be readily categorized or who refuse to be defined or classified by race? Hold a class debate on this proposition: "Students should never be forced by a school to assume a racial or ethnic identity."

Many people think that by allowing busing and limited affirmative action in education, the Court has followed through on the promise of *Brown*. Others, noting the Court's growing hostility to affirmative action and opposition to inter–school district remedies, think that the Court has taken up its former, passive role in the face of pervasive racism in society. Still others think that the Court should have no special commitment to racial integration and justice but should simply make sure that government is always "color-blind" in its policies. What do you think? Does the Court have a special responsibility to promote racial integration?

## Two Steps Forward, One Step Back: "Massive Resistance" and the Reaction to *Brown*

Although the *Brown* decision was met with jubilation in the African American community and among its civil rights allies in other racial groups, the decision set off a furious reaction among whites in the Deep South. Almost every elected official there—from governors to school board members—denounced the *Brown* decision and the Supreme Court. In Virginia, politicians and the white establishment declared a policy of "massive resistance" to federally sanctioned desegregation. Ku Klux Klan membership swelled across the South, and racist violence spread. Many cars featured bumper stickers that read: "Impeach Earl Warren."

**CHIEF JUSTICE EARL WARREN** (1891–1974) wrote the majority opinion in *Brown*. He was born to a working-class family in Los Angeles and labored on the railroads as a boy. He worked his way through college and law school at the University of California. He had served as a district attorney, state attorney general, and three-term governor when President Dwight Eisenhower appointed him to the Supreme Court in 1953. He retired in 1969.

HIGHLIGHTS

➣ Warren was the first governor of California to be elected three times. In one primary election, he won both the Republican and Democratic nominations.

➣ Justice Warren was chair of the commission that investigated the assassination of President John F. Kennedy, a commission that continues to be controversial today.

➣ As attorney general of California and a candidate for governor, Warren favored the internment and relocation of persons of Japanese ancestry on the West Coast during World War II. Yet he became a key force on the Court against racial discrimination and segregation. Justice Warren later called his decision to back the internment of Japanese Americans the major regret of his life.

In Arkansas white politicians swore they would never integrate. On September 2, 1957, Governor Orval Faubus declared that "blood will run in the streets" if black children tried to attend Central High School. He ordered the Arkansas National Guard to surround Central High to stop any attempt at integrating the student body. Elizabeth Eckford, an African American high school student at the time, was taunted and threatened when she tried to enter the school. Black students did not successfully integrate Central High School until the Supreme Court made it clear that the state had no power to stand in the way and President Dwight Eisenhower federalized the National Guard and ordered the troops to guarantee the safe passage of the students against the screaming mobs.

The following Supreme Court case determined that the defiance of government officials in Arkansas was unconstitutional, and that no state could exempt itself from the commands of equal protection and the supremacy clause, which makes the Constitution and federal laws supreme to state laws and power.

---

**COOPER**

**v.**

**AARON**

*Supreme Court of the United States*
Argued Sept. 11, 1958.
Decided Sept. 12, 1958.

[The school board of Little Rock, Arkansas, filed a petition to postpone desegregation plans of public schools due to "extreme public hostility." The district court granted the relief sought and the court of appeals reversed.]

Nine African American students leave the army station wagon that drove them to Central High School the morning of September 26, 1957. Paratroopers and two jeeps of the 101st airborne division form a tight cordon around the students as they enter the school.

Opinion of the Court by Chief Justice WARREN, Justice BLACK, Justice FRANKFURTER, Justice DOUGLAS, Justice BURTON, Justice CLARK, Justice HARLAN, Justice BRENNAN, and Justice WHITTAKER.

... We are urged to uphold a suspension of the Little Rock School Board's plan to do away with segregated public schools in Little Rock until state laws and efforts to upset and nullify our holding in *Brown v. Board of Education* have been further challenged and tested in the courts. We reject these contentions....

The constitutional rights of [the children] are not to be sacrificed or yielded to the violence and disorder which have followed upon the actions of the Governor and Legislature. As this Court said some 41 years ago in an unanimous opinion in a case involving another aspect of racial segregation: "It is urged that this proposed segregation will promote the public peace[,] ... this aim cannot be accomplished by laws or ordinances which deny rights created or protected by the Federal Constitution." Thus law and order are not here to be preserved by depriving the Negro children of their constitutional rights.

... The command of the Fourteenth Amendment is that no "State" shall deny to any person within its jurisdiction the equal protection of the laws.... "Whoever, by virtue of public position under a State government, ... denies or takes away the equal protection of the laws, violates the constitutional inhibition; and as he acts in the name and for the State, and is clothed with the State's power, his act is that of the State. This must be so, or the constitutional prohibition has no meaning." ...

It is, of course, quite true that the responsibility for public education is primarily the concern of the States, but it is equally true that such responsibilities, like all other state activity, must be exercised consistently with federal constitutional requirements as they apply to state action. The Constitution created a government dedicated to equal justice under law. The Fourteenth Amendment embodied and emphasized that ideal. State support of segregated schools through any arrangement . . . cannot be squared with the Amendment's command that no State shall deny to any person within its jurisdiction the equal protection of the laws. The right of a student not to be segregated on racial grounds in schools so maintained is indeed so fundamental and pervasive that it is embraced in the concept of due process of law. The basic decision in *Brown* was unanimously reached by this Court . . . and that decision is now unanimously reaffirmed. The principles announced in that decision and the obedience of the States to them, according to the command of the Constitution, are indispensable for the protection of the freedoms guaranteed by our fundamental charter for all of us. Our constitutional ideal of equal justice under law is thus made a living truth.

[*Reversed.*]

---

Just as white politicians in Arkansas used any legal or illegal means they could scare up to block the schoolhouse doors, white politicians in Virginia experimented with even more creative ways to stop desegregation. The school board in Prince Edward County, Virginia, simply closed down the public schools and reopened them as state-supported private schools. In *Griffin v. County School Board of Prince Edward County,* the Supreme Court also rejected that tactic. What was its reasoning?

—————

### GRIFFIN
### v.
### COUNTY SCHOOL BOARD OF PRINCE EDWARD COUNTY

*Supreme Court of the United States*
Argued March 30, 1964.
Decided May 25, 1964.

[In 1959, following the order of the Supreme Court to desegregate public schools, Prince Edward County, Virginia, closed its public schools. In their place, private, for-white-students-only schools opened with the support of state and local authorities.]

Justice BLACK . . .

. . . Having as early as 1956 resolved that they would not operate public schools "wherein white and colored children are taught together," the Supervisors of Prince Edward County refused to levy any school taxes for the 1959–1960 school year. . . . As a result, the country's public schools did not reopen in the fall of 1959 and have remained closed ever since, although the public schools of every other county in Virginia have continued to operate.... An offer to set up private schools for colored children in the county was rejected, the Negroes of Prince Edward preferring to continue the legal battle for desegregated public schools, and colored children were without formal education from 1959 to 1963, when federal, state, and county authorities cooperated to have classes conducted for Negroes and whites in school buildings owned by the county.

For reasons to be stated, we agree with the District Court that, under the circumstances here, closing the Prince Edward County school while public schools in all the other counties of Virginia were being maintained denied the petitioners and the class of Negro students they represent the equal protection of the laws guaranteed by the Fourteenth Amendment....

## II

... Virginia law, as here applied, unquestionably treats the school children of Prince Edward differently from the way it treats the school children of all other Virginia counties. Prince Edward children must go to a private school or none at all; all other Virginia children can go to public schools. Closing Prince Edward's schools bears more heavily on Negro children in Prince Edward County since white children there have accredited private schools which they can attend, while colored children until very recently have had no available private schools, and even the school they now attend is a temporary expedient. Apart from this expedient, the result is that Prince Edward County school children, if they go to school in their own county, must go to racially segregated schools which, although designated as private, are beneficiaries of county and state support.

A State, of course, has a wide discretion in deciding whether laws shall operate statewide or shall operate only in certain counties.... But the record in the present case could not be clearer that Prince Edward's public schools were closed and private schools operated in their place with state and county assistance, for one reason, and one reason only: to ensure, through measures taken by the county and the State, that white and colored children in Prince Edward County would not, under any circumstances, go to the same school. Whatever nonracial grounds might support a State's allowing a county to abandon public schools, the object must be a constitutional one, and grounds of race and opposition to desegregation do not qualify as constitutional.

... Accordingly, we agree with the District Court that closing the Prince Edward schools and meanwhile contributing to the support of the private segregated white schools that took their place denied petitioners the equal protection of the laws.

---

In cases like *Cooper* and *Griffin*, the Court was able to knock down the most overt brands of resistance to desegregating public schools. It also disallowed schemes that maintained separate black and white schools but gave individual students the freedom to "switch" from one to another. In *Swann v. Charlotte-Mecklenburg Board of Education* (1971), the Court also gave district courts enforcing *Brown* the green light to order the busing of students from one neighborhood to another—a controversial practice that led to brutal racist violence in many places, including Boston.

However difficult, courts tried to make integration work, in many places official attempts to evade *Brown*'s mandate were ingenious and successful. Yet even where desegregation did take hold, the underlying social dynamics often would not cooperate. In a sociological sense, the heart of the problem was "white flight," as countless white families decided to move rather than face the possibility of integration. With whites relocating across city and county lines in order to escape the implications of *Brown,* the question became whether courts could follow them by ordering desegregation and busing across school district lines.

In *Milliken v. Bradley* (1974), the Supreme Court found that federal courts may not normally order desegregation plans that cut across the lines of different school districts. A lower court had tried to order a desegregation plan that included not only Detroit but fifty-three neighboring suburbs. The Court rejected this approach, finding that municipal boundary lines were not automatically part of the problem of racial segregation and must be respected by the judiciary. Justice Marshall called the majority decision "a giant step backwards" that threatened to create black and white school districts. Many people believe that this decision encouraged white flight to the suburbs, halting the progress that had been made since 1954.

---

EXERCISE 7.3. As the Supreme Court grew more conservative in the last three decades of the twentieth century, it lost much of its fervor and energy for ending segregation in schools. In *Missouri v. Jenkins* (1995), the Court overturned an effort by a district court to encourage integration in Kansas City, Missouri, by ordering the creation of an urban magnet school with well-paid teachers that would attract students from the mostly white suburban and private schools. The majority in this decision found that such relief goes too far—that the district court exceeded its authority in ordering creation of the school and higher pay for the teachers. Do you agree?

EXERCISE 7.4. Write a one- to two-page letter to Chief Justice Warren in 1954 and the Reverend Martin Luther King, whose 1963 "I have a dream" speech at the Lincoln Memorial brought the civil rights movement's struggle alive for America. Tell them what your own city or county (or private) school system is like today—whether or not it is segregated or integrated or some mixture thereof. Include a description of the situation at your own school and indicate whether you think the teachers and students are living up to the ideals of integration championed by Chief Justice Warren and Dr. King. Give your school system a grade, somewhere between F and A+, on its efforts to break down racial and ethnic barriers. Hang the letters on your school's community bulletin board to share with your fellow students. What do people think of your observations?

---

**FOR THE CLASS**

THE FREDERICK DOUGLASS SCHOOL. In response to growing signs that African American teenaged boys are at disproportionate risk of academic failure, delinquency, depression, drug and alcohol abuse, and illiteracy, several cities have begun to experiment with special schools set up just for them. The theory is that this at-risk population needs African American male role models, closer supervision and discipline, and a curriculum geared to meet special needs. Private schools set up on this theory have had some impressive academic success.

Critics argue that not all young African American males are at risk, but many girls and kids from other backgrounds are at risk and could benefit from the same investment of resources. Further, critics maintain that setting up race- and sex-segregated schools violates the whole spirit and meaning of *Brown,* which insists that children learn best when they are not artificially segregated. Supporters of such schools note that schools are *de facto* segregated anyway, and that this formalized and positive group experience is the only possible solution to deal with a serious crisis within the most disadvantaged portion of the population.

Assume that a group of citizens in your city or town wants to charter a public school called the Frederick Douglass School that would admit only African American boys. Have two teams of students research and debate this issue as a matter of both policy and constitutional law. Would a city-funded, all-black, male school be a good idea where you live? Would it violate equal protection as described in *Brown*? Why or why not? Would such a school stigmatize its students? Would it stigmatize those students who are excluded? Are the answers the same when it comes to race and gender? Make sure that you distinguish between *policy* arguments ("it's a bad idea") and *constitutional* arguments ("it would violate equal protection"). Both kinds of arguments are acceptable, but know which is which.

After the debate, each member of the class should write a one- or two-page essay stating whether such a school is a good idea and whether it would be constitutional. (It is fine to say that it is a bad idea but constitutional or a good idea but unconstitutional.)

---

# The Right to Love

The laws segregating schools were not the only racially discriminatory statutes that the Supreme Court tackled in the second half of the last century. In 1967 the Court struck down as a violation of equal protection state laws forbidding interracial marriage between whites and nonwhites. These "antimiscegenation" statutes, which were common throughout the U.S., were used in the South to maintain the cultural system of white supremacy and to keep racial groups socially separate. Because they were based on racist notions of rigid biological differences among racial groups, these laws implicitly stigmatized and shamed children who were born to parents of different racial and ethnic ancestries.

In *Loving v. Virginia* (1967), the Court invalidated Virginia's law against interracial marriage. Virginia argued that its policy did not violate equal protection because it applied equally against whites and African Americans. That is, it was just as illegal for a white person to marry an African American as for an African American to marry a white. But the Court rejected this line of reasoning because it said that the whole purpose of the law was to continue "White Supremacy." This seems obvious today; why was it so controversial back then?

EXERCISE 7.5. In 1983 the Supreme Court upheld the decision of the Internal Revenue Service (IRS) to revoke Bob Jones University's charitable tax exemption because the private university in South Carolina had a rule expelling all students who dated or married "outside their own race" or who even advocated interracial dating. The Court found that the IRS acted properly in ruling that this policy brought Bob Jones University outside the class of "charitable" institutions. Similarly, some public high school principals have tried to ban interracial couples from attending their junior and senior proms. Would such a ban violate equal protection? Does *Loving v. Virginia* imply that young people should be able to date whomever they want? Why or why not?

## Affirmative Action—or "Reverse Discrimination"?

The dismantling of long-standing barriers to admission for African Americans in the 1960s did not mean automatic integration of public higher education. Most state (and private) colleges and universities were all white and many had racist campus cultures that did not create an inviting environment for minority students. Moreover, there were precious few minority students prepared to compete against their affluent white counterparts in the college and graduate school admissions process. To counter the awful legacies of segregation and white supremacy, many state and private universities voluntarily undertook a program of "affirmative action" to recruit and admit minority students in the 1960s and 1970s.

Affirmative action produced a backlash. Many white students who were not admitted to the college or graduate school of their choice blamed affirmative action. They felt cheated—why were minority students with lower test scores and grades being admitted when they were not? Of course, there was no way to prove that these white students would have been admitted in the absence of affirmative action—indeed, in many cases, most certainly would not have been. But they still felt that race now worked unfairly to the disadvantage of whites.

In 1978 the Supreme Court considered a challenge to affirmative action in *Regents of University of California v. Bakke*. In that case, Alan Bakke, a disappointed white applicant to the Medical School of the University of California at Davis, sued the school for reserving sixteen out of one hundred places in the entering class for minority students, including African Americans, Chicanos, Asian Americans, and Native Americans. Bakke successfully showed that many minority applicants, though certainly qualified to go to medical school, "were admitted with grade point averages [and] Medical College Admissions Test scores significantly lower than Bakke's." He did not show, and could not show, that he would have been admitted absent the program because many white applicants with scores lower than his were admitted.

The Court was deeply divided. Four justices thought that race-conscious admissions for the purposes of affirmative action and integration should not be subjected to strict scrutiny but to a lower level of examination. They found that the state's interests in cor-

Jennifer Gratz, one of two students challenging the admissions policies of the University of Michigan in a lawsuit, speaks with her lawyer, Terry Pell.

recting the historic underrepresentation of minorities in university life was surely important enough to justify the program. But four other justices would have imposed strict scrutiny and struck the program down as an unlawful use of race.

Justice Powell became the key justice in the case. He voted with the more conservative faction to find that the rigid numerical set-aside of sixteen places was unconstitutional and therefore ordered Bakke admitted. But he allowed that an affirmative action plan that uses a minority's race or ethnicity as a softer "plus" factor was acceptable to promote educational "diversity," which he said was a goal of "paramount importance" in a university. Citing the so-called "Harvard Plan," Powell argued that it took race and ethnicity into account as one factor among many, such as a student's home state or his or her parents' status as alumni, among other criteria not strictly meritoratic in nature. The conservatives felt—and have since come to argue strenuously—that any use of race in the admissions process violates equal protection. The liberals thought that this view twists equal protection to deny government the power to assist racial minorities who were victims of racial oppression for centuries. As Justice Marshall pointed out in *Bakke,* the same Congress that added the words "equal protection" to the Constitution in 1868 voted for the Freedmen's Bureau, whose explicit goal was to transfer resources to the recently freed black population. Marshall wrote that "it is inconceivable that the Fourteenth Amendment was intended to prohibit all race-conscious measures." Justice Blackmun's thoughts were especially cogent: "[In] order to get beyond racism, we must first take account of race."

The explosive political and legal controversy over affirmative action has not subsided. The Supreme Court is revisiting whether Justice Powell's celebrated "diversity" interest is indeed sufficiently compelling to justify using race as a factor in educational admissions. The occasion for the Court's reconsideration of affirmative action is *Gratz v. Bollinger* and *Grutter v. Bollinger,* a pair of challenges to affirmative action as practiced by the University of Michigan in its college and law school admissions. Consider the district court decision. What do you think of the constitutionality of the university's admissions policy?

— —

GRATZ
v.
BOLLINGER

*United States District Court,*
E.D. Michigan,
Southern Division
Dec. 13, 2000.

DUGGAN, District Judge. . . .

The University of Michigan ("University") is a public institution of higher education located in Ann Arbor, Michigan. Admission to the University is selective, meaning that many more students apply each year than can be admitted. The University received some 13,500 applications for admission to the LSA in 1997, from which it elected to enroll 3,958 freshmen. The University views diversity as an integral component of its mission. According to the University, diversity "increase[s] the intellectual vitality of [its] education, scholarship, service, and communal life." To facilitate the University's goal of diversity, it is undisputed that the LSA employs race as a factor in its admissions decisions.

. . . Jennifer Gratz [is a] Caucasian resident of the State of Michigan, who applied for admission into the 1995 and 1997 classes of the LSA, respectively. On January 19, 1995 . . . Gratz was notified that a final decision regarding her admission had been delayed until early to mid April 1995, as she was considered by the LSA as "well qualified, but less competitive than the students who ha[d] been admitted on first review." On April 24, 1995 . . . Gratz was notified that the LSA was unable to offer her admission. Thereafter . . . Gratz enrolled in the University of Michigan at Dearborn, from which she graduated in the spring of 1999.

The Defendant-Intervenors are seventeen African American and Latino students who have applied for, or intend to apply for, admission to the University, joined by the Citizens for Affirmative Action's Preservation, a nonprofit organization whose stated mission is to preserve opportunities in higher education for African American and Latino students in Michigan. According to Defendant-Intervenors, the resolution of this case directly threatens African American and Latino students' access to higher education.

Discussion

The Equal Protection Clause of the Fourteenth Amendment provides that no State shall "deny to any person within its jurisdiction the equal protection of the laws." The "central mandate" of the Fourteenth Amendment "is racial neutrality in governmental decisionmaking." Accordingly, the Supreme Court has explicitly clarified that "all racial classifications, imposed by whatever federal, state, or local governmental actor, must be analyzed by a reviewing court under strict scrutiny. In other words, such classifications are constitutional only if they are narrowly tailored measures that further compelling governmental interests."

Two interests have been asserted in support of the LSA's race conscious admissions policies. The University asserts that the LSA has a compelling interest in the educational benefits that result from having a diverse student body, whereas the Defendant-Intervenors assert that the LSA has a compelling interest in remedying the University's past and current discrimination against minorities. Therefore, the two issues this Court must decide in resolving the parties' motions for summary judgment are: (1) whether Defendants have asserted a compelling governmental interest in support of the LSA's use of race and (2) whether the measures by which the LSA has used race as a factor in admissions decisions were narrowly tailored to serve such interest.

### The Diversity Rationale

Both parties assert that with respect to the University's "diversity" rationale, the Supreme Court's decision in *Regents of the University of California v. Bakke* governs this dispute. In support of their motion for summary judgment, the University contends that under Justice Powell's decision in *Bakke,* the University has a compelling governmental interest in the educational benefits that flow from a racially and ethnically diverse student body. The University also contends that under *Bakke,* the LSA's admissions policies were properly tailored to achieve the University's stated interest in diversity.

Plaintiffs, however, contend that Justice Powell's decision in *Bakke* has never garnered a majority of support from the Justices and that subsequent Supreme Court cases have confirmed that "diversity" and "academic freedom" are not compelling governmental interests that can ever justify the use of race in the admissions process.

This Court is satisfied that, if presented with sufficient evidence regarding the educational benefits that flow from a diverse student body, there is nothing barring the Court from determining that such benefits are compelling under strict scrutiny analysis.

The University has presented this Court with solid evidence regarding the educational benefits that flow from a racially and ethnically diverse student body....

Plaintiffs have presented no argument or evidence rebutting the University's assertion that a racially and ethnically diverse student body gives rise to educational benefits for both minority and non-minority students. In fact, during oral argument, counsel for Plaintiffs indicated his willingness to assume, for purposes of these motions, that diversity in institutions of higher education is "good, important, and valuable." ...

... In this Court's opinion, the fact that the University cannot articulate a set number or percentage of minority students that would constitute the requisite level of diversity does not, by itself, eliminate diversity as a potentially compelling interest.

Furthermore, unlike the remedial setting, diversity in higher education, by its very nature, is a permanent and ongoing interest. As previously noted, diversity is not a "remedy." Therefore, unlike the remedial setting, where the need for remedial action terminates once the effects of past discrimination have been eradicated, the need for diversity lives on perpetually. This does not mean, however, that Universities are unrestrained in their use of race in the admissions process, as any use of race must be narrowly tailored. Hopefully, there may come a day when universities are able to achieve the desired diversity without resort to racial preferences. Such an occurrence, however, would have no affect on the compelling nature of the diversity interest. Rather, such an occurrence would affect only the issue of whether a university's race-conscious admissions program remained narrowly tailored. In this Court's opinion, the permanency of such an interest does not remove it from the realm of "compelling interests," but rather, only emphasizes the importance of ensuring that any race-conscious admissions policy that is justified as a means to achieve diversity is narrowly tailored to such interest. . . .

Having determined that the educational benefits flowing from a racially and ethnically diverse student body are a sufficiently compelling interest to survive strict scrutiny, the Court must now determine whether the LSA's admissions policies for the years at issue (1995–present) were narrowly tailored to achieving that interest.

As is clear from Justice Powell's opinion in *Bakke*, a university's interest in achieving the educational benefits that flow from a diverse student body does not justify an admissions program designed to admit a predetermined number or proportion of minority students. Instead, a university must carefully design its system to fall between these two competing ends of the spectrum, *i.e.*, between a system that completely fails to achieve a meaningful degree of diversity, under which the benefits associated with a diverse student body will never be realized, and a rigid quota system, which is clearly unconstitutional under Justice Powell's opinion in *Bakke*.

In striving to achieve such a system, "race or ethnic background may be deemed a 'plus' in a particular applicant's file," as long as this plus "does not insulate the individual from comparison with all other candidates for the available seats." As Justice Powell explained with reference to the Harvard plan, an admissions program that takes race into consideration must be "flexible enough to consider all pertinent elements of diversity in light of the particular qualifications of each applicant, and to place them on the same footing for consideration, although not necessarily according them the same weight." It is exactly because race need not necessarily be accorded the same weight as other objective factors that, in some instances, "race may tip the balance in an applicant's favor."

From 1998 through the present, the LSA has used a 150 point system, under which admission decisions were generally determined by the applicant's rank on the 150 point scale. Underrepresented minority applicants automatically receive 20 points based upon their membership in one of the identified under-represented minority categories. In 1999 and 2000, the LSA also added a system whereby certain applicants, including under-represented minority applicants, could be "flagged," thereby keeping such applicants in the review pool for further consideration.

Beyond the fact that rigid quotas are impermissible, Justice Powell's opinion in *Bakke* fails to set forth any bright line regarding what constitutes a permissible consideration of race in admissions decisions. Furthermore, in situations such as this, it is often a thin line that divides the permissible from the impermissible. Applying the principles set forth by Justice Powell in *Bakke*, this Court is satisfied that when examined in its entirety, the LSA's current admissions program (1999–present) represents a permissible use of race.

Foremost in the Court's decision that the LSA's current admissions program is constitutional is the fact that the LSA's current program does not utilize rigid quotas or seek to admit a predetermined number of minority students. Therefore, the LSA's current program does not contain the fatal flaw identified by Justice Powell in *Bakke*. Instead, race is taken into account in two ways under the LSA's current program. First, admissions counselors may assign each under-represented minority applicant twenty points in calculating their selection index score on account of their race. Second, under the LSA's current program, counselors may "flag" applicants that possess certain qualities or characteristics the LSA deems important to the composition of its freshman class, one of which is "under-represented race," thereby keeping an applicant who may not necessarily pass the LSA's initial admit threshold in the review pool for further consideration.

In response, Plaintiffs contend that the LSA's practice of adding twenty points to under-represented minority applicants' selection index scores really operates as the functional equivalent of a quota. Justice Powell, however, rejected essentially the same argument in *Bakke*. . . .

Minority applicants are not insulated from review by virtue of these twenty points any more than other applicants are insulated from review by virtue of the six points awarded for geographic factors, four points awarded for alumni relationship, three points awarded for an outstanding essay, five points awarded for leadership and service skills, twenty points awarded for socioeconomic status, or twenty points awarded for athletes. In fact, the Court notes that in certain circumstances, these points may be combined for a total of up to forty. The fact that these points may "tip the balance" in favor of a particular applicant, however, does not necessarily lead to a conclusion that such applicants have been insulated from competition in the sense that Justice Powell spoke of in *Bakke.*

What Plaintiffs really appear to contest is the fact that race is accorded twenty points, while other factors that may more consistently favor non-minority students are not typically accorded the same weight. However, as Justice Powell recognized in *Bakke,* universities may accord an applicant's race some weight in the admissions process and, in doing so, universities are not required to accord the same weight to race as they do other factors. As long as the admissions program does not work to isolate the applicants from review, it withstands constitutional muster, despite the fact that it may provide individuals with a "plus" on account of their race.

---

EXERCISE 7.6. One of the key arguments against affirmative action today is that it "stigmatizes" minority college and graduate students by making their fellow students assume that they were not admitted on the strength of their own intelligence and personal qualities. Do you think this is true? Does affirmative action stigmatize its intended beneficiaries?

---

# Rich Schools, Poor Schools: The Court's Treatment of "Separate but Equal" School Financing

Schools can be segregated along *economic* lines as well as racial lines. (In fact, economic lines sometimes closely parallel racial lines.) How should the Supreme Court deal with legal challenges to public school systems in which certain schools have a lot more money and resources than others?

The 1973 Supreme Court case, *San Antonio Independent School District v. Rodriguez,* held that wealth-based differences in public schools are *not* unconstitutional and that education is *not* a fundamental right. This holding is in tension with *Brown* and helps to explain why we still see tremendous disparities in public schools in different areas when it comes to teacher-student ratios, textbooks, science and art supplies, athletic equipment and fields, cleanliness, and so on.

The most common method of funding public schools is through local property taxes. This method favors residents of wealthier areas, where property taxes on real estate produce much more public revenue than taxes in poorer areas, where property values are lower. This means that students who go to school in areas with higher property values will enjoy a higher rate of spending on their education than will students in areas with

Demetrio Rodriguez and other Mexican American parents challenged the property tax–based system of financing schools in Texas as a form of wealth discrimination that violated the fundamental right to education. The Court rejected their equal protection claim in 1973, holding that wealth-based classifications do not warrant any special scrutiny and that education is no fundamental right under the equal protection clause.

lower property values. Does this violate the equal protection guarantee? In *San Antonio Independent School District v. Rodriguez* the Supreme Court found that it does not.

---

EXERCISE 7.7. Is the Supreme Court's decision in *Rodriguez* consistent with the *Brown* decision? Why or why not? What is the spirit of this case in relation to *Brown*?

EXERCISE 7.8. Many state supreme courts have done what the Supreme Court was unwilling to do: they have found that under their *state* constitutions students have a right to equal rates of spending in each school district. Do you agree with this approach? What would you think about a rule in your state that there has to be an equal number of dollars spent per pupil in each school district and school? Is that fair? What happens if a local parents' group wants to donate extra money or supplies? Is it okay for certain local public schools to acquire more resources by seeking private funding and/or holding fundraisers?

EXERCISE 7.9. More than 90 percent of children go to public school, but many also go to private schools that are funded by their families and by alumni contributions. Although some of these schools are relatively poor, many others are very rich and are able to give their students extraordinary resources and teacher attention. The Supreme Court in 1925 struck down an Oregon law that required all students to attend public schools rather than private ones. In *Pierce v. Society of Sisters*, the Court ruled that foreclosing alternatives to public school "unreasonably interferes with the liberty of parents and guardians to direct the upbringing and education of children under their control." Do you think that this decision was right, or should all students be required to go to public schools? What effect do private schools have on public schools? Should people have the right to send their children to any school they want, public or private, or do we lose something when families begin to sort themselves out according to wealth, religion, and race?

EXERCISE 7.10. In Justice Marshall's dissent in the *Rodriguez* case, he argues that equal spending on education is necessary to equip poorer students to participate on an equal basis in politics with more affluent students as they enter adulthood. Do you think education is in fact critical to a person's ability to participate effectively in voting, running for office, arguing for particular public policies, and persuading fellow citizens? Make a list of five ways your education has prepared you to be a capable citizen. Does the quality of your education influence the development of these skills?

---

FOR THE CLASS

SCHOOL VOUCHERS: PRO OR CON? The 1990s saw the growth of a movement in favor of "school vouchers," the policy of granting parents tax-financed vouchers that they can redeem to pay tuition for their children at any school, public or private. In Chapter Four we saw the Court uphold the constitutionality of the voucher plan against the charge that it violated the establishment clause.

The voucher idea, launched in 1955 in an essay penned by free-market economist Milton Friedman, has been adopted in Milwaukee, Wisconsin, and Cleveland, Ohio, as well as by the state of Florida. Proponents of vouchers say that every child, no matter how poor, should have the opportunity to attend the elite private schools typically reserved for the children of wealthy people and that the voucher program will stir a beneficial competition among schools for parents' voucher dollars. Opponents say that vouchers will simply strip the public schools of their best students, further undermine public support for public schools, and benefit only a tiny percentage of less affluent families, because the vast majority will still not have enough money to go to the elite private schools. The rhetoric of proponents is "free choice for all"; the rhetoric of opponents is "don't destroy the public schools."

Pair up with one of your classmates and do some research on all sides of the school voucher debate, then present a report to the class on your views. Are there ways that we could have vouchers without undermining public schools? Are there ways we could provide more choice and competition within the public schools?

DID THE CLINTONS MAKE THE RIGHT CHOICE? When Bill Clinton became president in 1993, he and his wife Hillary decided to send their daughter, Chelsea, to the private Sidwell Friends school in Washington, D.C. rather than to a public school. Senator Robert Dole, R-Kan., castigated the Clintons for sending Chelsea to private school while opposing school voucher programs that might allow poorer families to send their children to private school as well. In response, President Clinton told *Time* magazine that

Chelsea "had always been in public schools," but chose Sidwell Friends because it is "an extraordinary school" and Chelsea would "have a measure of privacy there that she would not have otherwise." He said that voucher advocates want "to take funds now going to the public schools and give them to the private schools, when the public schools are already underfunded, which will hurt more children than the relatively small number they propose to help. . . ."

Meanwhile, public school students and families in Washington expressed disappointment that the Clintons did not use the opportunity to show support for Washington's public schools and to get people who come to Washington for government purposes more invested in the city. What do you think? Did the Clintons make the right choice?

## "Suspect" Classes and Sex-Based Segregation

Since *Brown* was decided in 1954, the Supreme Court has developed different tests for equal protection claims brought under the Fourteenth Amendment. If a law distinguishes among people based on race, the Court reviews the case using "strict scrutiny," because the Court views race as an inherently suspect, or discriminatory, classification. To pass a strict scrutiny test the government must show that its racial classification advances a compelling public interest in an effective and necessary way.

If a law treats people differently according to their gender, the government must show that the law's classification advances an "important" public interest in a way that is substantially related to its purpose. This is "heightened" or "intermediate scrutiny."

If a law differentiates citizens based on physical handicap, wealth, sexual orientation, or many other categories, the Court reviews the case using only "rational basis scrutiny." This test asks, "Is there any conceivable rational basis for this law that is not an arbitrary burden on a particular group of people?"

The nuances of Supreme Court equal protection analysis are complicated and abstract. But it is important that you be able to conceptualize the underlying notion that classifications based on race are the most difficult for the government to justify, whereas classifications based on sex or citizenship status, though suspicious, are a little easier to justify. Classifications based on other categories, while still requiring some justification, are presumptively acceptable unless bigotry or animosity can be shown. If equal protection analysis were drawn on a continuum, it would look something like this:

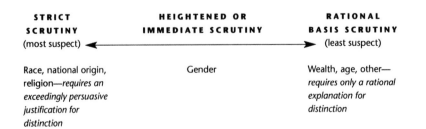

| STRICT SCRUTINY (most suspect) | HEIGHTENED OR IMMEDIATE SCRUTINY | RATIONAL BASIS SCRUTINY (least suspect) |
|---|---|---|
| Race, national origin, religion—*requires an exceedingly persuasive justification for distinction* | Gender | Wealth, age, other—*requires only a rational explanation for distinction* |

The Supreme Court has said that higher scrutiny is triggered when government draws lines that adversely affect a "discrete and insular minority." This is a group defined by some "immutable" (unchangeable) trait, a history of being the object of bias and discrimination, and political powerlessness in society.

Why are race classifications so much more suspect than gender classifications? Is it because the history of race oppression in the United States is more severe or detrimental than the history of sex discrimination? Is it because women, the undoubted targets of gender discrimination, are not a minority? Or is it because there are real differences between the sexes but not the races?

In *United States v. Virginia,* the Supreme Court heard arguments in January 1996 for and against the power of a state-funded military college to exclude women. Virginia Military Institute (VMI) was the sole single-sex school among Virginia's public institutions of higher learning. VMI's distinctive mission is to produce "citizen-soldiers," individuals prepared for leadership in civilian life and in military service.

Using a harsh, marinelike, "adversative" method of training not available elsewhere in Virginia, VMI endeavors to instill physical and mental discipline in its cadets and impart to them a strong moral code. This model of education features physical rigor, mental stress, absolute equality of treatment, absence of privacy, minute regulation of behavior, and indoctrination in "desirable values." The adversative method "dissects the young student," and makes him aware of his "limits and capabilities," so that he knows "how far he can go with his anger, . . . how much he can take under stress . . . exactly what he can do when he is physically exhausted." Because of this intense regimen, the alumni place high value on their VMI training, and VMI has the largest per-student endowment of all public undergraduate institutions in the nation.

The United States sued Virginia and VMI, alleging that VMI's males-only admission policy violated the Fourteenth Amendment's equal protection clause. VMI initially received a favorable ruling from the district court. On review, the Fourth Circuit reversed and ordered Virginia to remedy the constitutional violation. In response, Virginia proposed a parallel program for women: Virginia Women's Institute for Leadership (VWIL), located at Mary Baldwin college, a private liberal arts school for women. The district court found that Virginia's proposal satisfied the Constitution's equal protection requirement, and the Fourth Circuit affirmed. The appeals court deferentially reviewed Virginia's plan and determined that provision of single-gender educational options was a legitimate objective. Maintenance of single-sex programs, the court concluded, was essential to that objective. The court recognized, however, that its analysis risked bypassing equal protection scrutiny, so it fashioned an additional test, asking whether VMI and VWIL students would receive "substantially comparable" benefits. Although the court of appeals acknowledged that the VWIL degree lacked the historical benefit and prestige of a VMI degree, the court nevertheless found the educational opportunities at the two schools sufficiently comparable.

The Supreme Court rejected this attempt to create a parallel all-women's institution and instead insisted that VMI admit both men and women. Six justices made up the majority decision to find against Virginia in the VMI case: Justices Ginsburg, Stevens, O'Connor, Kennedy, Souter, and Breyer. Chief Justice Rehnquist filed an opinion concurring in the judgment. Justice Scalia dissented. (Justice Thomas abstained from both the consideration and the decision of the case because his son was a student at VMI at the time.)

Virginia Military Institute cadets stand at attention. Front and center is one of the first women admitted to VMI in the wake of the Court's landmark decision in *United States v. Virginia.*

The Court used intermediate scrutiny to evaluate the constitutionality of this gender-based discrimination in *United States v. Virginia*. The Court asked whether: (1) Virginia's interest in an all-male college is "important" to producing exemplary "citizen-soldiers," and (2) whether the all-male policy is "substantially related" to achievement of Virginia's goal of producing such soldiers.

Writing for the majority, Justice Ginsburg found that Virginia's arguments for a separate, all-female military college were unable to pass the test of intermediate scrutiny. Justice Ginsburg rejected Virginia's argument for a separate women's military college based on three principles. First, Justice Ginsburg held that, although gender-based classifications are not categorically prohibited, categorization by sex may not be used to create or reinforce the legal, social, or economic inferiority of women.

Second, Virginia failed to provide the Court with enough evidence that the exclusion of women was *substantially related* to the important state interest of VMI's adversative training method. In other words, the State had failed to offer enough proof that only an all-male setting would allow VMI's rigorous physical and mental conditioning program to operate. Why couldn't VMI continue to impose a tough set of academic and athletic protocols with women participating along with men? Still, the Court was willing to allow the all-male policy to continue if the State could show that women were offered an alternative to VMI that would produce female graduates with opportunities substantially equal to those afforded male graduates of VMI.

But Virginia was unable to clear this final hurdle. The Supreme Court rejected Virginia's proposed all-female school because the disparities in geographic location and physical and mental training, and the inferior reputation of the institution itself, would not allow for educational results comparable to attending VMI. Therefore, the Court's enunciation of its conclusion that "separate" produced a result far from "equal" left VMI holding the bag with an unconstitutional all-male policy.

Justice Scalia dissented from this analysis because, in his view, the school had met its burdens under intermediate scrutiny. He attacked the majority's view of the political vulnerability of women, pointing out that women constitute a majority of the electorate and have the power of the ballot to change educational policies they find disagreeable. Applying a weaker standard of scrutiny for Virginia's program, Justice Scalia concluded that VMI's program promoted the precise goal Virginia aspired to—the creation of leaders through a strict moral code—and that this goal clearly passed constitutional muster.

---

EXERCISE 7.11. What is your opinion of the validity of sex-segregated schools? Can all-female schools ever help women in a constitutionally permissible way? Is there ever justification for all-male schools?

EXERCISE 7.12. What would you think of single-sex classes within your school? Would the subject matter of the class—math, science, English—influence your decision? Are all-girls and all-boys sex-education classes appropriate to prevent embarrassment on both sides?

---

# Separating Citizens from Noncitizens under the Law

As we have seen, to legislate is to draw lines. One line we allow our government to draw is between citizens and noncitizens. When the nation began, there were very few distinctions between citizens and noncitizens. Indeed, noncitizens could vote in many states (so long as they were white male property owners). But anti-immigration sentiment became a powerful force in the twentieth century, and the Supreme Court often allowed terrible discrimination against aliens, perhaps the worst example being its permission in the *Korematsu* case (1944) for the relocation and internment of tens of thousands of Japanese Americans and Japanese resident aliens on the West Coast during World War II.

But the Court's formal constitutional doctrine today bans prejudiced discrimination against permanent resident aliens. Citing the fact that the equal protection clause covers "persons" (not "citizens"), the modern Court, in fact, uses heightened scrutiny to test laws that disadvantage lawful aliens. It has often struck down laws that make it harder for resident aliens to own property, to get fishing and hunting licenses, and so on. Only when laws touch on an important "government function" does the Court permit government to discriminate against noncitizens.

There are two ways to become an American citizen. The first is to be born here, even if it is to noncitizen parents, and this method of becoming a citizen is guaranteed by the Fourteenth Amendment. (Can you find the sentence that establishes this principle?) The other is to be "naturalized" by following the laws of the country. Generally, this means becoming a lawful permanent resident—a "green card holder"—and then taking a naturalization test in English, passing it, and then being sworn in at a naturalization

**JUSTICE WILLIAM J. BRENNAN** (1906–1997) was born in Newark, New Jersey, where his father was a popular local official in charge of public safety. Brennan attended Barringer High School and the Wharton School at the University of Pennsylvania. He went on to Harvard Law School. After a distinguished career as a labor lawyer, Brennan rose through the ranks of the New Jersey courts, landing on the New Jersey Supreme Court. President Dwight Eisenhower appointed him a justice of the U.S. Supreme Court in 1956, where he served until 1990.

HIGHLIGHTS

➤ Justice Brennan was a student of Justice Felix Frankfurter at Harvard Law School and later came to be both his colleague and frequent adversary on the Court.

➤ Unaware that President Eisenhower, a Republican, was considering nominating him to the Supreme Court, Brennan complained about having to travel to Washington, D.C., when Herbert Brownell mysteriously called him from the Attorney General's Office.

➤ Justice Brennan had a tremendous influence in promoting a progressive civil rights and civil liberties jurisprudence on the Court and was known as a great leader in forging consensus among his fellow justices.

ceremony. The non–U.S. born children of naturalized parents can then become citizens through application.

Public school systems all over America routinely accept children of lawful permanent residents. But what about the children of "illegal aliens" or "undocumented workers," that is, children who are not U.S. citizens and whose parents are not lawfully in the country? Do they have an equal protection right to go to public school? In 1975 Texas passed a law withdrawing state funds for the education of such children and gave schools the power to deny them enrollment. In *Plyler v. Doe,* the Court struck this law down as a violation of equal protection. How did it reach this conclusion?

---

**PLYLER**

v.

**DOE**

*Supreme Court of the United States*
Argued Dec. 1, 1981.
Decided June 15, 1982.

Justice BRENNAN delivered the opinion of the Court.

The question presented by these cases is whether, consistent with the Equal Protection Clause of the Fourteenth Amendment, Texas may deny to undocumented school-age children the free public education that it provides to children who are citizens of the United States or legally admitted aliens.

I

In May 1975, the Texas Legislature revised its education laws to withhold from local school districts any state funds for the education of children who were not "legally admitted" into the United States. The 1975 revision also authorized local school districts to deny enrollment in their public schools to children not "legally admitted" to the country.... These cases involve constitutional challenges to those provisions....

Plyler v. Doe

This is a class action, filed in the United States District Court for the Eastern District of Texas in September 1977, on behalf of certain school-age children of Mexican origin residing in Smith County, Tex., who could not establish that they had been legally admitted into the United States. The action complained of the exclusion of plaintiff children from the public schools of the Tyler Independent School District....

II

The Fourteenth Amendment provides that "[n]o State shall ... deprive any person of life, liberty, or property, without due process of law; nor deny to *any person within its jurisdiction* the equal protection of the laws." Appellants argue at the outset that undocumented aliens, because of their immigration status, are not "persons within the jurisdiction" of the State of Texas, and that they therefore have no right to the equal protection of Texas law. We reject this argument. Whatever his status under the immigration laws, an alien is surely a "person" in any ordinary sense of that term. Aliens, even aliens whose presence in this country is unlawful, have long been recognized as "persons" guaranteed due process of law by the Fifth and Fourteenth Amendments.... Indeed, we have clearly held that the Fifth Amendment protects aliens whose presence in this country is unlawful from invidious discrimination by the Federal Government....

... The more difficult question is whether the Equal Protection Clause has been violated by the refusal of the State of Texas to reimburse local school boards for the education of children who cannot demonstrate that their presence within the United States is lawful, or by the imposition by those school boards of the burden of tuition on those children. It is to this question that we now turn.

III

A

Sheer incapability or lax enforcement of the laws barring entry into this country, coupled with the failure to establish an effective bar to the employment of undocumented aliens, has resulted in the creation of a substantial "shadow population" of illegal migrants—numbering in the millions—within our borders.... This situation raises the specter of a permanent caste of undocumented resident aliens, encouraged by some to remain here as a source of cheap labor, but nevertheless denied the benefits that our society makes available to citizens and lawful residents.... The existence of such an underclass presents most difficult problems for a Nation that prides itself on adherence to principles of equality under law....

The children who are plaintiffs in these cases are special members of this underclass. Persuasive arguments support the view that a State may withhold its beneficence from those whose very presence within the United States is the product of their own unlawful conduct. These arguments do not apply with the same force to classifications imposing disabilities on the minor *children* of such illegal entrants. At the least, those who elect to enter our territory by stealth and in violation of our law should be prepared to bear the consequences, including, but not limited to, deportation. But the children of those illegal entrants are not comparably situated. Their "parents have the ability to conform their conduct to societal norms," and presumably the ability to remove themselves from the

State's jurisdiction; but the children who are plaintiffs in these cases "can affect neither their parents' conduct nor their own status.".... Even if the State found it expedient to control the conduct of adults by acting against their children, legislation directing the onus of a parent's misconduct against his children does not comport with fundamental conceptions of justice.

[V]isiting ... condemnation on the head of an infant is illogical and unjust. Moreover, imposing disabilities on the ... child is contrary to the basic concept of our system that legal burdens should bear some relationship to individual responsibility or wrongdoing. Obviously, no child is responsible for his birth and penalizing the ... child is an ineffectual—as well as unjust—way of deterring the parent....

... [This law] is directed against children, and imposes its discriminatory burden on the basis of a legal characteristic over which children can have little control. It is thus difficult to conceive of a rational justification for penalizing these children for their presence within the United States. Yet that appears to be precisely the effect of [the law].

Public education is not a "right" granted to individuals by the Constitution.... But neither is it merely some governmental "benefit" indistinguishable from other forms of social welfare legislation. Both the importance of education in maintaining our basic institutions, and the lasting impact of its deprivation on the life of the child, mark the distinction. The "American people have always regarded education and [the] acquisition of knowledge as matters of supreme importance.".... We have recognized "the public schools as a most vital civic institution for the preservation of a democratic system of government" ... and as the primary vehicle for transmitting "the values on which our society rests.".... "[A]s ... pointed out early in our history ... some degree of education is necessary to prepare citizens to participate effectively and intelligently in our open political system if we are to preserve freedom and independence.".... In addition, education provides the basic tools by which individuals might lead economically productive lives to the benefit of us all. In sum, education has a fundamental role in maintaining the fabric of our society. We cannot ignore the significant social costs borne by our Nation when select groups are denied the means to absorb the values and skills upon which our social order rests.

In addition to the pivotal role of education in sustaining our political and cultural heritage, denial of education to some isolated group of children poses an affront to one of the goals of the Equal Protection Clause: the abolition of governmental barriers presenting unreasonable obstacles to advancement on the basis of individual merit. Paradoxically, by depriving the children of any disfavored group of an education, we foreclose the means by which that group might raise the level of esteem in which it is held by the majority. But more directly, "education prepares individuals to be self-reliant and self-sufficient participants in society.".... Illiteracy is an enduring disability. The inability to read and write will handicap the individual deprived of a basic education each and every day of his life. The inestimable toll of that deprivation on the social, economic, intellectual, and psychological well-being of the individual, and the obstacle it poses to individual achievement, make it most difficult to reconcile the cost or the principle of a status-based denial of basic education with the framework of equality embodied in the Equal Protection Clause....

B

... [This law] imposes a lifetime hardship on a discrete class of children not accountable for their disabling status. The stigma of illiteracy will mark them for the rest of their lives. By denying these children a basic education, we deny them the ability to live within the structure of our civic institutions, and foreclose any realistic possibility that they will contribute in even the smallest way to the progress of our Nation. In determining the rationality of § 21.031, we may appropriately take into account its costs to the Nation and to the innocent children who are its victims. In light of these countervailing costs, the discrimination contained in § 21.031 can hardly be considered rational unless it furthers some substantial goal of the State. . . .

V

Appellants argue that the classification at issue furthers an interest in the "preservation of the state's limited resources for the education of its lawful residents.". . . . Of course, a concern for the preservation of resources standing alone can hardly justify the classification used in allocating those resources. . . . The State must do more than justify its classification with a concise expression of an intention to discriminate. . . . Apart from the asserted state prerogative to act against undocumented children solely on the basis of their undocumented status—an asserted prerogative that carries only minimal force in the circumstances of these cases—we discern three colorable state interests that might support [the provision]. . . .

First, appellants appear to suggest that the State may seek to protect itself from an influx of illegal immigrants. While a State might have an interest in mitigating the potentially harsh economic effects of sudden shifts in population. . . . [This law] hardly offers an effective method of dealing with an urgent demographic or economic problem. There is no evidence in the record suggesting that illegal entrants impose any significant burden on the State's economy. To the contrary, the available evidence suggests that illegal aliens underutilize public services, while contributing their labor to the local economy and tax money to the state fisc. . . . The dominant incentive for illegal entry into the State of Texas is the availability of employment; few if any illegal immigrants come to this country, or presumably to the State of Texas, in order to avail themselves of a free education. . . . Thus, even making the doubtful assumption that the net impact of illegal aliens on the economy of the State is negative, we think it clear that "[c]harging tuition to undocumented children constitutes a ludicrously ineffectual attempt to stem the tide of illegal immigration," at least when compared with the alternative of prohibiting the employment of illegal aliens. . . .

Second, while it is apparent that a State may "not . . . reduce expenditures for education by barring [some arbitrarily chosen class of] children from its schools" . . . appellants suggest that undocumented children are appropriately singled out for exclusion because of the special burdens they impose on the State's ability to provide high-quality public education. But the record in no way supports the claim that exclusion of undocumented children is likely to improve the overall quality of education in the State. . . . [T]he State failed to offer any "credible supporting evidence that a proportionately small diminution of the funds spent on each child [which might result from devoting some state funds to the education of the excluded group] will have a grave impact on the quality of education." . . . [B]arring undocumented children from local schools would not necessarily improve the quality of education provided in those schools. . . . Of course, even if improvement in the quality of education were a likely result of barring some *number* of children from the schools of the State, the State must support its selection of *this* group as the appropriate target for exclusion. In terms of educational cost and need, however, undocumented children are "basically indistinguishable" from legally resident alien children. . . .

Finally, appellants suggest that undocumented children are appropriately singled out because their unlawful presence within the United States renders them less likely than other children to remain within the boundaries of the State, and to put their education to productive social or political use within the State. Even assuming that such an interest is legitimate, it is an interest that is most difficult to quantify. The State has no assurance that any child, citizen or not, will employ the education provided by the State within the confines of the State's borders. In any event, the record is clear that many of the undocumented children disabled by this classification will remain in this country indefinitely, and that some will become lawful residents or citizens of the United States. It is difficult to understand precisely what the State hopes to achieve by promoting the creation and perpetuation of a subclass of illiterates within our boundaries, surely adding to the problems and costs of unemployment, welfare, and crime. It is thus clear that whatever savings might be achieved by denying these children an education, they are wholly insubstantial in light of the costs involved to these children, the State, and the Nation.

VI

If the State is to deny a discrete group of innocent children the free public education that it offers to other children residing within its borders, that denial must be justified by a showing that it furthers some substantial state interest. No such showing was made here. Accordingly, the judgment of the Court of Appeals in each of these cases is *Affirmed*. . . .

Chief Justice BURGER, with whom Justice WHITE, Justice REHNQUIST, and Justice O'CONNOR join, dissenting.

Were it our business to set the Nation's social policy, I would agree without hesitation that it is senseless for an enlightened society to deprive any children—including illegal aliens—of an elementary education. I fully agree that it would be folly—and wrong—to tolerate creation of a segment of society made up of illiterate persons, many having a limited or no command of our language. . . . However, the Constitution does not constitute us as "Platonic Guardians" nor does it vest in this Court the authority to strike down laws because they do not meet our standards of desirable social policy, "wisdom," or "common sense." . . . We trespass on the assigned function of the political branches under our structure of limited and separated powers when we assume a policymaking role as the Court does today. . . .

The Court makes no attempt to disguise that it is acting to make up for Congress' lack of "effective leadership" in dealing with the serious national problems caused by the influx of uncountable millions of illegal aliens across our borders. . . . The failure of enforcement of the immigration laws over more than a decade and the inherent difficulty and expense of sealing our vast borders have combined to create a grave socioeconomic dilemma. It is a dilemma that has not yet even been fully assessed, let alone addressed. However, it is not the function of the Judiciary to provide "effective leadership" simply because the political branches of government fail to do so. . . .

I

. . . I have no quarrel with the conclusion that the Equal Protection Clause of the Fourteenth Amendment *applies* to aliens who, after their illegal entry into this country, are indeed physically "within the jurisdiction" of a state. However, as the Court concedes, this "only begins the inquiry." . . . The Equal Protection Clause does not mandate identical treatment of different categories of persons. . . .

The dispositive issue in these cases, simply put, is whether, for purposes of allocating its finite resources, a state has a legitimate reason to differentiate between persons who are lawfully within the state and those who are unlawfully there. The distinction the State of Texas has drawn—based not only upon its own legitimate interests but on classifications established by the Federal Government in its immigration laws and policies—is not unconstitutional.

# A

The Court acknowledges that, except in those cases when state classifications disadvantage a "suspect class" or impinge upon a "fundamental right," the Equal Protection Clause permits a state "substantial latitude" in distinguishing between different groups of persons.... Moreover, the Court expressly—and correctly—rejects any suggestion that illegal aliens are a suspect class ... or that education is a fundamental right.... Yet by patching together bits and pieces of what might be termed quasi-suspect-class and quasi-fundamental-rights analysis, the Court spins out a theory custom-tailored to the facts of these cases.

In the end, we are told little more than that the level of scrutiny employed to strike down the Texas law applies only when illegal alien children are deprived of a public education.... If ever a court was guilty of an unabashedly result-oriented approach, this case is a prime example....

# 1

The Court first suggests that these illegal alien children, although not a suspect class, are entitled to special solicitude under the Equal Protection Clause because they lack "control" over or "responsibility" for their unlawful entry into this country.... Similarly, the Court appears to take the position that § 21.031 is presumptively "irrational" because it has the effect of imposing "penalties" on "innocent" children.... However, the Equal Protection Clause does not preclude legislators from classifying among persons on the basis of factors and characteristics over which individuals may be said to lack "control." Indeed, in some circumstances persons generally, and children in particular, may have little control over or responsibility for such things as their ill health, need for public assistance, or place of residence. Yet a state legislature is not barred from considering, for example, relevant differences between the mentally healthy and the mentally ill, or between the residents of different counties ... simply because these may be factors unrelated to individual choice or to any "wrongdoing." The Equal Protection Clause protects against arbitrary and irrational classifications, and against invidious discrimination stemming from prejudice and hostility; it is not an all-encompassing "equalizer" designed to eradicate every distinction for which persons are not "responsible." ...

The Court does not presume to suggest that appellees' purported lack of culpability for their illegal status prevents them from being deported or otherwise "penalized" under federal law. Yet would deportation be any less a "penalty" than denial of privileges provided to legal residents?... Illegality of presence in the United States does not—and need not—depend on some amorphous concept of "guilt" or "innocence" concerning an alien's entry. Similarly, a state's use of federal immigration status as a basis for legislative classification is not necessarily rendered suspect for its failure to take such factors into account....

The Court's analogy to cases involving discrimination against illegitimate children ... is grossly misleading. The State has not thrust any disabilities upon appellees due to their "status of birth.".... Rather, appellees' status is predicated upon the circumstances of their concededly illegal presence in this country, and is a direct result of Congress' obviously valid exercise of its "broad constitutional powers" in the field of immigration and naturalization.... This Court has recognized that in allocating governmental benefits to a given class of aliens, one "may take into account the character of the relationship between the alien and this country."... When that "relationship" is a federally prohibited one, there can, of course, be no presumption that a state has a constitutional duty to include illegal aliens among the recipients of its governmental benefits....

# B

Once it is conceded—as the Court does—that illegal aliens are not a suspect class, and that education is not a fundamental right, our inquiry should focus on and be limited to whether the legislative classification at issue bears a rational relationship to a legitimate state purpose....

The State contends primarily that § 21.031 serves to prevent undue depletion of its limited revenues available for education and to preserve the fiscal integrity of the State's school-financing system against an ever-increasing flood of illegal aliens—aliens over whose entry or continued presence it has no control. Of course such fiscal concerns alone could not justify discrimination against a suspect class or an arbitrary and irrational denial of benefits to a particular group of persons. Yet I assume no Member of this Court would argue that prudent conservation of finite state revenues is *per se* an illegitimate goal. Indeed, the numerous classifications this Court has sustained in social welfare legislation were invariably related to the limited amount of revenues available to spend on any given program or set of programs.... The significant question here is whether the requirement of tuition from illegal aliens who attend the public schools—as well as from residents of other states, for example—is a rational and reasonable means of furthering the State's legitimate fiscal ends....

... It simply is not "irrational" for a state to conclude that it does not have the same responsibility to provide benefits for persons whose very presence in the state and this country is illegal as it does to provide for persons lawfully present. By definition, illegal aliens have no right whatever to be here, and the state may reasonably, and constitutionally, elect not to provide them with governmental services at the expense of those who are lawfully in the state....

It is significant that the Federal Government has seen fit to exclude illegal aliens from numerous social welfare programs, such as the food stamp program ... the old-age assistance, aid to families with dependent children, aid to the blind, aid to the permanently and totally disabled, and supplemental security income programs ... the Medicare hospital insurance benefits program ... and the Medicaid hospital insurance benefits for the aged and disabled program.... Although these exclusions do not conclusively demonstrate the constitutionality of the State's use of the same classification for comparable purposes, at the very least they tend to support the rationality of excluding illegal alien residents of a state from such programs so as to preserve the state's finite revenues for the benefit of lawful residents....

The Court maintains—as if this were the issue—that "barring undocumented children from local schools would not necessarily improve the quality of education provided in those schools."... However, the legitimacy of barring illegal aliens from programs such as Medicare or Medicaid does not depend on a showing that the barrier would "improve the quality" of medical care given to persons lawfully entitled to participate in such programs. Modern education, like medical care, is enormously expensive, and there can be no doubt that very large added costs will fall on the State or its local school districts as a result of the inclusion of illegal aliens in the tuition-free public schools. The State may, in its discretion, use any savings resulting from its tuition requirement to "improve the quality of education" in the public school system, or to enhance the funds available for other social programs, or to reduce the tax burden placed on its residents; each of these ends is "legitimate." The State need not show, as the Court implies, that the incremental cost of educating illegal aliens will send it into bankruptcy, or have a "grave impact on the quality of education"...; that is not dispositive under a "rational basis" scrutiny. In the absence of a constitutional imperative to provide for the education of illegal aliens, the State may "rationally" choose to take advantage of whatever savings will accrue from limiting access to the tuition-free public schools to its own lawful residents, excluding even citizens of neighboring States....

Denying a free education to illegal alien children is not a choice I would make were I a legislator. Apart from compassionate considerations, the long-range costs of excluding any children from the public schools may well outweigh the costs of educating them. But that is not the issue; the fact that there are sound *policy* arguments against the Texas Legislature's choice does not render that choice an unconstitutional one.

---

EXERCISE 7.13. The dissenters in *Plyler v. Doe* accuse the majority of abandoning legal analysis and making a policy judgment to allow the children of illegal aliens to enroll in school. Was this in fact an improper policy intervention by the Court?

EXERCISE 7.14. In the eighteenth and nineteenth centuries, many states gave noncitizens the right to vote at all levels of government. Today the practice of noncitizen voting survives in community school board elections in Chicago and New York and in municipal elections in a number of communities, including Takoma Park, Maryland.

Assume that there is an upcoming referendum in your community on the issue of granting noncitizen parents of children in public schools the right to vote in local school board elections. Divide the class in half; research the issue and hold a debate on the referendum. Should we vote yes or no?

One issue to consider is whether we want noncitizens involved in local government. Why or why not? Recall that permanent residents pay federal, state, and local taxes, are subject to the draft and must obey all laws. But do we dilute the meaning of citizenship by giving aliens the right to vote?

The Supreme Court uses heightened scrutiny to examine discrimination against aliens who are lawfully present in the country. However, the Court does not use heightened scrutiny to test exclusions of aliens from "critical government functions," and the Court has considered teaching such a function. In *Ambach v. Norwick* (1979), the Court upheld New York's ban on employing as teachers any aliens who have become eligible to apply for citizenship but decline to do so. Justice Powell reasoned that because "a teacher has an opportunity to influence the attitudes of students toward government, the political process, and a citizen's social responsibilities," a noncitizen teacher who fails to apply for citizenship sends a negative message to students In dissent, Justice Blackmun argued that New York's rule was "irrational. Is it better to employ a poor citizen teacher than an excellent resident alien teacher? Is it preferable to have a citizen who has never seen Spain or a Latin American country teach Spanish to eighth graders and to deny that opportunity to a resident alien who may have lived for 20 years in the culture of Spain or Latin America?"

EXERCISE 7.15. What do you make of the dissenters' argument that all that should matter is the quality of the person's teaching? Assume that your class is the appointments committee at your high school looking for a new Spanish teacher. The choice has come down to two applicants. One is a forty-year-old El Salvadorean immigrant fluent in both Spanish and English who has a master's degree in Spanish literature. She has lived and worked as a Spanish teacher in the United States for fifteen years, but she declines to apply for citizenship because she still owns property in El Salvador and plans to retire there in twenty years. The other applicant is a twenty-five-year-old recent college graduate and a U.S. citizen by birth who majored in Spanish in college and speaks it very well but with a strong American accent. Unlike the first applicant, he is not certain that he wants to be a teacher for the rest of his career and may want to move into business. But he is a graduate of your school. Who do you select and why?

## Discrimination against Gays and Lesbians

The Supreme Court has never decided a case involving alleged equal protection violations by a public school or university against a gay or lesbian student. However, we know the general outline of the Court's thinking on the issue. On the one hand, the Court does not believe that there is a fundamental privacy right for gays and lesbians to be involved in homosexual relationships or to marry one another. On the other hand, the Court rejects laws and regulations that discriminate against gays out of animosity or prejudice. Ultimately, these two positions are probably irreconcilable, and the law is certain to evolve.

In a deeply polarizing 5–4 decision in 1986 called *Bowers v. Hardwick,* the Court upheld the criminal sodomy conviction of a gay man in Georgia and found that homosexuals have no fundamental due process privacy right to have same-sex relations. However, in 1996 the Court in *Romer v. Evans* struck down a Colorado state constitutional provision forbidding local jurisdictions to grant civil rights protections to gays and lesbians. In that case the Court found that, under equal protection, government actors cannot discriminate against gays and lesbians by denying them equal treatment under law simply based on prejudice and hostility. The *Bowers* and *Romer* decisions are obviously in tension and are likely to be on a collision course as the Court takes up a new generation of lawsuits challenging antigay discrimination.

Although federal civil rights laws do not forbid discrimination on the basis of sexual orientation, nine states—California, Connecticut, Hawaii, Massachusetts, Minnesota, New Jersey, Rhode Island, Vermont, and Wisconsin—have forbidden discrimination in places of public accommodation against gay citizens. The following case from New Jersey got its start when a young man named James Dale, an Eagle Scout, left home for college at Rutgers University. There he came out of the closet and told people he was gay. He soon became copresident of the Rutgers University Lesbian/Gay Alliance. After his name appeared in a newspaper article relating to his work in that capacity, he received a letter from the Boy Scouts revoking his adult membership in the organization. When he asked why, he was told that homosexuals were not allowed as members. Dale sued for readmission under the state's public accommodations law and, when the case went to the New Jersey Supreme Court, he won.

The Boy Scouts appealed to the United States Supreme Court, arguing that New Jersey was violating the First Amendment by forcing the Scouts to take gay members. They argued that being forced to take gay members offended the principles of the organization, which stood for "morally straight" conduct and against homosexuality. The Scouts invoked the Court's 1995 decision in *Hurley v. Irish American Gay, Lesbian and Bisexual*

Eagle Scout James Dale was removed as an assistant scoutmaster in New Jersey after the Boy Scouts learned he was active in Rutgers University's Lesbian/Gay Alliance.

*Group of Boston, Inc.,* which upheld the First Amendment right of the private organizers of the St. Patrick's Day parade in Boston to exclude a formal contingent of gay Irish Americans who wanted to march. In that decision Justice Souter found for the majority that a private speaker could control its own message by arranging or excluding particular elements of expression, much like a conductor putting together a symphony. The Boy Scouts argued that their overall message would be distorted and undermined by having to accept homosexual members. In another bitterly divided 5–4 opinion, the Supreme Court agreed with the Boy Scouts, finding that the group had a First Amendment right to exclude gays.

---

BOY SCOUTS OF AMERICA

v.

DALE

*Supreme Court of the United States*
Argued April 26, 2000.
Decided June 28, 2000.

Chief Justice REHNQUIST delivered the opinion of the Court.

Petitioners are the Boy Scouts of America and the Monmouth Council, a division of the Boy Scouts of America (collectively, Boy Scouts). The Boy Scouts is a private, not-for-profit organization engaged in instilling its system of values in young people. The Boy Scouts asserts that homosexual conduct is inconsistent with the values it seeks to instill. Respondent is James Dale, a former Eagle Scout whose adult membership in the Boy Scouts was revoked when the Boy Scouts learned that he is an avowed homosexual and gay rights activist. The New Jersey Supreme Court held that New Jersey's public accommodations law requires that the Boy Scouts readmit Dale. This case presents the question whether applying New Jersey's public accommodations law in this way violates the Boy Scouts' First Amendment right of expressive association. We hold that it does.

I

James Dale entered Scouting in 1978 at the age of eight by joining Monmouth Council's Cub Scout Pack 142. Dale became a Boy Scout in 1981 and remained a Scout until he turned 18. By all accounts, Dale was an exemplary Scout. In 1988, he achieved the rank of Eagle Scout, one of Scouting's highest honors.

Dale applied for adult membership in the Boy Scouts in 1989. The Boy Scouts approved his application for the position of assistant scoutmaster of Troop 73. Around the same time, Dale left home to attend Rutgers University. After arriving at Rutgers, Dale first acknowledged to himself and others that he is gay. He quickly became involved with, and eventually became the copresident of, the Rutgers University Lesbian/Gay Alliance. In 1990, Dale attended a seminar addressing the psychological and health needs of lesbian and gay teenagers. A newspaper covering the event interviewed Dale about his advocacy of homosexual teenagers' need for gay role models. In early July 1990, the newspaper published the interview and Dale's photograph over a caption identifying him as the copresident of the Lesbian/Gay Alliance.

Later that month, Dale received a letter from Monmouth Council Executive James Kay revoking his adult membership. Dale wrote to Kay requesting the reason for Monmouth Council's decision. Kay responded by letter that the Boy Scouts "specifically forbid membership to homosexuals."

In 1992, Dale filed a complaint against the Boy Scouts in the New Jersey Superior Court. The complaint alleged that the Boy Scouts had violated New Jersey's public accommodations statute and its common law by revoking Dale's membership based solely on his sexual orientation. New Jersey's public accommodations statute prohibits, among other things, discrimination on the basis of sexual orientation in places of public accommodation. [Dale ultimately won his claim before the New Jersey Supreme Court. The Boy Scouts appealed to the United States Supreme Court on First Amendment grounds.]

II

In *Roberts v. United States Jaycees*, we observed that "implicit in the right to engage in activities protected by the First Amendment" is "a corresponding right to associate with others in pursuit of a wide variety of political, social, economic, educational, religious, and cultural ends." This right is crucial in preventing the majority from imposing its views on groups that would rather express other, perhaps unpopular, ideas. Government actions that may unconstitutionally burden this freedom may take many forms, one of which is "intrusion into the internal structure or affairs of an association" like a "regulation that forces the group to accept members it does not desire." Forcing a group to accept certain members may impair the ability of the group to express those views, and only those views, that it intends to express. Thus, "[f]reedom of association . . . plainly presupposes a freedom not to associate."

The forced inclusion of an unwanted person in a group infringes the group's freedom of expressive association if the presence of that person affects in a significant way the group's ability to advocate public or private viewpoints. But the freedom of expressive association, like many freedoms, is not absolute. We have held that the freedom could be overridden "by regulations adopted to serve compelling state interests, unrelated to the suppression of ideas, that cannot be achieved through means significantly less restrictive of associational freedoms."

To determine whether a group is protected by the First Amendment's expressive associational right, we must determine whether the group engages in "expressive association." The First Amendment's protection of expressive association is not reserved for advocacy groups. But to come within its ambit, a group must engage in some form of expression, whether it be public or private.

The general mission of the Boy Scouts is clear: "[T]o instill values in young people." The Boy Scouts seeks to instill these values by having its adult leaders spend time with the youth members, instructing and engaging them in activities like camping, archery, and fishing. During the time spent with the youth members, the scoutmasters and assistant scoutmasters inculcate them with the Boy Scouts' values—both expressly and by example. It seems indisputable that an association that seeks to transmit such a system of values engages in expressive activity.

Given that the Boy Scouts engages in expressive activity, we must determine whether the forced inclusion of Dale as an assistant scoutmaster would significantly affect the Boy Scouts' ability to advocate public or private viewpoints. This inquiry necessarily requires us first to explore, to a limited extent, the nature of the Boy Scouts' view of homosexuality.

The values the Boy Scouts seeks to instill are "based on" those listed in the Scout Oath and Law. The Boy Scouts explains that the Scout Oath and Law provide "a positive moral code for living; they are a list of 'do's' rather than 'don'ts.' " The Boy Scouts asserts that homosexual conduct is inconsistent with the values embodied in the Scout Oath and Law, particularly with the values represented by the terms "morally straight" and "clean."

Obviously, the Scout Oath and Law do not expressly mention sexuality or sexual orientation. And the terms "morally straight" and "clean" are by no means self-defining. Different people would attribute to those terms very different meanings. For example, some people may believe that engaging in homosexual conduct is not at odds with being "morally straight" and "clean." And others may believe that engaging in homosexual conduct is contrary to being "morally straight" and "clean." The Boy Scouts says it falls within the latter category.

The New Jersey Supreme Court analyzed the Boy Scouts' beliefs and found that the "exclusion of members solely on the basis of their sexual orientation is inconsistent with Boy Scouts' commitment to a diverse and 'representative' membership . . . [and] contradicts Boy Scouts' overarching objective to reach 'all eligible youth.' " The court concluded that the exclusion of members like Dale "appears antithetical to the organization's goals and philosophy." But our cases reject this sort of inquiry; it is not the role of the courts to reject a group's expressed values because they disagree with those values or find them internally inconsistent.

The Boy Scouts asserts that it "teach[es] that homosexual conduct is not morally straight," and that it does "not want to promote homosexual conduct as a legitimate form of behavior." We accept the Boy Scouts' assertion. We need not inquire further to determine the nature of the Boy Scouts' expression with respect to homosexuality. . . .

We must then determine whether Dale's presence as an assistant scoutmaster would significantly burden the Boy Scouts' desire to not "promote homosexual conduct as a legitimate form of behavior." As we give deference to an association's assertions regarding the nature of its expression, we must also give deference to an association's view of what would impair its expression. That is not to say that an expressive association can erect a shield against antidiscrimination laws simply by asserting that mere acceptance of a member from a particular group would impair its message. But here Dale, by his own admission, is one of a group of gay Scouts who have "become leaders in their community and are open and honest about their sexual orientation." Dale was the copresident of a gay and lesbian organization at college and remains a gay rights activist. Dale's presence in the Boy Scouts would, at the very least, force the organization to send a message, both to the youth members and the world, that the Boy Scouts accepts homosexual conduct as a legitimate form of behavior.

Here, we have found that the Boy Scouts believes that homosexual conduct is inconsistent with the values it seeks to instill in its youth members; it will not "promote homosexual conduct as a legitimate form of behavior." The presence of Dale as an assistant scoutmaster would just as surely interfere with the Boy Scouts' choice not to propound a point of view contrary to its beliefs.

The New Jersey Supreme Court determined that the Boy Scouts' ability to disseminate its message was not significantly affected by the forced inclusion of Dale as an assistant scoutmaster because of the following findings:

> Boy Scout members do not associate for the purpose of disseminating the belief that homosexuality is immoral; Boy Scouts discourages its leaders from disseminating *any* views on sexual issues; and Boy Scouts includes sponsors and members who subscribe to different views in respect of homosexuality.

We disagree with the New Jersey Supreme Court's conclusion drawn from these findings.

First, associations do not have to associate for the "purpose" of disseminating a certain message in order to be entitled to the protections of the First Amendment. An association must merely engage in expressive activity that could be impaired in order to be entitled to protection.

Second, even if the Boy Scouts discourages Scout leaders from disseminating views on sexual issues—a fact that the Boy Scouts disputes with contrary evidence—the First Amendment protects the Boy Scouts' method of expression. If the Boy Scouts wishes Scout leaders to avoid questions of sexuality and teach only by example, this fact does not negate the sincerity of its belief discussed above.

Third, the First Amendment simply does not require that every member of a group agree on every issue in order for the group's policy to be "expressive association." The Boy Scouts takes an official position with respect to homosexual conduct, and that is sufficient for First Amendment purposes. In this same vein, Dale makes much of the claim that the Boy Scouts does not revoke the membership of heterosexual Scout leaders that openly disagree with the Boy Scouts' policy on sexual orientation. But if this is true, it is irrelevant. The presence of an avowed homosexual and gay rights activist in an assistant scoutmaster's uniform sends a distinctly different message from the presence of a heterosexual assistant scoutmaster who is on record as disagreeing with Boy Scouts policy. The Boy Scouts has a First Amendment right to choose to send one message but not the other. The fact that the organization does not trumpet its views from the housetops, or that it tolerates dissent within its ranks, does not mean that its views receive no First Amendment protection.

Having determined that the Boy Scouts is an expressive association and that the forced inclusion of Dale would significantly affect its expression, we inquire whether the application of New Jersey's public accommodations law to require that the Boy Scouts accept Dale as an assistant scoutmaster runs afoul of the Scouts' freedom of expressive association. We conclude that it does.

State public accommodations laws were originally enacted to prevent discrimination in traditional places of public accommodation—like inns and trains. Over time, the public accommodations laws have expanded to cover more places. New Jersey's statutory definition of "[a] place of public accommodation" is extremely broad. The term is said to "include, but not be limited to," a list of over 50 types of places. Many on the list are what one would expect to be places where the public is invited. . . . In this case, the New Jersey Supreme Court went a step further and applied its public accommodations law to a private entity without even attempting to tie the term "place" to a physical location. As the definition of "public accommodation" has expanded from clearly commercial entities, such as restaurants, bars, and hotels, to membership organizations such as the Boy Scouts, the potential for conflict between state public accommodations laws and the First Amendment rights of organizations has increased.

We have already concluded that a state requirement that the Boy Scouts retain Dale as an assistant scoutmaster would significantly burden the organization's right to oppose or disfavor homosexual conduct. The state interests embodied in New Jersey's public accommodations law do not justify such a severe intrusion on the Boy Scouts' rights to freedom of expressive association. That being the case, we hold that the First Amendment prohibits the State from imposing such a requirement through the application of its public accommodations law....

The judgment of the New Jersey Supreme Court is reversed, and the case is remanded for further proceedings not inconsistent with this opinion.

Justice STEVENS, with whom Justice SOUTER, Justice GINSBURG, and Justice BREYER join, dissenting....

## V

In its briefs, BSA implies, even if it does not directly argue, that Dale would use his Scoutmaster position as a "bully pulpit" to convey immoral messages to his troop, and therefore his inclusion in the group would compel BSA to include a message it does not want to impart. Even though the majority does not endorse that argument, I think it is important to explain why it lacks merit, before considering the argument the majority does accept.

BSA has not contended, nor does the record support, that Dale had ever advocated a view on homosexuality to his troop before his membership was revoked. Accordingly, BSA's revocation could only have been based on an assumption that he would do so in the future.

The majority, though, does not rest its conclusion on the claim that Dale will use his position as a bully pulpit. Rather, it contends that Dale's mere presence among the Boy Scouts will itself force the group to convey a message about homosexuality—even if Dale has no intention of doing so. The majority holds that "[t]he presence of an avowed homosexual and gay rights activist in an assistant scoutmaster's uniform sends a distinc[t] ... message," and, accordingly, BSA is entitled to exclude that message. In particular, "Dale's presence in the Boy Scouts would, at the very least, force the organization to send a message, both to the youth members and the world, that the Boy Scouts accepts homosexual conduct as a legitimate form of behavior."

The only apparent explanation for the majority's holding, then, is that homosexuals are simply so different from the rest of society that their presence alone—unlike any other individual's—should be singled out for special First Amendment treatment. Under the majority's reasoning, an openly gay male is irreversibly affixed with the label "homosexual." That label, even though unseen, communicates a message that permits his exclusion wherever he goes. His openness is the sole and sufficient justification for his ostracism. Though unintended, reliance on such a justification is tantamount to a constitutionally prescribed symbol of inferiority. As counsel for BSA remarked, Dale "put a banner around his neck when he ... got himself into the newspaper.... He created a reputation.... He can't take that banner off. He put it on himself and, indeed, he has continued to put it on himself."

The State of New Jersey has decided that people who are open and frank about their sexual orientation are entitled to equal access to employment as schoolteachers, police officers, librarians, athletic coaches, and a host of other jobs filled by citizens who serve as role models for children and adults alike. Dozens of Scout units throughout the State are sponsored by public agencies, such as schools and fire departments, that employ such role models. BSA's affiliation with numerous public agencies that comply with New Jersey's law against discrimination cannot be understood to convey any particular message endorsing or condoning the activities of all these people.

## VI

Unfavorable opinions about homosexuals "have ancient roots." Like equally atavistic opinions about certain racial groups, those roots have been nourished by sectarian doctrine. Over the years, however, interaction with real people, rather than mere adherence to traditional ways of thinking about members of unfamiliar classes, have modified those opinions.

That such prejudices are still prevalent and that they have caused serious and tangible harm to countless members of the class New Jersey seeks to protect are established matters of fact that neither the Boy Scouts nor the Court disputes. That harm can only be aggravated by the creation of a constitutional shield for a policy that is itself the product of a habitual way of thinking about strangers. As Justice Brandeis so wisely advised, "we must be ever on our guard, lest we erect our prejudices into legal principles."

If we would guide by the light of reason, we must let our minds be bold. I respectfully dissent.

---

**FOR THE CLASS**

PUBLIC DISPLAYS OF INTOLERANCE? In May 2003 Imaginary High School in Bismarck, North Dakota, held its senior prom. A week before the prom Principal Moffit received an anonymous letter indicating that several gay and lesbian couples were planning to attend the prom together, something that had never happened before. Principal Moffitt read this letter aloud at a school assembly and then announced that "any display of homosexual affection will upset many students, teachers, and parents and could create safety risks for the students involved. We want to remind everyone that we have a rule against public displays of affection here. And this kind creates a special danger."

Nonetheless, two same-sex couples arrived together at the prom—John Hargrove and Louis Spivak, and Elizabeth Warner and Paula Trahane. Like other prom dates, the couples danced together, which caused much whispering and gossiping at first. But as the night wore on, other students seemed to grow more comfortable with the same-sex couples, and some even invited the gay students to dance with them.

However, during the traditional last "slow dance" of the evening, Principal Moffit interrupted John and Louis and Elizabeth and Paula while they were dancing and escorted them brusquely out of the dance hall. He told them that they were violating rule twelve of the school code of sonduct, which forbids "public displays of affection at school-sponsored events." He told the students that they had been photographed "necking and making out" on the dance floor. They each admitted to "kissing" on the dance floor but protested that, as Elizabeth said, "half of the people on the dance floor are making out." The principal said, "if you're caught speeding, it's no defense to say other people were doing it too." The next day Principal Moffit conducted hearings and suspended each student for seven days for violating the rule. He rejected the students' arguments, which were uncontradicted, that no straight student was being suspended despite the fact that dozens had engaged in the same conduct. He also dismissed the argument, equally uncontradicted, that the school's usual punishment for first-offense public displays of affection was to issue a warning. Although Principal Moffit noted that no student had ever before been suspended for making out at school, he said there "were special circumstances, because I gave you specific warning and this type of contact could have been dangerous to you and others."

The four students appealed their suspensions to federal district court, alleging that their disparate treatment as gay students violated their equal protection rights. The school says that it had authority to punish the gay students more harshly because they were "on special alert," "their conduct could provoke violence against them in a very conservative community," and "homosexual sodomy is illegal in North Dakota anyway."

No federal court had ever ruled on this issue before, so it was a "case of first impression." Form a panel of three federal judges to hear the case, and make other students into witnesses or lawyers for either side. The judges should rule on the equal protection claim.

*Extra credit bonus question for future judges:* Do the students also have a First Amendment defense or a privacy defense? Is there a constitutional right to kiss or make other displays of affection in public?

---

### Read On

Bell, Derrick A., Jr. *Race, Racism, and American Law.* Boston: Little, Brown, 1980.

Carson, Clayborne, ed. *Eyes on the Prize: Civil Rights Reader.* New York: Penguin Books, 1991.

Kluger, Richard. *Simple Justice: The History of* Brown v. Board of Education *and Black America's Struggle for Equality.* New York: Knopf, 1975.

Kozol, Jonathan. *Savage Inequalities: Children in America's Schools.* New York: Crown Publishing, 1991.

Lagemann, Ellen C., and Lamar P. Miller, eds. Brown v. Board of Education: *The Challenge for Today's Schools.* New York: Teachers College Press, 1996.

Raskin, Jamin B. "Legal Aliens, Local Citizens: The Historical, Constitutional, and Theoretical Meanings of Alien Suffrage," *University of Pennsylvania Law Review 1391* 141 (1993).

Whitman, Mark. *The Irony of Desegregation Law 1955–1995.* Princeton: M. Wiener, 1998.

# 8 HARASSMENT IN THE HALLS: SEXUAL HARASSMENT AND BULLYING AT SCHOOL

"No person in the United States shall, on the basis of sex, be excluded from participation in, be denied the benefits of, or be subjected to discrimination under any education program or activity receiving federal financial assistance." TITLE IX (20 U.S.C. § 1681)

"There were two or three boys touching me ... and I'd tell them to stop but they wouldn't. This went on for ... months. Finally I was in one of my classes when all of them came back and backed me into a corner and started touching me all over.... After the class I told the principal, and he and the boys had a little talk. And after the talk was up, the boys came out laughing because they got no punishment." NAN STEIN AND LISA SJOSTRAM, *FLIRTING OR HURTING? A TEACHER'S GUIDE TO STUDENT-TO-STUDENT SEXUAL HARASSMENT IN SCHOOLS*

For most adults, high school evokes images of cramming for calculus tests, going to yearbook meetings, cheering on the home team, enjoying school musicals, and pinning on corsages at senior proms. But there has always been a dark side to high school: the teasing, put-downs, ridicule, and hazing that students sometimes inflict on one another, as well as the abuse of power over students practiced by a few bad-apple teachers and administrators. Sometimes these behaviors reach a point where they become illegal. This is the case with *sexual harassment*, which is defined as unwanted and unwelcome sexual advances and conduct that interfere with a student's education.

Sexual harassment is a serious and pervasive problem in American schools. In 1993 the American Association of University Women released a study done by Louis Harris and Associates called *Hostile Hallways*, which surveyed more than 1,600 American public high school students (grades 8 through 11). The findings were astonishing: 85 percent of the girls and 76 percent of the boys reported experiencing some kind of sexual harassment, including unwanted sexual touching, grabbing, comments, and gestures. All told, four out of five students had, to one degree or another, personally faced sexual harassment. Such harassment can undermine a student's academic performance and ruin his or her sense of physical, emotional, and mental well-being. Whereas student-on-student harassment is most common, some students face sexual harassment from teachers, coaches, advisers, staff, and even principals.

Although sexual harassment of students is not in any sense unconstitutional, it is illegal under Title IX of the Education Amendments of 1972, a federal statute passed by Congress. Under Title IX, sexual harassment in any school receiving federal funds, whether public or private, is considered a form of illegal sex discrimination. Thus any student, male or female, subjected to sexual harassment in any official school program or activity—whether in class or on the sports field, on campus or off campus—can bring suit against his or her school system under Title IX. The cases in this chapter define when a school system is liable for such harassment.

Under Title IX sexual harassment can assume two different forms: quid pro quo sexual harassment and hostile environment sexual harassment. Quid pro quo harassment occurs when a school employee, such as a teacher or staff member, tries to convince a student to submit to unwanted sexual advances as a condition for participating in a school program or extracurricular activity, as a means of getting ahead in some way (such as getting a better grade or a starting position on a team), or as a necessary way to avoid negative consequences (like getting a bad grade or having rumors spread about you). Hostile environment sexual harassment occurs when unwelcome hostile conduct of a sexual nature is so severe, persistent, or pervasive that it interferes with a student's ability to benefit from school or creates an intimidating, threatening, or abusive academic environment. Such an environment might be created by teachers, administrators, other students, or some combination thereof. Examples of conduct that create a hostile environment include leers, sexual banter and ridicule, use of pornography to embarrass and humiliate, unwanted touching, squeezing and fondling, sexual graffiti, persistent negative rumors, sexual "ratings" of students, sexual gestures and mooning, exhibitionist displays, and so on.

There is, of course, some ambiguity about when unwelcome juvenile sexual conduct actually crosses the line and creates a hostile learning environment. Obviously, a couple of bad jokes or a single unwelcome invitation to the movies are not Title IX violations. But the law considers severe and pervasive sexual harassment a serious problem and is willing to gamble that courts will be able to distinguish between an innocent (if undesired) love poem left at someone's desk and a pattern of sexually hostile and demeaning behavior.

**POINTS TO PONDER**

*How can schools and courts tell the difference between innocent teasing or joking and illegal sexual harassment?*

- If a teacher sexually pressures and harasses one of his or her students, should the school system be held legally and financially responsible even if the teacher's superiors were unaware of the situation?
- Should school authorities be held responsible for student-on-student sexual harassment if they know about it and do nothing to stop it? What if they are unaware of what is going on?

# When Teachers Harass Students

If a student brings a Title IX action alleging that she is being sexually harassed by a teacher and proves it, is the school automatically liable at that point for monetary damages? Or must the student first show that someone in authority at the school knew about the inappropriate behavior and failed to stop it? In *Gebser v. Lago Vista Independent School District* (1998), the Court found that a school district is liable for damages under Title IX for a teacher's sexual harassment of a student only if officials higher up in the school actually knew about it and chose to do nothing. Does this "deliberate indifference" standard leave students too vulnerable to predatory adults? See what you think by reading the majority and dissenting opinions.

---

GEBSER

v.

LAGO VISTA INDEPENDENT SCHOOL DISTRICT

*Supreme Court of the United States*
Argued March 25, 1998.
Decided June 22, 1998.

Justice O'CONNOR delivered the opinion of the Court.

The question in this case is when a school district may be held liable in damages in an implied right of action under Title IX of the Education Amendments (Title IX) for the sexual harassment of a student by one of the district's teachers. We conclude that damages may not be recovered in those circumstances unless an official of the school district who at a minimum has authority to institute corrective measures on the district's behalf has actual notice of, and is deliberately indifferent to, the teacher's misconduct.

I

In the spring of 1991, when petitioner Alida Star Gebser was an eighth-grade student at a middle school in respondent Lago Vista Independent School District (Lago Vista), she joined a high school book discussion group led by Frank Waldrop, a teacher at Lago Vista's high school. Lago Vista received federal funds at all pertinent times. During the book discussion sessions, Waldrop often made sexually suggestive comments to the students. Gebser entered high school in the fall and was assigned to classes taught by Waldrop in both semesters. Waldrop continued to make inappropriate remarks to the students, and he began to direct more of his suggestive comments toward Gebser, including during the substantial amount of time that the two were alone in his classroom. He initiated sexual contact with Gebser in the spring, when, while visiting her home ostensibly to give her a book, he kissed and fondled her. The two had sexual intercourse on a number of occasions during the remainder of the school year. Their relationship continued through the summer and into the following school year, and they often had intercourse during class time, although never on school property.

Gebser did not report the relationship to school officials, testifying that while she realized Waldrop's conduct was improper, she was uncertain how to react and she wanted to continue having him as a teacher. In October 1992, the parents of two other students complained to the high school principal about Waldrop's comments in class. The principal arranged a meeting, at which, according to the principal, Waldrop indicated that he did not believe he had made offensive remarks but apologized to the parents and said it would not happen again. The principal also advised Waldrop to be careful about his classroom comments and told the school guidance counselor about the meeting, but he did not report the parents' complaint to Lago Vista's superintendent, who was the district's Title IX coordinator. A couple of months later, in January 1993, a police officer discovered Waldrop and Gebser engaging in sexual intercourse and arrested Waldrop. Lago Vista terminated his employment, and subsequently, the Texas Education Agency revoked his teaching license. During this time, the district had not promulgated or distributed an official grievance procedure for lodging sexual harassment complaints; nor had it issued a formal anti-harassment policy. . . .

III

. . . When a teacher's sexual harassment is imputed to a school district or when a school district is deemed to have "constructively" known of the teacher's harassment, by assumption the district had no actual knowledge of the teacher's conduct. Nor, of course, did the district have an opportunity to take action to end the harassment or to limit further harassment. . . .

IV

. . . [W]e hold that a damages remedy will not lie under Title IX unless an official who at a minimum has authority to address the alleged discrimination and to institute corrective measures on the recipient's behalf has actual knowledge of discrimination in the recipient's programs and fails adequately to respond.

We think, moreover, that the response must amount to deliberate indifference to discrimination. The administrative enforcement scheme presupposes that an official who is advised of a Title IX violation refuses to take action to bring the recipient into compliance. The premise, in other words, is an official decision by the recipient not to remedy the violation. That framework finds a rough parallel in the standard of deliberate indifference. Under a lower standard, there would be a risk that the recipient would be liable in damages not for its own official decision but instead for its employees' independent actions. . . .

V

. . . [W]e will not hold a school district liable in damages under Title IX for a teacher's sexual harassment of a student absent actual notice and deliberate indifference. . . .

Justice STEVENS, with whom Justice SOUTER, Justice GINSBURG, and Justice BREYER join, dissenting.

. . . This case presents a paradigmatic example of a tort that was made possible, that was effected, and that was repeated over a prolonged period because of the powerful influence that Waldrop had over Gebser by reason of the authority that his employer, the school district, had delegated to him. As a secondary school teacher, Waldrop exercised even greater authority and control over his students than employers and supervisors exercise over their employees. His gross misuse of that authority allowed him to abuse his young student's trust.

... The Court's holding is also questionable as a factual matter. Waldrop himself surely had ample authority to maintain order in the classes that he conducted. Indeed, that is a routine part of every teacher's responsibilities. If petitioner had been the victim of sexually harassing conduct by other students during those classes, surely the teacher would have had ample authority to take corrective measures. The fact that he did not prevent his own harassment of petitioner is the consequence of his lack of will, not his lack of authority. . . .

. . . As long as school boards can insulate themselves from knowledge about this sort of conduct, they can claim immunity from damages liability. . . . Indeed, the rule that the Court adopts would preclude a damages remedy even if every teacher at the school knew about the harassment but did not have "authority to institute corrective measures on the district's behalf." . . .

IV

. . . A theme that seems to underlie the Court's opinion is a concern that holding a school district liable in damages might deprive it of the benefit of the federal subsidy—that the damages remedy is somehow more onerous than a possible termination of the federal grant. . . . It is not clear to me why the well-settled rules of law that impose responsibility on the principal for the misconduct of its agents should not apply in this case. As a matter of policy, the Court ranks protection of the school district's purse above the protection of immature high school students that those rules would provide. . . .

---

EXERCISE 8.1. What do you think of the dissenting justices' argument that the teacher, Frank Waldrop, is an authority figure within the school and therefore the school should be automatically (or "strictly") liable for his conduct? The majority believes that it is not fair to hold the school financially accountable, because school officials were not aware of the affair. Do you agree with the majority opinion (there must be actual knowledge and "deliberate indifference" before the school system becomes liable) or the dissenting opinion (the school must always be liable for the teacher's actions, even if there was no actual notice that a teacher was harassing a student or having an affair)?

---

# When Students Harass Students

If school systems are liable for their employees' sexual harassment of students when school authorities are aware of the offending behavior, what about when sexual harassment occurs at the hands of fellow students? One line of thought contends that schools are absolutely responsible and liable for anything that happens inside their walls; an opposing line of thought maintains that schools should never be responsible for actions taken by students (as opposed to employees). The Supreme Court has rejected both of these polar positions, ruling instead that, under Title IX, school systems will *sometimes* be liable for student-on-student sexual harassment. Under what conditions does the Court find schools responsible? As in *Gebser*, the Court in *Davis v. Monroe County Board of Education* found that a school can be held liable only when it knows about the harassment and acts with "deliberate indifference" to its existence. The Court also found that, in order for a plaintiff student to win her case, the harassment must be "severe, pervasive, and objectively offensive." The dissenters say that the decision opens the floodgates for litigation over trivial offenses. Do you agree?

———

# DAVIS
## v.
## MONROE COUNTY BOARD OF EDUCATION

*Supreme Court of the United States*
Argued Jan. 12, 1999.
Decided May 24, 1999.

Justice O'CONNOR delivered the opinion of the Court.

Petitioner brought suit against the Monroe County Board of Education and other defendants, alleging that her fifth-grade daughter had been the victim of sexual harassment by another student in her class. Among petitioner's claims was a claim for monetary and injunctive relief under Title IX of the Education Amendments of 1972. The District Court dismissed petitioner's Title IX claim on the ground that "student-on-student," or peer, harassment provides no ground for a private cause of action under the statute. The Court of Appeals for the Eleventh Circuit affirmed. We consider here whether a private damages action may lie against the school board in cases of student-on-student harassment. We conclude that it may, but only where the funding recipient acts with deliberate indifference to known acts of harassment in its programs or activities. Moreover, we conclude that such an action will lie only for harassment that is so severe, pervasive, and objectively offensive that it effectively bars the victim's access to an educational opportunity or benefit.

## I

### A

... According to petitioner's complaint, the harassment began in December 1992, when the classmate, G. F., attempted to touch LaShonda's breasts and genital area and made vulgar statements such as "I want to get in bed with you" and "I want to feel your boobs." Similar conduct allegedly occurred on or about January 4 and January 20, 1993. LaShonda reported each of these incidents to her mother and to her classroom teacher, Diane Fort. Petitioner, in turn, also contacted Fort, who allegedly assured petitioner that the school principal, Bill Querry, had been informed of the incidents. Petitioner contends that, notwithstanding these reports, no disciplinary action was taken against G. F.

G. F.'s conduct allegedly continued for many months. In early February, G. F. purportedly placed a door stop in his pants and proceeded to act in a sexually suggestive manner toward LaShonda during physical education class. LaShonda reported G. F.'s behavior to her physical education teacher, Whit Maples. Approximately one week later, G. F. again allegedly engaged in harassing behavior, this time while under the supervision of another classroom teacher, Joyce Pippen.

LaShonda Davis (right) with her mother in May 1999. Davis was only ten years old when she suffered through five months of crude sexual taunts and advances in the 1992–1993 school year.

Again, LaShonda allegedly reported the incident to the teacher, and again petitioner contacted the teacher to follow up.

Petitioner alleges that G. F. once more directed sexually harassing conduct toward LaShonda in physical education class in early March, and that LaShonda reported the incident to both Maples and Pippen. In mid-April 1993, G. F. allegedly rubbed his body against LaShonda in the school hallway in what LaShonda considered a sexually suggestive manner, and LaShonda again reported the matter to Fort.

The string of incidents finally ended in mid-May, when G. F. was charged with, and pleaded guilty to, sexual battery for his misconduct. The complaint alleges that LaShonda had suffered during the months of harassment, however; specifically, her previously high grades allegedly dropped as she became unable to concentrate on her studies, and, in April 1993, her father discovered that she had written a suicide note. The complaint further alleges that, at one point, LaShonda told petitioner that she "didn't know how much longer she could keep [G. F.] off her."

Nor was LaShonda G. F.'s only victim; it is alleged that other girls in the class fell prey to G. F.'s conduct. At one point, in fact, a group composed of LaShonda and other female students tried to speak with Principal Querry about G. F.'s behavior. According to the complaint, however, a teacher denied the students' request with the statement, "If [Querry] wants you, he'll call you."

Petitioner alleges that no disciplinary action was taken in response to G. F.'s behavior toward LaShonda. In addition to her conversations with Fort and Pippen, petitioner alleges that she spoke with Principal Querry in mid-May 1993. When petitioner inquired as to what action the school intended to take against G. F., Querry simply stated, "I guess I'll have to threaten him a little bit harder." Yet, petitioner alleges, at no point during the many months of his reported misconduct was G. F. disciplined for harassment. Indeed, Querry allegedly asked petitioner why LaShonda "was the only one complaining."

Nor, according to the complaint, was any effort made to separate G. F. and LaShonda. On the contrary, notwithstanding LaShonda's frequent complaints, only after more than three months of reported harassment was she even permitted to change her classroom seat so that she was no longer seated next to G. F. Moreover, petitioner alleges that, at the time of the events in question, the Monroe County Board of Education (Board) had not instructed its personnel on how to respond to peer sexual harassment and had not established a policy on the issue....

## II

... [A]t issue here is the question whether a recipient of federal education funding may be liable for damages under Title IX under any circumstances for discrimination in the form of student-on-student sexual harassment.

## A

We disagree with respondents' assertion, however, that petitioner seeks to hold the Board liable for G. F.'s actions instead of its own. Here, petitioner attempts to hold the Board liable for its own decision to remain idle in the face of known student-on-student harassment in its schools. In *Gebser,* we concluded that a recipient of federal education funds may be liable in damages under Title IX where it is deliberately indifferent to known acts of sexual harassment by a teacher. In that case, a teacher had entered into a sexual relationship with an eighth grade student, and the student sought damages under Title IX for the teacher's misconduct....

Accordingly, we rejected the use of agency principles to impute liability to the district for the misconduct of its teachers. Likewise, we declined the invitation to impose liability under what amounted to a negligence standard—holding the district liable for its failure to react to teacher-student harassment of which it knew or *should have known.* Rather, we concluded that the district could be liable for damages only where the district itself intentionally acted in clear violation of Title IX by remaining deliberately indifferent to acts of teacher-student harassment of which it had actual knowledge.... [W]e concluded in *Gebser* that recipients could be liable in damages only where their own deliberate indifference effectively "cause[d]" the discrimination....

We consider here whether the misconduct identified in *Gebser*—deliberate indifference to known acts of harassment—amounts to an intentional violation of Title IX, capable of supporting a private damages action, when the harasser is a student rather than a teacher. We conclude that, in certain limited circumstances, it does....

... The statute's plain language confines the scope of prohibited conduct based on the recipient's degree of control over the harasser and the environment in which the harassment occurs. If a funding recipient does not engage in harassment directly, it may not be liable for damages unless its deliberate indifference "subject[s]" its students to harassment. That is, the deliberate indifference must, at a minimum, "cause [students] to undergo" harassment or "make them liable or vulnerable" to it....

Where, as here, the misconduct occurs during school hours and on school grounds—the bulk of G. F.'s misconduct, in fact, took place in the classroom—the misconduct is taking place "under" an "operation" of the funding recipient.... In these circumstances, the recipient retains substantial control over the context in which the harassment occurs. More importantly, however, in this setting the Board exercises significant control over the harasser. We have observed, for example, "that the nature of [the State's] power [over public schoolchildren] is custodial and tutelary, permitting a degree of supervision and control that could not be exercised over free adults." ...

While it remains to be seen whether petitioner can show that the Board's response to reports of G. F.'s misconduct was clearly unreasonable in light of the known circumstances, petitioner may be able to show that the Board "subject[ed]" LaShonda to discrimination by failing to respond in any way over a period of five months to complaints of G. F.'s in-school misconduct from LaShonda and other female students.

B

… Having previously determined that "sexual harassment" is "discrimination" in the school context under Title IX, we are constrained to conclude that student-on-student sexual harassment, if sufficiently severe, can likewise rise to the level of discrimination actionable under the statute.…

The most obvious example of student-on-student sexual harassment capable of triggering a damages claim would thus involve the overt, physical deprivation of access to school resources. Consider, for example, a case in which male students physically threaten their female peers every day, successfully preventing the female students from using a particular school resource—an athletic field or a computer lab, for instance. District administrators are well aware of the daily ritual, yet they deliberately ignore requests for aid from the female students wishing to use the resource. The district's knowing refusal to take any action in response to such behavior would fly in the face of Title IX's core principles, and such deliberate indifference may appropriately be subject to claims for monetary damages. It is not necessary, however, to show physical exclusion to demonstrate that students have been deprived by the actions of another student or students of an educational opportunity on the basis of sex. Rather, a plaintiff must establish sexual harassment of students that is so severe, pervasive, and objectively offensive, and that so undermines and detracts from the victims' educational experience, that the victim-students are effectively denied equal access to an institution's resources and opportunities.

Whether gender-oriented conduct rises to the level of actionable "harassment" thus "depends on a constellation of surrounding circumstances, expectations, and relationships," including, but not limited to, the ages of the harasser and the victim and the number of individuals involved, moreover, must bear in mind that schools are unlike the adult workplace and that children may regularly interact in a manner that would be unacceptable among adults. Indeed, at least early on, students are still learning how to interact appropriately with their peers. It is thus understandable that, in the school setting, students often engage in insults, banter, teasing, shoving, pushing, and gender-specific conduct that is upsetting to the students subjected to it. Damages are not available for simple acts of teasing and name-calling among school children, however, even where these comments target differences in gender. Rather, in the context of student-on-student harassment, damages are available only where the behavior is so severe, pervasive, and objectively offensive that it denies its victims the equal access to education that Title IX is designed to protect.

The dissent fails to appreciate these very real limitations on a funding recipient's liability under Title IX. It is not enough to show, as the dissent would read this opinion to provide, that a student has been "teased," or "called offensive names[.]" Comparisons to an "overweight child who skips gym class because the other children tease her about her size," the student "who refuses to wear glasses to avoid the taunts of 'four-eyes,'" and "the child who refuses to go to school because the school bully calls him a 'scaredy-cat' at recess," are inapposite and misleading. Nor do we contemplate, much less hold, that a mere "decline in grades is enough to survive" a motion to dismiss. The drop-off in LaShonda's grades provides necessary evidence of a potential link between her education and G. F.'s misconduct, but petitioner's ability to state a cognizable claim here depends equally on the alleged persistence and severity of G. F.'s actions, not to mention the Board's alleged knowledge and deliberate indifference. We trust that the dissent's characterization of our opinion will not mislead courts to impose more sweeping liability than we read Title IX to require.

Moreover, the provision that the discrimination occur "under any education program or activity" suggests that the behavior be serious enough to have the systemic effect of denying the victim equal access to an educational program or activity. Although, in theory, a single instance of sufficiently severe one-on-one peer harassment could be said to have such an effect, we think it unlikely that Congress would have thought such behavior sufficient to rise to this level in light of the inevitability of student misconduct and the amount of litigation that would be invited by entertaining claims of official indifference to a single instance of one-on-one peer harassment. By limiting private damages actions to cases having a systemic effect on educational programs or activities, we reconcile the general principle that Title IX prohibits official indifference to known peer sexual harassment with the practical realities of responding to student behavior, realities that Congress could not have meant to be ignored. . . .

The fact that it was a teacher who engaged in harassment in *Franklin* and *Gebser* is relevant. The relationship between the harasser and the victim necessarily affects the extent to which the misconduct can be said to breach Title IX's guarantee of equal access to educational benefits and to have a systemic effect on a program or activity. Peer harassment, in particular, is less likely to satisfy these requirements than is teacher-student harassment.

C

Applying this standard to the facts at issue here, we conclude that the Eleventh Circuit erred in dismissing petitioner's complaint. Petitioner alleges that her daughter was the victim of repeated acts of sexual harassment by G. F. over a 5-month period, and there are allegations in support of the conclusion that G. F.'s misconduct was severe, pervasive, and objectively offensive. The harassment was not only verbal; it included numerous acts of objectively offensive touching, and, indeed, G. F. ultimately pleaded guilty to criminal sexual misconduct. Moreover, the complaint alleges that there were multiple victims who were sufficiently disturbed by G. F.'s misconduct to seek an audience with the school principal. Further, petitioner contends that the harassment had a concrete, negative effect on her daughter's ability to receive an education. The complaint also suggests that petitioner may be able to show both actual knowledge and deliberate indifference on the part of the Board, which made no effort whatsoever either to investigate or to put an end to the harassment.

Justice KENNEDY, with whom The Chief Justice, Justice SCALIA, and Justice THOMAS join, dissenting. . . .

B

. . . The practical obstacles schools encounter in ensuring that thousands of immature students conform their conduct to acceptable norms may be even more significant than the legal obstacles. School districts cannot exercise the same measure of control over thousands of students that they do over a few hundred adult employees. The limited resources of our schools must be conserved for basic educational services. Some schools lack the resources even to deal with serious problems of violence and are already overwhelmed with disciplinary problems of all kinds.

Perhaps even more startling than its broad assumptions about school control over primary and secondary school students is the majority's failure to grapple in any meaningful way with the distinction between elementary and secondary schools, on the one hand, and universities on the other. The majority bolsters its argument that schools can control their students' actions by quoting our decision in *Vernonia School District v. Acton* for the proposition that "the nature of [the State's] power [over public school children] is custodial and tutelary, permitting a degree of supervision and control that could not be exercised over free adults." Yet the majority's holding would appear to apply with equal force to universities, which do not exercise custodial and tutelary power over their adult students.

A university's power to discipline its students for speech that may constitute sexual harassment is also circumscribed by the First Amendment. A number of federal courts have already confronted difficult problems raised by university speech codes designed to deal with peer sexual and racial harassment....

The difficulties associated with speech codes simply underscore the limited nature of a university's control over student behavior that may be viewed as sexual harassment....

## II

... The law recognizes that children—particularly young children—are not fully accountable for their actions because they lack the capacity to exercise mature judgment. It should surprise no one, then, that the schools that are the primary locus of most children's social development are rife with inappropriate behavior by children who are just learning to interact with their peers. [Those] on the front lines of our schools describe the situation best:

> Unlike adults in the workplace, juveniles have limited life experiences or familial influences upon which to establish an understanding of appropriate behavior. The real world of school discipline is a rough-and-tumble place where students practice newly learned vulgarities, erupt with anger, tease and embarrass each other, share offensive notes, flirt, push and shove in the halls, grab and offend.

No one contests that much of this "dizzying array of immature or uncontrollable behaviors by students" is inappropriate, even "objectively offensive" at times ... and that parents and schools have a moral and ethical responsibility to help students learn to interact with their peers in an appropriate manner. It is doubtless the case, moreover, that much of this inappropriate behavior is directed toward members of the opposite sex, as children in the throes of adolescence struggle to express their emerging sexual identities.

It is a far different question, however, whether it is either proper or useful to label this immature, childish behavior gender discrimination. Nothing in Title IX suggests that Congress even contemplated this question, much less answered it in the affirmative in unambiguous terms....

The difficulties schools will encounter in identifying peer sexual harassment are already evident in teachers' manuals designed to give guidance on the subject. For example, one teachers' manual on peer sexual harassment suggests that sexual harassment in kindergarten through third grade includes a boy being "put down" on the playground "because he wants to play house with the girls" or a girl being "put down because she shoots baskets better than the boys." Yet another manual suggests that one student saying to another, "You look nice," could be sexual harassment, depending on the "tone of voice," how the student looks at the other, and "who else is around." Blowing a kiss is also suspect. This confusion will likely be compounded once the sexual-harassment label is invested with the force of federal law, backed up by private damages suits.

The only guidance the majority gives schools in distinguishing between the "simple acts of teasing and name-calling among school children," said not to be a basis for suit even when they "target differences in gender," and actionable peer sexual harassment is, in reality, no guidance at all. The majority proclaims that "in the context of student-on-student harassment, damages are available only in the situation where the behavior is so serious, pervasive, and objectively offensive that it denies its victims the equal access to education that Title IX is designed to protect." The majority does not even purport to explain, however, what constitutes an actionable denial of "equal access to education." Is equal access denied when a girl who tires of being chased by the boys at recess refuses to go outside? When she cannot concentrate during class because she is worried about the recess activities? When she pretends to be sick one day so she can stay home from school? It appears the majority is content to let juries decide....

The only real clue the majority gives schools about the dividing line between actionable harassment that denies a victim equal access to education and mere inappropriate teasing is a profoundly unsettling one: On the facts of this case, petitioner has stated a claim because she alleged, in the majority's words, "that the harassment had a concrete, negative effect on her daughter's ability to receive an education." In petitioner's words, the effects that might have been visible to the school were that her daughter's grades "dropped" and her "ability to concentrate on her school work [was] affected." Almost all adolescents experience these problems at one time or another as they mature.

III

... The majority seems oblivious to the fact that almost every child, at some point, has trouble in school because he or she is being teased by his or her peers. The girl who wants to skip recess because she is teased by the boys is no different from the overweight child who skips gym class because the other children tease about her size in the locker room; or the child who risks flunking out because he refuses to wear glasses to avoid the taunts of "four-eyes"; or the child who refuses to go to school because the school bully calls him a "scaredy-cat" at recess. Most children respond to teasing in ways that detract from their ability to learn. The majority's test for actionable harassment will, as a result, sweep in almost all of the more innocuous conduct it acknowledges as a ubiquitous part of school life.

The string of adjectives the majority attaches to the word "harassment"—"severe, pervasive, and objectively offensive"—likewise fails to narrow the class of conduct that can trigger liability, since the touchstone for determining whether there is Title IX liability is the effect on the child's ability to get an education. Indeed, the Court's reliance on the impact on the child's educational experience suggests that the "objective offensiveness" of a comment is to be judged by reference to a reasonable child at whom the comments were aimed. Not only is that standard likely to be quite expansive, it also gives schools—and juries—little guidance, requiring them to attempt to gauge the sensitivities of, for instance, the average seven year old.

... The problem is that the majority's test, in fact, invites courts and juries to second-guess school administrators in every case, to judge in each instance whether the school's response was "clearly unreasonable." ...

There will be no shortage of plaintiffs to bring such complaints. Our schools are charged each day with educating millions of children. Of those millions of students, a large percentage will, at some point during their school careers, experience something they consider sexual harassment....

The cost of defending against peer sexual harassment suits alone could overwhelm many school districts, particularly since the majority's liability standards will allow almost any plaintiff to get to summary judgment, if not to a jury. In addition, there are no damages caps on the judicially implied private cause of action under Title IX. As a result, school liability in one peer sexual harassment suit could approach, or even exceed, the total federal funding of many school districts....

Disregarding ... state-law remedies for student misbehavior and the incentives that our schools already have to provide the best possible education to all of their students, the majority seeks, in effect, to put an end to student misbehavior by transforming Title IX into a Federal Student Civility Code. I fail to see how federal courts will administer school discipline better than the principals and teachers to whom the public has entrusted that task or how the majority's holding will help the vast majority of students, whose educational opportunities will be diminished by the diversion of school funds to litigation. The private cause of action the Court creates will justify a corps of federal administrators in writing regulations on student harassment. It will also embroil schools and courts in endless litigation over what qualifies as peer sexual harassment and what constitutes a reasonable response.

In the final analysis, this case is about federalism. Yet the majority's decision today says not one word about the federal balance. Preserving our federal system is a legitimate end in itself. It is, too, the means to other ends. It ensures that essential choices can be made by a government more proximate to the people than the vast apparatus of federal power. Defining the appropriate role of schools in teaching and supervising children who are beginning to explore their own sexuality and learning how to express it to others is one of the most complex and sensitive issues our schools face. Such decisions are best made by parents and by the teachers and school administrators who can counsel with them. The delicacy and immense significance of teaching children about sexuality should cause the Court to act with great restraint before it displaces state and local governments....

---

EXERCISE 8.2. The majority holds that students suing over student-on-student sexual harassment must show that the harassment "is so severe, pervasive, and objectively offensive that it effectively bars the victim's access to an educational opportunity or benefit." Is this standard too tough to take care of many of the real sexual harassment problems that students face? Or is it too weak to prevent young people and their families from bringing federal court lawsuits over trivial issues like unwanted love poetry, overly suggestive valentine cards, and the kind of sexual banter and horseplay that take place in school hallways all over America?

EXERCISE 8.3. Find out if there is a sexual harassment policy at your school. If there is, consider how well it implements the holdings of these cases and the rules of Title IX. If no policy is currently in place, gather some model school policies from the Internet and the Department of Education and draft one for your school.

---

**FOR THE CLASS**

SEXUAL HARASSMENT? Consider the following examples of potentially objectionable behavior and try to determine whether each one constitutes Title IX sexual harassment—either quid pro quo or hostile environment—under *Gebser* and *Monroe County*. Could the students in each case sue? What would be the strengths and weaknesses of each case? Pretend your class is a law firm advising the students in each case on what to do. What advice do you give them?

A. Andy Algebra, the math teacher at North High, calls Sally Senior every night to talk about their respective social lives and tries to engage her in phone sex. One night he asks her to meet him at the beach. Although Andy is by far her favorite teacher, Sally tells him that she thinks "the relationship is going in the wrong direction." He says, "Gee, I was planning to nominate you for the math award, but I guess you're not really my prize pupil after all." Sally is upset about the situation and receives a C+ on her next exam, the first time she has received below a B+ in the class. She tells her academic adviser, the assistant principal, about the situation, but he tells her to just "ignore his comments, he flatters all the pretty girls." A week later, Andy sends Sally an email, saying: "I hope you meet me at the beach Friday night so we can discuss your poor grade on the last test. I know a way you can get your grades back up."

B. Albert Feinstein is slender and not athletically inclined. At gym, the other boys in the locker room tease him about his weight and clumsiness. Lately, they have taken to calling him "fag," "sissy," and "girl," and snapping their wet towels on his rear end. Several times when Albert has opened up his locker, he has found a bra or girl's panties with his name written on them. After another boy, forty pounds heavier than Albert, pounced on him on a wrestling mat and simulated sexual intercourse, Albert began to skip gym and complained about these events to his physical education teacher, who replied: "Come on, Albert, loosen up and take it like a man."

C. In a biology classroom discussion about the female reproductive system, Joe raised his hand and asked the teacher: "If girls are supposed to have mammary glands to feed their babies, why doesn't Mary have any?" The teacher immediately reprimanded Joe and demanded that he apologize to Mary, who was humiliated in front of her classmates.

D. Every day when girls at Reading High enter school, players on the football team sit on the curb with scorecards and hold up numbers, one through ten, "grading" them on their looks and appearance. Many girls feel embarrassed and humiliated by having to pass this gauntlet and have begun to come to school late to avoid being rated in this way. After receiving a number of "tardy" notices, several of the girls were given detention and other forms of discipline. When they objected to their discipline on the ground that they could not enter the school because of the rating game, the principal told them: "That's simply a fall homecoming tradition, and it's certainly no excuse for blatantly violating the rules of the school." The girls were disciplined. Meanwhile, the members of the team also took to pasting head shots of girl students onto the nude bodies of women pictured in pornographic magazines and placing them in the boys' locker room. After a few weeks the coach took them down but no one was disciplined.

---

# The Right of Gay and Lesbian Students
# against Harassment

Title IX's protections against sexual harassment apply to homosexual and heterosexual students alike. In 1996 an Ashland, Wisconsin, student named Jamie Nabozny received a $900,000 judgment against his school system for its failure to put an end to the violence

Nabozny endured at the hands of classmates from grades 7 through 11. At one point Nabozny was beaten so badly that he was hospitalized. Gay-bashing of this nature has, in some instances, led to murder.

Hostility toward gay, lesbian, and bisexual students—and anyone whom others think may belong to one of these groups—can also take nonviolent forms. The ridicule, relentless teasing, and put-downs that can occur may also be actionable in court if they are sufficiently severe and pervasive. Many states and counties have passed specific laws and ordinances protecting students against harassment based on sexual orientation. California has such a law, as does Massachusetts, which also promotes the creation of gay and lesbian support groups in public high schools. The state now has 180 Gay/Straight Alliances on campus.

Many people think that passing laws to protect gays, lesbians, and bisexuals against harassment encourages or promotes homosexuality. Do you agree? Do you believe that sexual orientation is innate or learned? How does this affect your position? Should gay and lesbian students have the right to form alliances on campus alongside other student clubs? Would it be viewpoint discrimination under the First Amendment to deny them the right to meet?

What can be done to prevent harassment of gay and lesbian students? Discuss with your classmates. (An interesting video on this issue, *It's Elementary,* is available from *www.womedia.org.*)

---

FOR THE CLASS

BULLY FOR YOU: COLUMBINE REVISITED. Sexual harassment is a sexualized form of the student-on-student bullying that is all too common in schools. Many students learn habits of cruelty—the infliction of pain on persons with less power—at home or in their neighborhoods and bring these destructive behaviors to school.

Many school systems trying to solve the puzzle of juvenile violence, truancy, and academic dysfunction have developed antibullying programs. Go online and find some resources that educators and young people have developed to stop bullying in their schools.

America heard a wake-up call about bullying in the infamous mass killings at Columbine High School by students Eric Harris and Dylan Klebold in April 1999. The two boys opened fire on teachers and fellow students, murdering thirteen people and wounding another twenty-one.

America mourned the slain youngsters and condemned the perpetrators of the massacre, but few people made the link between this insane explosion of gun violence and the problem of bullying. The next fall I received emails from a student at Columbine, who wrote that the school, in its recent back-to-school pep rally, had effectively banned mention of the deceased and the violence that took their lives the prior school year. My correspondent was convinced that the school had "learned nothing" and had specifically failed to confront the "bullying by jocks" that incensed Harris and Klebold and drove the boys over the brink.

Columbine High School gunmen Eric Harris (left) and Dylan Klebold in their 1999 yearbook photos.

A perceptive article in the *Washington Post,* written on June 12, 1999, by Lorraine Adams and Dale Russakoff, called "Dissecting Columbine's Cult of the Athlete; In Search of Answers, Community Examines One Source of Killers' Rage," confirmed my correspondent's sentiments. The reporters wrote of Columbine High that "some parents and students believe a schoolwide indulgence of certain jocks—their criminal convictions, physical abuse, sexual and racial bullying—intensified the killers' feelings of powerlessness and galvanized their fantasies of revenge. Dozens of interviews and a review of court records suggest that Harris's and Klebold's rage began with injustices of jocks."

The reporters found at Columbine an atmosphere in which jocks were lionized, coddled, and allowed to abuse other students. "The state wrestling champ was regularly permitted to park his $100,000 Hummer all day in a 15-minute space," they wrote. "A football player was allowed to tease a girl about her breasts in class without fear of retribution by his teacher," who also happened to be his coach. The wrestling team captain threw his girlfriend up against a locker in front of a teacher without getting in trouble; four football players were not punished by the school when they destroyed a man's apartment; and a handful of football players openly tormented a Jewish student in gym class with lyrics about Hitler and then escalated the abuse by pounding his body and threatening to set him on fire. In every case, school authorities essentially looked the other way because the jocks were at the top of the school's pecking order.

Friends of Harris and Klebold told the reporters that the boys grew increasingly angry and resentful over the bullying and the social system that tolerated it. "They just let the jocks get to them," one student said. "I think they were taunted to their limits."

Most of the boys' alleged taunters had graduated by the time Harris and Klebold unleashed their violence on the school, but six varsity athletes died in the attacks. No amount of bullying can ever excuse violence, and most bullied students never turn violent in response, much less kill anyone. But this background may help us focus on the brutish conditions under which many students attend school and a few end up losing their minds.

What is your school's policy on bullying? What can be done to end the social dynamics of bullying in our schools? What strategies work? Write a report on why bullying happens and how it can be stopped in your area.

---

***Read On***

Adams, Lorraine, and Dale Russakoff. "Dissecting Columbine's Cult of the Athlete; In Search for Answers, Community Examines One Source of Killers' Rage." *Washington Post.* June 12, 1999.

American Association of University Women. *Hostile Hallways: The AAUW Survey on Sexual Harassment in America's Schools.* Washington, D.C.: AAUW Educational Foundation, 1993.

Department of Education, Office of Civil Rights. *Sexual Harassment Guidance: Harassment of Students by School Employees, Other Students, or Third Parties.* Washington, D.C.: U.S. Government Printing Office.

Langelan, Martha. *Back Off: How to Confront and Stop Sexual Harassment and Harrassers.* New York: Simon and Schuster, 1993.

Stein, Nan, and Lisa Sjostram. *Flirting or Hurting? A Teacher's Guide to Student-to-Student Sexual Harassment in Schools.* Washington, D.C.: NEA Professional Library Publication, 1994. (Available from the National Education Association at 1-800-229-4200.)

***For Further Information***

American Association of University Professors, www.aaup.org

Lambda Legal Defense, www.lambdalegal.org

Gay, Lesbian and Straight Education Network, www.glsen.org

National Education Association, www.nea.org

National Organization for Women's Legal Defense and Education Fund, www.nowldef.org

National Women's Law Center, www.nwlc.org

# THE HEALTH OF THE
# STUDENT BODY:
# DISABILITY, PRIVACY,
# PREGNANCY, AND SEXUALITY

9

On any given day schools confront myriad health issues. Some students have physical disabilities, some have learning disabilities, some are pregnant, and some are sick. Any one of these students might need special accommodations or might feel exposed or embarrassed by their health problems. These concerns raise legal issues for the students, their families, and their schools.

For a long time schools ignored many student health problems. A lot of visually or hearing-impaired students, students with learning disabilities (diagnosed or not), and students with other kinds of problems simply dropped out of school or were institutionalized. Before the 1970s, when the disability rights movement arose, all students were assumed to be standard-issue, able-bodied children with no learning problems; for those who fell short of the norm, there was a thin safety net at best. For example, our understanding of learning disabilities was meager, and many bright students with dyslexia were classified as "slow." Girls who got pregnant sometimes faced ridicule, shame, ostracism, expulsion, and criminal laws against abortion. Students with physical, emotional, or cognitive problems often faced the additional nightmare of schools refusing to keep their medical and educational records private. Sensitive information might be shared with other government agencies, employers, recruiters, and businesses.

Today, students with serious health and learning disabilities have substantial legal protections. Section 504 of the Rehabilitation Act, passed in 1973, prevents discrimination on the basis of disability in programs receiving federal funds. The Americans with Disabilities Act (ADA), passed in 1990, blocks discrimination by both public and private schools on grounds of disability. It requires "reasonable accommodation" of student disabilities.

An even more dramatic improvement was the Individuals with Disabilities Education Act (IDEA), which was first enacted in 1975 as the Education for All Handicapped Children Act. The IDEA requires public schools to provide all disabled children with a special education and related services. Each disabled child's education must be free, appropriate, individualized, and conducted in the least restrictive appropriate setting.

There are also more options for pregnant girls. The Supreme Court has provided that women, including young women, have not only a right to bear children, but also a right to choose an abortion. However, as we shall see, states can condition exercise of this right on a parent's consent to the abortion or, in the absence of that, a judge's consent.

Finally, all students today enjoy the protections of the Family Educational Rights and Privacy Act of 1974 (FERPA), which establishes basic privacy protections for student records maintained by school administrators.

**POINTS TO PONDER**

*How far should schools go to provide "special services" to students with learning disabilities?*

*Does it violate the Family Educational Rights and Privacy Act for teachers to practice "peer grading" by having students mark each other's exams and quizzes?*

- Should girls younger than eighteen (considered "minors" under the law) be required to have the consent of one of their parents or a judge before obtaining an abortion?
- Should high schools make condoms available to sexually active teens as a way to curb teen pregnancy rates, or does this practice violate parents' right to control the raising of their children?

## The Rights of the "Differently Abled" under the Individuals with Disabilities Education Act

Under the IDEA, disabled students have a right to a free and appropriate special education and "related services." In *Irving Independent School District v. Tatro* (1984), the Supreme Court found that, under this "related services" language, a school district had to provide "clean intermittent catheterization"—an invasive medical substitute for urination—to an eight-year-old girl born with spina bifida, a congenital disorder that made it impossible for her to empty her own bladder. The Court also found that providing this catheterization was not a forbidden "medical service" (something that must be performed by a doctor, like surgery) under the IDEA but simply a "school health service" easily rendered by a nurse.

In the following case the Court considers whether the IDEA requires a school district to offer continuous one-on-one nursing services to a ventilator-dependent student in a motorized wheelchair who communicates by working a computer with head movements. The school's argument that it does not have a duty to provide nonstop nursing assistance to the student turns on the heavy costs of providing such a service. But, as you can see, the majority believes it is Garret F.'s right under the statute to receive the nursing care in school regardless of the cost. Justices Thomas and Kennedy disagree. What do you think?

## CEDAR RAPIDS COMMUNITY SCHOOL DISTRICT
### v.
## GARRET F.

*Supreme Court of the United States*
Argued Nov. 4, 1998.
Decided March 3, 1999.

Justice STEVENS delivered the opinion of the Court.

The Individuals with Disabilities Education Act (IDEA) ... was enacted, in part, "to assure that all children with disabilities have available to them ... a free appropriate public education which emphasizes special education and related services designed to meet their unique needs." Consistent with this purpose, the IDEA authorizes federal financial assistance to States that agree to provide disabled children with special education and "related services." The question presented in this case is whether the definition of "related services" in [the statute] requires a public school district in a participating State to provide a ventilator-dependent student with certain nursing services during school hours. ...

I

Respondent Garret F. is a friendly, creative, and intelligent young man. When Garret was four years old, his spinal column was severed in a motorcycle accident. Though paralyzed from the neck down, his mental capacities were unaffected. He is able to speak, to control his motorized wheelchair through use of a puff and suck straw, and to operate a computer with a device that responds to head movements. Garret is currently a student in the Cedar Rapids Community School District, he attends regular classes in a typical school program, and his academic performance has been a success. Garret is, however, ventilator dependent, and therefore requires a responsible individual nearby to attend to certain physical needs while he is in school.

... In 1993, Garret's mother requested the District to accept financial responsibility for the health care services that Garret requires during the schoolday. The District denied the request, believing that it was not legally obligated to provide continuous one-on-one nursing services.

[The administrative judge found that the IDEA required the school district to bear financial responsibility for all of the disputed services, including the disputed nursing services. The district and appeals courts agreed.]

II

The District contends that [the statute] does not require it to provide Garret with "continuous one-on-one nursing services" during the schoolday, even though Garret cannot remain in school without such care. However, the IDEA's definition of "related services," our decision in *Irving Independent School Dist. v. Tatro* and the overall statutory scheme all support the decision that as a recipient of federal funds under the IDEA, Iowa has a statutory duty to provide all disabled children a "free appropriate public education," which includes "related services."

The text of the "related services" definition broadly encompasses those supportive services that "may be required to assist a child with a disability to benefit from special education." As a general matter, services that enable a disabled child to remain in school during the day provide the student with "the meaningful access to education that Congress envisioned."

In *Tatro* we concluded that the Secretary of Education had reasonably determined that the term "medical services" referred only to services that must be performed by a physician, and not to school health services. Accordingly, we held that a specific form of health care (clean intermittent catheterization) that is often, though not always, performed by a nurse is not an excluded medical service. We referenced the likely cost of the services and the competence of school staff as justifications for drawing a line between physician and other services, but our endorsement of that line was unmistakable. It is thus settled that the phrase "medical services" in [the statute] does not embrace all forms of care that might loosely be described as "medical" in other contexts, such as a claim for an income tax deduction. ...

Instead, the District points to the combined and continuous character of the required care, and proposes a test under which the outcome in any particular case would "depend upon a series of factors, such as [1] whether the care is continuous or intermittent, [2] whether existing school health personnel can provide the service, [3] the cost of the service, and [4] the potential consequences if the service is not properly performed." ...

Finally, the District raises broader concerns about the financial burden that it must bear to provide the services that Garret needs to stay in school. The problem for the District in providing these services is not that its staff cannot be trained to deliver them; the problem, the District contends, is that the existing school health staff cannot meet all of their responsibilities and provide for Garret at the same time. Through its multifactor test, the District seeks to establish a kind of undue-burden exemption primarily based on the cost of the requested services. The first two factors can be seen as examples of cost-based distinctions: Intermittent care is often less expensive than continuous care, and the use of existing personnel is cheaper than hiring additional employees. The third factor—the cost of the service—would then encompass the first two. The relevance of the fourth factor is likewise related to cost because extra care may be necessary if potential consequences are especially serious.

The District may have legitimate financial concerns, but our role in this dispute is to interpret existing law. Defining "related services" in a manner that *accommodates* the cost concerns Congress may have had is altogether different from using cost *itself* as the definition. Given that [the statute] does not employ cost in its definition of "related services" or excluded "medical services," accepting the District's cost-based standard as the sole test for determining the scope of the provision would require us to engage in judicial lawmaking without any guidance from Congress. It would also create some tension with the purposes of the IDEA. The statute may not require public schools to maximize the potential of disabled students commensurate with the opportunities provided to other children, and the potential financial burdens imposed on participating States may be relevant to arriving at a sensible construction of the IDEA. But Congress intended "to open the door of public education" to all qualified children and "require[d] participating States to educate handicapped children with nonhandicapped children whenever possible."

This case is about whether meaningful access to the public schools will be assured, not the level of education that a school must finance once access is attained. It is undisputed that the services at issue must be provided if Garret is to remain in school. Under the statute, our precedent, and the purposes of the IDEA, the District must fund such "related services" in order to help guarantee that students like Garret are integrated into the public schools.

Justice THOMAS, with whom Justice KENNEDY joins, dissenting.

. . . a school nurse cannot provide the services that respondent requires, and continue to perform her normal duties. To the contrary, because respondent requires continuous, one-on-one care throughout the entire schoolday, all agree that the district must hire an additional employee to attend solely to respondent. This will cost a minimum of $18,000 per year. Although the majority recognizes this fact, it nonetheless concludes that the "more extensive" nature of the services that respondent needs is irrelevant to the question whether those services fall under the medical services exclusion. This approach disregards the constitutionally mandated principles of construction applicable to Spending Clause legislation and blindsides unwary States with fiscal obligations that they could not have anticipated.

For the foregoing reasons, I respectfully dissent.

---

EXERCISE 9.1. Assume a sixth-grade student with dyslexia suffers from anxiety and low-level depression because of her reading problems. Is she entitled to psychological counseling (along with her reading tutor) under the IDEA? Regulations issued by the U.S. Department of Education establish that psychological counseling is a necessary "related service" if it becomes essential to a child's ability to receive a quality education. Should psychological counseling be covered for *all* students, even those who have no other diagnosed learning or physical disability? Why or why not?

---

Many teachers conduct tests and quizzes by having their students grade each other's papers and then either shout out the grades or turn them in. But in the following case, the Falvo family, which lives outside Tulsa, Oklahoma, objected to the practice. One of the Falvo children, who had a learning disability, felt humiliated by having his grades calculated by a fellow student and then read aloud in front of the class. After the school refused to stop the practice or at least grant a special exemption for the Falvo children, the family sued, alleging that "peer grading" violates the Family Educational Rights and Privacy Act, which requires student "education records" to be kept confidential if they "are maintained by an educational agency or institution or by a person acting for such agency or institution." The question in this case became whether grades on a classroom quiz or test were such an institutional "record." What does the Court say?

---

## OWASSO INDEPENDENT SCHOOL DIST. NO. I-011
### v.
### FALVO

*Supreme Court of the United States*
Argued Nov. 27, 2001.
Decided Feb. 19, 2002.

Justice KENNEDY delivered the opinion of the Court.

Teachers sometimes ask students to score each other's tests, papers, and assignments as the teacher explains the correct answers to the entire class. Respondent contends this practice, which the parties refer to as peer grading, violates the Family Educational Rights and Privacy Act of 1974 (FERPA or Act)....

I

Under FERPA, schools and educational agencies receiving federal financial assistance must comply with certain conditions.... One condition specified in the Act is that sensitive information about students may not be released without parental consent. The Act states that federal funds are to be withheld from school districts that have "a policy or practice of permitting the release of education records (or personally identifiable information contained therein ...) of students without the written consent of their parents."... The phrase "education records" is defined, under the Act, as "records, files, documents, and other materials" containing information directly related to a student, which "are maintained by an educational agency or institution or by a person acting for such agency or institution."... The definition of education records contains an exception for "records of instructional, supervisory, and administrative personnel ... which are in the sole possession of the maker thereof...." The precise question for us is whether peer-graded classroom work and assignments are education records.

Three of respondent Kristja J. Falvo's children are enrolled in Owasso Independent School District No. I-011, in a suburb of Tulsa, Oklahoma. The children's teachers, like many teachers in this country, use peer grading. In a typical case, the students exchange papers with each other and score them according to the teacher's instructions, then return the work to the student who prepared it. The teacher may ask the students to report their own scores. In this case it appears the student could either call out the score or walk to the teacher's desk and reveal it in confidence, though by that stage, of course, the score was known at least to the one other student who did the grading. Both the grading and the system of calling out the scores are in contention here.

Respondent claimed the peer grading embarrassed her children. She asked the school district to adopt a uniform policy banning peer grading and requiring teachers either to grade assignments themselves or at least to forbid students from grading papers other than their own. The school district declined to do so, and respondent brought a class action ... against the school district, Superintendent Dale Johnson, Assistant Superintendent Lynn Johnson, and Principal Rick Thomas (petitioners). Respondent alleged the school district's grading policy violated FERPA....

... [We f]ind no violation of the Act....

II

... The parties appear to agree that if an assignment becomes an education record the moment a peer grades it, then the grading, or at least the practice of asking students to call out their grades in class, would be an impermissible release... Without deciding the point, we assume for the purposes of our analysis that they are correct. The parties disagree, however, whether peer-graded assignments constitute education records at all. The papers do contain information directly related to a student, but they are records under the Act only when and if they "are maintained by an educational agency or institution or by a person acting for such agency or institution."...

Petitioners ... contend the definition covers only institutional records—namely, those materials retained in a permanent file as a matter of course. They argue that records "maintained by an educational agency or institution" generally would include final course grades, student grade point averages, standardized test scores, attendance records, counseling records, and records of disciplinary actions—but not student homework or classroom work....

Respondent ... contends student-graded assignments fall within the definition of education records.... Grade books and the grades within, the court concluded, are "maintained" by a teacher and so are covered by FERPA.... The court recognized that teachers do not maintain the grades on individual student assignments until they have recorded the result in the grade books. It reasoned, however, that if Congress forbids teachers to disclose students' grades once written in a grade book, it makes no sense to permit the disclosure immediately beforehand....The court thus held that student graders maintain the grades until they are reported to the teacher....

The Court of Appeals' logic does not withstand scrutiny. Its interpretation, furthermore, would effect a drastic alteration of the existing allocation of responsibilities between States and the National Government in the operation of the Nation's schools. We would hesitate before interpreting the statute to effect such a substantial change in the balance of federalism unless that is the manifest purpose of the legislation. This principle guides our decision.

Two statutory indicators tell us that the Court of Appeals erred in concluding that an assignment satisfies the definition of education records as soon as it is graded by another student. First, the student papers are not, at that stage, "maintained" within the meaning of [the Act]. The ordinary meaning of the word "maintain" is "to keep in existence or continuance; preserve; retain." ... Even assuming the teacher's grade book is an education record ... the score on a student-graded assignment is not "contained therein"... until the teacher records it. The teacher does not maintain the grade while students correct their peers' assignments or call out their own marks. Nor do the student graders maintain the grades within the meaning of [the Act]. The word "maintain" suggests FERPA records will be kept in a filing cabinet in a records room at the school or on a permanent secure database, perhaps even after the student is no longer enrolled. The student graders only handle assignments for a few moments as the teacher calls out the answers. It is fanciful to say they maintain the papers in the same way the registrar maintains a student's folder in a permanent file.

The Court of Appeals was further mistaken in concluding that each student grader is "a person acting for" an educational institution for purposes of [the Act]. The phrase "acting for" connotes agents of the school, such as teachers, administrators, and other school employees. Just as it does not accord with our usual understanding to say students are "acting for" an educational institution when they follow their teacher's direction to take a quiz, it is equally awkward to say students are "acting for" an educational institution when they follow their teacher's direction to score it. Correcting a classmate's work can be as much a part of the assignment as taking the test itself. It is a way to teach material again in a new context, and it helps show students how to assist and respect fellow pupils. By explaining the answers to the class as the students correct the papers, the teacher not only reinforces the lesson but also discovers whether the students have understood the material and are ready to move on. We do not think FERPA prohibits these educational techniques. We also must not lose sight of the fact that the phrase "by a person acting for [an educational] institution" modifies "maintain." Even if one were to agree students are acting for the teacher when they correct the assignment, that is different from saying they are acting for the educational institution in maintaining it....

FERPA also requires recipients of federal funds to provide parents with a hearing at which they may contest the accuracy of their child's education records.... The hearings must be conducted "in accordance with regulations of the Secretary,"... which in turn require adjudication by a disinterested official and the opportunity for parents to be represented by an attorney.... It is doubtful Congress would have provided parents with this elaborate procedural machinery to challenge the accuracy of the grade on every spelling test and art project the child completes.

Respondent's construction of the term "education records" to cover student homework or classroom work would impose substantial burdens on teachers across the country. It would force all instructors to take time, which otherwise could be spent teaching and in preparation, to correct an assortment of daily student assignments. Respondent's view would make it much more difficult for teachers to give students immediate guidance. The interpretation respondent urges would force teachers to abandon other customary practices, such as group grading of team assignments. Indeed, the logical consequences of respondent's view are all but unbounded....

We doubt Congress meant to intervene in this drastic fashion with traditional state functions. Under the Court of Appeals' interpretation of FERPA, the federal power would exercise minute control over specific teaching methods and instructional dynamics in classrooms throughout the country. The Congress is not likely to have mandated this result, and we do not interpret the statute to require it.

For these reasons, even assuming a teacher's grade book is an education record, the Court of Appeals erred, for in all events the grades on students' papers would not be covered under FERPA at least until the teacher has collected them and recorded them in his or her grade book. We limit our holding to this narrow point, and do not decide the broader question whether the grades on individual student assignments, once they are turned in to teachers, are protected by the Act.

The judgment of the Court of Appeals is reversed....

---

EXERCISE 9.2. Assume your school uses "peer grading" in most classes. The Falvo decision has just come down upholding the practice. A student group still wants to debate whether it is a good idea for teachers to have their students grade each other's work. Form two teams to prepare to debate the issue at a schoolwide assembly. Have a group of students ask questions as if they were teachers and administrators.

EXERCISE 9.3. Under the No Child Left Behind Act of 2002, Congress required public high schools to give identifying information about their students to the United States Department of Defense for recruiting purposes. Parents have the right to "opt out" of this arrangement by writing a letter to the school asking for their children's information to be kept confidential. Do you want your information (name, address, phone number, grade) to be shared with the military recruiters? What do you tell your parents?

---

# Three Trimesters: Pregnant at School

Millions of American teenagers have sex every year. Consider this startling 2000 statistic from the Alan Guttmacher Institute in New York: Each year nearly one million U.S. teenaged girls become pregnant. Almost four out of five of these pregnancies are unintended. Some 55 percent of these pregnancies are carried to term, 31 percent end in abortions, and 14 percent end in miscarriage. Fortunately, however, the teen pregnancy rate is declining. Nonetheless, when girls in high school get pregnant, they are often shamed and belittled. Sometimes they experience official reactions as discriminatory. In the following case, Arlene Pfeiffer was dismissed from the National Honor Society in Marion Center Area High School in Marion, Pennsylvania, after the honor society learned she was pregnant. A model student with fine grades and activities, Pfeiffer was also president of the student council. The Society said she was being dismissed because of her premarital sexual conduct. Pfeiffer claimed that this was sex discrimination, because boys who engaged in premarital sex were not expelled from the honor society. Which way does the Third Circuit Court of Appeals rule on Pfeiffer's appeal from her expulsion from the society? Why?

—•—

PFEIFFER
v.
MARION CENTER AREA SCHOOL DISTRICT

*United States Court of Appeals for the Third Circuit*
Decided Oct. 30, 1990.

ALDISERT, Circuit Judge....

II

The appellant, Arlene Pfeiffer, was a member of the class of 1984 at the Marion Center Area High School in Marion, Indiana County, Pennsylvania. She was a good student who earned high grades and participated in a wide variety of school organizations, including serving as president of the student council. Based on her record, she was elected to her high school's chapter of the National Honor Society (NHS) in 1981.... The local chapter was governed by a faculty council composed of Robert L. Stewart, the principal of the high school, and Theda Lightcap, Jane Smith, Judith Skubis, and George Krivonick, all teachers at the Marion Center Area High School.

During the spring of 1983, Pfeiffer, who was unmarried, discovered that she was pregnant. She informed her school guidance counselor and principal and indicated that she wanted to rear her child but that she also wanted to finish high school. Principal Stewart told her that he saw no problem in her plan to continue school and graduate.

The handbook for the National Honor Society requires that students be selected for membership on the basis of scholarship, service, leadership and character. The constitution of the local chapter followed that of the national organization, requiring admission and maintenance be based on the same qualities....

Upon learning of Pfeiffer's pregnancy, Judith Skubis, a teacher and member of the faculty council, brought the matter to the attention of the other council members in the spring of 1983. That fall, when school resumed, the council scheduled a meeting for November 4, 1983, and Pfeiffer was invited to attend. The council members explained to her that her NHS membership was in question because premarital sex appeared to be contrary to the qualities of leadership and character essential for membership. When asked if her sexual activity leading to her pregnancy had been voluntary, the plaintiff answered in the affirmative. The council deferred further action.

On November 8, 1983, Pfeiffer's father, Delmont Pfeiffer, telephoned Principal Stewart requesting a prompt decision because an induction ceremony for seniors was scheduled for the next day and Arlene wanted to attend. The council met on the morning of November 9, 1983, and by secret ballot unanimously voted to dismiss her from the NHS chapter. By letter the council advised her:

> By action of the faculty council, you have been dismissed from the National Honor Society for the following reason:
>
> Failure to uphold the high standards of leadership and character required for admission and maintenance of membership. It is the opinion of the faculty council that a member must consistently set a positive example for others and, as outlined in the selection guidelines, always uphold all of the high standards of moral conduct.

On November 30, 1983, the council met with her parents, who requested that the subject be placed on the agenda of the school board meeting scheduled for December 12, 1983. Pfeiffer and her parents appeared at the meeting with counsel....

At the discussion, the board was asked to review the decision of the faculty council. On December 19, 1983, the board and the council met to consider the matter further and on January 16, 1984, the school board adopted a resolution unanimously affirming the action of the faculty council.

After graduation from high school, with honors, Pfeiffer elected not to go to college and began working with the Holiday Inn of Indiana, where she is presently a sales manager. She is married, but not to the father of the child conceived while she was in school.

III

Arlene Pfeiffer filed suit alleging discrimination in her dismissal from the local chapter of the NHS. The complaint included claims of gender discrimination.

## IV

At the onset of the case, the question arose whether Title IX applied because the School District did not receive federal funds for the operation of its chapter of the NHS, while it did receive federal funds for its school lunch program. . . .

Title IX of the Education Amendment of 1972 provides, in part, as follows:

No person in the United States shall, on the basis of sex, be excluded from participation in, be denied the benefits of, or be subjected to discrimination under any education program or activity receiving Federal financial assistance.

Regulations promulgated pursuant to Title IX specifically apply its prohibition against gender discrimination to discrimination on the basis of pregnancy, parental status, and marital status.

A recipient shall not apply any rule concerning a student's actual or potential parental, family, or marital status which treats students differently on the basis of sex. . . .

(b)(1) A recipient shall not discriminate against any student or exclude any student from its education program or activity, including any class or extracurricular activity, on the basis of such student's pregnancy, childbirth, false pregnancy, termination of pregnancy or recovery therefrom unless the student requests voluntarily to participate in a separate portion of the program or activity of the recipient.

## VI

[T]he appellant's entire argument before us rests upon her allegation that she was dismissed from the chapter because of her condition of pregnancy. Unfortunately for her theory, however, the district court found that the plaintiff was not dismissed for her pregnancy but because the council thought she had failed to uphold the standards already discussed as evidenced by Plaintiff's Exhibit 1 (the letter directed to her) and Plaintiff's Exhibit 3 (the resolution of the School Board dated January 16, 1984.)

. . . Supporting this finding is the stated reason given by the council for her dismissal: Failure to uphold the standards of leadership and character required for admission and maintenance of membership. Moreover, the finding is supported by the testimony of the faculty council members before the district court, each of whom testified at trial. Each faculty council member specifically denied that his or her dismissal vote was based anywhere on Pfeiffer's sex, on her pregnancy, or on her failure to marry after she had engaged in premarital sexual activity.

This factual finding is bolstered by the district court's reasoning that

[f]aced with the task of educating hundreds of young people, and with constant demand by the public that the schools instill attributes of good character as part of the educational process, the Council and the Board can scarcely be criticized for taking the action which was taken.

Indeed, the Supreme Court has given us express guidance in matters relating to student conduct in public schools:

The process of educating our youth for citizenship in public schools is not confined to books, the curriculum, and the civics class; schools must teach by example the shared values of a civilized social order. Consciously or otherwise, teachers—and indeed the older students—demonstrate the appropriate form of . . . conduct and deportment in and out of class. Inescapably, like parents, they are role models. The schools, as instruments of the state, may determine that the essential lessons of civil, mature conduct cannot be conveyed in a school that tolerates lewd, indecent, or offensive speech and conduct....

---

EXERCISE 9.4. In 1985 the Seventh Circuit Court of Appeals found in *Wort v. Vierling* that a school district's dismissal of a pregnant student from her National Honor Society *did* violate both Title IX and Equal Protection. The division between the Seventh and Third Circuit Courts of Appeal over the issue—a so-called "circuit split"—means that the law governing expulsions from the National Honor Society for being pregnant is different in different regions. A circuit split on a substantial issue will often provide the Supreme Court impetus to take up the issue case to resolve the split within the federal judiciary's appeals courts.

Imagine, therefore, that the Supreme Court takes a case in which a pregnant high school senior, who is an outstanding student and community leader, gets dismissed from Honor Society at Cape Cod High School. The society admits that it has only dismissed pregnant girls in the past because it cannot, and does not want to, investigate the sexual lives of its students, whether female or male. The society says it would exclude any student member who admitted to having premarital sex but, as of yet, no one had come forward to turn himself or herself in.

The student claims that this policy is a violation of her equal protection rights because, under the society's practice, only girls (who get pregnant) will be punished. Return to Chapter Seven and retrieve the standard for challenges to alleged governmental sex discrimination. Is this sex discrimination? If not, the case is over. If it is, the government can only win if it can show an "important interest"—an "exceedingly persuasive justification"—for its policy and that its means are "substantially related" to the interest.

Take oral arguments from lawyers on behalf of both the school and the girl. Other students should act as Supreme Court justices who must decide whether the society's dismissal of a pregnant student violates the equal protection clause or Title IX's ban on sex discrimination in schools. The justices should discuss the problem and then state their opinions and reasoning.

---

Some people place the blame for our high rates of teen pregnancy on the sexual images that saturate the media; others attribute teen pregnancy to an appalling lack of proper sexual education and knowledge about contraception. Very likely, these two factors go hand in hand to create a large number of unplanned pregnancies. Yet, the number is dropping now. Why? Many school systems have sought to promote abstinence or sex education; some have gone so far as to distribute contraceptives—specifically, condoms—to students when they ask for them.

In the next case the Supreme Judicial Court of Massachusetts held that a school program for voluntary distribution of condoms to male or female students who request them, without parental notification, did not violate the family's or student's privacy interests. The court determined that because the program was wholly voluntary and parents could instruct their children on whether or not to participate, there was no unlawful coercion or pressure for students to use the contraceptive services.

———

## CURTIS
### v.
### SCHOOL COMMITTEE OF FALMOUTH

*Supreme Judicial Court of Massachusetts*
Argued March 7, 1995.
Decided July 17, 1995.

Opinion: LIACOS, C.J.

The plaintiffs, students and parents of students in the Falmouth public school system, appealed from a grant of summary judgment in favor of the defendants, the school committee of Falmouth (school committee) and three individual defendants. We granted the school committee's application for direct appellate review. We affirm....

The plaintiffs alleged in their amended complaint, and now argue before this court, that the condom-availability program, as it stands, violates their right to familial privacy and their guaranteed liberties as parents in the control of the education and upbringing of their children, protected by the Fourteenth Amendment to the United States Constitution.... The plaintiffs ask us to reverse the judge's entry of summary judgment for the defendants and to enjoin the school committee from continuing to make condoms available to students without the inclusion of a provision which would permit parents to opt out of the program and without a system of parental notification of their child's requests for a condom.

The motion judge set forth the facts as follows: "On January 2, 1992, following an authorizing vote of the FSC [Falmouth school committee], the Superintendent of Schools issued a memorandum to the teaching staff of grades 7 through 12, detailing the condom availability program. At Lawrence Junior High School, students could request free condoms from the school nurse. Prior to receiving them, students would be counseled. The nurse was also instructed to give students pamphlets on AIDS/HIV and other sexually transmitted diseases. At Falmouth High School, students could request free condoms from the school nurse, or students could purchase them for $.75 from the condom vending machines located in the lower level boys' and girls' restrooms. Counseling by trained faculty members would be provided to students who requested it, and informational pamphlets were available in the [school] nurse's office. The Superintendent's memorandum instructed the staff to reserve their own opinions regarding condom availability in order to respect students' privacy. The memorandum also indicates that the Superintendent's presentation of the condom availability to the student body would stress abstinence as the only certain method for avoiding sexually transmitted diseases. The condom availability program took effect on January 2, 1992.

"The FSC condom program does not provide for an 'opt out' for students' parents whereby the parents have the option of excluding their student child from the availability of condoms. Nor is there a parental notification provision in the FSC program by which parents would be notified of their children's requests for condoms." ...

The judge concluded that the plaintiffs had failed to meet the threshold requirement for each of their claims because they were unable to demonstrate that the condom-availability program placed a coercive burden on their rights.... [T]hey argue, the State was required to prove the existence of a compelling State interest in maintaining the condom-availability program.

... [T]he condom-availability program in Falmouth is in all respects voluntary and in no way intrudes into the realm of constitutionally protected rights. Because no threshold demonstration of a coercive burden has been made, nor could have been made on these facts, the defendants properly were granted summary judgment....

We discern no coercive burden on the plaintiffs' parental liberties in this case. No classroom participation is required of students. Condoms are available to students who request them and, in the high school, may be obtained from vending machines. The students are not required to seek out and accept the condoms, read the literature accompanying them, or participate in counseling regarding their use. In other words, the students are free to decline to participate in the program. No penalty or disciplinary action ensues if a student does not participate in the program. For their part, the plaintiff parents are free to instruct their children not to participate. The program does not supplant the parents' role as advisor in the moral and religious development of their children. Although exposure to condom vending machines and to the program itself may offend the moral and religious sensibilities of the plaintiffs, mere exposure to programs offered at school does not amount to unconstitutional interference with parental liberties without the existence of some compulsory aspect to the program....

*Judgment affirmed.*

---

EXERCISE 9.5. Do you think that public high schools should participate in condom distribution programs? What about middle schools? What if students are required to meet with counselors first and discuss safe sexual behavior and proper use of contraceptives? In an older case from New York state, an appeals court struck down a similar condom distribution program that also had no parental notification requirement or opt-out option. Two courts came to opposite conclusions on the same issue. Which case had the better outcome? Why?

---

**FOR THE CLASS**

CONDOMS AND CONSENT. Imagine that you and your classmates are members of the school board in a district that sees 15 percent of its female students drop out before graduation as a result of pregnancy. How should the school district tackle the problem of teenage pregnancy? Do you favor condom distribution? Abstinence education? GED programs? Discuss the issue and your options with your classmates and see if you can develop an approach that you believe will remedy the problem.

Another deeply divisive issue is whether young women seeking an abortion should first have to obtain the consent and authorization of one of their parents. A variation on this approach charges health care providers with notifying parents. Currently, thirty states require some type of parental involvement.

---

# Abortion and the Privacy Rights of Teenagers

Few constitutional issues in our time have been as charged as that of abortion. In 1973, in *Roe v. Wade*, the Supreme Court upheld the fundamental right of a woman to choose an abortion in consultation with her doctor. In *Roe*, the Court derived the right to an abortion from the basic right to privacy. The right to privacy is founded in the liberty interest protected in the Fourteenth Amendment: "[N]or shall any state deprive any person of life, liberty, or property...."

The controversy over abortion has never really subsided, and the Supreme Court has dealt with repeated attempts by states to restrict a woman's abortion options. In the following 1992 decision, *Planned Parenthood of Southeastern Pennsylvania v. Casey*, however, the Court reaffirmed the essential "core" right of a woman to make a decision about terminating a pregnancy. But it did this in a way that allows greater regulation of abortion—specifically, when teenagers, or minor females, seek to have one. In *Casey*, the Court upheld, among other restrictions, the Commonwealth of Pennsylvania's rule that females under the age of eighteen must obtain the consent of either one of their parents or a judge before having an abortion. As a matter of constitutional law, does this holding damage the rights of women or simply uphold the rights of parents?

---

## PLANNED PARENTHOOD OF SOUTHEASTERN PENNSYLVANIA
### v.
## CASEY

*Supreme Court of the United States*
Argued April 22, 1992.
Decided June 29, 1992.

[The Court addressed the following sections of the Pennsylvania Abortion Control Act:]

Parental Consent for Abortion

... Except in the case of a medical emergency or except as provided in this section, if a pregnant woman is less than 18 years of age and not emancipated, or if she has been adjudged an incompetent ..., a physician shall not perform an abortion upon her unless, in the case of a woman who is less than 18 years of age, *he first obtains the informed consent both of the pregnant woman and of one of her parents.* ... In the case of a pregnancy that is the result of incest, where the father is a party to the incestuous act, the pregnant woman need only obtain the consent of her mother.

Consent to the performance of an abortion or if she elects not to seek the consent of either of her parents or of her guardian, [the Court] shall, upon petition or motion, after an appropriate hearing, authorize a physician to perform the abortion *if the court determines that the pregnant woman is mature and capable of giving informed consent* to the proposed abortion, and has, in fact, given such consent.

**JUSTICE HARRY A. BLACKMUN** (1908–1999) was born in Nashville, Illinois, and raised in St. Paul, Minnesota. Although he wanted to be a doctor rather than a lawyer, he went to Harvard Law School in 1929. He clerked on the Eighth Circuit Court of Appeals, practiced privately, and then actually took the place of his former employer and mentor, Judge Sanborn, on the Eighth Circuit. In 1970 President Richard Nixon appointed Blackmun to the Supreme Court after Nixon's two prior choices, both southern conservatives, were rejected by the Senate. Blackmun remained until his retirement in 1994.

HIGHLIGHTS

➤  Blackmun began a long-lasting friendship with fellow future Supreme Court justice Warren Burger in kindergarten and was even the best man at Burger's wedding. On the Court, the two were initially called "the Minnesota twins," but then their opinions began to diverge and their relationship cooled.

➤  In private practice Blackmun was resident general counsel for the Mayo Clinic, a prestigious research hospital in Minnesota. He described those ten years as "the happiest years of [my] professional experience."

➤  Though he regretted not going to medical school, Justice Blackmun had more of an impact on the field of medicine than most doctors because of his famous opinion in *Roe v. Wade*, upholding the right of a woman to choose abortion in consultation with her doctor. This was the opinion of which Justice Blackmun was most proud.

If the court determines that the pregnant woman is not mature and capable of giving informed consent or if the pregnant woman does not claim to be mature and capable of giving informed consent, the court shall determine whether the performance of an abortion upon her would be in her best interests. If the court determines that the performance of an abortion would be in the best interests of the woman, it shall authorize a physician to perform the abortion.

[Following is an excerpt from Justice O'CONNOR's majority opinion in *Casey* considering the above provision:] . . .

. . . Except in a medical emergency, an unemancipated young woman under 18 may not obtain an abortion unless she and one of her parents (or guardian) provides informed consent as defined above. If neither a parent nor a guardian provides consent, a court may authorize the performance of an abortion upon a determination that the young woman is mature and capable of giving informed consent and has in fact given her informed consent, or that an abortion would be in her best interests.

We have been over most of this ground before. Our cases establish, and we reaffirm today, that a State may require a minor seeking an abortion to obtain the consent of a parent or guardian, provided that there is an adequate judicial bypass procedure. Under these precedents, in our view, the one-parent consent requirement and judicial bypass procedure are constitutional.

The only argument made by [Casey] respecting this provision and to which our prior decisions do not speak is the contention that the parental consent requirement is invalid because it requires informed parental consent. For the most part, [Casey's] argument is a reprise of their argument with respect to the informed consent requirement in general, and we reject it for the reasons given above. Indeed, some of the provisions regarding informed consent have particular force with respect to minors: the waiting period, for example, may provide the parent or parents of a pregnant young woman the opportunity to consult with her in private, and to discuss the consequences of her decision in the context of the values and moral or religious principles of their family. . . .

Justice BLACKMUN, concurring in part, concurring in judgment in part and dissenting in part. . . .

. . . While the State has an interest in encouraging parental involvement in the minor's abortion decision, [the law] is not narrowly drawn to serve that interest.

Chief Justice REHNQUIST, joined by Justice WHITE, Justice SCALIA, and Justice THOMAS, concurring in the judgment in part and dissenting in part.

. . . [A] parental consent restriction certainly places very substantial obstacles in the path of a minor's abortion choice. . . . This may or may not be a correct judgment, but it is quintessentially a legislative one. . . . Under the guise of the Constitution, this Court will still impart its own preferences on the States in the form of a complex abortion code. . . .

---

Each year, more than one million American women between the ages of twelve and nineteen become pregnant. Studies show that most young women in this situation will approach one of their parents, usually their mother, to discuss their situation. But many young women do not, citing fear, embarrassment, and anxiety. Some women are in abusive or dysfunctional families and are afraid that their pregnancy will further complicate family dynamics or even provoke violence. As of July 1999, thirty states required some form of parental involvement in the teen's abortion decision—whether it was simple notice that the procedure was to take place or a requirement of consent (backed up by the "judicial bypass" option if consent was not forthcoming). The arguments for such laws focus on keeping parents closely connected to the lives of their children. Proponents of these laws say that children need help and support during times of crisis and that the parental involvement laws promote family decision making and protect parental rights. Many parents say that, if they are asked to consent to any other form of surgery for their minor children, why not abortion? They consider it a matter of their fundamental right to raise their children and set family values. In cases where abuse is a real danger, the minor can find her way to a judge in family court to authorize the procedure.

Opponents of mandatory parental involvement argue that although most young women facing an unwanted pregnancy will of their own accord talk to one or both parents, the laws traumatize and endanger precisely those young women who come from the most difficult family situations. They also argue that the laws turn many young women into criminals or outlaws who go to other states or jurisdictions to seek an abortion. The whole legal machinery here, they claim, delays the ability to get an abortion, increasing both the cost and the risk of the procedure. They also cite the embarrassment young women experience going before a judge (and a bailiff and a court reporter and anyone else who might be in the courtroom) to ask for the right to have an abortion. Some judges lecture and upbraid the young women, and many have found the young women not mature enough to get an abortion.

What do you think of this difficult issue?

EXERCISE 9.6. What do you think of "parental consent" requirements that force young women to obtain the consent of their parents or a judge to have an abortion? Does this violate their right to privacy? Will it make it more difficult to exercise the right, or will it foster greater family support and harmony? Although the *Casey* Court upheld the parental consent provision in the Pennsylvania law, it struck down the spousal notification provision that required women to attest that they had either notified their husbands of their plans to get an abortion or could not find them. Why do you think the Court treated the two provisions differently? One factor cited by Justice O'Connor was the high incidence of domestic violence and abuse by husbands of their wives, a problem often exacerbated by the decision of whether or not to proceed with a pregnancy. Does this argument sufficiently distinguish the two kinds of provisions? Do pregnant teenagers ever face domestic violence because of their predicament? On the other hand, if minors cannot obtain other kinds of surgery and medical procedures without parental consent, is there any reason—from a constitutional perspective—to treat abortion differently?

---

**FOR THE CLASS**

LEGISLATIVE DECISION MAKING. Turn your class into a state legislature. In the wake of the Supreme Court's decision in *Casey,* which upheld parental consent laws, your state is considering whether or not to require all females age eighteen and younger seeking an abortion to obtain the signature of both parents or, if her parents refuse, the consent of a state trial court judge before she is permitted to proceed. Would you vote for or against such a law? Make an inventory of all of the arguments available on both sides of the issue.

WHAT FACTORS ARE MOST IMPORTANT IN THE DECISION TO HAVE A CHILD? Assume you are a judge in a state with abortion judicial bypass proceedings. A fifteen-year-old girl, Sally, appears before you seeking your permission to have an abortion. She says she cannot get her parents' support because her father left the family long ago and has not been heard from, and her mother is a violently abusive alcoholic. You are charged with determining whether Sally is (1) mature enough to make her own decision and (2) if not, whether abortion or childbirth would be in her "best interests." Sally's boyfriend, also fifteen, very badly wants Sally to have the baby and promises to "help pay for diapers and stuff." He comes from a supportive family of financial means to back up his promises. But Sally says that she feels "way too young to have a baby and I wouldn't know how to take care of it. I'm overwhelmed right now." Sally says that her home situation is "pretty bad and I wouldn't want to bring a baby into it, but I would never give my child up for adoption." She says that she considers herself "a religious person, I definitely believe in God, and I will raise my children in a religious way when I get married and have kids." Sally's aunt, who is strongly opposed to abortion on religious grounds, told her she could help with babysitting on weekends if Sally had the baby. But Sally testifies that, "I just don't have a good support system. I may regret it one day, but I want an abortion." As the judge, what do you do? Go around the room and state your opinion. Would your decision be different if her boyfriend was poor or didn't want to support the child?

EXERCISE 9.7. If you are a judge who determines that a girl is *not* mature enough to decide for herself whether to have an abortion, under what conditions would it ever be in her "best interests" to have the child?

# Appendix A

# SUPREME COURT CONFIRMATION EXERCISE: YOU BE THE JUDGE

[The President] shall appoint . . . Judges of the supreme Court." ARTICLE II, SECTION 2

"The Judges, both of the supreme and inferior courts, shall hold their Offices during good behaviour. . . ." ARTICLE III, SECTION 1

Article II of the Constitution gives the president the power to appoint Supreme Court justices (and other federal judges) with "the Advice and Consent of the Senate." This means that the president's candidates for the Supreme Court have to receive a majority vote in the Senate in favor of confirmation before they are able to take office. Historically, the Senate has taken its duties seriously and has closely scrutinized presidential nominees to the Court. Indeed, over the centuries judicial nominees have generated heated controversy, and many have been rejected by the Senate.

Because Supreme Court justices have life tenure, Senate confirmation hearings are the single occasion upon which Congress can carefully probe the viewpoints of Supreme Court nominees. It is also the only opportunity the public and press have to witness and indirectly participate in a dialogue with nominees about justice, the Constitution, and the Court. This public educational function has become increasingly important since the 1939 confirmation hearing of Felix Frankfurter, the first nominee to appear personally before the Senate, and infinitely more important since the 1981 confirmation hearing of Sandra Day O'Connor, which was the first to be shown on television and broadcast on radio. Today Supreme Court confirmation hearings draw intense public interest and media scrutiny.

In the following exercise, students will assume the roles of key actors in a mock U.S. Supreme Court confirmation hearing before the U.S. Senate's Committee on the Judiciary. Select three students to play the roles of the U.S. Supreme Court justice nominees, nine students to be the Senate Committee on the Judiciary (with the teacher acting as the committee chair), three students to be television commentators, one student to act as the president of the United States, and three students to serve as counsel to the three Supreme Court nominees. In this exercise we are assuming that there are suddenly three vacancies on the Supreme Court. In fact, this scenario is highly unlikely; vacancies almost always occur one at a time. However, as of 2003 it has been ten years since a new justice joined the Court; we can expect a number of departures and nominations in the first decade of the new century.

The confirmation process for U.S. Supreme Court judicial nominees typically involves the following four-part sequence: First, the White House and the Federal Bureau of Investigation undertake several background checks on individuals identified as potential nominees;[1] second, the president makes his or her selection based on the outcome of these checks and on ideological and political grounds; third, a confirmation hearing to judge the fitness of the president's nominee (or, in our case, nominees) is conducted by the Senate Judiciary Committee; and fourth, the full Senate votes on whether to confirm the president's choice.

Start by having the student who is playing the president spend some time with his or her nominees to elicit background information. The president should then write and present a speech in a mock press conference introducing the nominees and trumpeting their virtues as potential justices. What are the outstanding qualities and experiences that qualify these persons to sit on the most important court in the land? What are the considerations and characteristics that the president cites as having informed his or her decision? The members of the media should ask questions about the president's choices and raise any issues of controversy surrounding the nominees. How does the president respond? (Note that the nominees should not make comments on their views at this time, but should wait to do so at the Senate Judiciary Committee hearings.)

Next, move on to the Senate Judiciary Committee hearing process. The nominees should fill out the Questionnaire for Judicial Nominees and distribute copies of their an-

**QUESTIONNAIRE FOR JUDICIAL NOMINEES**

1. Full name
2. Date and place of birth
3. Education
4. Marital status
5. Health: The physical and mental requirements of this position require you to prove that you are currently capable and do not foresee any likelihood of mental or emotional instability. Please disclose all information concerning this issue and provide the date of your last physical examination.
6. Memberships: List all organizations to which you belong and the positions you hold in each.
7. Public service: Provide your record of public service over the past five years.
8. Net worth: Provide a complete, current financial net worth statement.
9. Have you to your knowledge ever been under investigation for a possible violation of a civil or criminal statute? Have you ever been arrested or charged with a crime?
10. Please advise the committee on any unfavorable information that may influence public or congressional response to your nomination.
11. What is your judicial philosophy? Do you believe in "judicial activism," the idea that federal courts should actively intervene to enforce people's rights, or do you think that the Court should generally defer to the political branches of government?
12. What do you think are the best Supreme Court decisions involving the rights of students and young people? What do you think are the worst?

swers to every member of the Senate Judiciary Committee (and other students as well) for their consideration. Once the nominees' answers have been distributed, the confirmation hearing can begin.

The committee should consider one nominee at a time. Each nominee should make an opening statement thanking the president and the committee and describing his or her views and commitment to the Supreme Court. The students on the Senate Judiciary Committee should take turns posing two or three questions each to the nominee. The chair of the committee should call on senators in order of seniority (perhaps by age?), always making sure that order and protocol prevail throughout the proceedings. The nominees' counsels should be seated next to them during the hearings and be prepared to aid the nominees as necessary.

Senators can ask any questions they want, but the nominees always have the option of choosing not to answer. In fact, many nominees refuse to answer questions about their views of specific cases that will come before the Court, saying that such pointed answers would be inappropriate. Notwithstanding these objections, most nominees do their best to address the concerns of the senators. Oftentimes, senators will try to nail nominees down on their specific commitments and beliefs. The following are sample questions that the senators might ask. Feel free to change them or make up your own:

1. What are your qualifications to serve on the U.S. Supreme Court?
2. What aspects of law do you find the most intriguing?
3. What do you think are the greatest Supreme Court cases of all time?
4. Do you think that minors and students have constitutional rights? Are those rights equal to the rights of adults, or are they of less weight?
5. Do you think that it is unconstitutional for public universities to use race as a factor in admissions, even if it is to promote diversity in the incoming class? Does affirmative action violate equal protection?

When all of the senators have finished asking questions, the nominee should offer his or her closing thoughts. At this point the chair of the Senate Judiciary Committee should thank the nominee and excuse him or her.

Now bring on the next nominee and repeat the process.

When all the nominees have had their hearings, the committee should take a break, and the three television reporters and commentators should simulate a talk show and discuss how the nominees fared. What were their strengths and weaknesses as candidates? How did they handle hot issues and controversial questions? How will the senators react to their testimony?

The committee should then reconvene and discuss the legal philosophies and positions of the nominees and then vote on whether to confirm each of them. Now the classroom exercise is at an end. Of course, the nomination process is not yet complete. Normally, the names of the nominees who have passed the committee process are sent to the full Senate for a final vote. If you have a large class, have those students who were not selected to play any of the previous roles act as the full Senate and put the issue to them for a final vote. Which nominee or nominees did the class select?

The Supreme Court nominees (now justices, perhaps!) should discuss their experience: what they found difficult about the process, what they enjoyed, and what they learned. Would they do anything differently next time? What about the other actors? What did they learn? Do you think you would ever like to be a justice on the Supreme Court?

---

EXERCISE A.1. Write a one-page essay on any or all of the following questions: What is the most important thing people should know about the Constitution? How do you think learning about constitutional rights and responsibilities has changed your thinking about citizenship? Do you think there is a difference between young people who are constitutionally literate and those who are not? How would you convince a fellow teenager that it is important to study constitutional law? Is it important? Read your essay aloud.

EXERCISE A.2. Write a letter to a current Supreme Court justice detailing which of his or her decisions or opinions you admire and why.

---

*Note*

1. The first background check requires the nominee to complete numerous questionnaires that cover issues ranging from the nominee's address, education, and marital status to health conditions, legal activities, and ethical beliefs. The second background check is a computerized search for a nominee's criminal record or involvement in potentially embarrassing activities. The final background check is made by the FBI and includes a compilation of detailed interviews with current and previous employers and employees, family members, friends, colleagues, and neighbors. The FBI's background check is made available to the Senate Judiciary Committee chair and the ranking minority member only when the confirmation hearing exposes damaging information about the nominee.

# Appendix B

# UNITED STATES CONSTITUTION

We the People of the United States, in Order to form a more perfect Union, establish Justice, insure domestic Tranquility, provide for the common defence, promote the general Welfare, and secure the Blessings of Liberty to ourselves and our Posterity, do ordain and establish this Constitution for the United States of America.

## Article I

SECTION 1. All legislative Powers herein granted shall be vested in a Congress of the United States, which shall consist of a Senate and House of Representatives.

SECTION 2. The House of Representatives shall be composed of Members chosen every second Year by the People of the several States, and the Electors in each State shall have the Qualifications requisite for Electors of the most numerous Branch of the State Legislature.

No Person shall be a Representative who shall not have attained to the age of twenty five Years, and been seven Years a Citizen of the United States, and who shall not, when elected, be an Inhabitant of that State in which he shall be chosen.

[Representatives and direct Taxes shall be apportioned among the several States which may be included within this Union, according to their respective Numbers, which shall be determined by adding to the whole Number of free Persons, including those bound to Service for a Term of Years, and excluding Indians not taxed, three fifths of all other Persons.][1] The actual Enumeration shall be made within three Years after the first Meeting of the Congress of the United States, and within every subsequent Term of ten Years, in such Manner as they shall by Law direct. The Number of Representatives shall not exceed one for every thirty Thousand, but each State shall have at Least one Representative; and until such enumeration shall be made, the State of New Hampshire shall be entitled to chuse three, Massachusetts eight, Rhode-Island and Providence Plantations one, Connecticut five, New-York six, New Jersey four, Pennsylvania eight, Delaware one, Maryland six, Virginia ten, North Carolina five, South Carolina five, and Georgia three.

When vacancies happen in the Representation from any State, the Executive Authority thereof shall issue Writs of Election to fill such Vacancies.

The House of Representatives shall chuse their Speaker and other Officers; and shall have the sole Power of Impeachment.

SECTION 3. The Senate of the United States shall be composed of two Senators from each State, [chosen by the Legislature thereof,][2] for six Years; and each Senator shall have one Vote.

Immediately after they shall be assembled in Consequence of the first Election, they shall be divided as equally as may be into three Classes. The Seats of the Senators of the first Class shall be vacated at the Expiration of the second Year, of the second Class at the Expiration of the fourth Year, and of the third Class at the Expiration of the sixth Year, so that one third may be chosen every second Year; [and if Vacancies happen by Resignation, or otherwise, during the Recess of the Legislature of any State, the Executive thereof may make temporary Appointments until the next Meeting of the Legislature, which shall then fill such Vacancies.][3]

No Person shall be a Senator who shall not have attained to the Age of thirty Years, and been nine Years a Citizen of the United States, and who shall not, when elected, be an Inhabitant of that State for which he shall be chosen.

The Vice President of the United States shall be President of the Senate, but shall have no Vote, unless they be equally divided.

The Senate shall chuse their other Officers, and also a President pro tempore, in the Absence of the Vice President, or when he shall exercise the Office of President of the United States.

The Senate shall have the sole Power to try all Impeachments. When sitting for that Purpose, they shall be on Oath or Affirmation. When the President of the United States is tried, the Chief Justice shall preside: And no Person shall be convicted without the Concurrence of two thirds of the Members present.

Judgment in Cases of Impeachment shall not extend further than to removal from Office, and disqualification to hold and enjoy any Office of honor, Trust or Profit under the United States: but the Party convicted shall nevertheless be liable and subject to Indictment, Trial, Judgment and Punishment, according to Law.

SECTION 4. The Times, Places and Manner of holding Elections for Senators and Representatives, shall be prescribed in each State by the Legislature thereof; but the Congress may at any time by Law make or alter such Regulations, except as to the Places of chusing Senators.

The Congress shall assemble at least once in every Year, and such Meeting shall [be on the first Monday in December],[4] unless they shall by Law appoint a different Day.

SECTION 5. Each House shall be the Judge of the Elections, Returns and Qualifications of its own Members, and a Majority of each shall constitute a Quorum to do Business; but a smaller Number may adjourn from day to day, and may be authorized to compel the Attendance of absent Members, in such Manner, and under such Penalties as each House may provide.

Each House may determine the Rules of its Proceedings, punish its Members for disorderly Behaviour, and, with the Concurrence of two thirds, expel a Member.

Each House shall keep a Journal of its Proceedings, and from time to time publish the same, excepting such Parts as may in their Judgment require Secrecy; and the Yeas and

Nays of the Members of either House on any question shall, at the Desire of one fifth of those Present, be entered on the Journal.

Neither House, during the Session of Congress, shall, without the Consent of the other, adjourn for more than three days, nor to any other Place than that in which the two Houses shall be sitting.

SECTION 6. The Senators and Representatives shall receive a Compensation for their Services, to be ascertained by Law, and paid out of the Treasury of the United States. They shall in all Cases, except Treason, Felony and Breach of the Peace, be privileged from Arrest during their Attendance at the Session of their respective Houses, and in going to and returning from the same; and for any Speech or Debate in either House, they shall not be questioned in any other Place.

No Senator or Representative shall, during the Time for which he was elected, be appointed to any civil Office under the Authority of the United States, which shall have been created, or the Emoluments whereof shall have been encreased during such time; and no Person holding any Office under the United States, shall be a Member of either House during his Continuance in Office.

SECTION 7. All Bills for raising Revenue shall originate in the House of Representatives; but the Senate may propose or concur with Amendments as on other Bills.

Every Bill which shall have passed the House of Representatives and the Senate, shall, before it become a Law, be presented to the President of the United States; If he approve he shall sign it, but if not he shall return it, with his Objections to that House in which it shall have originated, who shall enter the Objections at large on their Journal, and proceed to reconsider it. If after such Reconsideration two thirds of that House shall agree to pass the Bill, it shall be sent, together with the Objections, to the other House, by which it shall likewise be reconsidered, and if approved by two thirds of that House, it shall become a Law. But in all such Cases the Votes of both Houses shall be determined by yeas and Nays, and the Names of the Persons voting for and against the Bill shall be entered on the Journal of each House respectively. If any Bill shall not be returned by the President within ten Days (Sundays excepted) after it shall have been presented to him, the Same shall be a Law, in like Manner as if he had signed it, unless the Congress by their Adjournment prevent its Return, in which Case it shall not be a Law.

Every Order, Resolution, or Vote to which the Concurrence of the Senate and House of Representatives may be necessary (except on a question of Adjournment) shall be presented to the President of the United States; and before the Same shall take Effect, shall be approved by him, or being disapproved by him, shall be repassed by two thirds of the Senate and House of Representatives, according to the Rules and Limitations prescribed in the Case of a Bill.

SECTION 8. The Congress shall have Power To lay and collect Taxes, Duties, Imposts and Excises, to pay the Debts and provide for the common Defence and general Welfare of the United States; but all Duties, Imposts and Excises shall be uniform throughout the United States;

To borrow Money on the credit of the United States;

To regulate Commerce with foreign Nations, and among the several States, and with the Indian Tribes;

To establish an uniform Rule of Naturalization, and uniform Laws on the subject of Bankruptcies throughout the United States;

To coin Money, regulate the Value thereof, and of foreign Coin, and fix the Standard of Weights and Measures;

To provide for the Punishment of counterfeiting the Securities and current Coin of the United States;

To establish Post Offices and post Roads;

To promote the Progress of Science and useful Arts, by securing for limited Times to Authors and Inventors the exclusive Right to their respective Writings and Discoveries;

To constitute Tribunals inferior to the supreme Court;

To define and punish Piracies and Felonies committed on the high Seas, and Offences against the Law of Nations;

To declare War, grant Letters of Marque and Reprisal, and make Rules concerning Captures on Land and Water;

To raise and support Armies, but no Appropriation of Money to that Use shall be for a longer Term than two Years;

To provide and maintain a Navy;

To make Rules for the Government and Regulation of the land and naval Forces;

To provide for calling forth the Militia to execute the Laws of the Union, suppress Insurrections and repel Invasions;

To provide for organizing, arming, and disciplining, the Militia, and for governing such Part of them as may be employed in the Service of the United States, reserving to the States respectively, the Appointment of the Officers, and the Authority of training the Militia according to the discipline prescribed by Congress;

To exercise exclusive Legislation in all Cases whatsoever, over such District (not exceeding ten Miles square) as may, by Cession of particular States, and the Acceptance of Congress, become the Seat of the Government of the United States, and to exercise like Authority over all Places purchased by the Consent of the Legislature of the State in which the Same shall be, for the Erection of Forts, Magazines, Arsenals, dock-Yards, and other needful Buildings;—And

To make all Laws which shall be necessary and proper for carrying into Execution the foregoing Powers, and all other Powers vested by this Constitution in the Government of the United States, or in any Department or Officer thereof.

SECTION 9. The Migration or Importation of such Persons as any of the States now existing shall think proper to admit, shall not be prohibited by the Congress prior to the Year one thousand eight hundred and eight, but a Tax or duty may be imposed on such Importation, not exceeding ten dollars for each Person.

The Privilege of the Writ of Habeas Corpus shall not be suspended, unless when in Cases of Rebellion or Invasion the public Safety may require it.

No Bill of Attainder or ex post facto Law shall be passed.

No Capitation, or other direct, Tax shall be laid, unless in Proportion to the Census or Enumeration herein before directed to be taken.[5]

No Tax or Duty shall be laid on Articles exported from any State.

No Preference shall be given by any Regulation of Commerce or Revenue to the Ports of one State over those of another; nor shall Vessels bound to, or from, one State, be obliged to enter, clear, or pay Duties in another.

No Money shall be drawn from the Treasury, but in Consequence of Appropriations made by Law; and a regular Statement and Account of the Receipts and Expenditures of all public Money shall be published from time to time.

No Title of Nobility shall be granted by the United States: And no Person holding any Office of Profit or Trust under them, shall, without the Consent of the Congress, accept of any present, Emolument, Office, or Title, of any kind whatever, from any King, Prince, or foreign State.

SECTION 10. No State shall enter into any Treaty, Alliance, or Confederation; grant Letters of Marque and Reprisal; coin Money; emit Bills of Credit; make any Thing but gold and silver Coin a Tender in Payment of Debts; pass any Bill of Attainder, ex post facto Law, or Law impairing the Obligation of Contracts, or grant any Title of Nobility.

No State shall, without the Consent of the Congress, lay any Imposts or Duties on Imports or Exports, except what may be absolutely necessary for executing it's inspection Laws: and the net Produce of all Duties and Imposts, laid by any State on Imports or Exports, shall be for the Use of the Treasury of the United States; and all such Laws shall be subject to the Revision and Controul of the Congress.

No State shall, without the Consent of Congress, lay any Duty of Tonnage, keep Troops, or Ships of War in time of Peace, enter into any Agreement or Compact with another State, or with a foreign Power, or engage in War, unless actually invaded, or in such imminent Danger as will not admit of delay.

# Article II

SECTION 1. The executive Power shall be vested in a President of the United States of America. He shall hold his Office during the Term of four Years, and, together with the Vice President, chosen for the same Term, be elected, as follows

Each State shall appoint, in such Manner as the Legislature thereof may direct, a Number of Electors, equal to the whole Number of Senators and Representatives to which the State may be entitled in the Congress: but no Senator or Representative, or Person holding an Office of Trust or Profit under the United States, shall be appointed an Elector.

[The Electors shall meet in their respective States, and vote by Ballot for two Persons, of whom one at least shall not be an Inhabitant of the same State with themselves. And they shall make a List of all the Persons voted for, and of the Number of Votes for each; which List they shall sign and certify, and transmit sealed to the Seat of the Government of the United States, directed to the President of the Senate. The President of the Senate shall, in the Presence of the Senate and House of Representatives, open all the Certificates, and the Votes shall then be counted. The Person having the greatest Number of Votes shall be the President, if such Number be a Majority of the whole Number of Electors appointed; and if there be more than one who have such Majority, and have an equal Number of Votes, then the House of Representatives shall immediately chuse by Ballot one of them for President; and if no Person have a Majority, then from the five highest on the list the said House shall in like Manner chuse the President. But in chusing the President, the Votes shall be taken by States, the Representation from each State having one Vote; A quorum for this Purpose shall consist of a Member or Members from two thirds of the States, and a Majority of all the States shall be necessary to a Choice. In every Case, after the Choice of the President, the Person having the greatest Number of Votes of the Electors shall be the Vice President. But if there should remain two or more who have equal Votes, the Senate shall chuse from them by Ballot the Vice President.][6]

The Congress may determine the Time of chusing the Electors, and the Day on which they shall give their Votes; which Day shall be the same throughout the United States.

No Person except a natural born Citizen, or a Citizen of the United States, at the time of the Adoption of this Constitution, shall be eligible to the Office of President; neither shall any Person be eligible to that Office who shall not have attained to the Age of thirty five Years, and been fourteen Years a Resident within the United States.

In Case of the Removal of the President from Office, or of his Death, Resignation, or Inability to discharge the Powers and Duties of the said Office,[7] the Same shall devolve on the Vice President, and the Congress may by Law provide for the Case of Removal, Death, Resignation or Inability, both of the President and Vice President, declaring what Officer shall then act as President, and such Officer shall act accordingly, until the Disability be removed, or a President shall be elected.

The President shall, at stated Times, receive for his Services, a Compensation, which shall neither be encreased nor diminished during the Period for which he shall have been elected, and he shall not receive within that Period any other Emolument from the United States, or any of them.

Before he enter on the Execution of his Office, he shall take the following Oath or Affirmation:—"I do solemnly swear (or affirm) that I will faithfully execute the Office of President of the United States, and will to the best of my Ability, preserve, protect and defend the Constitution of the United States."

SECTION 2. The President shall be Commander in Chief of the Army and Navy of the United States, and of the Militia of the several States, when called into the actual Service of the United States; he may require the Opinion, in writing, of the principal Officer in each of the executive Departments, upon any Subject relating to the Duties of their respective Offices, and he shall have Power to grant Reprieves and Pardons for Offences against the United States, except in Cases of Impeachment.

He shall have Power, by and with the Advice and Consent of the Senate, to make Treaties, provided two thirds of the Senators present concur; and he shall nominate, and by and with the Advice and Consent of the Senate, shall appoint Ambassadors, other public Ministers and Consuls, Judges of the supreme Court, and all other Officers of the United States, whose Appointments are not herein otherwise provided for, and which shall be established by Law: but the Congress may by Law vest the Appointment of such inferior Officers, as they think proper, in the President alone, in the Courts of Law, or in the Heads of Departments.

The President shall have Power to fill up all Vacancies that may happen during the Recess of the Senate, by granting Commissions which shall expire at the End of their next Session.

SECTION 3. He shall from time to time give to the Congress Information of the State of the Union, and recommend to their Consideration such Measures as he shall judge necessary and expedient; he may, on extraordinary Occasions, convene both Houses, or either of them, and in Case of Disagreement between them, with Respect to the Time of Adjournment, he may adjourn them to such Time as he shall think proper; he shall receive Ambassadors and other public Ministers; he shall take Care that the Laws be faithfully executed, and shall Commission all the Officers of the United States.

SECTION 4. The President, Vice President and all civil Officers of the United States, shall be removed from Office on Impeachment for, and Conviction of, Treason, Bribery, or other high Crimes and Misdemeanors.

# Article III

SECTION 1. The judicial Power of the United States, shall be vested in one supreme Court, and in such inferior Courts as the Congress may from time to time ordain and establish. The Judges, both of the supreme and inferior Courts, shall hold their Offices during good Behaviour, and shall, at stated Times, receive for their Services, a Compensation, which shall not be diminished during their Continuance in Office.

SECTION 2. The judicial Power shall extend to all Cases, in Law and Equity, arising under this Constitution, the Laws of the United States, and Treaties made, or which shall be made, under their Authority;—to all Cases affecting Ambassadors, other public Ministers and Consuls;—to all Cases of admiralty and maritime Jurisdiction;—to Controversies to which the United States shall be a Party;—to Controversies between two or more States;—between a State and Citizens of another State;—between Citizens of different States;—between Citizens of the same State claiming Lands under Grants of different States, and between a State, or the Citizens thereof, and foreign States, Citizens or Subjects.[8]

In all Cases affecting Ambassadors, other public Ministers and Consuls, and those in which a State shall be Party, the supreme Court shall have original Jurisdiction. In all the other Cases before mentioned, the supreme Court shall have appellate Jurisdiction, both as to Law and Fact, with such Exceptions, and under such Regulations as the Congress shall make.

The Trial of all Crimes, except in Cases of Impeachment, shall be by Jury; and such Trial shall be held in the State where the said Crimes shall have been committed; but when not committed within any State, the Trial shall be at such Place or Places as the Congress may by Law have directed.

SECTION 3. Treason against the United States, shall consist only in levying War against them, or in adhering to their Enemies, giving them Aid and Comfort. No Person shall be convicted of Treason unless on the Testimony of two Witnesses to the same overt Act, or on Confession in open Court.

The Congress shall have Power to declare the Punishment of Treason, but no Attainder of Treason shall work Corruption of Blood, or Forfeiture except during the Life of the Person attainted.

# Article IV

SECTION 1. Full Faith and Credit shall be given in each State to the public Acts, Records, and judicial Proceedings of every other State. And the Congress may by general Laws prescribe the Manner in which such Acts, Records and Proceedings shall be proved, and the Effect thereof.

SECTION 2. The Citizens of each State shall be entitled to all Privileges and Immunities of Citizens in the several States.

A Person charged in any State with Treason, Felony, or other Crime, who shall flee from Justice, and be found in another State, shall on Demand of the executive Authority of the State from which he fled, be delivered up, to be removed to the State having Jurisdiction of the Crime.

[No Person held to Service or Labour in one State, under the Laws thereof, escaping into another, shall, in Consequence of any Law or Regulation therein, be discharged from such Service or Labour, but shall be delivered up on Claim of the Party to whom such Service or Labour may be due.][9]

SECTION 3. New States may be admitted by the Congress into this Union; but no new State shall be formed or erected within the Jurisdiction of any other State; nor any State be formed by the Junction of two or more States, or Parts of States, without the Consent of the Legislatures of the States concerned as well as of the Congress.

The Congress shall have Power to dispose of and make all needful Rules and Regulations respecting the Territory or other Property belonging to the United States; and nothing in this Constitution shall be so construed as to Prejudice any Claims of the United States, or of any particular State.

SECTION 4. The United States shall guarantee to every State in this Union a Republican Form of Government, and shall protect each of them against Invasion; and on Application of the Legislature, or of the Executive (when the Legislature cannot be convened) against domestic Violence.

# Article V

The Congress, whenever two thirds of both Houses shall deem it necessary, shall propose Amendments to this Constitution, or, on the Application of the Legislatures of two thirds of the several States, shall call a Convention for proposing Amendments, which, in either Case, shall be valid to all Intents and Purposes, as Part of this Constitution, when ratified by the Legislatures of three fourths of the several States, or by Conventions in three fourths thereof, as the one or the other Mode of Ratification may be proposed by the Congress; Provided [that no Amendment which may be made prior to the Year One thousand eight hundred and eight shall in any Manner affect the first and fourth Clauses in the Ninth Section of the first Article; and][10] that no State, without its Consent, shall be deprived of its equal Suffrage in the Senate.

# Article VI

All Debts contracted and Engagements entered into, before the Adoption of this Constitution, shall be as valid against the United States under this Constitution, as under the Confederation.

This Constitution, and the Laws of the United States which shall be made in Pursuance thereof; and all Treaties made, or which shall be made, under the Authority of the United States, shall be the supreme Law of the Land; and the Judges in every State shall be bound thereby, any Thing in the Constitution or Laws of any State to the Contrary notwithstanding.

The Senators and Representatives before mentioned, and the Members of the several State Legislatures, and all executive and judicial Officers, both of the United States and of the several States, shall be bound by Oath or Affirmation, to support this Constitution; but no religious Test shall ever be required as a Qualification to any Office or public Trust under the United States.

# Article VII

The Ratification of the Conventions of nine States, shall be sufficient for the Establishment of this Constitution between the States so ratifying the Same.

Done in Convention by the Unanimous Consent of the States present the Seventeenth Day of September in the Year of our Lord one thousand seven hundred and Eighty seven and of the Independence of the United States of America the Twelfth. IN WITNESS whereof We have hereunto subscribed our Names,

George Washington,
President and deputy from Virginia.

| | |
|---|---|
| NEW HAMPSHIRE: | John Langdon, Nicholas Gilman. |
| MASSACHUSETTS: | Nathaniel Gorham, Rufus King. |
| CONNECTICUT: | William Samuel Johnson, Roger Sherman. |
| NEW YORK: | Alexander Hamilton. |

| NEW JERSEY: | William Livingston, |
| | David Brearley, |
| | William Paterson, |
| | Jonathan Dayton. |

PENNSYLVANIA: Benjamin Franklin,
Thomas Mifflin,
Robert Morris,
George Clymer,
Thomas FitzSimons,
Jared Ingersoll,
James Wilson,
Gouverneur Morris.

DELAWARE: George Read,
Gunning Bedford Jr.,
John Dickinson,
Richard Bassett,
Jacob Broom.

MARYLAND: James McHenry,
Daniel of St. Thomas Jenifer,
Daniel Carroll.

VIRGINIA: John Blair,
James Madison Jr.

NORTH CAROLINA: William Blount,
Richard Dobbs Spaight,
Hugh Williamson.

SOUTH CAROLINA: John Rutledge,
Charles Cotesworth Pinckney,
Charles Pinckney,
Pierce Butler.

GEORGIA: William Few,
Abraham Baldwin.

[The language of the original Constitution, not including the Amendments, was adopted by a convention of the states on September 17, 1787, and was subsequently ratified by the states on the following dates: Delaware, December 7, 1787; Pennsylvania, December 12, 1787; New Jersey, December 18, 1787; Georgia, January 2, 1788; Connecticut, January 9, 1788; Massachusetts, February 6, 1788; Maryland, April 28, 1788; South Carolina, May 23, 1788; New Hampshire, June 21, 1788.

Ratification was completed on June 21, 1788.

The Constitution subsequently was ratified by Virginia, June 25, 1788; New York, July 26, 1788; North Carolina, November 21, 1789; Rhode Island, May 29, 1790; and Vermont, January 10, 1791.]

# Amendments

**AMENDMENT I** *(First ten amendments ratified December 15, 1791.)*
Congress shall make no law respecting an establishment of religion, or prohibiting the free exercise thereof; or abridging the freedom of speech, or of the press; or the right of the people peaceably to assemble, and to petition the Government for a redress of grievances.

**AMENDMENT II**
A well regulated Militia, being necessary to the security of a free State, the right of the people to keep and bear Arms, shall not be infringed.

**AMENDMENT III**
No Soldier shall, in time of peace be quartered in any house, without the consent of the Owner, nor in time of war, but in a manner to be prescribed by law.

**AMENDMENT IV**
The right of the people to be secure in their persons, houses, papers, and effects, against unreasonable searches and seizures, shall not be violated, and no Warrants shall issue, but upon probable cause, supported by Oath or affirmation, and particularly describing the place to be searched, and the persons or things to be seized.

**AMENDMENT V**
No person shall be held to answer for a capital, or otherwise infamous crime, unless on a presentment or indictment of a Grand Jury, except in cases arising in the land or naval forces, or in the Militia, when in actual service in time of War or public danger; nor shall any person be subject for the same offence to be twice put in jeopardy of life or limb; nor shall be compelled in any criminal case to be a witness against himself, nor be deprived of life, liberty, or property, without due process of law; nor shall private property be taken for public use, without just compensation.

**AMENDMENT VI**
In all criminal prosecutions, the accused shall enjoy the right to a speedy and public trial, by an impartial jury of the State and district wherein the crime shall have been committed, which district shall have been previously ascertained by law, and to be informed of the nature and cause of the accusation; to be confronted with the witnesses against him; to have compulsory process for obtaining witnesses in his favor, and to have the Assistance of Counsel for his defence.

## AMENDMENT VII

In Suits at common law, where the value in controversy shall exceed twenty dollars, the right of trial by jury shall be preserved, and no fact tried by a jury, shall be otherwise re-examined in any Court of the United States, than according to the rules of the common law.

## AMENDMENT VIII

Excessive bail shall not be required, nor excessive fines imposed, nor cruel and unusual punishments inflicted.

## AMENDMENT IX

The enumeration in the Constitution, of certain rights, shall not be construed to deny or disparage others retained by the people.

## AMENDMENT X

The powers not delegated to the United States by the Constitution, nor prohibited by it to the States, are reserved to the States respectively, or to the people.

## AMENDMENT XI *(Ratified February 7, 1795)*

The Judicial power of the United States shall not be construed to extend to any suit in law or equity, commenced or prosecuted against one of the United States by Citizens of another State, or by Citizens or Subjects of any Foreign State.

## AMENDMENT XII *(Ratified June 15, 1804)*

The Electors shall meet in their respective states and vote by ballot for President and Vice-President, one of whom, at least, shall not be an inhabitant of the same state with themselves; they shall name in their ballots the person voted for as President, and in distinct ballots the person voted for as Vice-President, and they shall make distinct lists of all persons voted for as President, and of all persons voted for as Vice-President, and of the number of votes for each, which lists they shall sign and certify, and transmit sealed to the seat of the government of the United States, directed to the President of the Senate;—The President of the Senate shall, in the presence of the Senate and House of Representatives, open all the certificates and the votes shall then be counted;—The person having the greatest number of votes for President, shall be the President, if such number be a majority of the whole number of Electors appointed; and if no person have such majority, then from the persons having the highest numbers not exceeding three on the list of those voted for as President, the House of Representatives shall choose immediately, by ballot, the President. But in choosing the President, the votes shall be taken by states, the representation from each state having one vote; a quorum for this purpose shall consist of a member or members from two-thirds of the states, and a majority of all the states shall be necessary to a choice. [And if the House of Representatives shall not choose a President whenever the right of choice shall devolve upon them, before the fourth day of March next following, then the Vice-President shall act as President, as in the case of the death or other constitutional disability of the President.—][11] The person having the greatest number of votes as Vice-President, shall be the Vice-President, if such number be a majority of the whole number of Electors appointed, and if no person have a majority, then from the two highest numbers on the list, the Senate shall choose the Vice-President; a quorum for the purpose shall consist of two-thirds of the whole number of Senators, and a majority of the whole number shall be necessary to a choice. But no person constitutionally ineligible to the office of President shall be eligible to that of Vice-President of the United States.

AMENDMENT XIII  *(Ratified December 6, 1865)*

➤  SECTION 1.  Neither slavery nor involuntary servitude, except as a punishment for crime whereof the party shall have been duly convicted, shall exist within the United States, or any place subject to their jurisdiction.

➤  SECTION 2.  Congress shall have power to enforce this article by appropriate legislation.

AMENDMENT XIV  *(Ratified July 9, 1868)*

➤  SECTION 1.  All persons born or naturalized in the United States, and subject to the jurisdiction thereof, are citizens of the United States and of the State wherein they reside. No State shall make or enforce any law which shall abridge the privileges or immunities of citizens of the United States; nor shall any State deprive any person of life, liberty, or property, without due process of law; nor deny to any person within its jurisdiction the equal protection of the laws.

➤  SECTION 2.  Representatives shall be apportioned among the several States according to their respective numbers, counting the whole number of persons in each State, excluding Indians not taxed. But when the right to vote at any election for the choice of electors for President and Vice President of the United States, Representatives in Congress, the Executive and Judicial officers of a State, or the members of the Legislature thereof, is denied to any of the male inhabitants of such State, being twenty-one years of age,[12] and citizens of the United States, or in any way abridged, except for participation in rebellion, or other crime, the basis of representation therein shall be reduced in the proportion which the number of such male citizens shall bear to the whole number of male citizens twenty-one years of age in such State.

➤  SECTION 3.  No person shall be a Senator or Representative in Congress, or elector of President and Vice President, or hold any office, civil or military, under the United States, or under any State, who, having previously taken an oath, as a member of Congress, or as an officer of the United States, or as a member of any State legislature, or as an executive or judicial officer of any State, to support the Constitution of the United States, shall have engaged in insurrection or rebellion against the same, or given aid or comfort to the enemies thereof. But Congress may by a vote of two-thirds of each House, remove such disability.

➤  SECTION 4.  The validity of the public debt of the United States, authorized by law, including debts incurred for payment of pensions and bounties for services in suppressing insurrection or rebellion, shall not be questioned. But neither the United States nor any State shall assume or pay any debt or obligation incurred in aid of insurrection or rebellion against the United States, or any claim for the loss or emancipation of any slave; but all such debts, obligations and claims shall be held illegal and void.

➤  SECTION 5.  The Congress shall have power to enforce, by appropriate legislation, the provisions of this article.

AMENDMENT XV *(Ratified February 3, 1870)*

➤ *SECTION 1.* The right of citizens of the United States to vote shall not be denied or abridged by the United States or by any State on account of race, color, or previous condition of servitude.

➤ *SECTION 2.* The Congress shall have power to enforce this article by appropriate legislation.

AMENDMENT XVI *(Ratified February 3, 1913)*

The Congress shall have power to lay and collect taxes on incomes, from whatever source derived, without apportionment among the several States, and without regard to any census or enumeration.

AMENDMENT XVII *(Ratified April 8, 1913)*

The Senate of the United States shall be composed of two Senators from each State, elected by the people thereof, for six years; and each Senator shall have one vote. The electors in each State shall have the qualifications requisite for electors of the most numerous branch of the State legislatures.

When vacancies happen in the representation of any State in the Senate, the executive authority of such State shall issue writs of election to fill such vacancies: *Provided,* That the legislature of any State may empower the executive thereof to make temporary appointments until the people fill the vacancies by election as the legislature may direct.

This amendment shall not be so construed as to affect the election or term of any Senator chosen before it becomes valid as part of the Constitution.

AMENDMENT XVIII *(Ratified January 16, 1919)*[13]

➤ *SECTION 1.* After one year from the ratification of this article the manufacture, sale, or transportation of intoxicating liquors within, the importation thereof into, or the exportation thereof from the United States and all territory subject to the jurisdiction thereof for beverage purposes is hereby prohibited.

➤ *SECTION 2.* The Congress and the several States shall have concurrent power to enforce this article by appropriate legislation.

➤ *SECTION 3.* This article shall be inoperative unless it shall have been ratified as an amendment to the Constitution by the legislatures of the several States, as provided in the Constitution, within seven years from the date of the submission hereof to the States by the Congress.

AMENDMENT XIX *(Ratified August 18, 1920)*

The right of citizens of the United States to vote shall not be denied or abridged by the United States or by any State on account of sex.

Congress shall have power to enforce this article by appropriate legislation.

AMENDMENT XX *(Ratified January 23, 1933)*

➤ *SECTION 1.* The terms of the President and Vice President shall end at noon on the 20th day of January, and the terms of Senators and Representatives at noon on the 3d day of January, of the years in which such terms would have ended if this article had not been ratified; and the terms of their successors shall then begin.

> SECTION 2. The Congress shall assemble at least once in every year, and such meeting shall begin at noon on the 3d day of January, unless they shall by law appoint a different day.

> SECTION 3.[14] If, at the time fixed for the beginning of the term of the President, the President elect shall have died, the Vice President elect shall become President. If a President shall not have been chosen before the time fixed for the beginning of his term, or if the President elect shall have failed to qualify, then the Vice President elect shall act as President until a President shall have qualified; and the Congress may by law provide for the case wherein neither a President elect nor a Vice President elect shall have qualified, declaring who shall then act as President, or the manner in which one who is to act shall be selected, and such person shall act accordingly until a President or Vice President shall have qualified.

> SECTION 4. The Congress may by law provide for the case of the death of any of the persons from whom the House of Representatives may choose a President whenever the right of choice shall have devolved upon them, and for the case of the death of any of the persons from whom the Senate may choose a Vice President whenever the right of choice shall have devolved upon them.

> SECTION 5. Sections 1 and 2 shall take effect on the 15th day of October following the ratification of this article.

> SECTION 6. This article shall be inoperative unless it shall have been ratified as an amendment to the Constitution by the legislatures of three-fourths of the several States within seven years from the date of its submission.

## AMENDMENT XXI *(Ratified December 5, 1933)*

> SECTION 1. The eighteenth article of amendment to the Constitution of the United States is hereby repealed.

> SECTION 2. The transportation or importation into any State, Territory, or possession of the United States for delivery or use therein of intoxicating liquors, in violation of the laws thereof, is hereby prohibited.

> SECTION 3. This article shall be inoperative unless it shall have been ratified as an amendment to the Constitution by conventions in the several States, as provided in the Constitution, within seven years from the date of the submission hereof to the States by the Congress.

## AMENDMENT XXII *(Ratified February 27, 1951)*

> SECTION 1. No person shall be elected to the office of the President more than twice, and no person who has held the office of President, or acted as President, for more than two years of a term to which some other person was elected President shall be elected to the office of the President more than once. But this Article shall not apply to any person holding the office of President when this Article was proposed by the Congress, and shall not prevent any person who may be holding the office of President, or acting as President, during the term within which this Article become operative from holding the office of President or acting as President during the remainder of such term.

> SECTION 2. This article shall be inoperative unless it shall have been ratified as an amendment to the Constitution by the legislatures of three-fourths of the several States within seven years from the date of its submission to the States by the Congress.

**AMENDMENT XXIII** *(Ratified March 29, 1961)*

➤ *SECTION 1.* The District constituting the seat of Government of the United States shall appoint in such manner as the Congress may direct:

A number of electors of President and Vice President equal to the whole number of Senators and Representatives in Congress to which the District would be entitled if it were a State, but in no event more than the least populous State; they shall be in addition to those appointed by the States, but they shall be considered, for the purposes of the election of President and Vice President, to be electors appointed by a State; and they shall meet in the District and perform such duties as provided by the twelfth article of amendment.

➤ *SECTION 2.* The Congress shall have power to enforce this article by appropriate legislation.

**AMENDMENT XXIV** *(Ratified January 23, 1964)*

➤ *SECTION 1.* The right of citizens of the United States to vote in any primary or other election for President or Vice President, for electors for President or Vice President, or for Senator or Representative in Congress, shall not be denied or abridged by the United States or any State by reason of failure to pay any poll tax or other tax.

➤ *SECTION 2.* The Congress shall have power to enforce this article by appropriate legislation.

**AMENDMENT XXV** *(Ratified February 10, 1967)*

➤ *SECTION 1.* In case of the removal of the President from office or of his death or resignation, the Vice President shall become President.

➤ *SECTION 2.* Whenever there is a vacancy in the office of the Vice President, the President shall nominate a Vice President who shall take office upon confirmation by a majority vote of both Houses of Congress.

➤ *SECTION 3.* Whenever the President transmits to the President pro tempore of the Senate and the Speaker of the House of Representatives his written declaration that he is unable to discharge the powers and duties of his office, and until he transmits to them a written declaration to the contrary, such powers and duties shall be discharged by the Vice President as Acting President.

➤ *SECTION 4.* Whenever the Vice President and a majority of either the principal officers of the executive departments or of such other body as Congress may by law provide, transmit to the President pro tempore of the Senate and the Speaker of the House of Representatives their written declaration that the President is unable to discharge the powers and duties of his office, the Vice President shall immediately assume the powers and duties of the office as Acting President.

Thereafter, when the President transmits to the President pro tempore of the Senate and the Speaker of the House of Representatives his written declaration that no inability exists, he shall resume the powers and duties of his office unless the Vice President and a majority of either the principal officers of the executive department or of such other body as Congress may by law provide, transmit within four days to the President pro tempore of the Senate and the Speaker of the House of Representatives their written declaration that the President is unable to discharge the powers and duties of his office. Thereupon Congress shall decide the issue, assembling within forty-eight hours for that purpose if not in session. If the Congress, within twenty-one days after receipt of the latter written declaration, or, if Congress is not in session, within twenty-one days after Congress is required to assemble, determines by two-thirds vote of both Houses that the President is unable to discharge the powers and duties of his office, the Vice President shall continue to discharge the same as Acting President; otherwise, the President shall resume the powers and duties of his office.

**AMENDMENT XXVI** *(Ratified July 1, 1971)*

➤ *SECTION 1.* The right of citizens of the United States, who are eighteen years of age or older, to vote shall not be denied or abridged by the United States or by any State on account of age.

➤ *SECTION 2.* The Congress shall have power to enforce this article by appropriate legislation.

**AMENDMENT XXVII** *(Ratified May 7, 1992)*

No law varying the compensation for the services of the Senators and Representatives shall take effect, until an election of Representatives shall have intervened.

### Notes

1. The part in brackets was by section 2 of the Fourteenth Amendment.
2. The part in brackets was changed by the first paragraph of the Seventeenth Amendment.
3. The part in brackets was changed by the second paragraph of the Seventeenth Amendment.
4. The part in brackets was changed by section 2 of the Twentieth Amendment.
5. The Sixteenth Amendment gave Congress the power to tax incomes.
6. The material in brackets has been superseded by the Twelfth Amendment.
7. This provision has been affected by the Twenty-fifth Amendment.
8. These clauses were affected by the Eleventh Amendment.
9. This paragraph has been superseded by the Thirteenth Amendment.
10. Obsolete.
11. The part in brackets has been superseded by section 3 of the Twentieth Amendment.
12. See the Nineteenth and Twenty-sixth Amendments.
13. This Amendment was repealed by section 1 of the Twenty-first Amendment.
14. See the Twenty-fifth Amendment.

*Source:* U.S. Congress, House, Committee on the Judiciary, *The Constitution of the United States of America, as Amended,* 100th Cong., 1st sess., 1987, H Doc 100-94.

# Appendix C
# GLOSSARY

AD HOC. Created for a singular and temporary purpose.

ADVISORY OPINION. An opinion issued by a court in which it states how it would rule on a legal matter that is not actually ripe for decision; significantly, the Supreme Court and other federal courts do not issue advisory opinions.

ALIEN. A person who lives within the borders of a country but is not a citizen. Legal aliens are lawfully present, illegal aliens unlawfully so.

ANTIMISCEGENATION STATUTE. A law that forbids people of different races to marry or have children. In *Loving v. Virginia* (1967), the Supreme Court ruled state antimiscegenation laws unconstitutional.

APPELLANT. The party that appeals a lower court's decision. This party is usually seeking reversal of the lower court's decision. *See also* petitioner.

APPELLEE. The party that responds to an appeal. This party is generally seeking affirmation of a lower court's decision. *See also* respondent.

ARGUENDO. For the sake of argument.

ATTORNEY GENERAL, U.S. Head of the Department of Justice, appointed by the president. Responsibilities include representing the United States in legal matters, standing before the Supreme Court in cases where the United States is a party, and counseling the president and others within the executive branch as needed. Each state also has its own attorney general.

BILL OF RIGHTS. The first ten amendments of the Constitution guaranteeing citizens basic constitutional rights and liberties.

CASE-OR-CONTROVERSY REQUIREMENT. The constitutional requirement that cases before the federal courts must involve an actual, and not hypothetical, dispute between parties.

CASTE. A rigid social class or stratum; characteristic of a stratified classbound society.

CERTIORARI. *See* writ of certiorari.

CIVIL SUIT. A lawsuit undertaken to protect an individual's private legal rights. Also known as a civil action.

CLASS ACTION. A lawsuit in which a large group of people with a common interest and complaint join together to sue.

COMMERCIAL SPEECH. Expression that proposes a sale or other commercial transaction. Commercial speech receives less constitutional protection than political speech.

COMMON LAW. Body of law that develops over time from the judgments of courts. Contrasted with statutory law, which is written by legislatures.

COMPLAINT. The document that a plaintiff serves upon a defendant and submits to court. It details a "cause of action," meaning the alleged legal injury in a case; the facts that give rise to it; and the relief or damages sought.

CONCURRING OPINION. Opinion written by a justice or judge that agrees with the judgment of the majority in a case but that offers a separate explanation or process of reasoning for arriving there.

CONSTITUTIONAL INJURY. A harm caused by violation of an individual's constitutional rights that gives rise to standing to sue.

CONSTRUCTIVE KNOWLEDGE. Knowledge that a reasonable person in the same circumstances would have.

CONTRABAND. Goods that are illegal to obtain, possess, or distribute.

CRIMINAL PROSECUTION. Process by which the government charges a person with a criminal violation and brings him or her to trial.

DE FACTO. A state of affairs that exists as a matter of fact, rather than law, without official compulsion behind it.

DE MINIMIS. A trivial or insignificant thing that a court may choose to overlook in deciding an issue.

DECLARATORY RELIEF. A binding declaration by a court defining the rights and duties of parties in a case.

DEFENDANT. Person or party that is sued in a civil case or prosecuted in a criminal case.

DELIBERATE INDIFFERENCE. Ignoring something on purpose.

DESIGNATED PUBLIC FORUM. Public property that the government opens up for free speech purposes. Unlike traditional public forums—streets, sidewalks, parks—

this is property that the government does not have to use for expressive purposes but chooses to in any event.

DISCLAIMER. A statement that one disclaims or refuses responsibility for some liability, eventuality, or risk.

DISSENTING OPINION. Opinion written by a justice or judge that disagrees with the ruling of the majority opinion in a case. One can dissent without filing a dissenting opinion.

DOUBLE JEOPARDY. The prosecution of an individual twice for the same criminal offense. This practice is outlawed by the Fifth Amendment to the Constitution.

DUE PROCESS CLAUSE. Clause in the Fifth and Fourteenth Amendments that declares that no person may be deprived of life, liberty, or property without due process of law. Interpreted to mean that every individual is entitled to a fair trial with significant protections, such as the right to be heard, to call witnesses, to cross-examine witnesses, and so forth.

EMPIRICAL. Based on experience or observation.

ENJOIN. To stop or restrain by injunction.

EQUITABLE REMEDY. When a court enforces a right in a way that does not involve the award of money damages, as when it orders someone to stop committing an unlawful act.

EXCLUSIONARY RULE. The rule under the Fourth Amendment in which evidence obtained unlawfully, in violation of a suspect's rights, may be suppressed and excluded in court.

EXPRESSIVE CONDUCT. Actions that do not literally involve speaking or writing but that nonetheless send a message. Picketing a store, wearing a political button, and painting a picture are all examples of expressive conduct.

FEDERALISM. The system of divided and allocated powers between the states and the federal government.

GENERAL COUNSEL. The most senior lawyer in a government or private legal department.

GRAND JURY. A body of citizens that sits to review relevant evidence and testimony to determine whether a person should be formally charged with a crime.

HOLDING. A court's decision on a matter of law in a case.

ILLEGAL. Actions or conduct that are in violation of municipal, state, or federal law.

IN LOCO PARENTIS. Literally, in the place of a parent. Teachers and school authorities act *in loco parentis* in the school domain when there is no direct supervision by a parent or guardian.

INJUNCTION. An order from a court commanding or preventing an action.

INJURY. The violation of another party's legal rights or its legally protected interests. If the government puts you in prison without a trial, it has violated your due process rights, and you have been injured by its actions.

INVIDIOUS DISCRIMINATION. Discrimination that is objectionable and offensive, usually involving prejudice and stereotyping.

JUDICIAL RESTRAINT. The theory and practice whereby judges defer to the political branches and strive not to invalidate democratically chosen public policies and laws.

JUDICIAL REVIEW. The constitutional power of a court to examine laws and policies made by other branches of government and to invalidate them if they are unconstitutional or unlawful.

JURISDICTION. A court's power to hear a case; also, territory over which a government exercises authority.

JURISPRUDENCE. The fundamental and linked principles of a body of law or legal system.

LEGISLATIVE HISTORY. The specific legislative background and events leading to passage of a statute, including hearings, committee reports, floor statements, and debates. Legislative history is sometimes used by a court as an aid in interpreting a statute or a constitutional provision.

LIABILITY. A legal obligation or responsibility. Liability is enforceable by a court in a civil or criminal trial.

MAGISTRATE. A judicial officer, like a judge, but with lesser and circumscribed authority.

MAJORITY OPINION. Opinion written by a justice or judge indicating the court's ruling in a case and offering an explanation for that ruling.

MANDAMUS. Latin for "we command." Usually, a writ of mandamus is issued from a court to force another court or government official to undertake a specific action.

MEDIATOR. A neutral party that helps to bring opposing sides to agreement by suggesting solutions and fostering productive negotiations.

MOOT. Descriptive of a case that is no longer fit for judicial resolution because an actual controversy no longer exists.

MOTION. An oral or written request for a court to rule on an issue or to compel a party in a case to do something.

NARROWLY TAILORED. A government policy that is closely linked to its objective and so restricts only so much liberty as is necessary to achieve it.

NONSECULAR. Religious.

NOTICE. Adequate warning, a "head's up."

ONEROUS. Difficult or burdensome.

ORDINANCE. Local law enacted by a city, suburb, town, municipality, or other local entity.

OVERBROAD. A law that sweeps too far by proscribing conduct or speech that is constitutionally protected.

PER CURIAM. By the court as a whole, rather than by a single author. It generally indicates the majority or plurality opinion (if not the unanimous opinion of the court), but there can still be concurring or dissenting opinions.

PETITIONER. Party that presents a petition to a court in an effort to seek appeal of a judgment. *See also* APPELLANT.

PLAINTIFF. Party that brings an original civil suit in a state or federal court.

PLURALITY OPINION. An opinion that does not receive support from enough justices (or judges) to constitute a majority on a court but receives more votes than any other opinion. Such an opinion will usually state the "judgment of the court" and may be accompanied by other opinions concurring in the judgment or dissenting from it.

POLITICAL QUESTION. Doctrine that compels federal courts to avoid deciding cases involving the discretionary powers of the executive or legislative branches.

PRECEDENT. Prior case law.

PRELIMINARY INJUNCTION. A temporary court order for a party to a case to do something or to stop doing something. The injunction lasts until the case has been fully decided on its merits.

PRESUMPTION. When something is assumed (rather than proven).

PRIOR RESTRAINT. The restriction of speech or press before it is actually published or expressed. Analogous to censorship.

PROBABLE CAUSE. Sufficient reason to believe that a person has committed, or is committing, a crime or that a place contains evidence connected with a crime.

PROMULGATE. To put a law or regulation into effect; to make known.

PROSCRIBE. To prohibit or ban.

PUBLIC ACCOMMODATIONS LAW. A law providing that a business must provide lodging, meal service, entertainment, or other services to all members of the public. In federal law, the Civil Rights Act of 1964 is the key example.

QUID PRO QUO. Something for something else; this for that. Quid pro quo campaign contributions ("I will give your campaign $1,000 if you vote for the farm bill") are illegal bribes.

RATIONAL BASIS REVIEW. The standard by which a court will uphold a nondiscriminatory law, under equal protection or due process, if it bears a reasonable relationship to the attainment of a legitimate public objective.

REASONABLE SUSPICION. The level of suspicion required for school officials to search a student's belongings or person, a weaker standard than probable cause.

RECORD. The facts and evidence assembled by a trial court in a case.

RELIEF. The monetary benefit or other restitution that a court in a civil suit grants to a party that has suffered damages or injury.

RESPONDEAT SUPERIOR. Doctrine that allows an employer (or superior) to be liable for an employee's actions committed in the course of employment.

RESPONDENT. Party that answers to a petition for review in court. *See also* APPELLEE.

RESTITUTION. Making someone whole, usually by giving them their money back.

RIPENESS. Doctrine requiring that an actual live case or controversy be present—as opposed to a hypothetical or potential controversy—for a case to be heard. A case will not be heard unless it is ripe for adjudication.

SECULAR. Not related to religion.

SEIZURE. Under the Fourth Amendment, government confiscation of property or arrest of a person.

SEPARATION OF POWERS. The constitutional doctrine establishing that each of the three branches of the government—legislative, executive, and judicial—is essentially independent and exercises unique powers.

SETTLEMENT AGREEMENT. Resolution of a legal dispute outside of court.

SEXUAL HARASSMENT. Sexual conduct, sometimes accompanied by promises or threats, that (1) creates a hostile learning or workplace environment and/or (2) involves express or implied conditions in which rejection of, or submission to, said conduct will affect an individual's employment or academic status (quid pro quo harassment).

SOLICITOR GENERAL. Attorney in the Department of Justice who represents the government in cases that go before the U.S. Supreme Court.

STANDING. The doctrine requiring that an individual show that he or she suffered a direct and concrete injury that is traceable to the government and that can be redressed through court-ordered relief before a person's constitutional case against the government may be heard.

STATE ACTION. Action undertaken by a government agency or actor, whether federal, state, or local. State action is required to bring a constitutional case against the government.

STATUTE. A law passed by a federal or state legislature.

STATUTORY. Relating to a statute.

STRICT SCRUTINY. The legal standard applied to suspect classifications, such as race, under equal protection and to burdens on fundamental rights, such as reproductive freedom, under due process in which the government must show that it has used the least restrictive means to advance a compelling state interest.

SUMMARY JUDGMENT. Judicial resolution of a case without trial where all of the significant facts of the case are uncontested and one party is entitled to win as a matter of law.

TORT. A civil wrong. If you drive recklessly and knock down your neighbor's mailbox, he or she can sue you for committing a tort.

TRADITIONAL PUBLIC FORUM. A public place traditionally open to citizen communication, expression, and assembly: specifically, streets, sidewalks, and parks.

UNCONSTITUTIONAL. Descriptive of actions that are in violation of the commands or guarantees of the Constitution.

UNITED STATES CIRCUIT COURTS OF APPEAL. Body of courts consisting of thirteen federal circuits, including the Court of Appeals for the District of Columbia and the Court of Appeals for the Federal Circuit. These appellate courts hear cases that have been appealed from the United States District Courts.

UNITED STATES DISTRICT COURTS. Body of trial courts in which cases involving federal lawsuits are first tried.

UNITED STATES SUPREME COURT. Highest court in the United States. The Supreme Court is made up of a chief justice and eight associate justices and is charged with ruling on appeals from the United States Circuit Courts of Appeal and from state supreme courts. The Court also functions as a trial court in certain cases, including those that occur between states or those that involve ambassadors.

VAGUENESS. A law is unconstitutionally vague under due process if it is so ambiguous as not to give people notice of what is forbidden and what is allowed.

VERDICT. A jury's decision in a case or, in a nonjury trial, a judge's decision.

VIEWPOINT NEUTRALITY. The First Amendment requirement that government may not suppress or censor speech based on the point of view taken.

WARRANT. A writ or an order authorizing an officer to conduct a search of a place or to execute an arrest.

WRIT. A court's written order commanding someone to do, or refrain from doing, something.

WRIT OF CERTIORARI. A writ issued by the U.S. Supreme Court to a lower court directing the lower court to deliver the case for review. *Certiorari* is Latin and means "to be more fully informed."

# Appendix D
# BIBLIOGRAPHY

Abraham, Henry J., and Barbara Perry. *Freedom and the Court: Civil Rights and Liberties in the United States.* New York: Oxford University Press, 1998.

American Association of University Women. *Hostile Hallways: The AAUW Survey on Sexual Harassment in America's Schools.* Washington, D.C.: AAUW Educational Foundation, 1993.

Arbetman, Lee, and Edward O'Brien. *Street Law.* St. Paul, Minn.: West Educational Publishing, 1999.

Axelrod, Alan. *Minority Rights in America.* Washington, D.C.: CQ Press, 2002.

Ball, Howard. *The Bakke Case: Race, Education, and Affirmative Action.* Lawrence: University Press of Kansas, 2000.

Bell, Derrick A., Jr. *Race, Racism, and American Law.* Boston: Little, Brown, 1980.

Biskupic, Joan, and Elder Witt. *Guide to the U.S. Supreme Court.* 3d ed. Washington, D.C.: Congressional Quarterly, 1997.

Bollinger, Lee C., and Geofrey R. Stone, eds. *Eternally Vigilant: Free Speech in the Modern Era.* Chicago: University of Chicago Press, 2002.

Bosmajian, Haig. *The Freedom Not to Speak.* New York: New York University Press, 1999.

Bosworth, Matthew H. *Courts as Catalysts: State Supreme Courts and Public School Finance Equity.* Albany: State University of New York Press, 2001.

Carson, Clayborne, ed. *Eyes on the Prize: Civil Rights Reader.* New York: Penguin Books, 1991.

Chih Lin, Ann, ed. *Immigration.* Washington, D.C.: CQ Press, 2002.

Chin, Gabriel Jack. *Affirmative Action and the Constitution.* New York: Garland, 1998.

Clark, Charles S. "Charter Schools," *CQ Researcher,* December 20, 2002, 1033–1056.

Cole, David. *No Equal Justice: Race and Class in the American Criminal Justice System.* New York: New Press, 1999.

Cortner, Richard C. *Civil Rights and Public Accommodations: The Heart of Atlanta and McClung Cases.* Lawrence: University Press of Kansas, 2001.

Cushman, Clare, ed. *Supreme Court Decisions and Women's Rights.* Washington, D.C.: CQ Press, 2001.

———. *The Supreme Court Justices: Illustrated Biographies, 1789–1995.* 2d ed. Washington, D.C.: Congressional Quarterly, 1995.

Department of Education, Office of Civil Rights. *Sexual Harassment Guidance: Harassment of Students by School Employees, Other Students, or Third Parties.* Washington, D.C.: U.S. Government Printing Office.

Devine, John. *Maximum Security: The Culture of Violence in Inner-City Schools.* Chicago: University of Chicago Press, 1996.

Douglas, Davison. *Reading, Writing, and Race: The Desegregation of the Charlotte Schools.* Chapel Hill: University of North Carolina, 1995.

———. *School Busing: Constitutional and Political Developments.* New York: Garland, 1997.

Epps, Garrett. *To An Unknown God: Religious Freedom on Trial.* New York: St. Martin's Press, 2001.

Finkelman, Paul, ed. *Religion and American Law: An Encyclopedia.* New York: Garland, 2000.

Finkelman, Paul, and Melvin I. Urofsky. *Landmark Decisions of the United States Supreme Court.* Washington, D.C.: CQ Press, 2003.

Fish, Stanley. *There's No Such Thing as Free Speech and It's a Good Thing Too.* New York: Oxford University Press, 1994.

Foersel, Herbert N. *Free Expression and Censorship in America: An Encyclopedia.* Westport, Conn.: Greenwood, 1997.

Freyer, Tony. *The Little Rock Crisis: A Constitutional Interpretation.* Westport, Conn.: Greenwood, 1984.

Friendly, Fred W. *Minnesota Rag: The Dramatic Story of the Landmark Supreme Case That Gave New Meaning to Freedom of the Press.* New York: Random House, 1981.

Garcia, Alfredo. *The Sixth Amendment in Modern American Jurisprudence: A Critical Perspective.* Westport, Conn.: Greenwood, 1992.

Hall, Kermit. *The Oxford Companion to the Supreme Court of the United States.* New York: Oxford University Press, 1992.

Heins, Marjorie. *Not in Front of the Children: "Indecency," Censorship, and the Innocence of Youth.* New York: Hill and Wang, 2001.

Hentoff, Nat. *Free Speech for Me—But Not for Thee.* New York: HarperCollins, 1992.

Heumann, Milton, Thomas Church, and David Redlawsk, eds. *Hate Speech on Campus: Cases, Case Studies, and Commentary.* Boston: Northeastern University Press, 1997.

Hyman, Irwin A. *Corporal Punishment in American Education: Readings in History, Practice, and Alternatives.* Philadelphia: Temple University Press, 1979.

Johnson, John W. *The Struggle for Student Rights:* Tinker v. Des Moines *and the 1960s.* Lawrence: University Press of Kansas, 1997.

Jost, Kenneth. "Affirmative Action," *CQ Researcher,* September 21, 2001, 737–759.

———. "School Vouchers Showdown," *CQ Researcher,* February 15, 2002, 121–144.

———. "Single-Sex Education," *CQ Researcher,* July 12, 2002, 569–592.

————, ed. *The Supreme Court A to Z*. 2d ed. Washington, D.C.: Congressional Quarterly, 1998.

Kalven, Harry. *A Worthy Tradition: Freedom of Speech in America*. New York: Harper and Row, 1988.

Kluger, Richard. *Simple Justice: The History of* Brown v. Board of Education *and Black America's Struggle for Equality*. New York: Knopf, 1975.

Kousser, J. Morgan. "Separate but *Not* Equal: The Supreme Court's First Decision on Racial Discrimination in Schools," *Journal of Southern History* 17 (1980).

Kozol, Jonathan. *Savage Inequalities: Children in America's Schools*. New York: Crown Publishing, 1991.

LaFave, Wayne R. *Search and Seizure*. 2d ed. St. Paul, Minn.: West Publishing, 1987.

Lagemann, Ellen C., and Lamar P. Miller, eds. Brown v. Board of Education: *The Challenge for Today's Schools*. New York: Teachers College Press, 1996.

Landsberg, Brian K. *Enforcing Civil Rights: Race, Discrimination, and the Department of Justice*. Lawrence: University Press of Kansas, 1997.

Langelan, Martha. *Back Off: How to Confront and Stop Sexual Harassment and Harrassers*. New York: Simon and Schuster, 1993.

Lantieri, Linda, and Janet Patti. *Waging Peace in Our Schools*. Boston: Beacon Press, 1998.

Larson, Edward J. *Trial and Error: The American Controversy over Creation and Evolution*. New York: Oxford University Press, 1985.

Leonard, Arthur S., ed. *Homosexuality and the Constitution*. New York: Garland, 1997.

Levy, Leonard W. *Origins of the Fifth Amendment*. New York: Oxford University Press, 1968.

————. *The Establishment Clause: Religion and the First Amendment*. New York: Macmillan, 1986.

Lewis, Anthony. *Gideon's Trumpet*. New York: Random House, 1964.

————. *Make No Law: The Sullivan Case and the First Amendment*. New York: Random House, 1991.

Lofgren, Charles A. *The Plessy Case: A Legal-Historical Interpretation*. New York, Oxford University Press, 1987.

Manfredi, Christopher P. *The Supreme Court and Juvenile Justice*. Lawrence: University Press of Kansas, 1998.

Manwaring, David. *Render Unto Caesar: The Flag Salute Controversy*. Chicago: University of Chicago Press, 1962.

Marshall, Patrick. "Homework Debate," *CQ Researcher*, December 6, 2002, 993–1012.

————. "Religion in Schools," *CQ Researcher*, January 12, 2001, 1–24.

Masci, David. "Evolution and Creationism," *CQ Researcher*, August 12, 1997, 745–768.

————. "Preventing Teen Drug Use," *CQ Researcher*, March 15, 2002, 217–240.

Metcalf, George R. *From Little Rock to Boston: A History of School Desegregation.* Westport, Conn.: Greenwood Press, 1983.

Murdoch, Joyce, and Deb Price. *Courting Justice: Gay Men and Lesbians v. The Supreme Court.* New York: Basic Books, 2001.

Patterson, James T. Brown v. Board of Education: *A Civil Rights Milestone and Its Troubled Legacy.* New York: Oxford University Press, 2001.

Raskin, Jamin B. "Legal Aliens, Local Citizens: The Historical, Constitutional, and Theoretical Meanings of Alien Suffrage," *University of Pennsylvania Law Review 1391* 141 (1993).

Ravitch, Frank S. *School Prayer and Discrimination: The Civil Rights of Religious Minorities and Dissenters.* Boston: Northeastern University Press, 1999.

Schwartz, Bernard. *Swann's Way: The School Busing Case and the Supreme Court.* New York: Oxford University Press, 1986.

Shiell, Timothy C. *Campus Hate Speech on Trial.* Lawrence: University Press of Kansas, 1998.

Sitkoff, Harvard. *The Struggle for Black Equality, 1954–1992.* Rev. ed. New York: Hill and Wang, 1993.

Stein, Nan, and Lisa Sjostram. *Flirting or Hurting? A Teacher's Guide to Student-to-Student Sexual Harassment in Schools.* Washington, D.C.: NEA Professional Library Publication, 1994.

Strum, Phillippa. *Women in the Barracks: The VMI Case and Equal Rights.* Lawrence: University Press of Kansas, 2002.

Tushnet, Mark V. *The NAACP's Strategy Against Segregated Education, 1925–1950.* Chapel Hill: University of North Carolina Press, 1987.

Tyack, David B. "The Perils of Pluralism: The Background of the Pierce Case," *American Historical Review* 74 (1968).

Wallenstein, Peter. "Race, Marriage, and the Supreme Court: From *Pace v. Alabama* to *Loving v. Virginia*," *Journal of Supreme Court History* 65 (1998).

Wheeler, Stanton, and Leonard S. Cottrell Jr. *Juvenile Delinquency: Its Prevention and Control.* New York: Russell Sage Foundation, 1966.

Whitman, Mark. *The Irony of Desegregation Law 1955–1995.* Princeton: M. Wiener, 1998.

Wilkinson, J. Harvie. *From* Brown *to* Bakke: *The Supreme Court and School Integration, 1954–1978.* New York: Oxford University Press, 1979.

Wills, Garry. *Under God: Religion and American Politics.* New York: Simon and Schuster, 1990.

Yudof, Mark G., David L. Kirp, and Betsy Levin. *Educational Policy and the Law.* 3d ed. St. Paul, Minn.: West Publishing, 1992.

# Appendix E

# MARSHALL-BRENNAN
# FELLOWS 1999–2003

The following lawyers and law students have served as Marshall-Brennan fellows, teaching the "We the Students" constitutional literacy course in public schools in Maryland and Washington, D.C. Their hard work and commitment have been extraordinary.

Aisha Braithwaite
Alison Accettola
Alison Hillman
Amanda Howe
Amit Chugh
Andrea Harrington
Andrew Fausett
Angela Conyers
Anita Nigam
Ariele Cohen
Artemis Moutsatsos
Babatunde Williams
Belinda Harris
Beth McGinn
Beth Roma
Beverly Hudnut
Bill Kamens
Bruce Halloway Cork
Carmen Forrest
Cassandra Capobianco
Cedar Carlton
Chris Campos
Chris Caple
Chris Rose
Christian Levesque
Christianna Lewis
Christopher Fetgatter
Cynthia Hamra
Dan Habib
Daniel Jawor

Danny Alvarez
Dave Mikhail
David Maloney
Delicia Reynolds
Dena Marshall
Divya Murthy
Ed Cho
Eden Segal
Edna Yang
Elna Santos
Emily Caplan
Emily Marlow
Eric Lerum
Fahryn Hoffman
Fatema Yeganeh
Gabrielle de la Gueronniere
Hani Demetrious
Heather Collier
Herbert Rouson
Hillary Taylor
Ilona Coleman
Jackson Toof
James Prince
Jane Leiphart
Jason Chang
Jeanette Manning
Jenifer Leaman
Jennafer Neufeld
Jennifer Beall
Jennifer Kraham

Jennifer McKeever
Jennifer Saubermann
Jessica Strasnick
Jessica Swartz
Jessica Waters
Jill Imgrund
Jill Lavacchia
Jim Ferg-Cadima
Joanna Day
Jodi Weiler
Joe Ferretti
Joel Blank
John DiIorio
John Fieldsend
John Thompson
Josh Krintzman
Julie Flamant
Juria Jones
Kaleb Kasperson
Karen Hassinger
Kate Ellis
Kathleen Monaghan
Keith Fredlake
Kim McManus
Kristen Pezone
La Shon Cole
Laura Fajardo
Laura Rinaldi
Lisa Cox
Lori Sher
Luis Clavijo
Marci Jones
Maria Mirabal
Mary Ellen Tsekos
Maryam Ahranjani
Maureen Dimino
Melissa Maker
Michael Haas
Michael Jacob
Mike Will
Miles Granderson
Missy Bernheim
Misty Carter
Miya Nazzaro
Moira Lee
Mononique Tervalon
Moxi Upadhyaya
Myriah Habeeb

Nancy Faulkner
Natalie Watson
Nicole Bacon
Nicole Laquintano
Olga Kats
Oscar Gonzalez
Pamala Micheaux
Pedro Medrano
Peter Young
Quoc Vuong
Raanan Weintraub
Rachel Cantillon
Rachel Raymond
Raymond Jones
Rebecca Goldfrank
Rebecca Shankman
Rena Scheinkman
Richard Mooradian
Riqueza Feaster
Ryan Borho
Sari Maltz
Sasha Mehra
Scott Lee
Seigrid Rich
Serwat Perwaiz
Sharmalee Rajakumaran
Shawn Thompson
Sheila Bedi
Sheila Moreira
Sheila Siegel
Spencer Hamlin
Stephanie Joseph
Stephen Cooper
Sujay Mooss
Tan Alam
Theresa Steed
Tracey Rogers
Trevor Rose
Tyler Rauert
Umesh Jani
Valorie Perez
Wendy Jamison
Whetanah Tucker
Wilder Leavitt
Will Taylor
William Duston
Zack Rosenburg
Zandria Jacobs-Conyers

# Index

Note: Page numbers in *italics* indicate photos.

# Photo Credits

| Page number | Credit |
|---|---|
| x, xiii, xv | Jamin Raskin |
| xi, xii, 57, 88, 98, 118, 131, 133, 175, 221 | Associated Press |
| 2, 9, 26, 29, 36, 164, 165, 166, 168, 186 | Library of Congress |
| 5 | National Archives |
| 7 | Ken Heinen |
| 13, 18, 40, 62, 73, 76, 234 | Collection of the Supreme Court of the United States |
| 16 | Bentley Historical Library |
| 19 | Bill Pierce |
| 22, 38, 74, 77, 113, 167, 169 | Corbis |
| 27 | Mary Beth Tinker |
| 42 | Chris Pyle |
| 45 | Newsday |
| 50 | Steven Aden |
| 79, 83 | *Providence Journal-Bulletin* |
| 109, 125, 195, 217 | Reuters |
| 116 | Ankers Photographers, Inc. |
| 137 | *Time,* Andre Lambertson/SABA |
| 148 | *Columbus Evening Dispatch* |
| 154 (top, bottom) | *Miami Herald* |
| 156 | W&L Archive |
| 180 | Institute of Texan Cultures |
| 184 | File photo |
| 208 | Alan Weiner |